Indian Advertising Laughter & Tears

Indian Advertising Laughter & Tears

1950
to
2013

Arun Chaudhuri

NIYOGI
BOOKS

Published by
NIYOGI BOOKS
D-78, Okhla Industrial Area, Phase-I
New Delhi-110 020, India
Tel: 91-11-26816301, 49327000
Fax: 91-11-26810483, 26813830
Email: niyogibooks@gmail.com
Website: www.niyogibooksindia.com

Editorial and Design: Write Media

ISBN: 978-93-83098-47-7
Year of Publication: 2014

Printed at: Niyogi Offset Pvt. Ltd., New Delhi, India

To Urmimala,

for sharing three decades of challenges in Kolkata where we saw advertising die

Contents

Preface

Indian Advertising 1780 to 1950 was published by Tata McGraw Hill in 2007. This sequel covers the subsequent period in the history of Indian advertising from 1950 till the present—immediately after Independence, going on to the new millennium.

I would like to share with readers how I selected the profiles of those eminent men and women who shaped the character of advertising in India. The world of Indian advertising has been dominated by a cluster of ad agencies whose clients comprised the big budget advertisers for years. J. Walter Thompson (JWT), which later became Hindustan Thompson Associates (HTA) and then reverted to JWT; Ulka (now FCB Ulka Advertising); Clarion McCann Advertising (now Bates) and Lintas were initially the most visible in print advertisements. The persons who managed the business of these agencies naturally figure in this book with the proviso that each person selected left some significant impression on the advertising of his or her times. I deliberately omitted those who merely managed the business of the agency without making any professional contribution to advertising. This remains a contentious issue. For who am I to determine whether a person's contribution has been significant enough?

The managing directors of JWT/HTA, sandwiched between Peter Fielden and Subhas Ghosal, were minor actors. The appellation of managing director or CEO given by an agency does not automatically elevate a person to the stature of Ghosal. I applied the same yardstick to Ogilvy & Mather (O&M). In my view, the last of the Mohicans in O&M was Mani Ayer.

Indian advertising was transformed by the sudden arrival of Mass Communication and Marketing (MCM); this agency turned advertising into a glamorous profession. It threw away the norms followed by the lead agencies. MCM solicited business aggressively, which was unheard of. MCM parties were the talk of the town; clients and prospects hoped to get invitations. MCM attracted talent. When the agency closed, burning out like a meteor in the firmament, three other agencies—Rediffusion, Trikaya and Enterprise—

were born from its embers. These agencies, which were remarkable for path-breaking creative work, were formed by young enterprising professionals and some of the most memorable ads of the late 1970s and 1980s were crafted by them.

A different kind of agency came into existence with R.K. Swamy Associates. The founder, who named the agency after himself, was middle-aged when he decided to float his own outfit. He was unlike any other ad personality of the times; he did not wear the creative hat. Swamy persuaded a number of young people who were his colleagues in HTA to work for him. The agency opened the business potential of public sector units, which up until then had remained indifferent to advertising.

In this brief history of Indian advertising, my attempt has been to present the profiles of people who may be called the movers and shakers of the profession. I have included memorable campaigns which showcase Indian advertising in each decade. On the other hand, I have also included a lot of advertisements that are poor in creative content. Since few advertisement campaigns stand out in any period of history and most advertisements are average in creative merit, the feel of the standards in a decade is important.

Though I deliberately excluded more recent celebrities in the profession, who regularly feature in the society columns of newspapers and magazines, it is not to belittle them. I left them out because they are no longer independent; they work for large international conglomerates. Those who own these conglomerates are more important than the faces hired to manage their various Indian ad agencies. For example, Sir Martin Sorrell, the owner of the WPP Group (WPP stems from Wire and Plastic Products, a UK manufacturer of wire baskets), is more important than the chief executives he pays to manage the day-to-day business of his leading Indian agencies. I had to mention him because he is shaping the course of Indian advertising since 1992.

I confess I no longer understand how one agency differentiates the way it arrives at the creative platform from another when both come under the same international umbrella. Once upon a time, the creative at Ogilvy, Benson & Mather (OBM) followed a distinctive pattern that owed its origin to David Ogilvy. We wrote long headlines that summed up the proposal of the entire advertisement; a headline could have as many as 25 words. Times have changed. Now O&M ads don't have the look and feel of the Ogilvy *gharana*. Ulka ads between 1960 and 1980 were different from the ads created at HTA. Rediff ads had a distinctive feel that was different from the ads created at Trikaya. Enterprise and Frank Simoes crafted ads with their magic creative touch. The client ultimately decides on the look and feel of advertising. Perhaps clients with more linear backgrounds—all MBAs—have lost the calibre to judge good advertising.

To reiterate—times have indeed changed. My daughter who chose a career in copywriting tells me a creative portfolio of a copywriter today has to include ads with long copy. That is reassuring since clients invariably ask, 'Who reads copy?' This amazes me because I am yet to come across a consumer who is persuaded without a single verbal impulse.

Advertising is influenced by certain extraneous factors. These are:

The political scene in India

When the Central Government had strong reservations about anything that smacked of an alien democratic culture, advertising was dubbed as bad for society. Then again, when periods are marked by religious tensions and there is a preponderance of religion in the social sphere, almost every image of a woman seen in an advertisement is regarded as promoting wanton sexuality.

The state of technologies in various spheres that are used in the making of advertisements

Between the early 1980s and early 1990s, printing technology went through a complete transformation in India. First, the process of printing newspapers changed. The age of giving advertising material in zinc and copper blocks or in matrices was past. Positives were now handed over to newspapers. Similarly, job printing also saw these changes. Master printers visited Germany every year and invested in more advanced printing machines. Despite the high import duty imposed on these machines, printing companies did good business and managed their books of accounts intelligently to remain profitable without showing good profits. Advertisements, whether in newspapers or as Point of Sale material, could now present high quality reproduction, which gave art directors greater scope to explore ideas based on photography.

Television replaced print as the most favoured medium of advertisers and agencies

Technologies came in that enabled the making of films for television rather than adapting films for cinema viewing into television formats. Technically the cost of making a commercial came down but clients continued to pay a steadily rising cost for film production. This remains one great mystery!

The emergence of new media

This is an inevitable offshoot of the development of new forms of communication such as the internet and mobile telephone. It added a new level of aggressiveness in advertising, encroaching into the personal sphere without permission.

However, in this book I have not gone into details pertaining to technology. Critics of my previous book felt rather strongly that there is no need to mention zinc and copper blocks, matrices and to fill up pages with the development of the camera, the moving picture and so on when the author has the scope to write a gripping novel with so much material available in old ads. I owe them an apology. I wrote the book for advertising professionals believing that some day we will have people in the profession who like reading books and who may desire to know how ads were fashioned in the past with the technology then available.

The focus in this book is on those individuals who made Indian advertising what it is today. In a way, it is a celebration of the individual efforts of brilliant minds crafting memorable campaigns and creating brands which are still strong in their market presence. But even here I am aware of the exclusion rather than inclusion of a vast majority of art directors across the major advertising centres namely, Bombay (now Mumbai), Madras (now Chennai) and Delhi because I lacked the financial strength to research my subject better. There is enormous scope to improve on this but time is passing and with the passage of time information on people in the profession will be lost.

I am grateful to Niyogi Books for publishing this book quickly and making it available at the current price. I am especially indebted to Tultul Niyogi and her husband Bikash Niyogi for their infectious enthusiasm. I am grateful to my friend and colleague Sujan Datta for helping me with re-touching old pictures. This was not an easy job. The old papers and magazines from where the photographs have been sourced are yellow with age. Besides, the photographs were initially printed on the cheapest quality of newsprint with what were even then vintage printing machines.

I hope this book will be useful to those wishing to enter the profession. I also hope that more advertising people in India will begin writing about the profession.

Arun Chaudhuri
Kolkata
31 December 2013

1

1950–1960 Overview

The period under review covers the state of advertising in India immediately after Independence in 1947. The trauma of Partition was fresh in public memory. It was bloody and no less cruel than the attacks by Amir Timur in 1398, when he is said to have butchered 100,000 adult male captives in Delhi.[1] Or the massacre ordered in Delhi by the brigand-turned-king of Persia, Nadir Shah, in 1739, when his soldiers mowed down citizens of Delhi regardless of whether they were Mohammedans or Hindus and enslaved their wives and daughters.[2] Like obdurate donkeys, the people of India through the ages choose to play up divisions between themselves only to realise when they are under the sword of adventurers that they may suffer less if they face the enemy as one nation.

The ethnic cleansing of minorities with the active support of those in governance in Pakistan resulted in over two million deaths and the displacement of over 17 million persons across the new borders that now divided the political map of the Indian subcontinent. A comparative study of the census of 1941 with 1951 shows the extent of change in the religious mix of the population in the region.[3] For example, in the 1941 census for the Punjab province, which included Punjab and Bhawalpur, non-Muslims accounted for 24.58 per cent of the population, whereas in the 1951 census the non-Muslim population was a mere 2.77 per cent. In the province of Sind, which included Sind, Khairpur and the Karachi Federal Area, in 1941

[1]Majumdar R.C., H.C. RayChaudhuri and Kalikinkar Datta. *An Advanced History of India.* Third edition, p. 328. Macmillan, 1967. This seems unlikely. What was the population of Delhi if he killed 1,00,000 male captives?

[2]*Ibid.* p. 524–526.

[3]Sporadic communal violence continued for three to four years. Jawaharlal Nehru was worried about flare-ups in Calcutta in 1950. *The Statesman* dated 22 February 1950 quotes the prime minister while paying tribute to Sarat Bose immediately following his death, 'All of us today are living under great stress because of the news we receive from day-to-day happenings in Bengal.' Copies of *The Statesman* in the first three months of 1950 are replete with appeals made by Dr B.C. Roy and Liaquat Ali Khan to people on both sides of divided Bengal to maintain peace.

non-Muslims accounted for 28.60 per cent of the population; in the 1951 census they accounted for only 8.53 per cent. However, in this province, non-Muslims fared better than in other provinces of the region. This was probably due to non-Muslims living in concentrated demographic enclaves, which made it possible for them to find strength in numbers against killer mobs.

In the North West Frontier Province (NWFP), which included settled districts as well as states, in 1941 non-Muslims comprised 4.60 per cent of the population; in 1951 they were a meagre 0.10 per cent. In 1941 in Baluchistan, which included districts and states, non-Muslims accounted for 8.53 per cent of the total population, and after the trauma of Partition it came down to 1.47 per cent.[4]

The situation in the East was marginally better. Mahatma Gandhi's fast unto death stopped the killings in Calcutta (now Kolkata), orchestrated by the Muslim League premier of Bengal, Hussain Shaheed Suhrawardy. In East Bengal, that became East Pakistan, over 40 per cent of the population was ethnically cleansed despite Gandhiji's much touted presence in Noakhali where he camped in the hope of stopping the bloodbath.

In comparison with the Hindu minority in Pakistan, an estimated 18 per cent of the total Muslim population in India either migrated to Pakistan or were killed. This is not to suggest that the situation on the ground was significantly better. Eighteen per cent of India's population then may have comprised over six crore persons. How many migrated as opposed to how many lost their lives is a subject that does not really concern our narrative, but deserves serious consideration by historians who are focussed on these unhappy events. However, the Congress government in New Delhi was committed to a secular India. There was no connivance, on the part of the government in Delhi, in uprooting the Muslim minority and in misusing the administrative machinery for this purpose.

The cloud of Partition cast a long shadow in the new era of political freedom. Refugees from Punjab tried to reconstruct their lives with little help from an impoverished Central Government.[5] The Sikhs are a proud race; they do not beg for a living. They proved their mettle, doing whatever they could lay their hands on—as petty traders, pushing vegetable carts

---

[4]Sridhar N. 'Ethnic Cleansing in Pakistan during Partition: A Preliminary Statistical Analysis.' *Bharat Rakshak Monitor*, vol. 6 (2), September–October 2003.

[5]There is a long-held belief in West Bengal that the people displaced from East Pakistan received far less from the Central Government than displaced persons from Punjab. In a letter to the editor published in *The Times of India*, Bombay, on 11 January 1950 this is expressed forcefully. Here is an excerpt: 'Truncated, West Bengal is today economically the most handicapped unit in the country. The strained economy is almost verging on collapse with the tremendous influx of refugees from East Bengal. While the refugees from West Punjab have been receiving aid from the Centre in addition to that from the East Punjab government, no such aid has been made available to the East Bengal refugees.' (Signed Samir Ganguli from Calcutta.)

across New Delhi roads, doing odd jobs in transport organisations, as carpenters or electricians, setting up eateries across highways, or turning their hands to agriculture and other vocations wherever they could find work. This set them apart as toilers and entrepreneurs. To survive, they followed their economic instincts across India, and chose not to remain tied to only the states in the north of the country, adjoining or adjacent to undivided Punjab.

In the east, displaced persons from East Pakistan fared worse than their Punjabi brethren. Calcutta had little to offer by way of relief. Yet they came to the city and its suburbs by the thousands and tried to find shelter and work; both were scarce. Soon the City of Palaces began to resemble a large ghetto, with its characteristic stench, the breakdown of civic services, along with other attendant evils that accompany unchecked migrations of people. In the decades following, this influx from East Pakistan continued unabated and began to fester like an infected wound. There followed other fundamental changes after Partition. Expatriates, uncertain of their place in free India, started returning home. The Central Government was immediately called upon to wage a war with Pakistan in Kashmir, while a number of princely states within India, ruled by Muslim kings, were undecided which way to turn. Revenues were meagre, the coffers empty, agriculture (which was the chief occupation of over 90 per cent of the population) was entirely monsoon fed, and predominantly single cropping. Use of fertilisers other than cow dung was almost unknown. There were millions to feed with insufficient food grains. The Green Revolution in the Indian state of Punjab was two decades into the future. Memories of the great famines that decimated the population were a recent scar in the minds of people in every province, especially the people living in West Bengal, Tamil Nadu and Gujarat.

The Congress Party, which was in the forefront of civil disobedience movements prior to Independence, naturally succeeded the British government in New Delhi and in all the states that formed the Republic of India. It was a political party without ideology; there were as many shades of political divide within the party as there were members, as is evident in this cartoon.[6]

[6]*The Times of India*, Bombay, carried this cartoon on the front page of its issue dated 15 January 1950.

The first chapter traces the socio-economic condition of India in the decade immediately following Independence. Advertising is examined as a useful tool that is interlinked with the overall economic condition of Indian society.

15 August 1947 is a watershed in our nation's political history in the twentieth century. Newspapers flagged off the great day with poster headlines capturing images of national leaders, especially Nehru making his 'Tryst with destiny' speech in the middle of the night (introducing the unfamiliar word 'tryst' in Indian English). There were great expectations of the future ahead as a free nation, although the bloody partition of the country that left millions dead and many thousands homeless worried the leaders of the new government.

Advertising was not a profession quite in the public eye. Not too many people regarded the profession as important; no one considered it glamorous, which may seem unbelievable today. In fact, not many people would have heard of advertising as a profession. However, by the early 1950s, professional competency in advertising had developed in three major metro towns. Cities in India that had the infrastructure to provide advertising support were Bombay, Madras and Calcutta. Delhi did not develop as a centre for advertising until the 1970s. From 1905 onwards, foreign and Indian advertising agencies were operating in these cities. Proficiency in art, account servicing and media scheduling had developed. Most of the larger agencies recruited young people and trained them. JWT, L.A. Stronach, L.R. Swamy in Madras and D.J. Keymer followed this policy. Artists came from the art colleges that were training young men in fine arts and commercial art in Bombay, Calcutta and Madras from around the 1860s and 1870s. Account executives, media personnel and copywriters had to be trained because there was no institution where such training was provided. In 1961, *Admars* published a chronological list of ad agencies in India since the beginning of the twentieth century.[7]

[7]*Admars*, June 1961 (*Admars* was a publication of the Advertising Agencies Association of India). I have taken this from 'The Advertising Brief' dated 30 December 1999.

CHRONOLOGICAL LIST OF AGENCIES IN INDIA

1905	B. Dattaram & Company, Bombay
1925	L.A. Stronach & Company Pvt Ltd, Bombay
1925	L.R. Swami & Company, Madras
1928	D.J. Keymer & Company Ltd (Bomas Ltd subsequently)
1929	J. Walter Thompson
1931	National Advertising Service Pvt Ltd, Bombay
1931	Universal Publicity Company, Calcutta
1935	Indian Publicity Bureau Pvt Ltd, Calcutta
1936	Studio Ratan Batra Pvt Ltd, Bombay
1936	Krishna Publicity Company Pvt Ltd, Kanpur
1938	Jayendra Publicity, Kolhapur
1939	The Press Syndicate Ltd, Bombay
1940	Navanitlal & Company, Ahmedabad
1941	Green's Advertising Service Agents, Bombay
1943	Advertising & Sales Promotion Company, Calcutta
1944	Dazzle, Bombay
1944	Ranjit Sales & Publicity Pvt Ltd, Bombay
1945	Efficient Publicities Pvt Ltd, Madras
1945	Tom & Bay Advertising Pvt Ltd, Poona (now Pune)
1946	Eastern Psychograph Pvt Ltd, Bombay
1946	Everest Advertising Pvt Ltd, Bombay
1947	Grant Advertising Inc, Bombay
1947	Swami Advertising Bureau, Sholapur
1948	R.C. Advertising Company, Bombay
1948	Phoenix Advertising Pvt Ltd, Calcutta
1952	Shantilal G. Shah & Company, Bombay
1954	Express Advertising Agency, Bombay
1954	India Publicity Company Pvt Ltd, Calcutta
1956	Aiyars Advertising & Marketing, Bombay
1956	Clarion Advertising Services Pvt Ltd, Calcutta
1958	Shree Advertising Agency, Bombay
1959	Associated Publicity, Cuttack
1959	General Publicity Service, Bombay
1960	Advertising Accessories, Trichur
1960	Marketing Advertising Associates, Bombay
1961	Industrial Advertising Agency, Bombay

The Advertising Brief from which the table on the previous page has been copied mentions that there may well have been other agencies that do not feature here. The article also mentions that agencies which closed down before 1961 may not have been included. We assume, on the basis of this comment, that apart from JWT all the older agencies, namely B. Dattaram, L.A. Stronach and L.R. Swamy were functioning till the 1960s. *The Illustrated Weekly of India*, 16 January 1972, which had a full coverage of the Bangladesh war, carried the key number 'STRONACHS' for Parksons Playing Cards.

When we consider print advertising in the period immediately after Independence we see a continuation of the kind of advertising before 1947. Brand names which were popular in the early 1940s generally remained popular in the late 1940s and in the decade following. Market demand for consumables and durables was limited since consumers had little disposable income. There was no dramatic change because political transition in India began to have an impact on society gradually, only after the new political class settled down to the business of governance.[8] In the advertising business there were very few Indians in senior administrative positions in the leading agencies. In the early 1950s the legendary D.K. Gupta was the senior-most Indian professional in Calcutta in a large foreign-owned agency, D.J. Keymer. At the time he was assistant manager. In an interview, Bal Mundkur, who later set up Ulka Advertising, commented that he was the only 'covenanted officer in Keymer', which he joined after quitting Air India.[9]

What was the general economic condition of India? Which were the major occupations? What was the financial market like? Understanding these fundamentals will help us analyse whether advertising played any major role in improving lifestyles of people; helping companies meet the actual and latent demand of the consuming classes. Which companies were major advertisers and where were these companies or their businesses located? Which media found favour with advertisers and agencies? These are some of the questions we shall seek answers for as we explore the history of Indian advertising in the 1950s.

State of Indian economy in 1950

Independence from British rule in 1947 led to far-reaching change in Indian society. The English as rulers of India were used to a lifestyle that was very different from the way Indians lived. The impoverished Indian farmer, who constituted over 90 per cent of India's population then, was so poor that he

[8]The fact that Lord Mountbatten was requested to stay on as governor general in independent India reflects a lack of confidence in Nehru and the leaders around him to assume full charge.
[9]I interviewed Bal Mundkur in Delhi in the mid-1990s when he said this.

did not eat two square meals a day. The middle class was a tiny segment in this ocean of poverty.[10] The creamy layer within the middle class did not share a lifestyle that was uniform in terms of quality throughout the country. A person belonging to this category, domiciled in Bombay, was likely to have a different lifestyle and habits of consumption of consumer goods than someone living as far away as Madras or Calcutta or as close as Nasik or Thane. Consumption of goods varied in accordance with a person's vocation, education and his place of residence. We should perhaps also include language, religion, sex and even caste.[11]

With the departure of the British from India, consumables imported from the UK declined over a period of time. It dried up entirely after the Central Government began to promulgate a socialist slant in its handling of the Indian economy. It was at best fuzzy thinking ardently supported by Nehru, who was a proponent of socialism.[12] As other stalwarts of the Congress died, Nehru emerged as the uncrowned king of the party and the government at the Centre.[13]

Reading this drivel in the footnote, it would surprise few that under Nehru's premiership, from 1947 to 1964, a period of 17 long years, Indians in a newly-freed nation actually had their freedom restricted. The nation turned into a prison; stifling ambition, curbing industry, with free Indians being governed

[10]George Mathew in his 'Introduction' to *India at 50*, published by Express Publications (Madurai) Ltd (1997), writes, 'According to the Planning Commission, only five per cent of India's population in 1947 had a satisfactory living standard ... Beneath this layer was a sea of poverty comprising about 300 million people.' He also mentions that not even one in three children in the primary school age was attending school and there was one doctor among 25,000 people in rural India. Adult literacy was poor; one adult among seven could read and write.

[11]The Indian Constitution especially favoured an end to casteism in any form—unfortunately, contemporary India seems to be beset with reverse casteism, nurtured by politicians, that deliberately makes for inequality of opportunity for those who are born into high caste families. As we shall see, the extent and diversity of use of consumer products in the following years became more and more restricted to a class of people who enjoyed financial, political or administrative power; some of the availability percolated down to lackeys who surrounded these social parasites.

[12]In his presidential address to the Congress Party in Lucknow in 1936, he had said grandiloquently, 'I am convinced that the only key to the solution of the world's problems and of India's problems lies in socialism and when I use the word I do so not in a vague humanitarian way but in the scientific, economic sense. Socialism is, however, something even more than an economic doctrine; it is a philosophy of life and as such also it appeals to me. I see no way of ending poverty, the vast unemployment, the degradation and the subjection of the Indian people except through socialism. That involves vast and revolutionary changes in our political and social structure, the ending of vested interests in land and industry, as well as the feudal and the autocratic Indian states' system. That means the ending of private property, except in a restricted sense, and the replacement of the present profit system by a higher ideal of cooperative service. It means ultimately a change in our instincts and habits and desires. In short, it means a new civilisation, radically different from the present capitalist order.'

[13]Every nation follows a unique style of governance. Democracy in India carries a lot of the regal aura of the Mughal era. A prime minister is treated like royalty and people are forever bending over backwards to please dignitaries. In recent years this has reached comic proportions.

like a subject people. The Central Government controlled by the Congress for 50 years was a democracy only in name.[14]

The Congress at the Centre as well as state governments, where also the Congress constituted the majority party in most states, gradually began setting up barriers to a free market economy by restricting free movement of goods across states, especially scarce agricultural produce such as rice.[15] The objective behind this exercise was to insulate rural areas from the frequent occurrence of famine. The distribution chain that was entrenched in India over a long period of time and controlled by banias ensured that the bulk of the agricultural produce found a way into towns and cities. There was rampant black marketing in commodities.[16] As early as January 1950, Nehru had to answer questions on black marketing in parliament.[17]

In the 1950s Indian society had a larger proportion of unproductive consumers than productive ones. The latter contribute to national income; the former consumers comprise people who do not contribute to national income. Children, older persons who can no longer work and, in India, *also persons who can find no work* are grouped in the unproductive category. If we go by the figures given in the census reports of 1961 and 1971, we may assume that the unproductive population in the 1950s was more than half of the total population.

Press was by far the most important medium. About 90 per cent of media expenditure was allocated to print advertising alone. In this the major share of fund allocation was earmarked for newspaper advertisements; magazines received a very small portion of the budget. This does not imply that as publications magazines were inferior to newspapers in quality. Indeed, some

---

[14] 1 February 1953: This Sunday edition of *The Times of India* carried a news item on the front page with a bold subhead stating, 'Chaos in Film Industry: Dr Keskar Calls for Reform'. The report continues, 'He defended measures to tighten censorship rules as the government wanted to take prompt action against errant producers.' Whatever may have been the cause of irritation of the Minister of Information & Broadcasting, Dr B.V. Keskar, the fact that he wanted to impose censorship is a pointer to the mindset of the leaders of the time.

[15] It took a long while to persuade Bengalis to introduce wheat (chapati) in their meal. Prafulla Sen, who succeeded Dr Bidhan Chandra Roy as chief minister of West Bengal, became unpopular after he suggested that people have chapatis along with rice. In North India, the generic term 'Madrasis', which includes Tamil, Telegu, Malayali and Kanarese, are believed to share a common preference for rice as opposed to wheat in their food habit.

[16] I stumbled upon an interesting piece of news in *The Times of India* of 13 January 1950. This came in page 7 with a subheading 'Hoarder Flogged'. 'For the first time in Srinagar,' so the story went, 'flogging was administered in public yesterday for black marketing and hoarding of food grains. Charged under the government's recent food grains enhanced penalty ordinance, Abdullah Butt got 12 strokes with the cane.' While caning is even now resorted to in Pakistan, where the Shariat law is followed, I found this piece of news almost unbelievable for India.

[17] *The Times of India*, Bombay, dated 2 January 1950, reported: 'Pandit Nehru was asked about the steps taken by the government to deal with black marketing. He said that so far as the government was concerned, any person found guilty, however eminent or influential he might be, should be proceeded against.'

of the magazines were remarkably good in the reproduction of advertisements even though high-quality paper for printing books and periodicals was not available. Many magazines prospered; growth in circulation attracted more advertising as discerning advertisers and media planners realised that a magazine advertisement remained in circulation longer than an advertisement in a daily, and was indispensable as reminder medium for a campaign. Media availability was confined to press, magazines, cinema and outdoor. There was no TV. Radio advertising was available through Radio Ceylon but not over All India Radio. With the benefit of hindsight we observe that agencies and advertisers rarely did justice to running an adequate number of ads in magazines. The media mix generally was loaded in favour of press advertising.

The *INS Press Handbook* carries an interesting summary of developments related to newspapers and advertising agencies. I reproduce a graph that gives a perspective of accredited advertising agencies from 1939 to 2000. The graph shows there were around 14 publications accredited to the Indian Newspaper Society (INS; former Indian and Eastern Newspaper Society, IENS) at the turn of the decade (1950), whereas at its close (1959–60) there were 85. In the same issue of the handbook we also have a summary of the number of agencies accredited to INS. There are 14 agencies in 1950, which goes up to

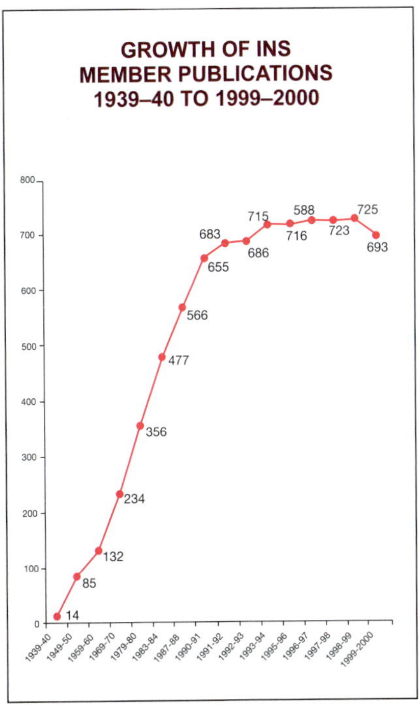

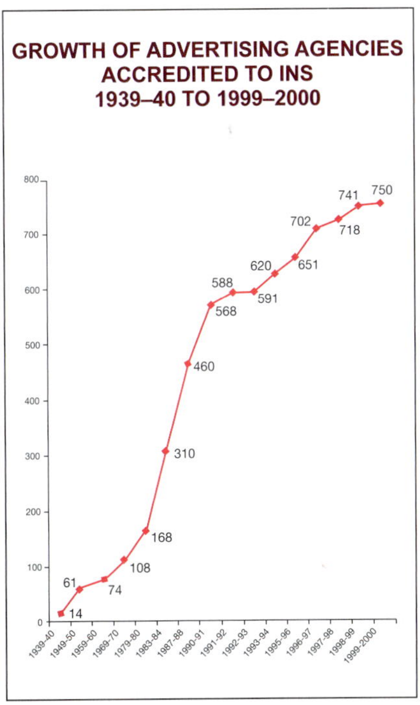

74 by 1959–60. The total expenditure on advertising, all India, amounted to only Rs 5 crore. Compared to the present total expenditure of around Rs 40,000 crore, it looks very small indeed. But in the 1950s, Rs 5 crore must have been regarded as more than adequate for agencies and publications since many new agencies and publications were started in the fifties.

Until fairly recent times it was possible to start an agency business with hardly any capital. All it required was to secure one or two clients who would entrust work to a person they liked and in whom they had confidence.[18]

PRODUCTIVE AND UNPRODUCTIVE CONSUMERS IN INDIA[19]

	Total Working Population (Productive Consumers)	Total Non-working Population (Unproductive Consumers)
1961 Census	188 million (42.7 per cent)	251 million (57.3 per cent)
1971 Census	180.4 million (32.9 per cent)	367.6 million (67.1 per cent)

Measured by other yardsticks such as life expectancy, literacy, housing, clothing and per capita availability of food grains, Indian society was poor materially and could not look beyond the present day. The burden of mere existence weighed heavily upon the minds of common citizens. Life expectancy at birth for men in the period 1941–1950 was 32.5 years, for women it was 31.7 years and average life expectancy was only 32 years. In the next decade, 1951–1960, life expectancy went up. For men it was about 42 years and for women, around 41 years. Together, it averaged 41.2 years, which is substantial compared to the previous decade.

The mean age for marriage in India in 1951 for males was 19.9 years, for females it was only 15.6 years. The standard of living for the vast majority of Indians was very low. And, between 1950 and 1965, there was a decline in the general standard of living. Consider the following table on clothing:

PERCENTAGE EXPENDITURE ON CLOTHING IN INDIA[20]

	1950	1960	1965
Rural	9.14	8.44	7.22
Urban	8.10	6.08	5.76

[18] I started an agency with zero capital in 1984. A client gave me Rs 50,000 (which was very generous for the times). With this as seed capital, I ran the agency for close to 15 years when I decided to exit the business. By then my operation had spread from Calcutta to all the metro cities with the exception of Hyderabad. This is not to suggest that I was an outstanding businessman. On the contrary, I was woefully inadequate. But I could manage to run a business for so long only because it was advertising, where interpersonal relationships play such a large part and cover up other deficiencies.

[19] Datt, Ruddar and K.P.M. Sundharam. *Indian Economy*. p. 60. S. Chand & Co. Ltd, 1978.

[20] Ganguli, B.N. and Davendra B. Gupta. *Levels of Living in India*. p. 95. I found this reference also in *Indian Economy* by Ruddar Datt and K.P.M. Sundharam.

People spent the greater part of their scarce earning on food. Clothes were regarded as luxury. A vast majority of people went through the year with one or two sets of clothes. Generally advertising on branded textiles coincided with festivals such as Diwali or Dussehra when people bought clothes for themselves and their families. For every earning member of a family, the purchase of almost every item of consumption, including primary articles such as food grains, was planned.

At the time the proportion of *pucca* houses to the total number of houses was as low as 36.8 per cent.[21] The best states were Punjab with 94 per cent, Jammu and Kashmir with 80 per cent, Rajasthan with 62.6 per cent, Maharashtra with 56.2 per cent, Kerala with 52.1 per cent and Gujarat with 51.8 per cent of *pucca* houses to the total number of houses. The laggards were Assam with 9.5 per cent, Orissa with 10.6 per cent and Bihar with 15.1 per cent. West Bengal registered a low 24.7 per cent of *pucca* houses despite Calcutta being the state capital.

The National Sample Survey, eighteenth round, presented a table on the percentage distribution of population by daily expenditure classes. This table, which is included in a footnote, shows that in 1956–57 the poorest people who spent up to 50 paise per day comprised about 56 per cent of the rural population and 36 per cent of the urban population. Life in cities was far better, with the poorest comprising 11 per cent of the population in 1956–57. It is not surprising that the cities continued to experience large migrations from smaller towns and villages, especially Calcutta in the east, Delhi and Kanpur in the north, Bombay and Ahmedabad in the west and Madras and Hyderabad in the south.

If the first group is combined with the next group, that is, those whose per capita daily expenditure was between 50 paise and 70 paise, the two groups combined account for 77 per cent for rural, 58 per cent for urban and about 28 per cent in cities.[22]

J.L. Azad of the Planning Commission had calculated that the per capita expenditure on education in 1950–51 was a meagre Rs 3.2. This rose to Rs 34.8 in 1974–75, which reflects poorly on society and social priorities set by the government at the time, which continued to harp on socially inclusive development for all.

---

[21] *Ibid.*
[22]

Daily per capita Expenditure Class in Paise	Rural 1956–57	Rural 1963–64	Urban 1956–57	Urban 1963–64	Cities 1956–57	Cities 1963–64
Up to 50 p	55.9	32	36	16.4	11.2	4.8
50 p to 70 p	22	27.3	22.2	21	16.6	7.7
70 p to 93 p	11.7	19.4	15.7	21.3	16.4	15.7
93 p to 143 p	7.3	14.7	14.6	21.2	25.1	26.1
143 to 183 p	1.7	3.7	4.6	7.3	10.5	11.8
183 p and above	1.4	2.9	6.9	12.8	20.2	33.9
All classes	100.0	100.0	100.0	100.0	100.0	100.0

Main occupations

The National Income Committee,[23] set up by the government of India in 1949, observed in its report that the principal occupations in 1950–51 were:

1. Agriculture, which contributed nearly half the national income; 72.4 per cent of the working force was employed in agriculture.
2. Mining, manufacturing and hand trades, which contributed about 16 per cent of the national income; 10.6 per cent of the working force was employed in this category.
3. Services sector, including commerce, transport and communications accounted for about 18 per cent of the national income.
4. Yet another head, 'Other Services', which included professional services such as administrative services, house and property along with more everyday services such as domestic services and, inexplicably, the liberal arts, accounted for 15 per cent of the national income.

Therefore, if all services are combined under a common head, the service sector accounted for as much as 33 per cent of the national income, as opposed to a cumulative total of 16 per cent for the manufacturing sector.[24] The average per capita income in 1950 at 1948–49 prices was estimated to be Rs 250.[25]

The Planning Commission was constituted in 1951 by a resolution of the government of India. This was a milestone in post-independent India as it led to the First Five Year Plan. This concept of Five Year Plans owed much to Soviet Russia. Members of the Planning Commission presented an outline of the First Five Year Plan in July 1951. The Commission proposed a plan outlay of Rs 1,493 crore at the initial stage followed by a further outlay of Rs 300 crore in the second stage, provided external assistance was available. Of all the subsequent and at most times grandiose Five Year Plans, the First Five

[23]Members of the committee included Professor P.C. Mahalnobis, Professor D.R. Gadgil and Professor V.K.R.V. Rao. Datt, Ruddar and K.P.M. Sundharam. *Indian Economy*. p. 35. S. Chand & Company, 1978.

[24]I reproduce a chart from *Indian Economy*:

Productivity per Person in Different Occupations (1950–1951)

Occupation	Percentage of Working Force Employed	Percentage of Net National Product Produced	Productivity per Person
Agriculture	72.4	51.3	Rs 500
Mining, manufacturing and hand trades	10.6	16.1	Rs 1,000
Commerce, transport and communication	7.7	17.7	Rs 1,500
Other services	9.3	15.1	Rs 800

[25]Leading economists in the 1960s and 1970s differed in their calculation of per capita income (average). Arora and Iyengar estimated average income at Rs 249, while K. Mukherjee and M. Mukherjee placed it Rs 4 and Rs 3 higher, respectively. S.J. Patel estimated an average income at Rs 259. For our purposes Rs 250 would not be too far out, indicating how little people had to live on. The majority agree that there was a decline in average income compared to 1945. *Ibid.*

Year Plan was outstanding because of what it achieved.[26] The expenditure planned under specific heads indicates (a) priorities in economic development and (b) the state of the economy.

In the early 1950s, the industrialisation of India in the Nehruvian era had begun. Basic parameters of living such as availability of food,[27] health care, housing, communication and education were scarce; but the founders of modern India felt that industrialisation must go on in full swing.

In the late 1950s, India had only 11,800 miles (18,986.2 km) of highways. The First Five Year Plan envisaged work only on 750 miles (1,206.75 km) of roads, unbelievable in our day and age when politicians and planners talk about thousands of kilometres of road construction with outlays in excess of a few hundred thousand crores of rupees. The Indian Roads & Transport Development Association (IRTDA) in its representation to the government proposed only Rs 23 crore as expenditure for the National Highways, and a total of less than Rs 120 crore for allocations proposed for states and the Centre combined.[28]

---

[26]Summing up the achievements of the First Five Year Plan were the following key factors:

1. Growth of national income by 18 per cent (admittedly on a very modest base).
2. Growth of per capita income by 11 per cent and per capita consumption by 9 per cent (which in reality does not mask general indigence).
3. Increase in food production by 20 per cent (which is surprising considering single cropping and poor irrigation over much of agricultural land across India).
4. Extension of irrigation facilities over 160 lakh acres. (A significant achievement under difficult conditions.)
5. Rise in industrial production—139 points over the base year, 1950–51—resulting in an annual growth of 8 per cent. Source: *India at 50*. p. 46. General Editor: T.J.S. George. Express Publications (Madurai) Ltd, 1997.

[27]In the December 1951 issue of the *Dunlop Gazette* (an in-house magazine of the company), a description of the Sahaganj factory states, 'The facilities include cheap electricity, running water, up-to-date sanitary arrangements, separate kitchens and a plot of land for kitchen gardening. In these days of food shortage, the last item is of some importance. The soil is fertile and it is gratifying to note that practically everybody living on the estate makes an effort to augment the vegetable supply.' The same issue devotes half a page to Noel Newsome, PR manager of Harry Ferguson Ltd, who was visiting various places in India to promote mechanised farming (use of tractors). He says, 'The chronic food scarcity in our country has made it clear that the long-term solution of our food problem lies in improved farming and higher productivity on land.' At the time India had neither the technology nor the infrastructure to make all this possible.

[28]These figures have been taken from an old issue of *Dunlop Gazette* dated December 1951. I reproduce the table to show the kind of monetary allocation that was made for various states; some such as Bombay and West Bengal were economically advanced while Uttar Pradesh and Bihar were relatively backward.

States	NPC's Allocation (Rs. crores)	Increase recommended by IRTDA (Rs. crores)
Central Government: National Highways	23.00	-
West Bengal	13.85	-
Bombay	11.64	-
Bihar	8.00	-
Uttar Pradesh	5.22	5.00
Madras	5.00	5.00
Assam	2.13	2.00
Madhya Pradesh	2.00	2.00
Orissa	2.00	-
East Punjab	0.75	2.00
Part B and C States	20.15	10.00
Total	93.74	26.00

The Indian capital market in the fifties

Since advertising is integral to business, a brief review of the Indian capital market is necessary to understand the environment in which business was conducted in the 1950s. There were 1,125 listed companies in 1956 of which 576 were listed with the Calcutta Stock Exchange, 197 with the Bombay Stock Exchange and 192 with the Madras Stock Exchange. Besides these there were 81 listed at the Ahmedabad Stock Exchange, 73 with Delhi and 40 companies each with the Uttar Pradesh and Nagpur Stock Exchanges. The total paid-up capital was only Rs 270 crore.

Most of the industries had over 50 per cent of their capital in the form of ordinary shares. The Tata Iron & Steel Company had an unusually high percentage of its capital (73 per cent) in the form of preference shares. The other leading industries, namely, chemical, paper and engineering, also depended to a considerable extent on preference shares. The jute industry, which was largely controlled by British companies, had a more balanced capital structure with 60 per cent of capital from ordinary shares, 30 per cent in the form of preference shares and 10 per cent from debentures.[29]

[29]Cirvante V.R. *The Indian Capital Market*. p. 108. Oxford University Press, 1956. I reproduce the table of industries and their methods of raising capital.

Industry	Total Number of Companies	Ordinary Capital (Rs lakh)	Ordinary Capital as per cent of Total Capital Employed	Number of Companies	Preference Capital (Rs in lakh)	Preference Capital as per cent of Total Capital Employed
Jute	61	1,304	60.5	49	622	28.9
Cotton Mills	167	2,817	81.5	57	487	14.1
Iron and Steel	5	874	42.8	2	889	43.5
Engineering and Construction	25	336	71	10	124	26.2
Coal	55	495	87.9	9	43	7.6
Electric	70	1,682	73.5	27	394	17.2
Tea	133	524	89.7	23	51	8.7
Cement	4	1,225	91.8	2	40	3
Sugar	49	640	66.7	23	172	17.9
Chemical	7	231	63.5	5	113	31
Paper	8	177	57.8	5	68	22.2
Steamship	6	306	90.3	2	18	5.3
Timber	4	111	95.7	1	3	2.6
Match	2	77	100	-	-	-
Radio and Cable	1	54	75	-	-	-

Media in the 1950s: Press

The Press Commission carried out one of the first surveys on advertising expenditure in India in 1953. According to this report, the size of the advertising expenditure was estimated at Rs 5 crore annually. It seems incredible today when total advertising expenditure nationally is estimated to be in the region of over Rs 40,000 crore. In the decade of the 1940s, 65 new publications were born; quite a few were destined to leave their mark in the next three decades. The more notable publications were:

Blitz, English (Bombay), 1941

Daily Jagran, Hindi (Jhansi and Kanpur), 1942

Thanthi, Tamil (Madras, Madurai and Trichy, also called Tiruchirappalli), 1942

Tarun Bharat, Marathi (Nagpur and Poona), 1944

Sanmarg, Hindi (Calcutta), 1945

Cinema Masika, Malayalam (Kottayam), 1946

Eve's Weekly, English (Bombay), 1947

Sport & Pastime, English (Madras), 1947

Kumudam, Tamil (Madras), 1947

Matrubhumi, Oriya (Cuttack), 1947

Nai Duniya, Hindi (Indore), 1947

Prajatantra, Oriya (Cuttack), 1947

Swatantra Bharat, Hindi (Lucknow), 1947

Amar Ujala, Hindi (Agra), 1948

Deccan Herald, English (Bangalore, now Bengaluru), 1948

Lokasatta, Marathi (Bombay), 1948

Prajavani, Kannada (Bangalore), 1948

Auto-Spark, English (Bombay), 1949

It is clear from the names mentioned that magazines were beginning to come into the newsstands. Some such as *Sport & Pastime*, *Cinema Masika*, *Eve's Weekly* and *Auto-Spark* were already targeting special interest groups.

Compared to the 1940s, the next decade saw fewer new newspapers and magazines, but among the 46 publications listed, there were quite a few that prospered later. Not surprisingly, a number of publications belong to The Times of India Group. They had both the resource and the talent to diversify into language dailies and magazines.

Year	Publication (Name, Language)	Where Published
1950	*Dharmayug*, Hindi	Bombay
1950	*Saptahik Hindustan*, Hindi	Delhi
1950	*Amrita Patrika*, Hindi	Allahabad
1950	*Jagran*, Hindi	Indore
1950	*Janashakti*, Gujarati	Bombay
1950	*Navbharat Times*, Hindi	Bombay and Delhi
1950	*Phulchhab*, Gujarati	Rajkot
1951	*Screen*, English	Bombay
1951	*Loksatta*, Gujarati	Baroda
1951	*Tamil Nadu*, Tamil	Madurai
1951	*Yugadharma*, Hindi	Nagpur and Jabalpur
1952	*Andhra Prabha Illustrated Weekly*, Telegu	Madras
1952	*Amrit*, Marathi	Nasik
1952	*Filmfare*, English	Bombay
1952	*Navaneet*, Hindi	Bombay
1952	*Trend*, English	Bombay
1952	*Daily Akali*	Jullundur
1952	*Ultorath*, Bengali	Calcutta
1953	*Cine Advance*, English	Calcutta
1953	*Janasatta*, Gujarati	Ahmedabad
1953	*Advance*, English	Kanpur
1954	*Prapancha*, Kannada	Hubli
1954	*Reader's Digest*, Indian Edition, English	Bombay
1954	*Cinema Rangam*, Telegu	Madras
1954	*Bhavan's Journal*, English	Bombay
1954	*Vir Arjun*, Hindi	Delhi
1954	*Cinema Jagat*, Hindi	Calcutta
1955	*Vasanti*, Hindi	Benaras (now Varanasi)
1955	*Assam Bani*, Assamese	Gauhati (now Guwahati)
1955	*Rekha*, Hindi	Nagpur
1955	*Sansar*, Gujarati	Anand
1955	*Current Events*, English	Dehradun
1955	*Shrirang*, Gujarati	Ahmedabad

Year	Publication (Name, Language)	Where Published
1955	*Suprabhat*, Hindi	Calcutta
1955	*Chandani*, Gujarati	Ahmedabad
1956	*India Magazine*, English	Madras
1956	*Bharati*, Hindi	Bombay
1956	*Kasturi*, Kannada	Hubli
1956	*Navabharat*, Gujarati	Baroda
1956	*Jagriti*, Sindhi	Bombay
1956	*Dipika*, English	Bombay
1957	*Kerala Janatha*, Malyalam and English	Trivandrum (now Thiruvananthapuram)
1957	*Madhya Pradesh Chronicle*, English	Bhopal
1957	*Hyphen*, English	Bombay
1958	*Flair*, English	Bombay
1958	*Parag*, Hindi	Bombay

In February 1956, D.J. Keymer sent letters to all employees in Calcutta that the agency could no longer continue to function in the city as its earning from the branch was declining. This decision was to lead to the formation of a strange kind of company: a company owned by its employees, a company that was a cooperative. The name chosen by the leading owner-entrepreneurs was Clarion Advertising Services Private Limited.

I mention this here because the agency soon became a leading national agency. From the 1950s till about the mid-1980s it remained number two in billing to JWT (renamed HTA). It trained new recruits, thereby developing a talent pool of professionals for the advertising industry; created exciting advertising and earned the trust of some of the best companies in the country. Clarion also set benchmarks on what a company should not do. It evolved into a peculiar agency that had the rare ability to kick itself in the backside rather too frequently.

Clarion had an enviable start. The men who were at the helm were held in high regard by the major companies in Calcutta. Dunlop India Limited and ITC decided to back the new agency since the men who were working on their account would continue to work for them. *The Statesman*, which in 1956 was not only a major daily in Calcutta but was recognised as a premier national paper, also decided to support the young agency. *The Statesman* offered 15 per cent commission and extended credit even though the agency had not earned its accreditation from the IENS. Even the chief minister of West Bengal, Dr B.C. Roy, who did not share the leftist political leaning of some of the founder directors, told the team members when they called on him that he would support their agency.

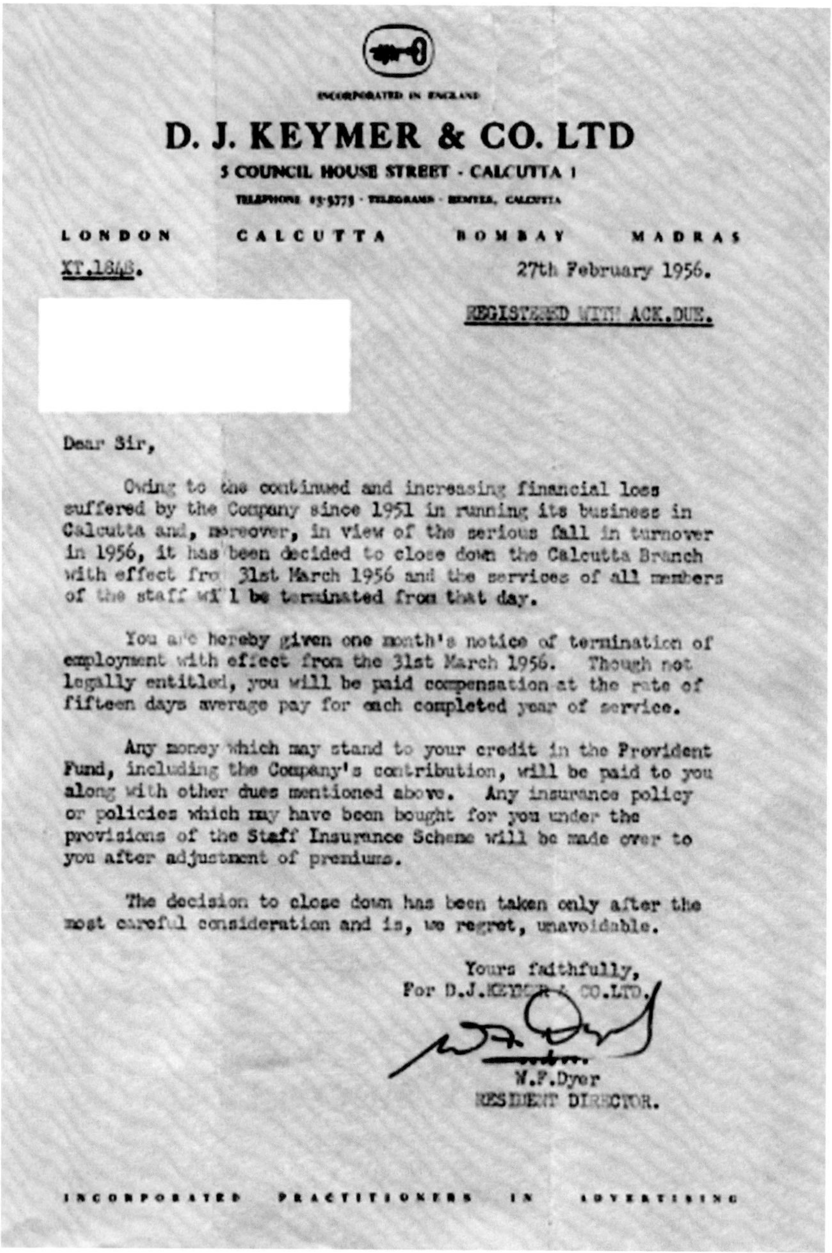

INCORPORATED IN ENGLAND

D. J. KEYMER & CO. LTD

5 COUNCIL HOUSE STREET · CALCUTTA 1

LONDON CALCUTTA BOMBAY MADRAS

XT.1848. 27th February 1956.

REGISTERED WITH ACK.DUE.

Dear Sir,

Owing to the continued and increasing financial loss suffered by the Company since 1951 in running its business in Calcutta and, moreover, in view of the serious fall in turnover in 1956, it has been decided to close down the Calcutta Branch with effect from 31st March 1956 and the services of all members of the staff will be terminated from that day.

You are hereby given one month's notice of termination of employment with effect from the 31st March 1956. Though not legally entitled, you will be paid compensation at the rate of fifteen days average pay for each completed year of service.

Any money which may stand to your credit in the Provident Fund, including the Company's contribution, will be paid to you along with other dues mentioned above. Any insurance policy or policies which may have been bought for you under the provisions of the Staff Insurance Scheme will be made over to you after adjustment of premiums.

The decision to close down has been taken only after the most careful consideration and is, we regret, unavoidable.

Yours faithfully,
For D.J.KEYMER & CO.LTD.

W.F.Dyer
RESIDENT DIRECTOR.

INCORPORATED PRACTITIONERS IN ADVERTISING

The letter mentions that business for D.J. Keymer in Calcutta was declining since 1951. Is this factual or is it a mere pretext to make an unpleasant decision more acceptable to those employees who were served this notice of termination of service?[30] What was the total expenditure on advertising in the country in the early 1950s? What were the major expense heads for an agency operation? How many agencies ceased to operate in a year? What were the major business risks in running an ad agency? How many new ad agencies came into existence in a year or in a decade? What was the expectation of profit in running an ad agency? How much capital was required to start and operate an agency?

Like any other business, the ad agency business also has to negotiate good times with the not-so-good times. The flight of business capital from one metro to others reduces the overall business available in advertising. However, in the 1950s there was not any significant flight of capital from Calcutta. After the communists came to power in Calcutta in the mid-1970s, militant trade union activity, marked by *gheraos*,[31] drove capital away from the city and the state to other places such as Bombay, Delhi and Bangalore, which offered a better work environment.

The subsequent success of Clarion proves that the business climate was not so bad as to warrant the closure of D.J. Keymer's Calcutta branch. A common problem that leads to sickness of ad agencies is over-staffing. Too often an agency that does well takes on more and more undesirable persons on board with the aim of providing the best possible service to clients. Unfortunately, a great many people does not mean service efficiency. It is quite possible that D.J. Keymer from the early 1950s till the time it declared the closure of its Calcutta branch had too many undesirable people, resulting in paring of profit. At the time, 'laying off' surplus staff was not unknown in industry practice. Later laws were promulgated that made layoffs ridiculously difficult. When Clarion commenced operation it absorbed everyone in D.J. Keymer, which suggests that over-staffing was not regarded as an insurmountable problem by the new entrepreneur managers.

[30]In a commemorative collection of essays published in 1979 on Dilip Kumar Gupta, who was the advertising manager of Bata India, Nripenda Sanyal recalls, 'I heard from D.K. himself that Keymer had requested him to stay on and represent the company in Calcutta as the resident director. He declined since he didn't wish to stay on alone where all other colleagues were asked to leave. When the employees of Keymer formed Clarion it came as a surprise to many that they did not request D.K. to join them.' Till that time, D.K. Gupta was perhaps the senior-most Indian officer in D.J. Keymer in Calcutta. He was designated assistant manager.

[31]Forced detention of management staff and employers. They were surrounded by aggrieved workmen; very often those detained were not allowed to use the toilet. The police turned a blind eye to this condemnable illegal action. Sometimes *gheraos* lasted 8 or 12 hours.

L.A. Stronach

L.A. Stronach started his advertising agency named after him in 1925. He was a Eurasian who probably liked Bombay better than London. He also had an office in London. Unlike the present day, when American, British, French and Japanese agencies have offices in India, buying up majority stake in India's best agencies, Stronach went to London after consolidating his business in Bombay.

The few references about Stronach the man paint him in poor light. Subhas Ghosal, in his recollections, spoke about Stronach being a miserly fellow. Ghosal recounted that he bullied his employees who were scared of him. But which agency head in India ever managed an office without scaring people down the line?

L.A. Stronach was a leading agency, it did sizeable business. Without good work and without a proper service structure it could not have retained its place as a leading agency as long as it did.

Sylvester daCunha, who has played such an important role in the development of Indian advertising in many different ways—as business manager, brand creator, scribe on advertising and as a respected professional setting standards of 'best practice'—spent his formative years in L.A. Stronach in London where he learnt the basics of advertising. He must have felt comfortable at L.A. Stronach since he did not shift to any other agency.

L.R. Swamy

Another agency which commenced operation in 1925 sharing the name of its founder was L.R. Swamy Advertising. It was based in Madras. Between 1925 and the 1950s, it was a leading agency. It is probable that L.R. Swamy started operations as an outdoor agency, taking up mainstream advertising later. Most ad men who started agencies in the early twentieth century began their careers with some major newspaper. For instance, B. Dattaram, who founded the first Indian ad agency, worked for *The Times of India*.

The media scene

At the time print media comprised:

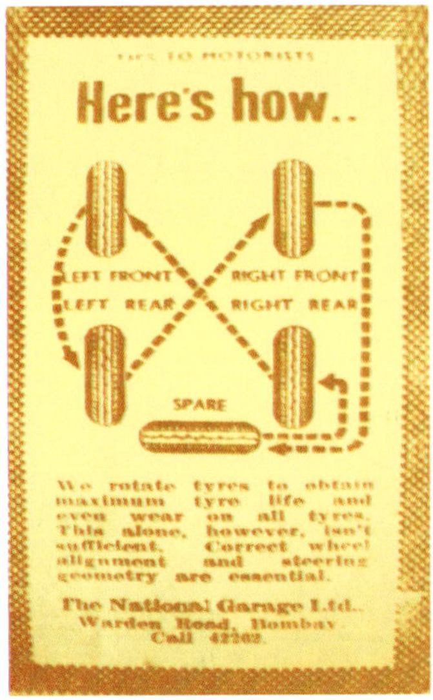

- Newspaper advertisements

These were mostly black and white. *The Times of India* used a single second colour for small single-column width advertisements that appeared as solus ads on the cover page. Here is an example.[32]

Line illustrations were more common than half-tones in advertisements. Illustrators were generally very proficient.[33]

- Advertisements in magazines

There were hardly any periodicals at the time that offered colour option to advertisers. Four-colour processing, though not unknown—and quite often used in printing point-of-purchase (POP) materials such as posters, danglers, leaflets and so on—was rare for advertisements in newspapers and periodicals.[34] On special occasions newspapers published supplements that provided a colour option to advertisers. But newsprint quality was poor and the advertisements lost visual clarity especially if pictures were in half-tone.

Reader's Digest was one of the few magazines that gave advertisers the option of colour ads. Most of the colour advertisements featured line illustrations. The Brylcreem advertisement is an early example of a testimonial ad using a celebrity. Tenzing Norgay, after climbing Mount Everest, became a national celebrity. Brylcreem was quick to capitalise on his stature. The picture in the ad was a half-tone which was touched up and converted to a quarter-tone before the final assembly of the advertisement.

---

[32]We shall present different kinds of advertisements at the end of this chapter—grouping them to enable the reader to assess the creative merits of ads so featured.

[33]They had no computers or software available that enables a graphic artist today to download a line illustration by the mere click of the mouse.

[34]Subrata Banerjee, writing in the *International Handbook of Advertising*, McGraw Hill, edited by S. Watson Dunn, 1964, observes, 'Because of import restrictions newsprint is in short supply and quality cannot be guaranteed. As a result, reproduction of half-tones even in major English dailies is difficult … This situation acts as a brake on designing, presentation and the use of photographs … Even publications which are printed in colour cannot effectively reproduce a wide range of colours—even in photogravure.'

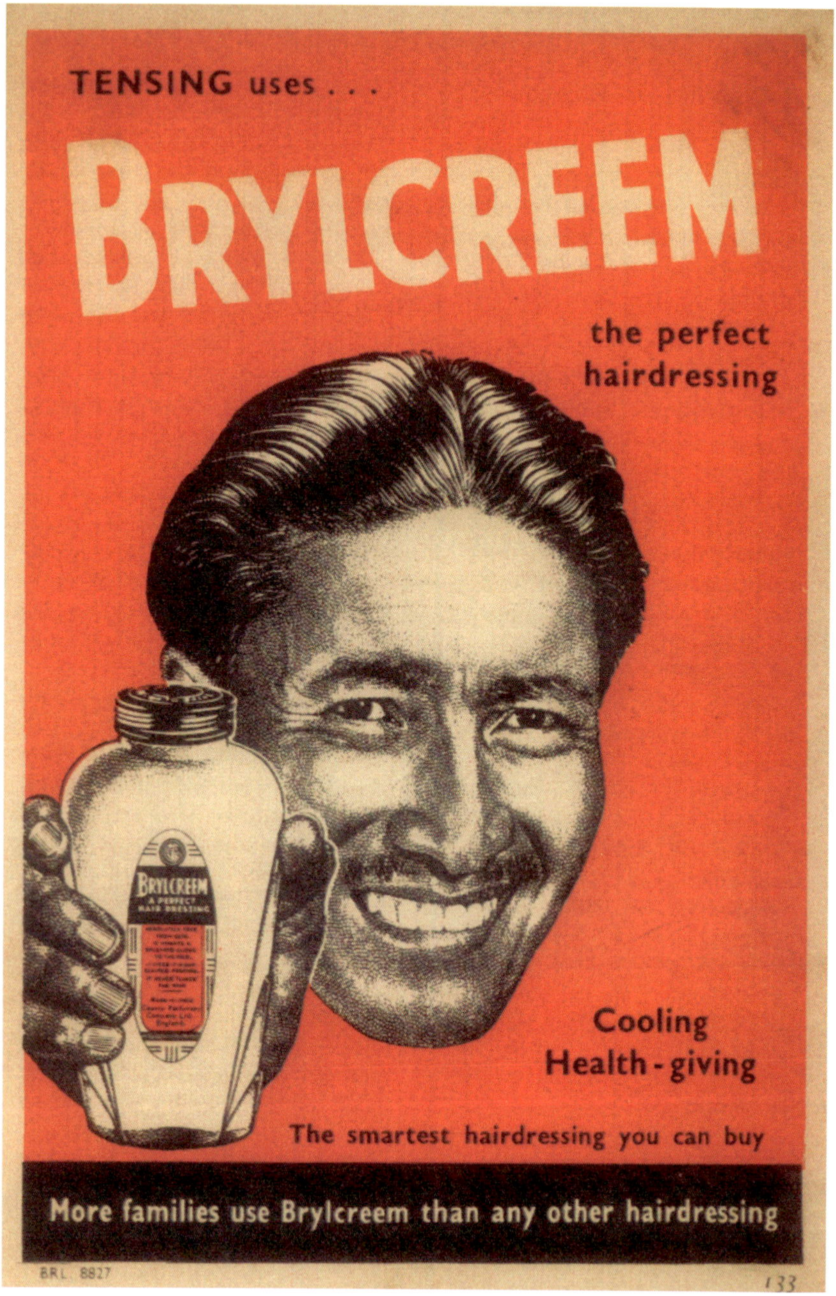

Hairstyles such as sartorial styles keep coming back. Youngsters today who use gel to pursue hairdos that remain in place even in stormy conditions would surely approve of the shiny well-groomed look of Tenzing.

- Posters/POP items such as shelf stickers, show cards, eye-catchers and danglers[35]

It is difficult to believe that the picture in the poster, showing a worker manually *making a tyre, represents the state of the tyre-making industry in the fifties. Dunlop's Sahaganj factory was one of the most highly mechanised factories in Asia. Or is the visual supporting the claim of perfect workmanship by showing a person working with his hands?*

---

[35]The Dunlop posters are from 1948/1949. Apart from the Hindi Eveready poster the other Eveready items displayed are examples of contemporaneous POPs from American Eveready Works. Eveready printed these in 2005 to commemorate 100 years of the company. As part of the B.M. Khaitan Group of Companies, Eveready continues to be a leader in dry cells in India, but after the Bhopal gas tragedy the organisation downed shutters in the USA.

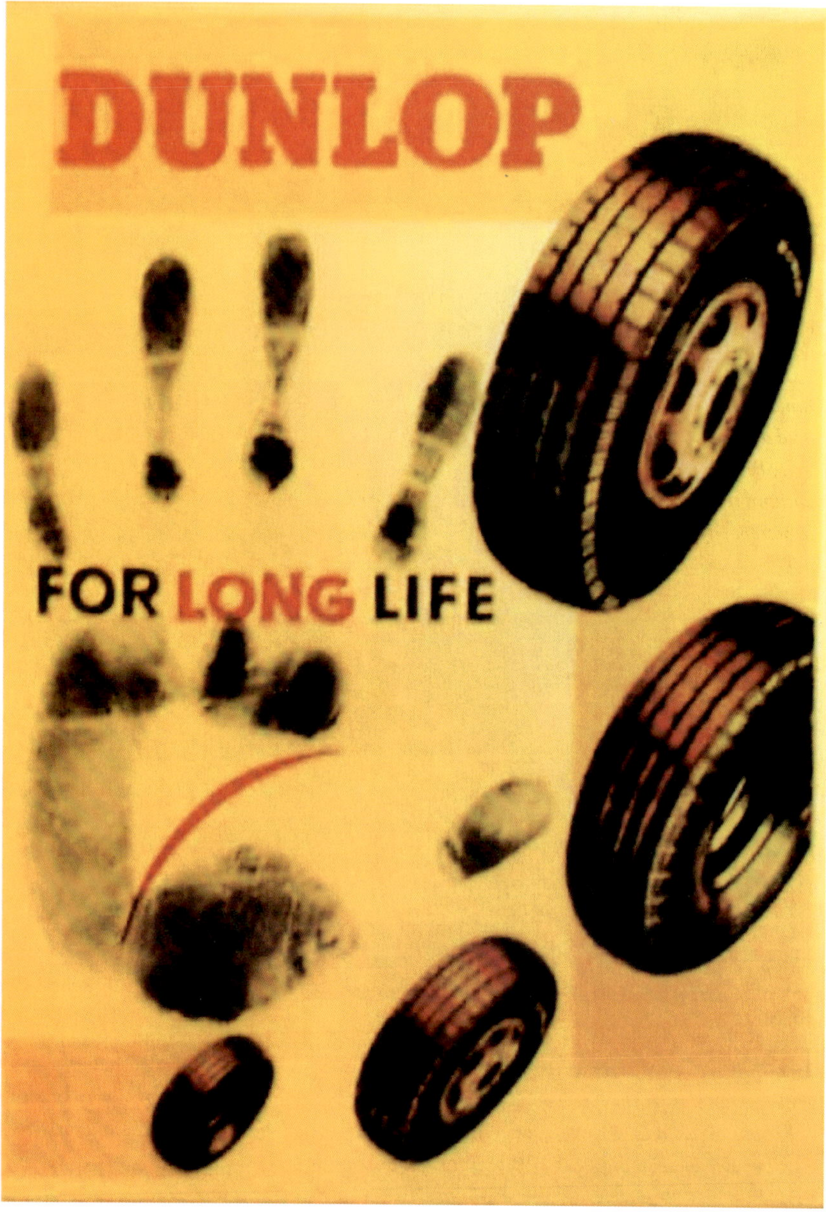

Art directors often forget that advertising should be simple and easy to grasp. I wonder how many truck and bus drivers or for that matter tyre dealers would have figured out that the open palm showing a red line indicates a long life line, which is the message in the caption. It is an untidy poster with the smudgy black palm, tyres that are naturally black in colour against a bright yellow ground.

Dunlop used tin plates when the objective was to retain the message for some time. Tin plates lasted longer, often years, till someone decided to remove them. Although the photograph lacks clarity the display above was possibly a tin plate. Printing on tin was done in Bombay and Calcutta. Note the use of bright contrasting colours. John Boyd Dunlop's bearded face features at the bottom right-hand corner.

This poster is intriguing. The owner driver of a heavy vehicle, if he knew English, would surely ask the dealer how such a tyre would benefit him. Do the teeth increase road grip? Is the tyre safer to run on? Company salesmen spent a good deal of their time interacting with dealers, selling new concepts of products so that the dealers could present these ideas forcefully to truckers.

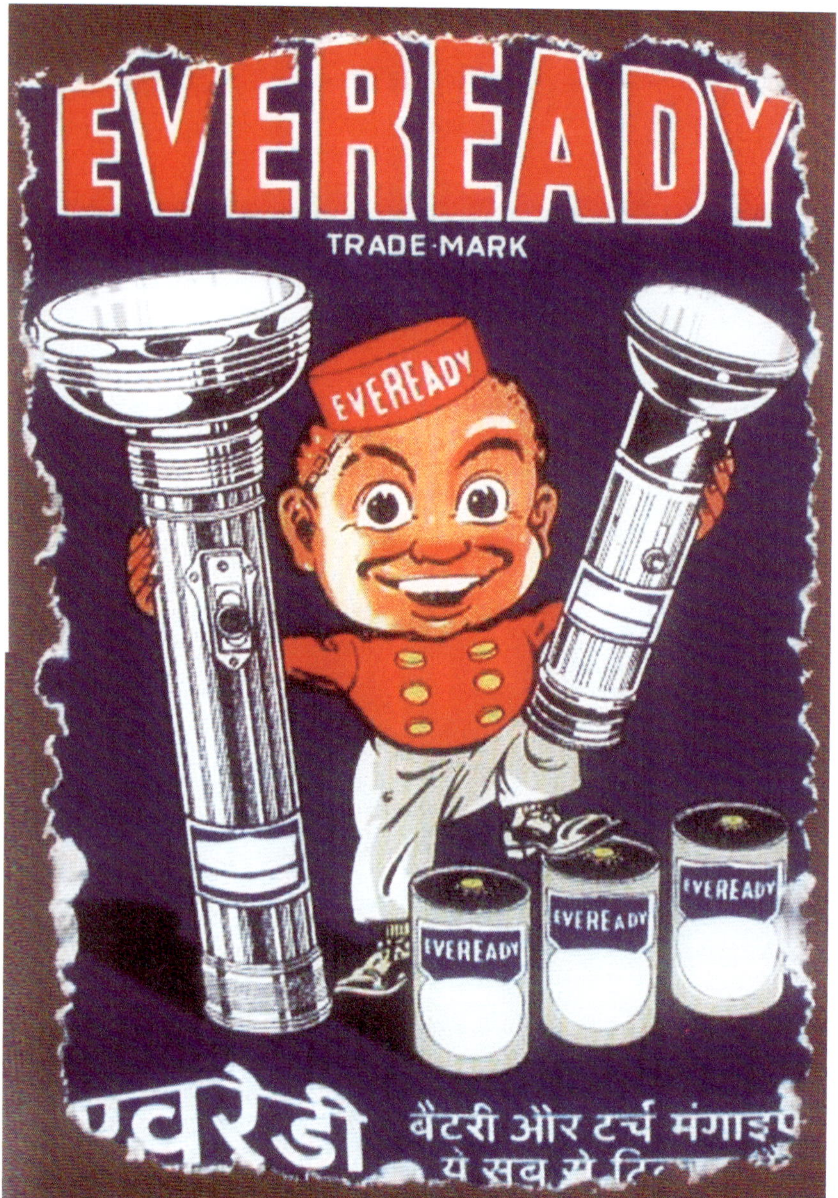

Eveready battery and Jeevan Sathi torch became very popular in the country. These were early branded products that found customers in towns and villages because they served a real need. Electricity was unknown in villages. Snakes wandered into homes especially during the monsoons when low-lying land was inundated. Incidents of snake bite were quite common across the country.

These are examples of high-end products. I am not sure whether electric candles were ever launched in India. Nine Lives battery with a black cat as a motif was launched with a lot of advertising support.

Marketers had a choice of options for POP display materials and other support print literature. The common point-of-sale (POS) items were:

- Folders and pamphlets, most of which were designed to educate consumers on product attributes or benefits
- Direct mail

It may surprise a twenty-first century marketer to learn that in the mid-fifties there were many companies that spent effort and money to maintain a mailing list. Regular mails were sent to shareholders. Ads were released for brands with a response coupon built in, which had an address column. *Reader's Digest* carried one of the most effective mail campaigns for its magazine and other books. It gave a token gift to respondents and also ran a free trial offer.

Besides the print media, other media options available at the time were:

- Cinema slides
- Advertising films. Initially these films were not of any fixed duration; over time, 100 ft films were made, which took 60 seconds to exhibit.

Ad films were exhibited in cinema halls; infrequently, as shown here, by a mobile exhibition van that toured the countryside, covering villages and towns. I suspect that among those sitting on the ground, the majority were company people who travelled with the film exhibition unit.

- Hoardings

The brand of tyre shown in the hoarding, Dunlop Fort, had a fairly long run of popularity. Brand attrition was unknown in the 1950s, unless aided by the marketer's loss of interest in the brand.

- Signage on roads, buildings, and bridges. In Calcutta one prominent railway bridge, which displayed the company logo, prompted people to call the place Dunlop Bridge. Buses plying the route today still display the same name although the company is moribund for the past so many years.

How we miss those old times! Pedestrians crossing any street in Calcutta in 2013 do so at the risk of their lives. In the 1950s a policeman was posted at the crossing to ensure the safety of pedestrians. This picture was published in a Dunlop Gazette *of the early 1950s.*

- Sometimes companies participated in exhibitions, which were spectacular. Exhibitions showcased a company's strengths and, unlike now, exhibitions were not regarded as forums for serious business transaction.

Dunlop played a catalytic role in rural development. Since the most basic forms of transportation such as handcarts and bullock carts moved goods and people in India, which was 90 per cent an agricultural economy, enabling these basic forms of transport to move smoother by replacing wooden wheels with tyres was a significant achievement. The handcart running on tyres reduced the physical effort of the poor men who pulled these carts. Bullock carts on tyres helped to increase the productive life of animals. However, animal-drawn vehicles on tyres also required better road surfaces. During the monsoons village roads were generally impassable on anything save bullock carts with large wooden wheels.

The stands used in this photograph seem to have been of the re-usable kind. Product leaflets and posters for dealer outlets have been pasted on the display boards. Actual products were also displayed at the stall. The tyre displayed on the left looks like a truck tyre; the tyre with white sidewall on the right is a car tyre.

In these pictures we see an actual display of items, as is common in trade fairs organised today. However, this exhibition took place in the UK in the late 1940s.

Print media: Content, format, scheduling and constraints

Newspaper advertisements constituted the primary medium for most campaigns. The options available were:

- Classified columns. In this category there were papers whose columns were structured as display classified advertisements. These generally appeared on the first page, were of single column width and frequently within 10 cm length.

A number of these advertisements that appeared in the section meant for small advertisers pertain to eateries. Dining out, especially over the weekend, must have been popular among those who lived in the four metropolitan cities.

We must remember that till the late 1950s and well into the early years of the 1960s, a sizeable expatriate population remained in India. While employment opportunity in government services was no longer attractive for expatriates, they continued to hold important positions in private companies. Upper class Indians tended to emulate their lifestyle. The kind of fare offered by these restaurants indicates popular choice.[36]

DINE AND DANCE
AT THE
AMBASSADOR
STARLIT ROOF GARDEN
On Saturday the 17th
With Molly O'Conner
HECKE KINGDOM & HIS BAND
OUR AIRCONDITIONED GRILL ROOM SPECIALITIES
Today: Souvaraine Soup
Lobster a la Tourville
Tomorrow: French Onion Soup
Australian Turkey & York Ham
For reservation phone 26091[37]

[36]Chinese cuisine or for that matter South Indian dishes or typical Punjabi food were not as common as now. By the 1970s preference of foods changed, especially when dining out. But by the 1970s most expatriates had left India.

[37]Obviously Australian turkeys and York hams were still being imported, despite the Indian government cutting down on imports because India's economy was in a precarious situation. *The Times of India*, Bombay, carried this advertisement on 16 January 1953. In the next advertisement we are again greeted by the Australian roast turkey.

The same paper on the same day carried a number of similar advertisements. A second advertisement offered special dinner at Apollo Bunder:

> CHEZ CAROLINE
> Dhunraj Mahal, Apollo Bunder
> Tonight Dinner Special
> **MILAN MINESTRONE SOUP**
> **CHICKEN A LA KING WITH**
> **WAFFLE**
> Tomorrow Dinner Special
> **DUCK A L'ORANGE WITH**
> **JUMPING POTATOES**
> Reserve your table for Republic Night Dinner
> **AUSTRALIAN ROAST**
> **TURKEY & HAM**
> Phone: 35362

It is gratifying to see that Republic Day was being marketed as an occasion for dining out. In later years Indians forgot to celebrate the two most important days in the calendar—Republic Day and Independence Day—allowing politicians to be perfect killjoys with pontifical speeches.[38]

- Personal column advertisements. In the early 1950s, ads in personal columns were truly 'personal' in nature unlike ads in the personal column in dailies today where most of them are commercial.

Under 'Kennel, Pets and Livestock', *The Times of India* of 16 January 1953 carried this delightful notice:

> **For Sale Healthy and Talkative**
> Cockatoo and African parrot. Please telephone 75126

People seeking jobs or looking for servants and, surprisingly, for the times, even young ladies wanted for modelling assignments appeared in personal column advertisements.

The Times of India of 31 January 1953 carried the following advertisements:

1. Wanted An Efficient Bearer—well trained—Salary Rs 65/- with room and without food.

I have retained the capitals as used in the actual advertisement. Readers today may wonder whether the advertiser was indeed offering a salary that an efficient and well-trained bearer could live on besides saving some to send home to his own family.

[38]Republic Day celebrations revolve around display of military might, which perhaps is necessary in view of India's 'friendly' neighbours.

2. Oxford Undergraduate, British ex-Guards officer, finishing June, wants to join import-export merchant or agency house, India, South East Asia, Hong-Kong.

The Second World War had ended just eight years prior to the release of the advertisement. By the time a lot of army men had been discharged and were on the lookout for suitable employment. This person seems to be one who likes the sunshine in Asia compared to the mist and cold of England. Of all the Asian countries mentioned, he probably had the highest preference for India since it comes first in his list of places. At the time many Indian medical graduates migrated to England where they were welcome because England had a shortage of doctors. And Indians continued to live and die without adequate medical facility or proper medical attention for decades after Independence.[39]

3. Wanted Young Ladies Residing in Bombay with attractive and expressive features and good teeth to pose for photographs for commercial advertisements. Good remuneration paid. Apply with full details.

Bombay has always been more progressive than any other Indian city especially with regard to the ready acceptance of women at work. Women generally felt safe taking up jobs and other assignments and were never unduly worried even if they worked late. In 1953 we are unlikely to come across a similar advertisement in the leading dailies of Madras, Delhi or Calcutta.

- Tender advertisements. These were used by government agencies to register bids from vendors for a host of supplies including services.
  The Hindu of 1 January 1957 carried the following tender ads:

CHIT TENDER NOTICE
Highways Department, Madras

Sealed Tenders are invited by the undersigned at his Office at Sivaganga for the road maintenance works for '57–'58 (both Highways and District Board) in the Ramnad Highways Division up to 1 p.m. on 25.1.'57 for the Highways Works and 26.1.'57 for District Board Works. They will be opened at 1.30 p.m. on the above dates, in the presence of Contractors or their Agents.

Tender forms can be had on application from the Manager of the Divisional Engineer's Office at Sivaganga on payment of Re 1-0-3 (not refundable) during working hours from 21-1-1957 to 24-1-1957 (both days inclusive). Application received after 24-1-1957 will be rejected.

[39]In the 1970s, engineers, especially from the Indian Institutes of Technology (IITs), ran away from India to the USA. While the government of India (and therefore the Indian taxpayer) provided excellent technical education at little cost it benefitted the USA more than India. It is time some social historian covered this singular migration often called 'brain drain' to examine the impact it had on India's development.

(Sd) G.A. VENKATACHALAM,
Divisional Engineer (Highways)[40]

TENDER
NANGAL FERTILIZERS &
CHEMICALS PRIVATE LTD
157/48 Diplomatic Enclave, New Delhi

NOTICE
Sealed Item Rate Tenders are invited up to 3 p.m. on 16th January, 1957, for the construction of Intake Well-cum-Pump House and Quarter Million Gallons Clear Water Low-level Reservoir and Pump House on the right bank of River Sutlej 2000 feet upstream of Nangal Dam.

Detailed plans, specifications and schedule of quantities can be had from the Office of the Chief Civil Engineer on payment of Rs 7-8 per set.

Estimated cost Rs 1,03,200/-

Earnest money[41] Rs 2,580/-

K.C. WADIA
Chief Civil Engineer

The Hindu continued to adhere to the then conventional format of displaying advertisements and nothing else on its front page. By the late 1950s, *The Times of India*, Bombay and *The Statesman*, Calcutta, had moved away from the conventional format, in line with major international newspapers. These major national dailies displayed the most important political news of the day on the front page. The recent trend in major national English dailies is to feature a full-page advertisement on the front page. Political headlines are displayed on the following page.

If we study the advertisements displayed, we find that there are as many as 24 separate heads under which advertisements are placed. Displaying the typical orderliness of the Tamil intellect, each head is clearly mentioned and the rate for release neatly printed right underneath the category so that every advertiser knew the cost of release under a specific head.[42]

[40]These days of mega-projects such as the 'Golden Quadrilateral' or whatever grandiloquent names they are given, expenditure is calculated in thousands of crore, whereas government projects immediately after Independence were very modest in outlay and generally implemented better than now because executors were immeasurably more honest.

[41]Earnest money here is 2.5 per cent of the total estimated project cost.

[42]The other mainline English dailies probably printed these rates in separate rate cards. At least that is how I saw them in the early 1970s. By printing the rates of advertisements in the main paper, *The Hindu* allowed the reader, if he wanted to advertise, to calculate what he had to pay without visiting the newspaper's office.

The Hindu of 2 January 1957 inserted the following advertisements on the front page:

1. *PERSONAL (Rs 6 per word Rs 9 for business minimum Rs 4-8-0 & Rs 6-12-0 respectively)*
   TREETEX Insulation Board for partitions, ceilings, cold storage and air conditioned rooms and Cinema halls. Available at Spencer & Co. Ltd, Mount Road, Madras-2.
   This advertisement appearing in the personal column is no different from ads we see in papers today that occupy space in personal columns which are trade advertisements.[43]
2. *AGRICULTURAL MACHINERY & TRACTORS Rs 6 per word minimum Rs 4-8-0*
   For Sale: One Second-hand International Harvester Farma 1 Super A model, 15 H.P. Tractor with four wheeled Trailer—Simpson model, and three discs—Harrow plough with seeding attachment at Coimbatore. For particulars contact Box No. 4955. C/o THE HINDU.
   It is a little surprising that for farm machinery there is no significant reduction in the rate—especially when raising agricultural production was *the* primary concern of the government both in New Delhi as well as in the states of the Indian republic.
3. *AUTOMOTIVE Rs 6 per word, minimum Rs 4-8-0*
   For Sale: Humber Super Snipe 1947 Model in excellent condition. Please contact: M/s Gulamali Abdul Hussein & Co. 28 Linghi Chetty Street, Madras. Phone No. 3598.
4. *BUSINESS FOR SALE: Rs 6 per word, minimum Rs 4-8-0*
   For Sale: One Hosiery Factory with all equipment as a running concern with five acres of land with buildings at Trichur Town limit. Can be inspected with previous appointment. Apply Post Box No. 20, Trichur.
5. *BUSINESS OFFERS: Rs 6 per word, minimum Rs 4-8-0*
   Can supply experienced Erectors, Fitters, Welders, Masons etc. for Boiler and Chimney erection work. Contracts also undertaken. P.L. Bery & Co. 13 Canning Street, Calcutta.[44]

The Hindu reveals a very advertiser-friendly face. If we notice that 'Business For Sale' and 'Business Offers' are two advertisements that are clearly *business-related* and that the charge for insertion in both is exactly the same, the one reason for having two separate heads for release must have been to facilitate visibility of each advertisement so that those to whom each advertisement is meant would not need to search through the paper. Similarly,

[43]I do not follow the rate card here. It seems to imply for truly personal ads the advertiser was required to pay Rs 6 per word whereas for business ads the rate charged was only Rs 9 per word.
[44]This is an unusual advertisement dealing with a highly specialised area of an industrial service provider.

another advertisement that follows these two under a separate subhead, 'Electroplating', is also a business advertisement and carries the same price for release.

6. *DRESS-MAKING AND MILLINERY: Rs 6 per word, minimum Rs 4-8-0*
   English all worsted five shades Trousers, made for Rs 29/8. Royal Tailoring Co. Bangalore 1.
7. *ELECTROPLATING: Rs 6 per word, minimum Rs 4-8-0*
   We solve your Electroplating problems. Refer: The Best Electroplates, Mount Road, Madras.
8. *EDUCATIONAL: Rs 6 per word, minimum Rs 4-8-0*
   Practical Radio Training home-study courses now available for candidates in India. Radio and Tool Kits provided. Write for prospectus to British Institute of Engineering Technology (India) Private Ltd Dept 3/PR 359 D Naoroji Road, Bombay 1.

The advertisements were positioned alphabetically, according to the specific headline or subject matter of each.

9. *FINANCIAL: Rs 6 per word, minimum Rs 4-8-0*
   Hire Purchase Motor Vehicles arranged. Rate 9 per cent. P.V. Gajapati Raj & Co. Purushotham Building, Mount Road, Madras 85286.
10. *FLOWERS, SEEDS AND GARDENING: Rs 6 per word, minimum Rs 4-8-0*
   Three "Wonderful" "Blue" "Black" & "Violet" Rosegrafts Rs 10. Giant "Human Head" Rosegrafts Doz Rs 25 Mullick's Nursery, Salkia, Howrah.

Why did Mullick's Nursery, based in West Bengal, choose to advertise in *The Hindu*? Did Mullick have regular clients in Madras? How were these rose grafts transported? How were they sent to different destinations in Madras after they reached there (assuming they went by train)? Thanks to courier services and better and faster modes of communication these questions are no longer asked. But in the 1950s none of these services existed.

11. *LEGAL NOTICES: Re 1-10-0 per line, minimum Rs 4-14-0*

I have not included any example here because legal notices generally have the same tone and are likely to interest few people.

The Hindu, like all right thinking newspapers and individuals, felt justified in charging a higher rate for legal notices compared to other kinds of advertisements.

12. *MACHINERY & TOOLS: Rs 6 per word, minimum Rs 4-8-0*
   No example is necessary under this head.
13. *MEDICAL: Rs 6 per word, minimum Rs 4-8-0*
   For Cough Syrup, liked for its taste and welcomed for its relief, in all cases of Coughs, Whooping Cough, Asthma, Bronchitis, etc. Consult Sreevatsas, Madras-30.

Sreevatsas was either a precocious doctor or vendor of cough remedy. If only he had divined the importance of branding, he might have bequeathed to his successors enormous wealth to fight over after his own demise.[45]

14. *MATRIMONIAL: Rs 5 per word, minimum Rs 3-12-0*

    WANTED fair, beautiful girl, to marry wealthy Vellala boy of 20 in South India. Dowry no bar.

The interesting thing about this advertisement is that despite the passage of time Indian males, if they are of marriageable age, still look for fair partners. The wealthier the groom's family, the higher the bar on how fair is passable fair. Any reader of *The Hindu* or *The Times of India*, in 2013, looking at the matrimonial columns will find a majority of the advertisements very similar to the advertisement here. Note also that dowry is mentioned quite openly; anti-dowry laws were passed much later.

Of course, the other notable aspect of the matrimonial column in *The Hindu* is that the rate is lower than for other types of advertisements. Even toughened newspaper men have a soft corner for prospective brides and grooms.

In another advertisement the advertiser reveals the preference given to those employed in government services in the southern states. This particular advertisement indicates what salary levels were regarded as adequate by the bride's family. In modern times similar preferences are mentioned in matrimonial ads when people talk of NRIs settled in the USA or prospective grooms earning six-figure salaries. Indians are generally sound in arithmetic and with the passing years have not forgotten to add zeroes to their salary to increase eligibility.

Wanted Balija or Telegu girl, to marry a boy, aged 26, in Govt. Executive line, drawing Rs 110 with bright prospects. Parents in sound position.

Is the salary mentioned not as impressive as it should be? Why do the parents state that they are sound financially?

15. *PHOTOGRAPHY: Rs 6 per word, minimum Rs 4-8-0*
16. *PUBLIC NOTICES: Re 1-10-0 per line, minimum Rs 4-14-0*

    These notices include subjects like loss of insurance policy and so on. The rate is less than the usual of Rs 6 per word.

17. *PUBLIC AUCTIONS: Re 1-10-0 per line, minimum Rs 4-14-0*

    Why should auctions find a separate mention, especially as the rate charged is identical to public notices? And these, too, are notices of a specific type. Is this again a reflection of the orderly mind of the ad department managers in *The Hindu*?

18. *PROFESSIONAL: Rs 6 per word, minimum Rs 4-8-0*

[45]A news item in *The Economic Times* (in 2006), it was noted that cough remedies constituted Rs 200 crore per annum among OTC products.

For Accurate Predictions, consult Kavaseri Subramania Sastrigal in person (no correspondence) at 'Siddhasraman' Abhiramapuram, behind Gurukulam, Mylapore, Madras.

Fortune-tellers are recognised as 'professionals'. It is no mumbo jumbo, but serious business that even today marks every activity of our elite in Chennai and New Delhi. Ah! Who would not wish to avoid Rahukalam, and set forth to conquer the world in the most auspicious hour? Sastrigal is no ordinary soothsayer. He does not believe in quick-fix solutions by sending postcards.

19. *RENTALS: Rs 6 per word, minimum Rs 4-8-0*
20. *RADIOS & GRAMOPHONES: Rs 6 per word, minimum Rs 4-8-0*
    Sound investments. Murphy Radios. Gramophon House 26/27 Rattan Bazaar Madras-3

It is not unlikely that for this advertisement the dealer received the cost of release from Murphy.[46]

21. *REAL ESTATE: Rs 6 per word, minimum Rs 4-8-0*
22. *SITUATION REQUIRED: Rs 5 per word, minimum Rs 3-12-0*
    For this column the rate charged is lower than for most other columns, reflecting a social concern by the publication.
23. *SITUATIONS VACANT: Rs 6 per word, minimum Rs 4-8-0*
    Hindustan Lever Limited require the services of experienced male stenographers with a minimum speed of 100 words per minute and 40 words per minute in typewriting. The candidate should be able to read and write Telegu. Knowledge of Kanarese would be an added advantage.

We must remember that jobs were scarce in the late 1950s. Here Hindustan Lever Limited, HLL (Lever Brothers, then Unilever, then Hindustan Lever and now Hindustan Unilever—the one and the same company assuming different names as it suited it from the nineteenth century to the twenty-first) not only wanted a very experienced steno-typist, but also a linguist who would know at least two southern languages. Some people with socialist leanings may see exploitation in the advertisement.

24. *TENDERS: Re 1-10-0 per line, minimum Rs 4-14-0*
25. *TRADE ANNOUNCEMENTS: Rs 6 per word, minimum Rs 4-8-0*
    Single and Double Door Steel Almirahs of various sizes. Contact Lalluram & Co. 2/156, Broadway, Madras-1.
26. *WANTED: Rs 6 per word, minimum Rs 4-8-0*
    This particular head includes a number of miscellaneous items such as steel doors, binoculars and even typists, although for typists there already was a situations vacant column. There was no difference in the rates.

[46]In the mid-1970s, when I handled Philips' radios, they had a budget for dealer promotion advertisements. The dealers only paid a small portion of the release cost, if at all they paid anything.

While looking at the advertisements in *The Hindu*, let us turn to two advertisements released by Lintas, for advertising professionals. Both the advertisements were well laid-out and were typographical, with a lot of white space and use of bold headlines to draw attention. Both were in 10 cm x 3 column size and were given almost solus positioning on 4 January 1957.

LINTAS need a
Head for their Films Department

LINTAS, Bombay announce that one of their senior positions, Head of Films Department, will shortly fall vacant.

Applicants should be conversant with every aspect of film-making and possess sound administrative ability.

A candidate with the right talents would justify a generous starting salary and be appointed on a Senior Management grade. He should not be over 40 years of age.

Applications—which will be treated in strict confidence—must be made in writing to 'The Manager, LINTAS LIMITED, Post Box No. 758, Bombay-1, before January 21, 1957. Mark the envelope "Personal".'

It was quite unusual for an advertising agency, in the late 1950s, to be looking for a man dedicated to film production, and one who would obviously lead a team of people devoted entirely to making advertising films. At the time Lintas was a captive agency of HLL. In being a captive unit of India's largest marketer of fast moving consumer products, it probably made more films than most agencies.

Another appointment advertisement released the same day by Lintas in *The Hindu* gives us an insight into the way an agency operated at the time. Let us first read the advertisement.

LINTAS need
Junior Account Executive
The person we are looking for is between 26 and 33 years of age. It would be an advantage if he has advertising experience—preferably in an Advertising Agency (whatever the department)—and has executive ability and is equipped to make a creative contribution to the Advertising that he handles.

He will be appointed as an Assistant on the Managerial level.

(The conclusion is the same as the previous Lintas advertisement).

There were no management graduates in India. Generally those who joined advertising came from well-to-do families. Ad agencies had not become so compartmentalised that they hired people after meticulous screening so that they would clearly fit specific requirements of specialised functions. For example, a copywriter was given a copy test and was selected on the basis of his ability to write grammatical English. A wholly subjective evaluation of his ability to ideate determined the agency's choice. If his uncle or father happened to be an important client of the agency, then he was unquestionably talented. A media person was selected on the basis of his nimbleness in simple arithmetic. An account executive was chosen on his outgoing personality, his fluency in spoken English, including the Englishness of his accent, and not infrequently, on his looks for which he was in no way responsible, but in which his parents played an important part.

As for the creative contribution expected of the junior account executive, he briefed the creative departments, namely, art and copy, on what the client wanted. He then followed up on the execution of the job, seeing that the copywriter wrote the copy, the art director did the layout and on approval of the layout followed up on the execution of the artwork.[47] He was also responsible for following up with the media for the release of the advertisement as scheduled.[48]

The Hindu dated 5 January 1957 had a small news item tucked away in one of the inside pages at the bottom. It is included here because it was published to commemorate the tenth anniversary of Everest Advertising, which was among the leading agencies till about the middle of the 1980s. In the 1970s, Everest was often cited as an agency that was managed profitably, which implied that it did not allow clients to pay as and when able.[49]

EVEREST ADVERTISING COMPANY BOMBAY 3 JANUARY

Presiding over the tenth anniversary celebrations of the Everest Advertising Co. (P) Ltd here this evening, Murarji J. Vaidya, president of the Indian Merchant Chamber, said that with the growing development of industry in the Second Five Year Plan, publicity was bound to play a great role in the country.

---

[47]The account executive interacted with the client. If there were any delays he was held accountable. Most account executives have a ready stock of stories regarding how difficult it is to get copywriters and art directors deliver jobs in time. I have seen for myself at two of the leading Indian agencies I have worked in that there were art directors who started looking at jobs requisitioned after downing a few pegs at lunch. Lunch predictably was an extended affair of two to three hours.

[48]Bal Mundkur told me in an interview in 2000, that Lintas was the only agency in the 1950s and 1960s to send its executives to England for training. On their return they either joined HLL as brand managers or were assigned the function of account executives in Lintas.

[49]Indian advertising agencies suffered on the financial front because clients too often showed a callous disregard of paying on time. This is not a problem faced by agencies anywhere else, in the USA, Europe or Japan. For smaller agencies it meant overdrawing from the bank, which resulted in a punitive rate of interest—often 21.25 per cent, where agencies at the time earned 15 per cent from the media. The INS savaged the arm that brought in the business, namely the agencies. Getting INS accreditation was a long and complicated process. I had the sad experience of having to bribe the INS eastern zone representative to get accreditation for my agency. It is a happy thing that no agency requires INS accreditation to be in business any more as newspapers now directly negotiate with advertisers and agencies.

Mr A.M. Patel, Chairman of the Company, welcomed Mr Vaidya and other guests.

H.A. Kharas proposed a vote of thanks.

Homi Kharas

Homi Kharas was an eminent copywriter of Bombay. He had an irrepressible sense of humour, which may be described as a typical Parsi trait. He became the copy chief in Clarion Bombay and for a considerable period of time was a pivot in its creative department. He worked with Subrata Sengupta during the formative days of the Bombay branch and helped the agency bag a number of prestigious accounts.

Not much should be made of what the president of the Merchant Chamber of Commerce said. He was only making an appropriate sounding statement for the occasion. The total volume of advertising spend was around Rs 5 crore annually. The Congress government regarded advertising as a social evil to be endured because it could not be stopped. But the Congress Party had no problem in employing propaganda, preferably through government-owned media, to convey the official line on various subjects to people.

A number of products available in the 1950s continue to be leaders in their category even now, such as Colgate Dental Cream.

NOW! PROOF that brushing teeth right after eating with

COLGATE
Dental Cream

HELPS STOP TOOTH DECAY!

(This is followed by an illustration of two persons looking at an X-Ray plate)

Caption: X -RAYS SHOW HOW PROPER USE OF COLGATE'S HELPS STOP TOOTH DECAY.

Body copy: Now dental science offers proof that always brushing teeth with Colgate's right after eating helps stop tooth decay before it starts!

Under the direction of eminent dental authorities, one group of college men and women always brushed their teeth with Colgate Dental Cream right after eating—while another group followed their usual dental care. The average of the group using Colgate's as directed was a startling reduction in number of cavities—far less tooth decay! The other group developed new cavities at a much higher rate.

No claim is made that using Colgate's can stop all tooth decay, or help cavities already started. But brushing teeth with Colgate Dental Cream right after eating is the proved way to help stop tooth decay.

(Visual of pack follows) **A COLGATE QUALITY PRODUCT**
Always Use Colgate's to Clean Your Breath While You Clean Your Teeth
And HELP STOP TOOTH DECAY!
GET COLGATE'S Nylon Toothbrush
(Visual of Toothbrush)

Nylon bristles to protect your gums

This vintage 1950 advertisement has many similarities with modern toothpaste advertisements in print (although television has become the primary medium for this product category).

- To sell Colgate the advertisement takes recourse to a quasi-medical claim. Colgate's platform of tougher enamel because of use of Colgate is a quasi-medical claim. In most toothpaste advertisements the ubiquitous dentist in his uniform is presented recommending a specific brand with the intention of reinforcing the brand with customers who are ready to believe any professional claim.[50]
- Toothbrush is also given a technology platform; nylon toothbrushes must have been a fairly recent introduction in the market.[51]

However, there is a significant point of departure between the Colgate ad of the 1950s and a Colgate or Pepsodent ad in 2013. The earlier ad is more honest as it declares that the ad does not claim Colgate can stop all tooth decay, an honest admission that any contemporary toothpaste advertisement would regard as inadmissible.

The observation that after Independence Indian markets entered a non-competing mode may sound strange, but with increasing bureaucratisation this gradually became the norm throughout the country. The Central Government invested in gigantic steel plants and other industries that from the start had no compulsion to be profitable. The president of this great nation, like the Mughal monarch of yore, was head of the armed forces, the government as well as of the many industries in the public sector that were being built everywhere. Most presidents probably had no inkling of their role

[50]In the late 1990s, Pepsodent released a campaign that included TV and print in which the stated claim was there were fewer germs in the mouth if a person used this brand of toothpaste. Colgate objected to the claim and the regulatory authorities advised Pepsodent to withdraw the campaign. The company did so but after requesting for a grace period so that it could instruct TV channels to withdraw, giving the channels minimum time. When this was acceded to, Pepsodent increased the ad's showing within the grace period threefold. Consumers lapped it up. Pepsodent sales increased dramatically at the expense of Colgate.

[51]I recollect when polyester first came into the market there was quite a demand as people were amazed to see a cloth that dried fast after washing and retained the crease of the shirt or pair of trousers washed. Polyester in all probability was the result of research carried out by ICI in the UK.

in these businesses, although tender advertisements were issued in the name of his august personage.[52]

The private sector mastered the fine art of living with bureaucrats. They no longer invested their own capital to start an industry, relying on banks and government funds to provide the necessary capital, from which again they kept something aside for personal use, instead of investing the whole amount in business.

In the 1950s India was beginning its long and tortuous journey into chaos. There were fewer brands in the market than now. Large multinational companies advertised not because they felt any acute need to do so, but in a gentlemanly way to help a friend in an agency, who happened to be a fellow club member or because the company for years had a budget for the purpose. Most print ads were brand advertisements. Larger companies allocated a budget for corporate campaigns as well. Public relations (PR) was part of the ad manager's responsibility.

Subhas Ghosal

It is impossible to think of modern Indian advertising without Subhas Ghosal. He was the son of a physician who spent his childhood in Patna. His father bought him a ticket to advertising. He sent Ghosal to JWT and agreed to pay the agency if it hired him as an apprentice. He was quite obviously a rare middle class Indian who was acquainted with advertising or had heard of JWT.

Ghosal remembered his early days in JWT under Peter Fielden. He was sent to the pan shops in Bombay to understand how they carried on the business of selling cigarettes. It was a long trudge but exposure to business this way gave him an uncanny ability to understand the critical aspects of any business. He became a leader who inspired his team; a thinker who looked years ahead for his profession; a communicator who excelled in both the written and the spoken word. He wrote Bengali and English with equal proficiency.

Ghosal was based in Calcutta for a long time, where he headed the Calcutta branch operation of HTA. He moved to Bombay in the early 1970s

[52]A few industries are now called Navaratnas, a few are called mini-Navaratnas, but most public sector companies are sick or ailing. Unfortunately, the communist/socialist members of parliament raise a hue and cry whenever anyone proposes these be sold or shut down to stop them from bleeding the exchequer. They fear if the government is allowed to do this, their comrades, who have never done an honest day's work in their entire careers, feeding off the taxpayer's money, will be inconvenienced.

rather reluctantly, when the top job of leading the company was thrust upon him. He developed a visionary perspective of advertising as a profession, which was much larger than the immediate interests of the agency he served, although HTA showcased the best in Indian advertising for close to four decades.

Ghosal's contemporary Alyque Padamsee noted that brilliant as he undoubtedly was, with Fielden around, his rise to the top of the pecking order in JWT was not as easy as it should have been. In his autobiography *A Double Life*, Padamsee, reminiscing about Fielden's style of running his outfit, writes: 'He had long ago *mastered the British principle of divide and rule* ... He never appointed a deputy, so brilliant Subhas Ghosal had to wait till Greg Bathon, John Gaynor and Morris Mathias had completed their tenures before assuming the mantle of managing director.'

Because of the increasing socialist slant of Indian foreign policy, most multinational companies lost interest in the country as the economy plodded along with what was sarcastically termed the 'Hindu rate of growth'. JWT was no exception. Thanks to Ghosal, the New York office continued to consider its ties with its Indian office as still existing, despite the fact that no profit was shared with it.

Most appropriately, Ghosal was the spokesman for Indian advertising in the Asian Advertising Congress. He was feted with the highest awards in advertising by both Bombay and Calcutta Advertising Clubs. After retiring from HTA (JWT had renamed itself as HTA and was again to become JWT in the 1990s) he was made chairman emeritus and left to set up Contract, a subsidiary of HTA, which he did with aplomb. Contract, too, came into the list of the first 10 advertising agencies in the country in a short time. It evolved as a highly creative agency and like HTA bagged numerous awards for advertising excellence. Some of Ghosal's addresses to advertising professionals will be included in their appropriate place.

He built long-term relationships with other advertising professionals who were leaders of competing agencies. None of them lost sight of the fact that they were colleagues in the larger perspective of the advertising profession. During the most trying times of dissension and trade union activity in Clarion, which was then the number two agency to HTA in terms of billing, Ghosal realised how important it was to help Clarion come out of its self-created mess because competition was good for advertising. He asked his team not to pitch for Clarion accounts in those stressful days.

Not many would know that Ghosal may be called a product of the Bengal Renaissance. He was a close relation of Satyajit Ray and a nephew of the great mathematician and founder of the Indian Statistical Institute, Prasanta Mahalanobis.

Ghosal, who stood the tallest among advertising greats of the twentieth century, writing a foreword for a series of institutional advertisements published in *Reader's Digest* in 1954, mentions that, 'Institutional or corporate advertising, though much in evidence today, was not so common 30 years ago.' (This foreword was written in 1985.)

A series comprising six advertisements was created for Imperial Chemical Industries (ICI). The company was marketing an anti-malarial drug, Paludrine. The advertisements were published in *Reader's Digest* between March and August 1954. The style of writing followed the editorial style of the magazine.[53] R.P. Gupta, who worked as a freelance copywriter at the time, wrote the advertisements. He later joined JWT Calcutta as a copywriter, where he worked from 1954 to 1956 before moving to Tata Steel where he became the chief of PR.

Satyajit Ray drew the illustrations for a Paludrine campaign, when he was art director in D.J. Keymer.

These illustrations portray life in two very different types of well-to-do homes in Calcutta in the 1950s in a humourous vein. Look at the pictures closely: you will see there are three male attendants in the picture on the right. One seems to be the chauffeur, the man next to him a bearer while the third man wearing a pugree *is possibly a* khansama. *In the same frame we see an ayah holding a child, also a second female attendant. There is a tiger skin on the floor. How many tigers gave up their lives every year to adorn rich homes! The picture on the left shows an Indian home which has fewer people in the frame.*

[53]This is a precursor to the editorial style of advertisements that became quite popular in magazines and in the special supplements carried by major dailies since the 1990s. The rider today is that advertisements of this genre have the word 'Advertisement' written above them to warn an unsuspecting reader that what he is reading is not editorial content.

Ghosal, recalling the campaign 30 years later, wrote: 'Mr Gupta, or RP as he is fondly known, met the top man in charge of marketing Paludrine, a noted authority on parasitology. He gave RP some authoritative books on malaria with the stern order not to venture beyond introductions and the historical chapters of the book.'

R.P. Gupta was an intellectual in the Bengal Renaissance mould. He was an avid collector of Kalighat 'Pot' paintings and rare manuscripts. As a copywriter he believed in expressing himself simply: he rendered even technical copy into a form that was easily understood by non-technical readers. He mastered writing in English and Bengali and authored many articles and books in both languages. His Bengali book on the cries of street vendors in Calcutta is a delight to read and is considered by many to be a minor classic in modern Bengali literature. He was one of the pioneer practitioners in PR and was the PR chief of Tata Steel.

R.P. Gupta

The advertisement released in *Reader's Digest* in the issue dated March 1954 is quite boring. It is a full-page advertisement with a mass of closely typed text matter. I am not sure many readers would have cared to read what was published, however well it may have been written, unless he happened to be a near cousin of the Anopheles mosquito. I reproduce the advertisement (facing page) as it appeared.

Reading the ad makes us think how little man knows about his environment. Malaria is back. New anti-malarial drugs are prescribed because the older drugs do not seem to cure the disease any more. The sure-cure feel of R.P. Gupta's advertisement rings hollow in the light of malaria emerging once more as one of the deadliest killers in the world.

Editorial style of advertising

The editorial style of advertising is generally effective because of the way an advertisement is written. While this particular style of advertising was not in vogue, copywriters did occasionally attempt the presentation of campaigns with an editorial slant. Dunlop also released an advertisement with a similar editorial slant. This too was published in the same magazine, which seems to have featured quite regularly in most media plans of multinational companies then operating in India.[54]

[54]Considering that the magazine started its Indian edition in Bombay in 1954, it had in two years consolidated its position as the top English magazine in India.

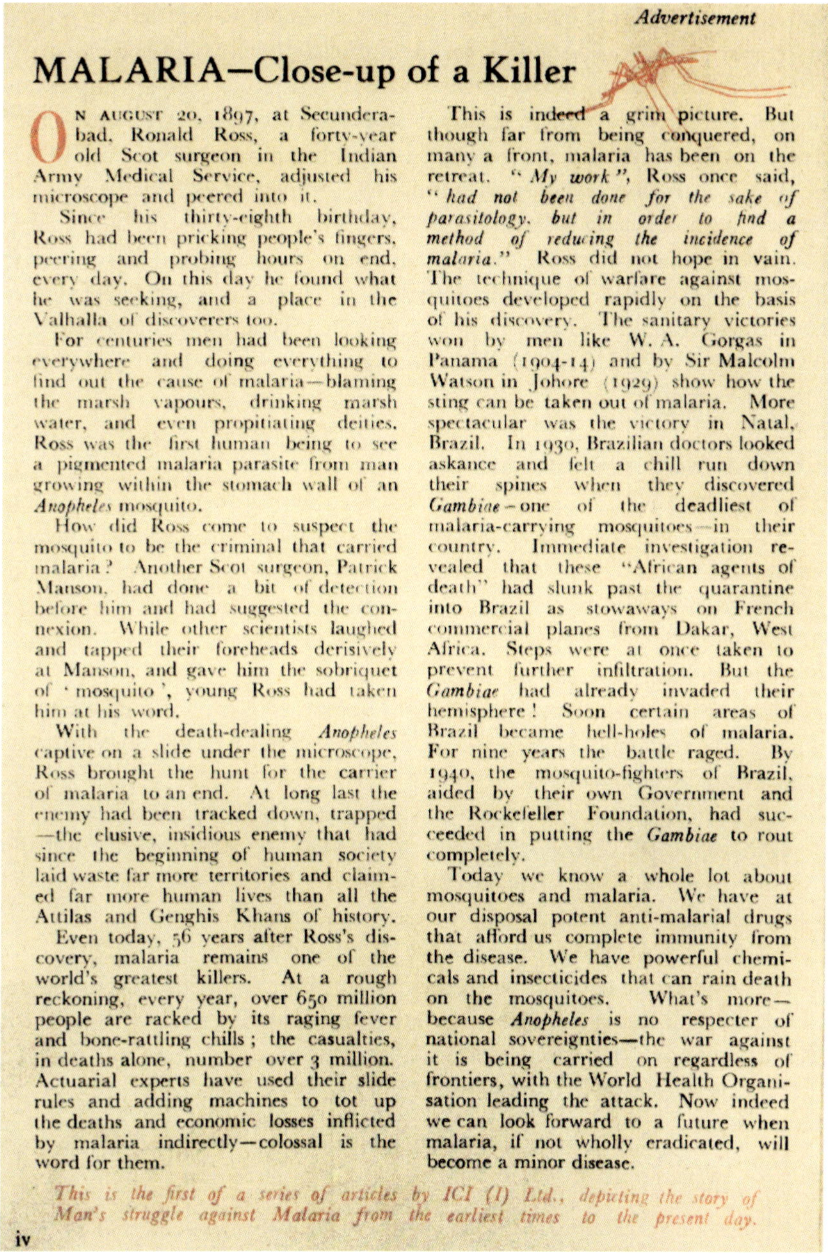

Advertisement

MALARIA—Close-up of a Killer

ON AUGUST 20, 1897, at Secunderabad, Ronald Ross, a forty-year old Scot surgeon in the Indian Army Medical Service, adjusted his microscope and peered into it.

Since his thirty-eighth birthday, Ross had been pricking people's fingers, peering and probing hours on end, every day. On this day he found what he was seeking, and a place in the Valhalla of discoverers too.

For centuries men had been looking everywhere and doing everything to find out the cause of malaria—blaming the marsh vapours, drinking marsh water, and even propitiating deities. Ross was the first human being to see a pigmented malaria parasite from man growing within the stomach wall of an *Anopheles* mosquito.

How did Ross come to suspect the mosquito to be the criminal that carried malaria? Another Scot surgeon, Patrick Manson, had done a bit of detection before him and had suggested the connexion. While other scientists laughed and tapped their foreheads derisively at Manson, and gave him the sobriquet of 'mosquito', young Ross had taken him at his word.

With the death-dealing *Anopheles* captive on a slide under the microscope, Ross brought the hunt for the carrier of malaria to an end. At long last the enemy had been tracked down, trapped—the elusive, insidious enemy that had since the beginning of human society laid waste far more territories and claimed far more human lives than all the Attilas and Genghis Khans of history.

Even today, 56 years after Ross's discovery, malaria remains one of the world's greatest killers. At a rough reckoning, every year, over 650 million people are racked by its raging fever and bone-rattling chills; the casualties, in deaths alone, number over 3 million. Actuarial experts have used their slide rules and adding machines to tot up the deaths and economic losses inflicted by malaria indirectly—colossal is the word for them.

This is indeed a grim picture. But though far from being conquered, on many a front, malaria has been on the retreat. "*My work*", Ross once said, "*had not been done for the sake of parasitology, but in order to find a method of reducing the incidence of malaria.*" Ross did not hope in vain. The technique of warfare against mosquitoes developed rapidly on the basis of his discovery. The sanitary victories won by men like W. A. Gorgas in Panama (1904-14) and by Sir Malcolm Watson in Johore (1929) show how the sting can be taken out of malaria. More spectacular was the victory in Natal, Brazil. In 1930, Brazilian doctors looked askance and felt a chill run down their spines when they discovered *Gambiae*—one of the deadliest of malaria-carrying mosquitoes—in their country. Immediate investigation revealed that these "African agents of death" had slunk past the quarantine into Brazil as stowaways on French commercial planes from Dakar, West Africa. Steps were at once taken to prevent further infiltration. But the *Gambiae* had already invaded their hemisphere! Soon certain areas of Brazil became hell-holes of malaria. For nine years the battle raged. By 1940, the mosquito-fighters of Brazil, aided by their own Government and the Rockefeller Foundation, had succeeded in putting the *Gambiae* to rout completely.

Today we know a whole lot about mosquitoes and malaria. We have at our disposal potent anti-malarial drugs that afford us complete immunity from the disease. We have powerful chemicals and insecticides that can rain death on the mosquitoes. What's more—because *Anopheles* is no respecter of national sovereignties—the war against it is being carried on regardless of frontiers, with the World Health Organisation leading the attack. Now indeed we can look forward to a future when malaria, if not wholly eradicated, will become a minor disease.

This is the first of a series of articles by ICI (I) Ltd., depicting the story of Man's struggle against Malaria from the earliest times to the present day.

iv

Today, unless a reader happens to be inquisitive, he will skip this advertisement and amuse himself with something else that contains less prose and more fun. But the copywriter in the 1950s wrote for people who had little by way of amusement. Reading was very much an accepted part of recreation among the literate folk in the country. Life was slower; people worked regular hours and were not expected to attend to official duties round-the-clock.

Seeing films of the 1950s or listening to music gives us an impression of a slower paced world. In ad films storyboards concentrated on a story. The storyboard unravelled before the eager and captive audience for a whole minute. Theatregoers were loath to miss the commercials that were screened before the actual show commenced. The Films Division of the Central Government presented documentary films on any subject that seemed to have propaganda value for the government. These documentaries were in black and white, exceedingly boring, unimaginative in the manner in which they were conceived. The viewing public generally took a toilet break when these were shown.

Display advertisements

There were many different kinds of display advertisements in any leading daily. Toothpastes, biscuits, women's lingerie, tonics, and not too frequently, industrial products, general announcements of exhibitions pertaining to specific trading fraternities, cigarettes, tyres and even haute couture were all to be seen in dailies such as *The Times of India* in Bombay, *The Statesman* in Calcutta and *The Hindu* in Madras.

Here are some advertisements of different categories of products. A display advertisement in 10 cm x 2 columns about a newly released book makes interesting reading.[55]

FAMILY PLANNING
Fully Illustrated - 125 Easy Methods
By Lady Dr K. Satyavati, M. Ms. England.
1-G CONNAUGHT PLACE, NEW DELHI
Foreword by Gen Cariappa. Appreciation from Pandit Jawaharlal Nehru, Shri K.M. Munshi, contains all the latest easy methods. Price Eng 5/- Hindi 3/-. Besides getting the book and appliances you can consult the Author as well.
Phones: 48646, 46557 & 24855

General Cariappa was roped in to support the national effort on population control. What appliances were offered may interest family planning experts in our times.[56]

[55] *The Hindu*, 7 January 1957.

[56] We assume appliances include more than condoms. For those who are interested, condoms date back to the sixteenth century, and even earlier to ancient Egypt. It is not unlikely that the Indian civilisation had its own scientific or metaphysical variant, considering this great civilisation produced the erotic masterpiece, the *Kamasutra*. Surely, Indian courtesans in temples and palaces did not wish to be encumbered by progenies any more than their sisters around the world.

The Scott's Emulsion advertisement shows the quality of illustrations in the fifties. Illustrators were highly regarded in agencies. How did the creative group tackle the matter of appeal? Remember there was no market research. Companies such as HLL may have experimented with consumer feedback on a few occasions, but most advertising agencies based their 'appeal' on product attributes or benefits. In Scott's Emulsion the product attribute is pure cod liver oil while the benefits are (1) Vitamin D builds bones (2) Vitamin A builds resistance to infections.

The Times of India published a self-advertisement on 16 January 1953 in which the newspaper announced that an edition was soon to be published from Calcutta. Since this particular advertisement was repeated a number of times in the following days, we may assume that the paper was actually published from Calcutta also, though the Calcutta edition may have been short-lived. *The Statesman* was a formidable competitor and captured the hearts and intellect of regular readers of the English press.

SOON from
CALCUTTA
(Illustration in line of The Times of India, *folded)*

The Times of India, famed nationally and internationally, as Asia's leading daily, with the largest readership in the East, is widening its scope. A new edition makes its appearance to give further proof of its growing popularity. Regarded as the faithful mirror of Indian public opinion in every sphere of activity, its impartial and independent editorial policy, its balanced expression of Indian thought has won for it the highest esteem in the journalistic world. This coupled to its exclusive News coverage by The Times of India News Service, its special reports from able correspondents the world over and other features such as city news, market reports and quotations make *The Times of India* an incomparable leader in Indian journalism. The Calcutta edition will now give an on-the-spot service to the vast areas of Eastern India, hitherto served from either Bombay or Delhi.

(In bold, 20 points U/L); **Watch for Opening Date**

(Box, in reverse): **The Times of India** *(In logo type, 24 points)*

AT PRESENT SIMULTANEOUSLY PUBLISHED FROM BOMBAY & DELHI

Available from all agents of *The Illustrated Weekly of India*, leading newsagents and book stalls or direct from *The Times of India*, 21 Convent Road, Calcutta.

Also at: 13/1 & 13/2 Govt. Place East, Calcutta

(Within a box) Other allied publications:[57]
The Illustrated Weekly of India
Dharmayug
Navbharat Times
Filmfare
Satyayug

This advertisement was probably drafted by a journalist. A copywriter would have presented it differently; the sentences would have been shorter; the product features would not have been buried in the copy. He may have included a lead-in or subhead to highlight its claimed leadership status.[58]

In the early 1950s, cigarette smoking was not injurious to health. To give complete satisfaction to brand loyal smokers here is a brand, declaring in a front page solus advertisement in *The Times of India*[59] its single-mindedness in packing a punch:

Puff by Puff
Taj (Brand name. But the logo type on the pack face is not used. It is upper-lower here as opposed to all caps used on the pack).

Gives you more smoking pleasure

(The visual is in the centre of the frame showing an open pack with an ashtray close by on which a lit cigarette is perched. All pictures are in line illustration. The pack face has the brand name in Hindi.)

Body Copy:

1. This brown, oval-shaped cigarette contains more tobacco, burns slow and gives you more puffs.
2. It has a true tobacco flavour which adds zest to every puff. Ideal for heavy and chain smokers.

---

[57]Every publication goes through a process of brand erosion like all other FMCG products. Decay of a publication catches even the best managed media houses unprepared. By the time someone wakes up the brand is already in such poor health that owners decide to kill it. *The Illustrated Weekly* and *Dharmayug* were leading periodicals in their times; the first in English and the second in Hindi. In fact, in 1980, *The Illustrated Weekly* marked its centenary year. In a single issue dated 12–18 February 1978 there were 42 advertisements—39 black and white and 3 colour ads. This issue had 80 pages including the covers, which were also printed on poor quality of newsprint. The advertisements took up 28 pages. At the time Khushwant Singh was the editor. I tried to check out with *The Times of India* office in Kolkata on the two publications which folded up. I was told that *The Illustrated Weekly* started as *The Times of India* weekly edition in 1880, was renamed *The Illustrated Weekly* in 1923 and closed down in 1993. They had not heard of *Satyayug*. Sometimes a truly successful editor determines the lifecycle of a paper. *The Illustrated Weekly* had three high profile editors in M.V. Kamath, Khushwant Singh and Pritish Nandy. The publication probably died of ennui with the departure of Nandy.

[58]I handled the account for the magazine *Sunday*, when M.J. Akbar was its editor during my stint at OBM. I recall he was very critical of what ad agencies produced and generally spoilt a perfectly good ad by tinkering with the copy. However, the best ads carried headlines sent by the agency.

[59]16 January 1953.

3. More puffs from every cigarette and more zest in every puff mean maximum smoking pleasure for you.

The only cigarette of its kind.
BEWARE OF IMITATIONS

(Key No. Greens' Advertising).

Advertisements are a reflection of the times. But a newspaper carries other news items that have a direct bearing on a particular day. A political or economic decision which has far-reaching implications for the future may be of utmost interest to readers. The following news item appeared in *The Times of India* on the same day as the cigarette ad:

Congress debate on forming linguistic states

A resolution welcoming the decision of the government of India to form Andhra state and recommending planned and cautious implementation of the programme of linguistic re-distribution of the country will be placed before the Subjects Committee and later, before the open session of the Congress here.

In 2014, the Andhra issue revisits us once more. Those who belong to Telengana wish to form a new state. The Telegu are a divided lot. The anger that was aroused between Hindi and Non-Hindi speaking states is no longer central to regional or national politics. Politicians have rediscovered 'caste' as a useful tool to garner votes.

Consider the advertisements of the 1950s according to product or service category. This would enable us to catch a glimpse of market dynamics and to see how agencies handled like and unlike products and attempted to provide a competitive edge to their brand through advertising.

Fast moving consumer non-durables

A direct message with the text supporting the promise that Vitex grows hair. The product claims to arrest dandruff and even grow hair on bald patches, which is certainly untrue. One of the wonders of the twenty-first century are Dr Batra's Hair Clinics which have gone on a mission of eradicating baldness from the country. I hope their claims are more honest. It would be a sad day if bald men are seen in India 10 years hence.

The Brylcreem man is as nattily presented as his twenty-first century descendant. But cricketers in the fifties generally looked more like players at the end of a hard day's cricket than film stars as they do now. Sunil Gavaskar commentating on the subject observed that in his times players did not hug other players closely when they took a wicket or scored a century because they did not use body spray to smell like flowers. If a batter scored runs in a game he could not have his hair so settled even if he used Brylcreem.

Brylcreem advertised in *Reader's Digest* very regularly. One such advertisement that was published in the *Digest* issue of July 1957 included very long copy. It began, inexplicably, with a hat and ended with the brand. The connection between the two was rather contrived. It must have taken a keen purveyor of advertising to read the ad.

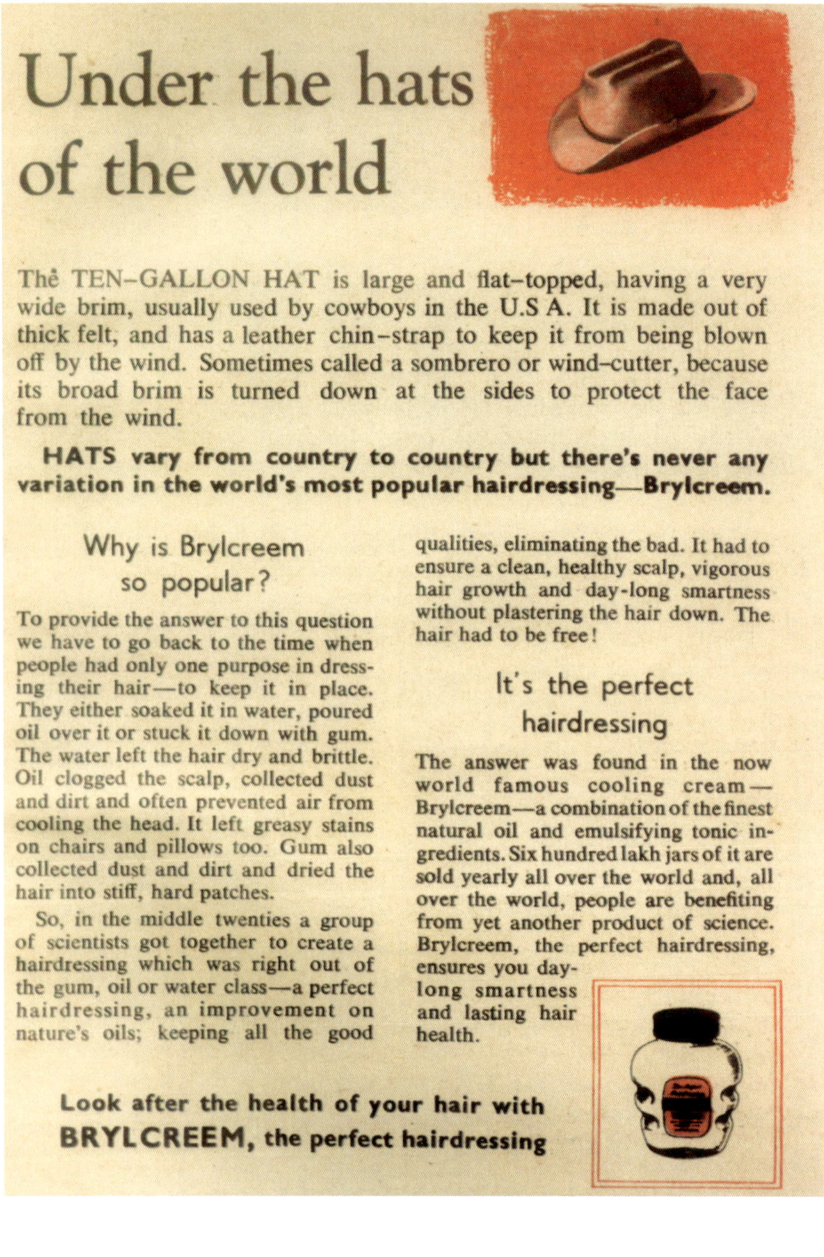

The headline presents a beauty plan and looks as modern as many of the contemporary brands. The ad talks of 'skin types' and promises a discernible benefit of a lovelier skin. This is a precursor to HLL's campaign for Fair & Lovely in the 1980s that was positioned as a cream that made people fairer.

Every soap company and every brand of soap from time immemorial has promised 'glowing beauty' or 'glowing skin'. Lux followed its international creative platform by positioning the brand as the soap used by film stars who have a glowing complexion. The concept covers both continuity and change. HLL has steadfastly adhered to the same creative platform. Continuity is in presenting the most popular film stars; while change is the natural change of people's preference as one film star fades out and a new one becomes the favourite. Bollywood has given Lux an unending reservoir of heroines through the ages. In the 1950s, Lux presented the popular film stars of the times.

There were some Indian brands of toilet soap which enjoyed sizeable markets nationally. Godrej owned Cinthol, a popular brand then, which remains popular today.

The concept of body odour was not Indian. Since the late 1930s HLL was trying to familiarise Indians with this novel concept.[60] By the 1950s the term may have entered popular usage since the ad mentions it prominently in the copy and the copywriter builds the ad on this proposition. The Cinthol ad also mentions the Godrej range of products: toilet powder (which I presume

[60]P.L. Tandon in his memoirs *Beyond Punjab* mentions how he tried explaining to his boss in 1937 how impossible it would be to popularise the concept of BO (body odour). He maintained that in a hot country such as India everyone perspired and people accepted that as a fact of life. It didn't mean anyone was dirty or didn't bathe every day (Hind Pocket Books, 1971).

This was after the tremendous success of Pakeezah, *where Meena Kumari played the lead role. HLL and its in-house agency Lintas were forerunners in using the popularity of box office hits.*

is talcum powder), hair tonic and shaving stick (not shaving cream). The talcum powder and the shaving stick both contain a mysterious ingredient, 'G 11'.

A fizzy drink that did wonders as it cooled, titillated the taste buds, bucked-up the drinker, and also made his mornings beautiful acting as a laxative. 'Laxative' in extra-bold typeface at the bottom of the tin may have deterred a cautious person from trying the brand as a cool refreshing summer drink.

Food advertising has to look appetising. It is easier to do it now with colour transparencies and special shoots in studios, using the best lenses, employing various paints and colours for heightened visual effect and then using computers to touch up. How difficult it was to carry over the same effect through line illustrations and in black and white. A recipe in the ad may have attracted most women readers to glance through the advertisement: Rex Jelly Crystals offer six different flavours.

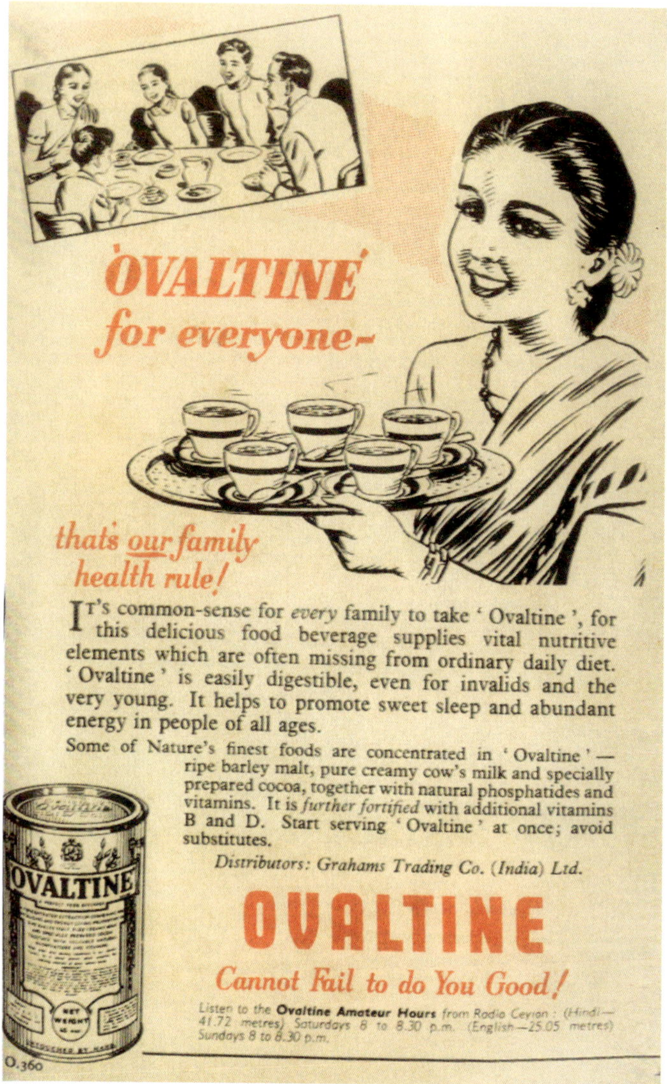

It was Ovaltine long before Cadbury's Drinking Chocolate became a popular feature on kitchen shelves of middle-class folk. Ovaltine was competing with Horlicks as the preferred health drink, a milk supplement, in the house. The interesting feature in the ad is the mention of Ovaltine Amateur Hours programme from Radio Ceylon, which was managed by Ameen Sayani. All India Radio took a long time to break through the preconceived mindset of Congress ministers in New Delhi who believed that it was morally incorrect to allow people to enjoy Hindi film songs, which advertisers such as Ovaltine were so willing to sponsor.[61]

[61] I covered this subject in my book *Indian Advertising 1780 to 1950*. pp. 228, 230-231 and 235.

Ovaltine ran ads to present brand use in different situations. Here, the brand is shown against the backdrop of an adult who leads a vigorous life.

Amul was establishing its brand image. The Amul girl was to follow in 1967, a year after Sylvester daCunha bagged the account for his agency, daCunha Communications. The agency also created the memorable tag line, 'Utterly Butterly Delicious Amul'. Bharat Dabholkar produced some of the smartest copy for Amul hoardings and small press advertisements month after month, based on contemporary topics, for 15 years on the trot. The length of time one copywriter sustained his craft may itself be regarded as setting some sort of world record. Great ad men of the West such as David Ogilvy produced brilliant print concepts all their lives, but not a fresh concept on the same brand, every single month without fail!

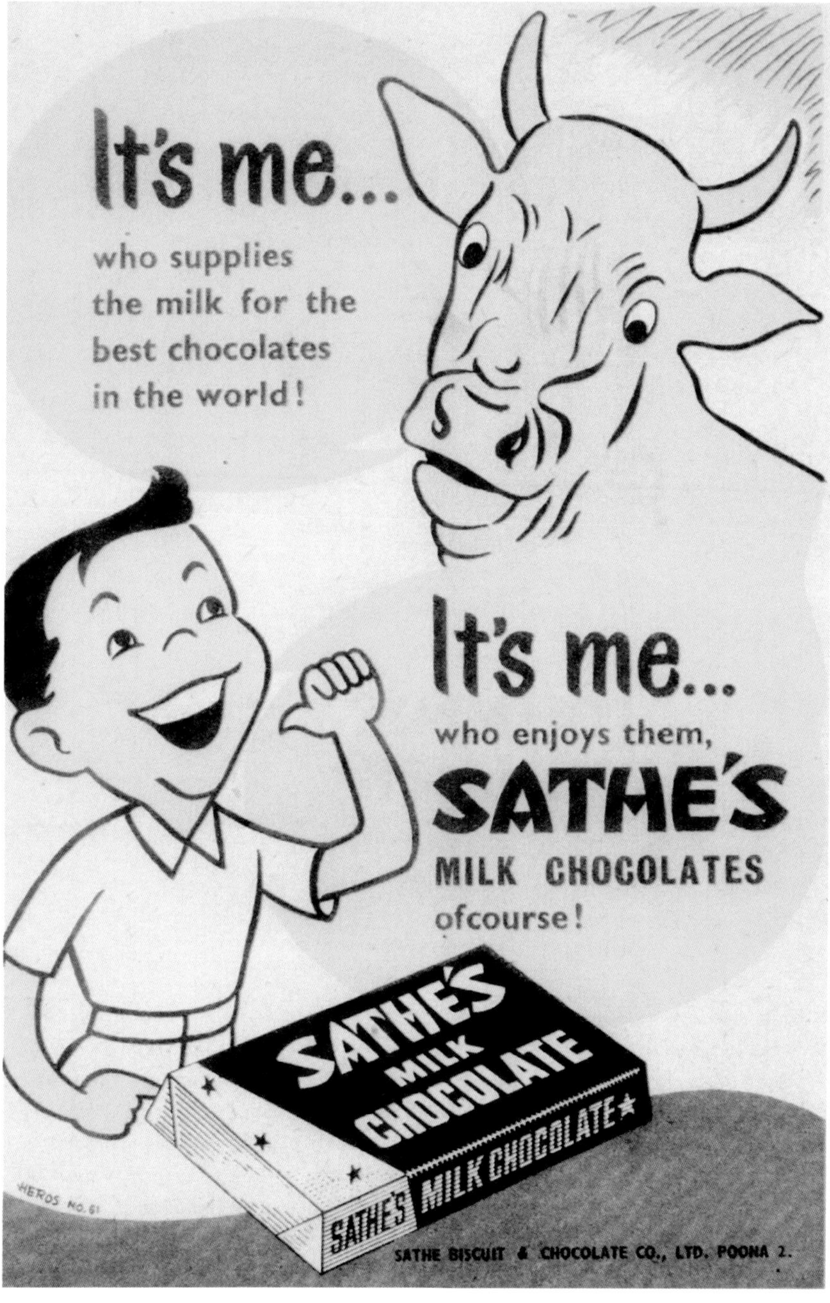

Sathe was a less-known brand of chocolates. Cadbury was the brand leader but there were not too many varieties available then. Only Milk Chocolate was available in small and regular size slabs.

Whiskies were advertised in print. Although in the Congress credo drinking was unacceptable, the administration in the 1950s did not ban liquor advertising, as they were to do post-1970. However, liquor consumption in middle-class homes was not very common. May be in Punjab people did not frown upon social drinking, but in the rest of the country there were inhibitions with regard to public consumption of alcohol. People in the highest socio-economic class and people in the lowest drank more openly and more regularly than middle-class folk. Whisky, after toddy, was the favourite drink of Indians. The presence of expatriates probably influenced government policy with regard to the import of whisky, and therefore the availability of brands in the open market as well as advertising in media available. In the coming decades all this was to change. More conservative Congress leaders frowned upon social drinking. They had their way. In some states such as Madras (later to become Tamil Nadu), Gujarat and Maharashtra local governments promulgated prohibition, resulting in avoidable tragedies among people in the economically weaker sections of society who died drinking hooch.

Gin seems to have been quite popular considering the frequency and variety of advertisements released by Hayward's for its brand. Social drinking among expats was common, especially over weekends. Gin and tonic was a popular midday drink before lunch. Gin was also considered to be a lady's drink for reasons unknown to this author.

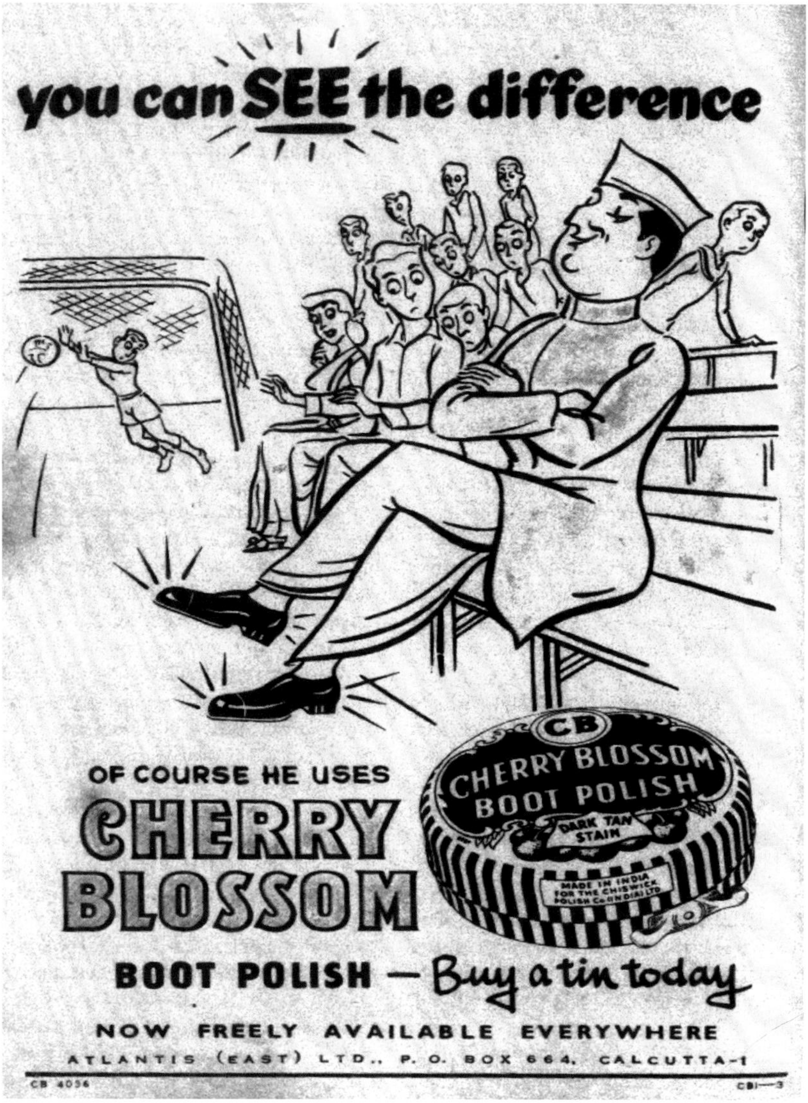

The tin is illustrated with an eye to detail. It may have been retouched by hand from a hard black and white print. The illustration may also have been a scrapper board drawing for which the artist used a stylus to cut the image on a specially coated surface. He used a hard print of the pack or object to trace the outline and then he created relief using deft lines. Scrapper board drawings were extensively used for packs of all sorts of products. They ensured hi-fidelity reproduction in newspapers. Even products such as tyres, which were all black, were drawn ensuring every detail. Few artists specialised in scrapper board, but those who did had far more work than they could handle. In Calcutta, the best scrapper board man, Shamiullah, was a full-timer with HTA. He also did freelance work for other agencies.

Art directors very often try to support copy with visuals that have a direct association with the copy. Unfortunately, when the ad reaches the reader he either overlooks the visual or does not understand the connection. In the Flex ad, see the faded visuals of cars on top. The obvious implication is change from an old style British car to a new style American limousine. After all, the shoe advertised is Americano. Flex had a tannery based in Kanpur, which was and still remains a major leather processing centre. Vikram Seth's famous novel The Suitable Boy *has a Kanpur setting where the hero—a leather technologist—is employed at a tannery similar to Flex.*

The ad looks somewhat strange with the figure at the top cut off from below his neck. The second fellow at the bottom looks the executive-type as he walks down in a suit. Notice the prominence given to the brand name, which is positioned in the centre. The styles of footwear presented are quite detailed. It could not be difficult for the buyer to match these styles when he visited an actual Bata outlet. But the way the shoe is laced is not the normal way shoes are generally presented in any footwear advertisement. The art director may have been new to the Bata account. The account executive and the client should not have missed this detail.

Retail outlets: Layout, colour scheme, window display, customer flow

In India of the twenty-first century, retail is the big cash cow looming large on the horizons of the largest companies in the country as elsewhere. Walmart and Reliance have taken the first initiatives to enter the sector where economists are looking at a total market potential in excess of Rs 16,000 crore per annum. Every modern retail outlet is offering a slew of in-store surprises to deliver ultimate satisfaction to the customer. However, the idea of delivering a uniform standard of service across a sizeable number of stores spread all over a vast country belongs to the Bata shoe company.

Bata is a brand name derived, as brand names so often are, in Europe and the USA, from an individual who mechanised the process of shoe-making and formatted a standardised distribution network. Bata became a global name with retail stores across continents. The company settled in India quite early and was one of the few that carried on its business with a degree of comfort that other foreign companies in the country may have envied.

Bata set new standards in retail. It presented the same shop exterior wherever you happened to be. The Bata name was prominently displayed in reverse against a red ground. The company had different categories of stores but with the same look and similar service. It segmented the market. Stores stocked a range of high-end products in an upscale environment while other stores stocked lower-priced footwear in the same metro in a different locality. It was not that an identical amount was spent on every store or that all stores were the same size and had the same standard frontage. Bata's store models were admirably adaptable. Some were larger, some were double-storeyed,[62] but they all delivered the same effect.

Bata ran effective in-store campaigns, a combination of displays with posters and other POP material highlighting individual brands. During monsoons, all the shops stored and displayed monsoon wear prominently, thus inviting customers. In festive seasons, a wider variety of products was displayed, with quite a few being priced a little above the standard range.

Unlike Christian or Muslim countries, India is complex in its many festivals which take place throughout the year. These include festivals of all major religions of the world. Bata seized upon these occasions as an opportunity. People had so little to spare they converted the bigger festivals

[62]In Calcutta, Bata in College Street was two-storeyed; its outlets in the Grand Hotel lobby and close by New Market were upscale stores.

such as Diwali and Pongal into buying occasions for footwear. In West Bengal, the company's unforgettable Puja campaigns declared, '*Pujoe chai notun juto*. Bata.'[63]

In-store layout was standardised by Bata; it ensured adequate seating capacity because people came in with their families to purchase footwear. Footwear, not infrequently, was bought for every family member at the same time. Bata stores generally had one or two rows of seats with some space for the salesman to help a customer slip on his new pair. The stores ensured a person buying a new pair had sufficient space to walk a few steps to 'feel' the shoe well.

Display windows, wherever a store had them, were decorated with gay ribbons and in up-market stores windows had revolving display stands with special lighting on the shoes. While window displays were not uncommon, Bata standardised the shop look and experience across the country. Indeed, the company modernised retailing in India.

The importance of illustrations

In the 1950s and 1960s, advertisements depended on drawings rather than on photography for visual support. As noted elsewhere, half-tones were difficult to reproduce because of the poor quality of newsprint available in the country. Drawings in line were easier to reproduce. Art directors and agencies utilised a large variety of drawings, depending on what was required.[64]

In the following advertisements that have been scanned mostly from *Reader's Digest*, since this particular magazine normally carried a large number of advertisements, the variety and quality of illustrations is evident. Some of

[63]Translated, it will read, 'In Pujas we want new shoes. Bata.' In a way the feeling conveyed by the line is a demand of children in a family for new shoes. 'Pester power,' as marketers term it today, was translated into this memorable line in the 1950s.

[64]In the early 1970s, when I worked in Clarion in Calcutta, I remember quite a number of specialist illustrators. There was an illustrator who executed realistic photographic drawings with paint and brush; another who turned out fast pencil illustrations. Reputed art directors in the 1950s to the 1970s such as Samir Sarkar, who initially worked with Clarion and then went over to JWT and Ronen Ayan Dutta, art director with JWT before he set up his own creative unit, were illustrators with a distinctive style of drawing. The importance of illustrators in Indian advertising has been dealt with incisively by P.N. Sarma in his *The Role of an Art Director*, reproduced in Chapter 2.

the illustrations are in realistic style; some are stylised; some are typically comic-strip drawings. A few come close to looking like photographs.

Drawings of packs are generally executed with care and with an eye to detail. Some of the packs may have been based on hard prints of actual packs, which were afterwards carefully re-touched by the illustrator. Very few artists were available for scrapper board work. Only the largest agencies such as JWT and Clarion had permanent artists on their roll for this kind of work.

There were a number of good still photographers in Bombay, Madras and Calcutta in the 1950s. The larger agencies such as JWT and Clarion set up their own studios with very competent photographers. Some of these photographers, after working in the agency for a few years, became freelancers and offered their services to all agencies, big and small.

Ahmed Ali was one of the early independent photographers in Calcutta. He had a large studio just off Park Street and was much in demand for his work, especially during certain times of the year. In the 1950s to the 1970s, many leading companies produced sleek calendars designed around themes. The themes could relate to the businesses pursued by companies; though not infrequently they could be totally unrelated. Photographers such as Ali and art directors had scope to explore their combined creative skills.

Bourne & Shepherd, one of the oldest studios in Bombay and Calcutta, also undertook advertising work that was assigned either from agencies or received as direct commissions from advertisers. Bombay Photo Stores was another studio that enjoyed a fair share of the business in cities such as Bombay and Calcutta.

Other than annual calendars, art directors used photographs for posters, exhibition panels and for window display cut-outs. Colour photography was not too common. The cost of processing colour bromides was heavy; the time taken to process bromides was also long because colour film processing was not done everywhere. Photographers mainly shot black and white rolls. They used light and shade in different ways to create moods and effects. In ad agencies most bromides went through a process of retouching. This was common practice with product photographs such as gramophones, tyres, cigarette packs, toothpaste, hair oil (shampoos were not so prevalent), branded teas in tins or cartons and so on. Model photography was also done, but models were shot more often in Bombay compared to the other metros.

ENO was an old brand that adapted to changing times. It was similar to Andrew's, but the illustration of an Indian family was a change from the earlier visuals of English men and women in ENO ads of the late nineteenth century and the early years of the twentieth century.[65]

[65]I have shown them in my book *Indian Advertising 1780 to 1950.*

This particular brand of cigarettes was evoking nostalgia of old England. Englishmen were around and many Indians working in British trading houses were sometimes too eager to ape their sahibs. The standard of illustrations was very good when executed by any of the leading agencies. This was a JWT ad.

A brilliant ad! The illustration is simple, done in a bold stroke. The Gold Flake smoker is no ordinary person; he is an intellectual. Look at the Gold Flake pack—a tin that is a pen sketch. The artist maintains realistic rendering of the various type styles on the tin.

This ad is equally delightful. Here the man of intellect, the Gold Flake smoker, is obviously more taken up by the smoke he inhales in a cabaret where dancing girls do not seem to draw his attention. The Gold Flake tin in the foreground is prominent. The illustrator surely enjoyed drawing the visual.

The setting is very European with a woman shown in riding breeches. The woman's figure is an illustration. The packs may also have been line drawings, skilfully executed.

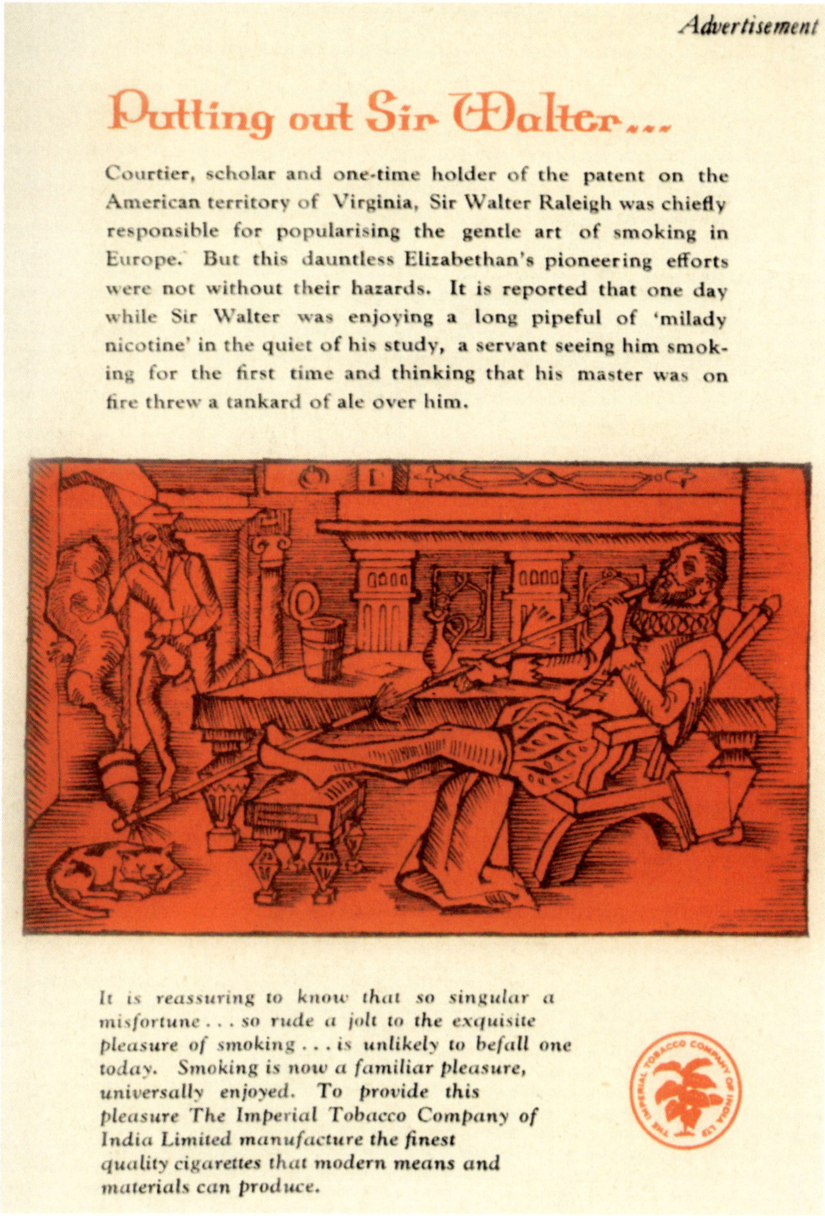

You may be amused to read the text that says Walter Raleigh's servant threw a tankard of ale on him thinking he was on fire. Did they not drink water in Elizabethan England? Or did they normally douse flames with ale?

Reading the text transports us back to a time when smoking was regarded as a harmless pleasure; there were no health warnings on packs. Doctors did not associate cancer and heart attacks with smoking.[66] It was not rare for wives whose husbands were non-smokers to bewail the fact that they did not smoke. Film actors turned smoking into a lifestyle habit, since they were seen to smoke so frequently in films. Old Bengali films in the late fifties show heroes lighting up so often that one wonders whether they ever needed to breathe God's air to live. In the early fifties, doctors and the US government were alive to the association of smoking with a number of diseases which included cancer and heart attacks. The cigarette lobby, which was enormously powerful, used every trick it could find to stall the inclusion of the surgeon general's warning on cigarette packs. I find it strange that doctors in India had not woken up to the studies conducted in the USA linking smoking with various serious ailments. Even the Indian government in Delhi seems to have been blissfully unaware. Unlike the political leaders and bureaucrats who run the government machinery today, those at the helm in the fifties were far more responsible and honest. Had they been aware of these studies they might have taken some action to restrict the consumption of tobacco.

Using a comic strip format to illustrate a story became popular in the following decades. In this particular story (facing page) the expressions on the faces and the background within the small space in each frame shows how good illustrators were at the time. The first two frames depict two different scenes in the typist's office. The third frame shows him in a bus where he has to go standing. The fourth frame illustrates his home as also frame number seven.

Horlicks released comic strip advertisements in a series. The drift of the story is similar to the one above. The setting is different. In this one the Horlicks hero is a social worker. From constantly being tired, he changes to a vibrant activist—thanks to his doctor who advises him to drink Horlicks regularly.

[66]I find the US surgeon general had connected smoking to both cancer and heart attacks from the early 1950s. Why India took so long to introduce warning on packs is perhaps indicative of the power of lobbyists working on behalf of major multinational organisations.

In yet another ad that was released in *The Hindu* on 5 February 1953, Kedar, who is the hero, does not have the energy to scout around for a groom for his sister Roma. He always feels tired; till his doctor prescribes Horlicks. And then he gets the nephew of a zamindar to marry Roma. Many modern young women will be offended by the sexist tone of the ad.

This advertisement is unusual for the times when baby and infant foods were sold in the black market. An anxious parent heard, on the grapevine, news about tins being sold by a retailer. He would slip away from office or leave home early to get to the store before others, often seeing himself hundredth in a queue of eager buyers waiting for the shop to open.

Britannia was already a reputed brand in the confectionery market in the country.

Parle was another sizeable player in the confectionery market. Both Britannia and Parle had an excellent national distribution network.[67]

[67]I am a little uncertain about Kerala and the north-eastern states, barring Assam. Despite a poor communication network, wholesale dealers and distributors developed an efficient distribution network throughout the country. This was both a blessing and a curse—blessing because products by and large were available if the buyer was willing to pay the price. And curse because this same network was turned into a mighty apparatus for profiteering, which led to frequent famines engineered by unscrupulous traders.

Service industries (airlines)

Bobby Kooka's maharaja is already making waves. Here he declares regally he's flying Air India. 'Pachyderm' precedes Asterix, in tongue-in-cheek use of big words in a humourous vein. This ad is reproduced in a size that allows readers to appreciate the easy manner in which the facial expressions of the characters are drawn, especially those who are upfront. Look at the elephant's eye and the mahout's crestfallen expression.[68]

[68]S.K. Kooka's speech in the first Indian advertising convention held in Calcutta in 1960 delightfully recounts the branding element derived from the maharaja. This along with a short biographical sketch of Kooka features in Chapter 2.

A promotional ad! The illustrations give the advertisement a busy look.

This particular advertisement is a true reflection of India in the 1950s. People could only dream of flying to foreign destinations. It took almost half-a-century for Indians to be freed from governmental shackles, enabling easy foreign tours.

Compared to Air India advertisements, ads of other airlines look run-of-the-mill. Most tried to position an airline either by destinations covered or by the type of aircraft flown by them. Here are some examples. Why so many airlines chose to advertise in Indian magazines, particularly *Reader's Digest* and national English dailies, is not clear since there were few Indian travellers. However, a large number of expatriates were still around and they may have constituted the bulk of travellers out of India.

This aircraft ad firmly identifies its brand image with a particular make of aircraft, which flies faster than other comparable ones, besides being the preferred choice of most airlines.

This is different. It uses a testimonial route. And in choosing an Indian who was then a frequent flyer it may have caught the attention of those who were planning visits abroad. In the early 1950s till the late 1980s such Indians represented a very select group.

This advertisement positions PAA for its great cuisine. Then the ad details all other pluses that come with the airline. Perhaps in doing so the agency, very likely JWT, misses out on the fundamental principle in advertising that one advertisement should carry a single message as memorably as possible.

Bad advertising cannot get worse than this! I suspect the agency either did a rush job or was so friendly with the client that it could get anything approved.

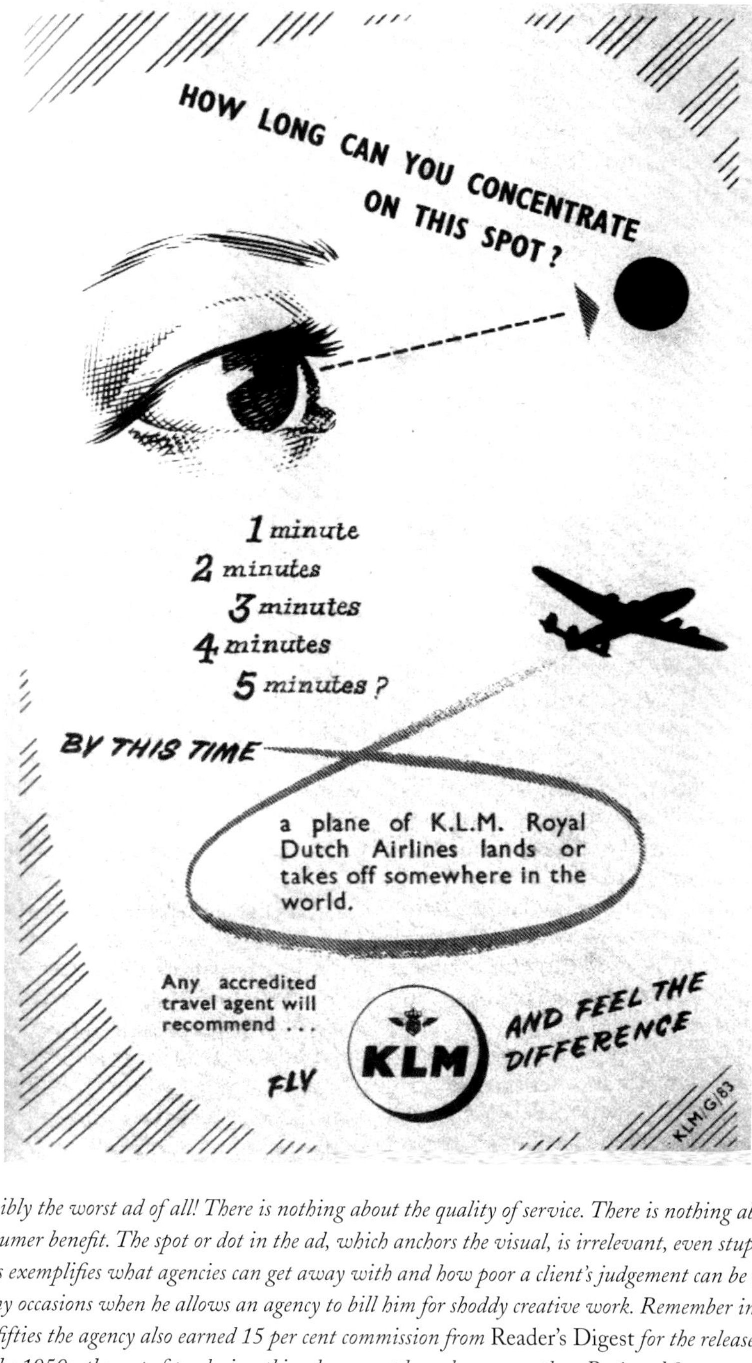

Possibly the worst ad of all! There is nothing about the quality of service. There is nothing about consumer benefit. The spot or dot in the ad, which anchors the visual, is irrelevant, even stupid. This exemplifies what agencies can get away with and how poor a client's judgement can be on many occasions when he allows an agency to bill him for shoddy creative work. Remember in the fifties the agency also earned 15 per cent commission from Reader's Digest *for the release. In the 1950s, the cost of producing this ad may not have been more than Re 1 and 8 annas, taking studio time, cost of settings and the copywriter's time.*

Fast moving consumer goods (FMCGs) in 1950

India of the 1950s was a sellers' market. There were few companies with national distribution spread. Competition in some categories was high. Despite the low purchasing power of the average Indian, there existed an unfulfilled demand for FMCGs. Companies such as HLL had the right environment to prosper in, provided they satisfied the consumer.[69] One of the most competitive markets was the toothpaste market. Consumers had many choices. Yet the market was in a nascent stage as a vast majority of people used traditional products such as neem twigs, salt, oil and even ash from their *chullas* to clean their teeth.

The Times of India dated 16 January 1953 carried the following Pepsodent ad:

Headline: **Brush away**
the risk of DECAY *(with each alphabet of the last word visually showing the idea of decay)*
...with wonder-working IRIUM

Nothing else cleans teeth so WHITE *(Bold lettering in outline, emphasising the word 'white').*

Body copy: Look, the *cleanest* teeth are *safest* from decay—and nothing else can clean so clean as Irium, famous all over the world, strips away stain and film from your teeth. Irium cleans teeth really white, cleans teeth really clean, cleans teeth safest from decay. No matter what toothpaste you're using now you MUST BENEFIT by changing to Pepsodent with Irium.

PEPSODENT

(Not the logo type used on the pack)

Line illustration in reverse on top right of the ad showing a woman brushing her teeth.

Main visual: Large quarter-tone. A couple with the lady having her palm read by an astrologer who resembles a sardarji from the profile presented. Lady smiling. Her teeth heavily re-touched.

Visual of dentist in box: Blurb, as if dentist is saying:

The truth about tooth decay

---

[69] P.L. Tandon in his reminiscences of HLL mentions how in his initial stint as a young executive kicking off market research in the company, he told his immediate boss that in India it was the male who did the monthly purchase of household goods, a conviction his boss did not share with him. When they decided to actually probe the incidence of purchase, one of their lady investigators got an insight into the process. When she asked housewives who actually bought household items she received the reply that it was the man in the house. But when asked how he purchased things that were generally used by women, a thoughtful respondent clarified the position by saying, 'Oh, I now follow what you are asking. Yes he does the buying, but I tell him what to buy.'

Copy: Science has proved that acid-producing bacteria cause most decay. There is only one way to safeguard your teeth—they must be kept clean from bacteria. *(Visual of a pair of dentures in reverse within a tight frame.)*

Irium is the registered trademark of Pepsodent Ltd. It is a special ingredient for giving greater cleansing power. Thus the surest way to fight tooth decay is to use Pepsodent immediately after eating. *(Visual of pack with a portion of the tube sticking out.)*

This is followed by an oval-shaped visual with leaves around it and copy in reverse which is in all capitals:

THE ONLY TOOTHPASTE CONTAINING IRIUM

This particular advertisement is rather forced. The copy is repetitive and questions the intelligence of the reader. There is a single feature that it over-sells—Irium—which is what most toothpaste ads continue to do even today. In fact, the repetitiveness of the text reminds us of some of our modern TV commercials on toothpastes, where the tendency is to over-sell a single feature or ingredient.

With a clutter of visuals in one ad it is not surprising that the ad is in size 50 cm x 4 columns, which is the half-page size of the paper.

Generally toothpaste ads took a lifestyle approach, as the following examples show:

Forhan's occupied a niche positioning. It became identified as a brand especially suitable for keeping gums healthy. While the visual of the lady is drawn in line, the artist creates a person who looks upmarket. Her dressing gown is a European concept and, like the European women of the day, she has bobbed hair.

In fact, most toothpaste and toothbrush ads of the time look very contemporary. The difference is that whereas print ads today carry photographs in colour, in the 1950s these were generally line sketches or retouched black and white photographs. Yet line drawings show a degree of realism which modern illustrators may find difficult to match. In advertising it is so often seen that with the passage of time a set of skills weakens or disappears altogether as new skills replace the older ones with technical improvements in production and media.

The visual conveys freshness, much like a TV commercial, if one sees the expression in the eyes of the model. A promotion aimed at children is likely to make mothers respond positively. The headline cleverly combines a product benefit through its ingredient 'chlorophyll'. It says a modern toothpaste arrests 'decay germs'. Pepsodent in 2007 fights germs 'Dhishoom Dhishoom'. Compare these ads with the most recent toothpaste ads. You may arrive at the conclusion that there is nothing new.

Marketing research

Did the agencies and their clients arrive at the advertising platform by gut feel? Or were most brands from multinational companies primed for advertising in New York or London? Did agencies undertake marketing research? How else would they know what platform they should use for a campaign? True, there were fewer products available to customers, but the customer still had his preference. It was the most major task of the marketer and the agency to get as close to his need as possible if they wanted to make their brand a success.

HLL was the first to employ marketing research in the country. This was in the early forties of the twentieth century. The company understood the importance of getting feedback from consumers in developing and marketing new products. By the early 1960s, JWT and Clarion opened independent marketing research departments to provide deeper insight into consumer psyche for clients. These departments later functioned as companies. This enabled agencies to project their research units as independent units that could be relied upon to be objective in their work, a primary requirement for every marketing research activity.

A number of eminent media planners began their careers in marketing research or moved to it from media functions. The important names in marketing research from the 1960s to the 1980s include Ramesh Thadani, who in a brief life worked for both CORE (the independent research company of Clarion) and Indian Market Research Bureau (IMRB; the independent research company of JWT), doing path-breaking projects; Manoranjan Dutta, a brilliant statistician who helped CORE become a leading marketing research company; and Arup Ray, also associated with CORE, who introduced qualitative research and remains unsurpassed in his ability to draw information from consumer panels through group discussions or personal interviews.

Arup Ray

Arup Ray joined the marketing research division of Clarion after completing his post-graduate studies in England. Along with Manoranjan Dutta, he helped establish the credentials of the department in marketing research. The two major contenders for research projects then were JWT and Clarion. He resigned from Clarion in the late 1970s to work for ACIL, a sister concern of Clarion. He set up his own marketing research company based in Calcutta a short while later. Ray is a visiting faculty to a number of reputed management institutes. He remains passionate about research and teaching. The author acknowledges his debt of gratitude for the training he received from Arup Ray when he joined Clarion in the early 1970s.

In Ajit Haksar's autobiography[70] he dwells on his own involvement in enabling JWT to set up IMRB as a separate company. Subhas Ghosal was the prime mover behind IMRB. He always held market research to be absolutely necessary for effective advertising. JWT and Clarion showed their farsighted perspective in asking clients to look at research as a touchstone to consumer demands, brand acceptance and campaign deliverables in terms of top-of-mind awareness and reach. These agencies incurred considerable expense in setting up the infrastructure for research.

Unfortunately, the media, though their earnings were immeasurably greater than the combined earnings of ad agencies, did very little for market research. Newspapers were the worst offenders for this since print was for all campaigns the primary medium. Newspapers spent little to understand the fundamentals of who were their readers, what they particularly liked in their newspapers of choice, whether they saw advertisements and, if yes, what they recalled. Tara Sinha in her characteristic forthright manner spoke about how little the newspapers were doing to support agencies and clients with useful information in her address to the first advertising congress in Calcutta.

M.K. Khanna, who was the managing director of HTA, in his foreword to the *Thompson Urban Market Index*, published in 1986, wrote: 'In 1960, J. Walter Thompson company's pioneering efforts produced the first-ever compilation of data on consumer markets in the country. It thereby fulfilled the vital need for assessing accurate market potential. *The Gazetteer* was incorporated, for the first time, in the new series in 1963, as an independent guide to the understanding and interpretation of markets.'

The *Urban Market Index* of 1986 covered all markets, nationally, with a population of one lakh and above. It supplemented information available in the census report by providing information on 46 demographic and socio-economic variables for each city. Additional data was collected on a variety of items such as LPG gas connections, post offices, hospital beds, eating houses, hotels, workshops, factories, places of communal gatherings and locations of residential houses. The *Urban Market Index* carried a trove of information of value to agencies and their clients.

Clarion combined market rating indices with media information for Class I towns. The report was updated in 1972, based on census 1971 data and urban consumer expenditure figures. Like in HTA, those who helped with the research attempted to understand the smaller markets. The agencies included professionals from teaching institutions, government bodies

[70]Ajit Haksar was the chairman of ITC. His autobiography is titled *Bite the Bullet.*

and management consultancy companies to ensure the quality of published material.

Those associated with the *Urban Market Index* included the eminent economist Dr R.K. Hazari, who had served the Reserve Bank of India as a deputy governor; Dr Vasant Patnakar, management services consultant; Suren Chawla, then media director of HTA and Ramesh Thadani, then general manager of IMRB.

It is strange that none of the national newspapers were in any way associated with either HTA or Clarion in their endeavour to develop a knowledge base that would contribute to the quality of media planning. However, the Clarion study mentions that for information pertaining to cinema it received help from Blaze Advertising Private Limited.

After the late 1970s, when Clarion went into a steady tailspin, which ended in the final eclipse of the company, R.K. Swamy Associates wore the mantle of research. Hansa was a company formed to undertake research. Under Dr Vasumathi, Hansa Research undertook many studies which they marketed to clients successfully. R.K. Swamy valued market research and spared no expense in initiating research studies.

Since market research enabled companies to earn substantial profit, a number of entrepreneurs entered this market. Some of these smaller research companies became well-known and received orders from multinational companies that invested steadily in market research. Market research studies in India in the 1960s to 1990s were inexpensive compared to research spending in Europe and the USA. IMRB was generally the most expensive.

This advertisement mentions 'glowing skin—healthier skin'. Do we notice any difference between product claims made then with product claims now?

The inventiveness of marketers and copywriters never ceases to amaze! Here they highlight 'Lipoid' solvent. If every brand had its own specific magic ingredient, scientists in formulation must have been extraordinarily busy with their discoveries. Some may wonder how many Nobel Laureates dedicated their lives to oral hygiene, although most geniuses are naturally reticent in wishing their wives 'good morning' before they brush their teeth; quite a few even after they have brushed their teeth.

Toothpaste packaging in the 1950s was simple with bold typefaces ensuring shelf visibility. While most typefaces used were chunky, the 'Kolynos' brand name in italics looked modern. In 'Rexona', we have an example of an italicised script form of typeface; with the visual of a smiling woman, it conveys a feminine bias. 'Forhan's' included a stylised serif typeface with a delicate body.

The years immediately following Independence were not deficient in subjects pertaining to lifestyle. Advertisements regarding fashion parade, hair styling and so on indicate that among the wealthy were fashion-conscious people. Gradually, as living became more difficult and the government began to squeeze out personal freedom, such events become rarer from the mid-1960s.

In 1953, *The Times of India* carried the following ads on 30 January:

Extended for another week
FASHIONS FOR '53
Incorporating an exclusive display of recent FASHION PARADE
NEW ERA MILLS
And the model sarees shown at the
Recent **FASHION PARADE**
Which are now on sale
From February 1st
VEENA PUROHIT
Will be in attendance between
4 & 6 pm to carry out
LADIES INDIAN HAIR STYLES
(By previous appointment)
Evans Fraser & Co. (India) Ltd.
FORT HOUSE, BOMBAY

The ad is rather shoddy in composition; it seems the copywriter was making an attempt to highlight an event that had taken place with the display of sarees shown at the fashion parade. Veena Purohit was probably a hairdresser who was well-known to fashionable people and catered to upmarket customers. This is a promotional add-on, which may have attracted visitors to the sale. What is not clear is whether Evans Fraser was the owner of New Era Mills or the owner of an event management company.

Cinema

The Bombay film industry taught Indian advertising the art of postering. Since few people read English, it is not clear why the industry took the trouble and paid the expense of translating Hindi film titles into English. The clarity of film posters remains unmatched to this day; each poster dominated by a single visual representing the lead characters. The letters used in framing a Hindi or Urdu word in English were at times innovative just as at other times they tested the viewer's ability to decipher what the nearest Hindi words were likely to be. The Bombay film industry provided the only entertainment for the masses. A ticket to the cinema was something a cinemagoer had to fight for, especially if the movie was a new release or a popular one with enthralling songs. Film ads in newspapers, hoardings and posters appealed to a large captive audience that was eager for entertainment.

Education

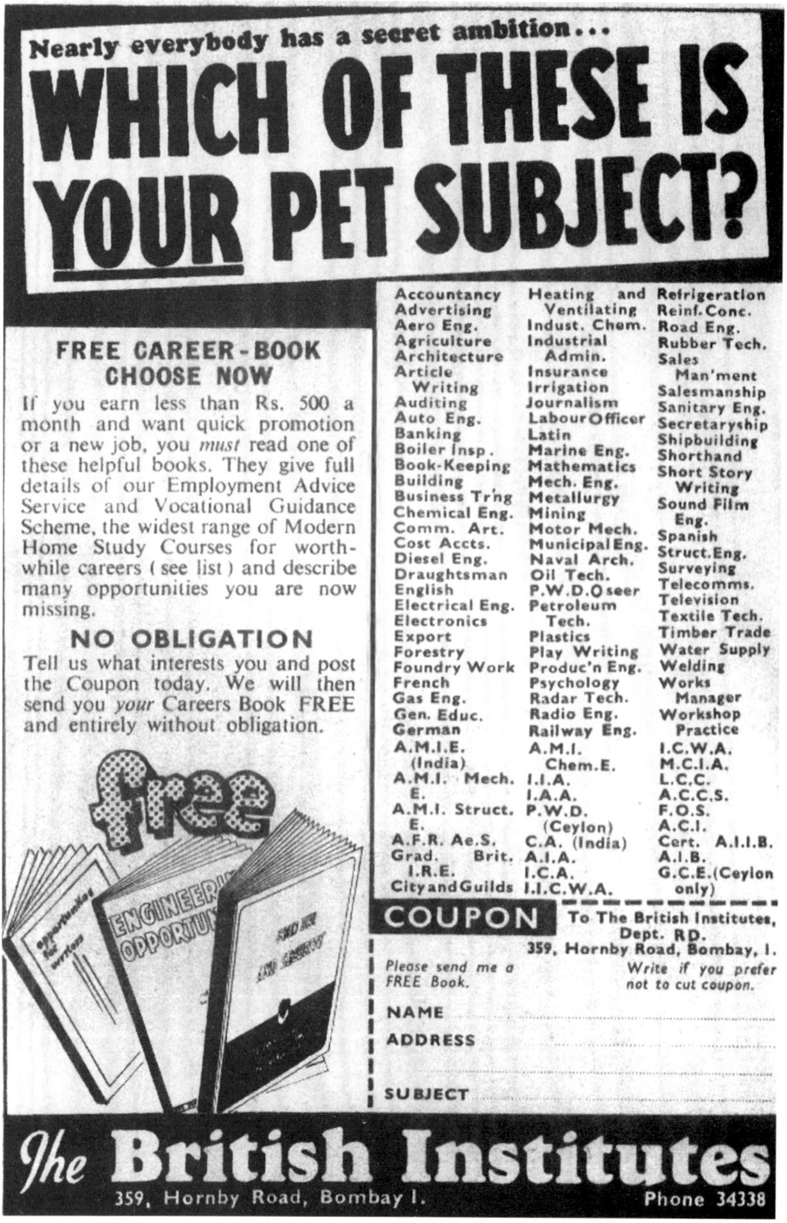

The British Institutes advertised quite heavily, soliciting students to take up any of their career-oriented subjects. They must have had a good response to their coupons, judging by the frequency of ads in a single newspaper.

Linguaphone Institute was also heavily into print advertising and released ads in the mainline English dailies as well as in Reader's Digest. *People must have opted for language courses since the campaign was sustained for a number of years.*[71]

[71]I consider it a singular misfortune that I have never come across a single individual who learnt a foreign language by taking up a postal course.

Non-prescription drugs

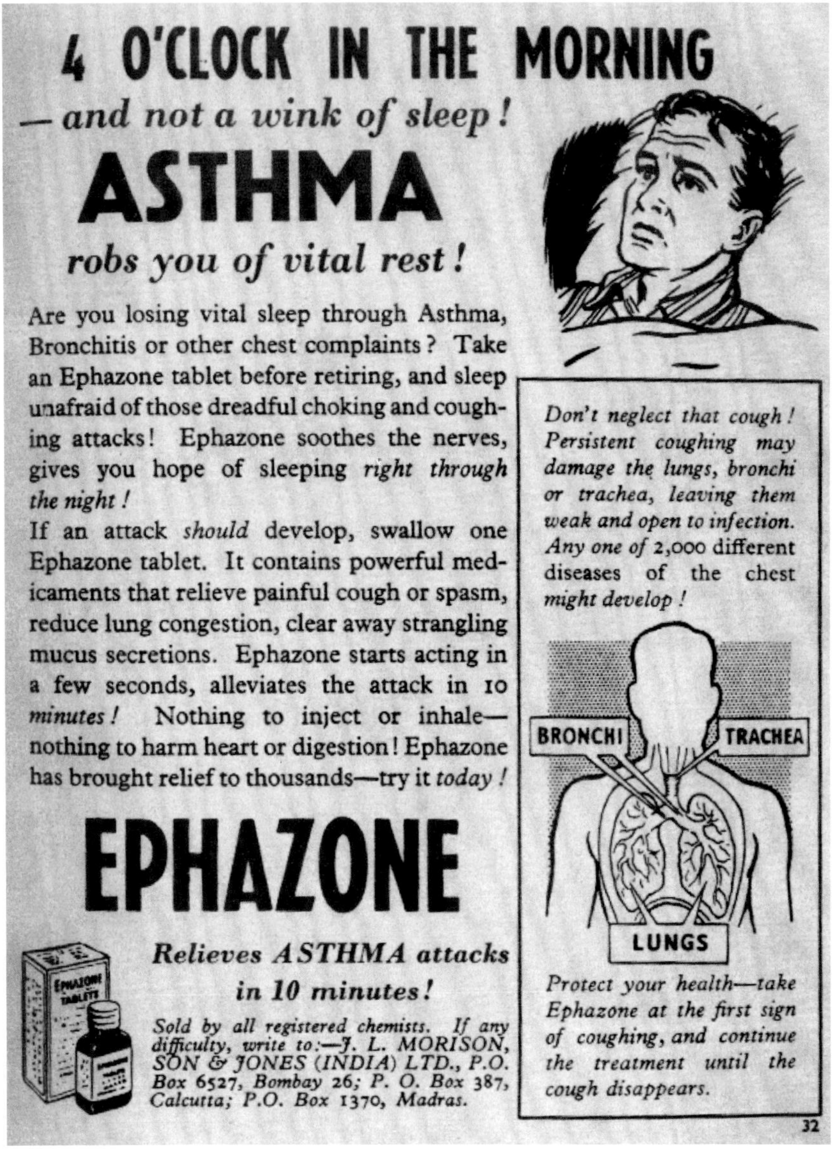

The copy is lucid. Line illustrations add to the serious look of the advertisement. The pack though small is not lost. The baseline includes a promise for cure that may be more compelling than the headline.

Angier's is some sort of tonic recommended for those convalescing after a bout of malaria. It was heavily advertised. Unlike the previous advertisement, this is not a serious medical composition. At the bottom of this advertisement are two lines that draw our attention. 'Angier's Emulsion contains no animal oil, and its preparation is untouched by hand. It is therefore acceptable to all castes and religions.' This is a casteist statement, which will be condemned by liberal intellectuals of the twenty-first century. But the statement reflects the social conditions prevailing then and is a commentary on why the founding fathers of the Indian Constitution attempted to eradicate casteism in independent India. The paradox is that our leaders have only strengthened caste consciousness by creating a new set of Brahmins who are the Other Backward Class (OBC) and others who receive preferential treatment in every sphere of life.

Advertisements in English were lucid in style. This was true of advertisements between the 1950s and the 1970s. Modern day advertisements in English are rarely written so well. The drawing is realistic and represents a lady who appears to be in her forties. The packs are prominently displayed along with the promotional item—a free eye bath with every bottle.

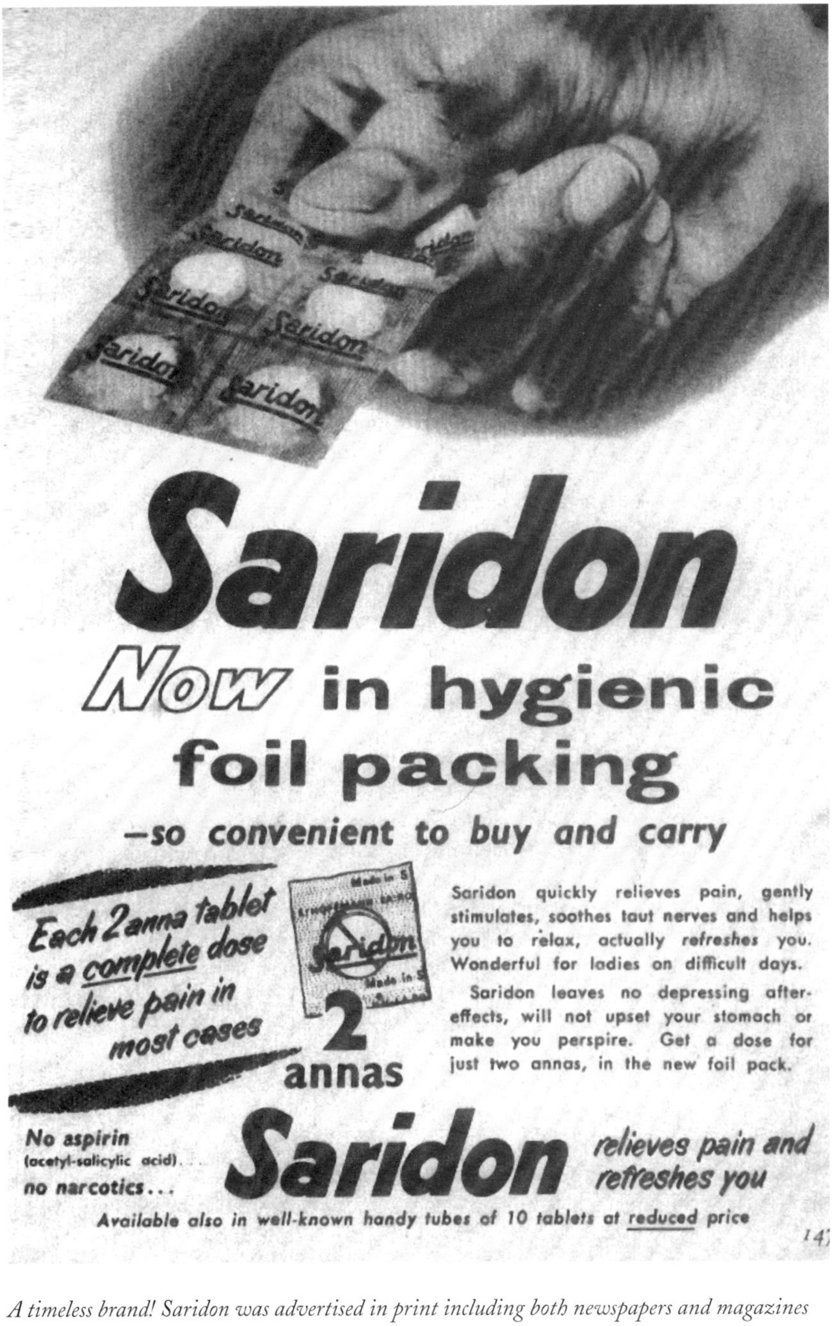

A timeless brand! Saridon was advertised in print including both newspapers and magazines and, very memorably, over radio. Foil packing may have been new and becomes the platform on which the ad rests. The tablets were also available in tubes, mentioned in the baseline beneath the brand name. Note how various other messages in the advertisement are played up.

This ad, based on a village doctor serving humanity, is a myth. There were no village doctors then. Villagers lived and died without healthcare quite contentedly—just as they do now. The difference is there is some primary healthcare available for most village communities today, but there is no dearth of quacks. Villages that have access to practitioners of alternative systems of medicine such as homeopathy or ayurveda are fortunate.

We present two advertisements from a series campaign released by ICI. The first appeared in Reader's Digest *in January 1957, the second a month later in the same magazine. At the time ICI had a significant presence in India with a medical department to sell its products made in the UK. It manufactured paints in Rishra, near Calcutta. Dulux and Duco were leading brands in the decorative and automotive segments. These companies manufactured a few chemicals as well and later set up a factory for industrial explosives at Gomia, now in Jharkhand. The point to note here is that many of the large business groups set aside certain sums for corporate campaigns. They were not hard pressed to sell products; demand generally far exceeded supply. These last two ads obviously targeted doctors; to make them feel important and to note the association of ICI with modern medicine.*[72]

---

[72]My own experience with corporate advertisements aimed at doctors has largely been that they are rarely noticed, let alone read. Busy medical practitioners do not have the time to read even the medical literature given to them by medical reps of various companies. It is so bad now that every pharmaceutical company gives a present while reminding doctors to prescribe their brand of medicine. I often wonder what doctors do with their many similar presents—pen-stands, thermos flasks, wrist watches and blood pressure instruments. Their favourite places of family holiday, sponsored by medical companies, now go beyond Thailand and Malaysia and extend to Australia, New Zealand and Europe.

Here is another example of a corporate campaign where the company tries to build an association, however far-fetched or blatantly stupid, with national goals or national pride.[73]

The copy is forced. No 'Bhai sahib' would enjoy going through the advertisement. This is typical of the times when every large company allocated a budget for corporate advertising. Agencies were appointed to handle corporate advertising for companies such as Brooke Bond, Lipton, ITC and Bata. Among Indian companies, the Tata Group was in the forefront in developing and sustaining a dynamic image for the whole group. Why the Birlas, who dominated the business scene, had very little corporate presence remains a mystery. The Birlas were reviled for being the manufacturers of the Ambassador car and were the favourite target for left trade union leaders.

The Tata Group also advertised for individual companies in a decentralised manner, where each company advertised in accordance with its strategic business objectives. Most corporate campaigns excelled in their presentation and content and senior art directors and copywriters were assigned to work on these campaigns.

[73]This advertisement was carried in the October issue of *Reader's Digest* in 1957.

Art directors

JWT and Clarion and somewhat later Ulka, Everest and MCM, carried the most talented art directors and copywriters on their staff. Lintas, though an agency with sizeable billing, was regarded more as a house agency of HLL. Lintas changed after Gerson daCunha and Alyque Padamsee joined the agency. The management at HLL also realised that it was necessary for Lintas to work for other companies besides HLL to take its rightful place as a major ad agency in the country.

Art directors and copywriters earned good money moonlighting for smaller agencies. This was an open secret and the top management of the leading agencies turned a blind eye to the practice. Since each art director had his distinctive style, it was not easy to hide artworks executed for other companies, especially in an age when illustrations were so important in layouts that any ad professional would have easily identified the art director who had created it.

O.C. Ganguli was a renowned illustrator. This particular illustration was created for Dunlop. When we look at it today we are drawn by the grace, charm and beauty of the tribal men and women. Although poverty was acute among the santhals in Bengal and Jharkhand, the men and women depicted here are healthy and colourful. Ganguli must have been inspired by his many visits to Santiniketan and the Santhal Parganas. There were many stories about him. One that was often repeated with variants was how a client barged into O.C.'s office to see how his work was progressing. O.C. had done nothing about it. He quickly dipped his brush into a simmering cup of tea next to his easel and started painting. He disregarded the presence of the man. The client left highly impressed that the great O.C. was totally absorbed in his work.

What prompted HLL to release a corporate campaign? Could it be that the company was not sure what the government's policy would be with regard to foreign companies? Or was the company informing people that its business was in the national interest? The important point to note in the ad is the mention of market research. Long before IMRB was formed, HLL started market research in India. Indeed, Prakash Lal Tandon, the first Indian chairman of HLL, mentions in his autobiography that he joined the company in the late 1930s and was inducted into the market research department, which commenced operation with him.[74]

[74]P.L. Tandon observes in his memoirs that, being a chartered accountant qualified in England, he was first introduced to the head of the accounts department, an Englishman, who was not a qualified accountant. He naturally did not wish an overqualified Indian to be working under him. The general manager of HLL then found an easy escape route by pushing him into market research, about which nobody in the company knew anything. Tandon had the good fortune of meeting another Englishman there who had been given an India posting to set up a market research cell. Tandon's book, now out of print, is a must read for every management student.

The other interesting point raised in the ad is the question of the quality of products sold to consumers and of gaining their trust. Indian markets were flooded with substandard products across all price segments for close to 50 years since Independence. Not infrequently, newspapers come out with stories of people being blinded, maimed or even killed because of spurious food products. Even today, spurious medicines are a menace in many northern states, especially Uttar Pradesh and Bihar. The legal system in India moves with the speed of an arthritic turtle on land. Unscrupulous businessmen who indulge in selling spurious food products or fake medicines go unpunished. If we remember the social context within which HLL operated in the 1950s, we realise the significance of what the company was doing by setting quality standards for products sold under its brand name.

The average purchasing power was so low among people that few companies could generate large sales volumes. HLL was a large organisation, with 8,500 employees; it had extensive distribution coverage. Its distribution may not have covered every village but its brands were present nationally across most states. To ensure territory coverage, its sales officers and salesmen travelled extensively.[75] They travelled by train and bus, lived in government dak bungalows when they did not find a good hotel and managed to survive on local water that was not bottled in a special factory. Tandon does not tell us how many died of diarrhoea, cholera or suffered from chronic gastro-intestinal diseases. He remained healthy and died in his nineties in Pune.

[75]P.L. Tandon recounts the weary hours of travel that he had to put in every month when the general mode of travel was rail. Few marketing whiz kids today are likely to survive such a punishing routine.

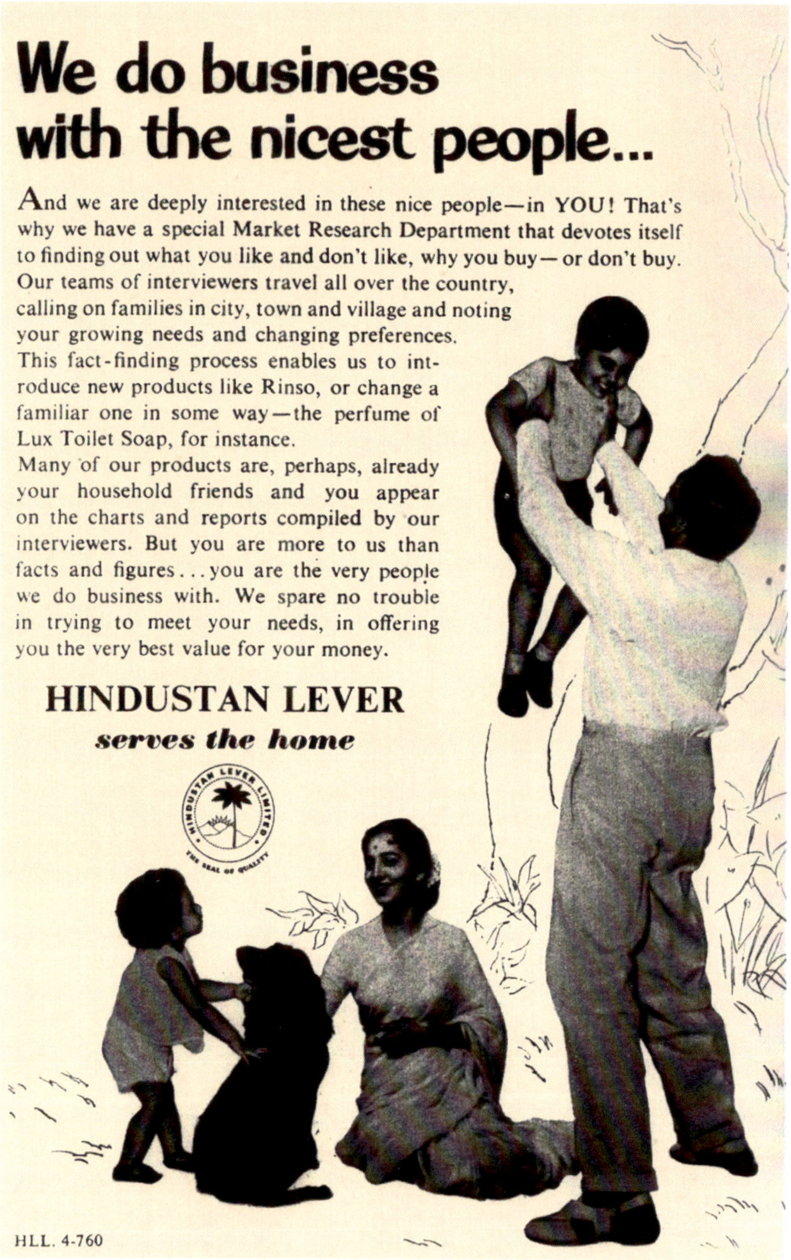

This is a rather unusual advertisement and there may not be quite another like it anywhere in the world. Researchers would feel flattered reading an advertisement dedicated to market research. It appeals to the reader directly while extolling the company's involvement with its customers.

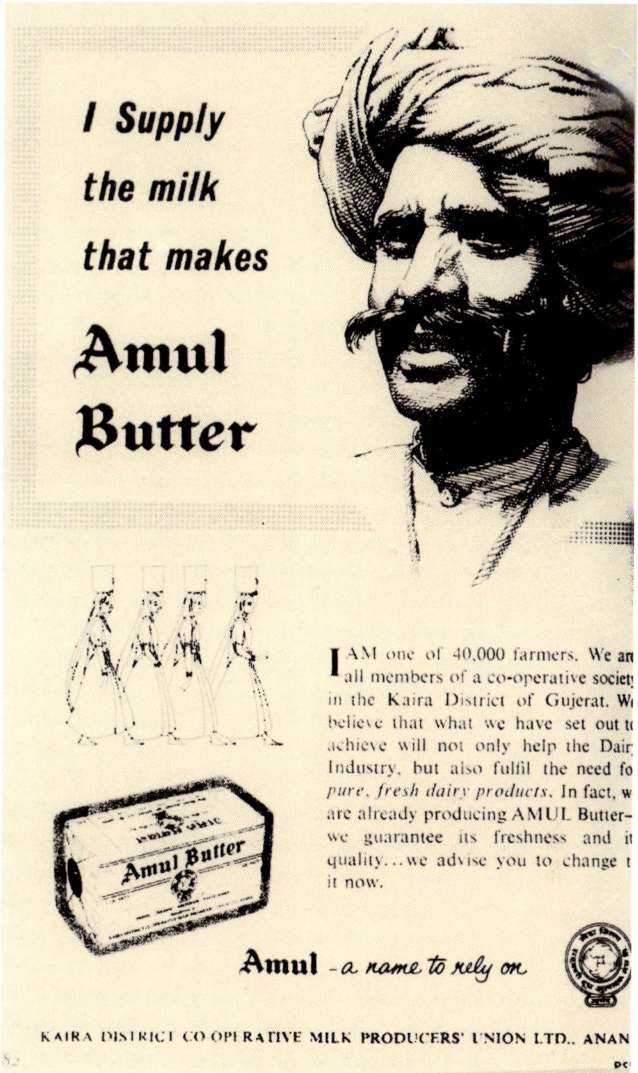

This appeared at a time when Dr Kurien was establishing Amul Butter as a household brand and before the Amul girl was born. The advertisement dwells on the cooperative experiment that was being successfully implemented by the farmers of the Kaira district in Gujarat, which became a milestone in cooperative management in India.[76] *The eminent film-maker, Shyam Benegal, made* Manthan, *an award-winning film based on the Kaira cooperative experiment.*

[76]Dr Kurien's association with Amul unfortunately ended bitterly. He was forced out of the board of Amul. Dr Kurien groomed capable persons but was reluctant to give up command, which resulted in his ouster. The strength of the Amul movement is evident in that despite serious quarrels it has not affected the everyday management at Amul.

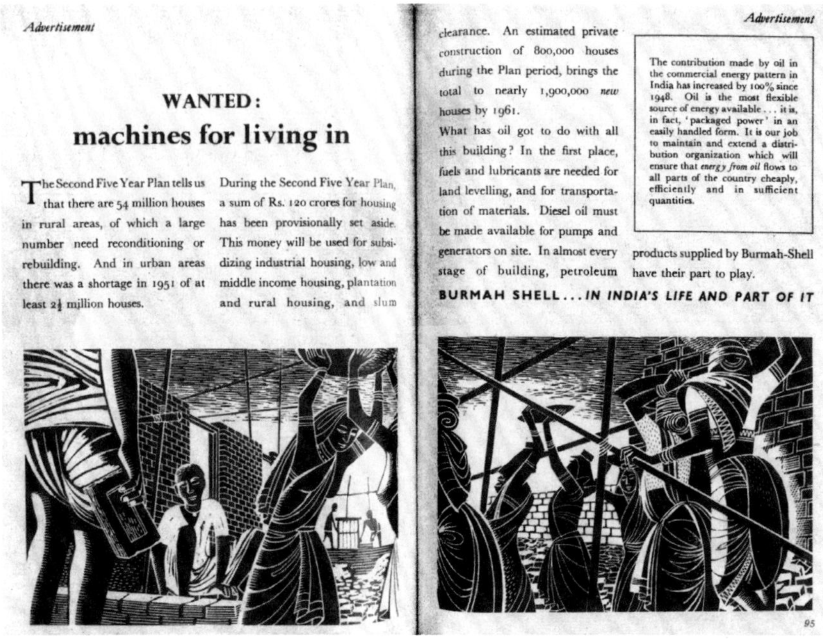

The copy of this advertisement connects Burmah Shell and its business of supplying oil and lubricants to rural housing that seemed to be a prime focus of the Second Five Year Plan. The effort is forced, which the copywriter was aware of since he asks, 'What has oil got to do with all this building?' and his answer lacks depth and conviction. In the inset the company asserts why its role is important in the Indian economy. A lot of posturing was inevitable as Nehru's government constantly posed the threat of nationalisation of foreign-owned companies.

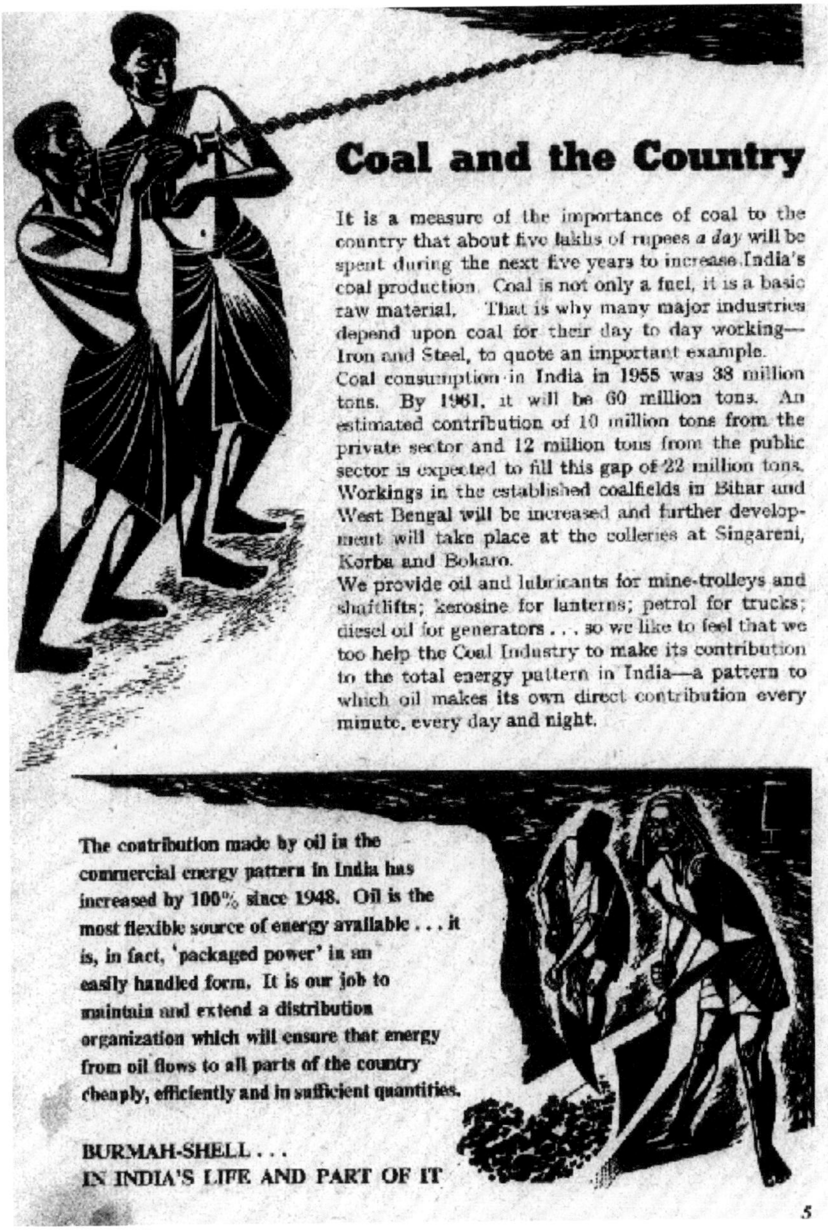

Another advertisement in which Burmah Shell associates its functions with the coal industry, which was obviously regarded as vital to India's energy needs. Indeed one might ask, reading the text, whether Burmah Shell mandarins felt their role was only secondary in the energy sector. Since then oil has become far more critical in the energy sector, not only in India but globally.

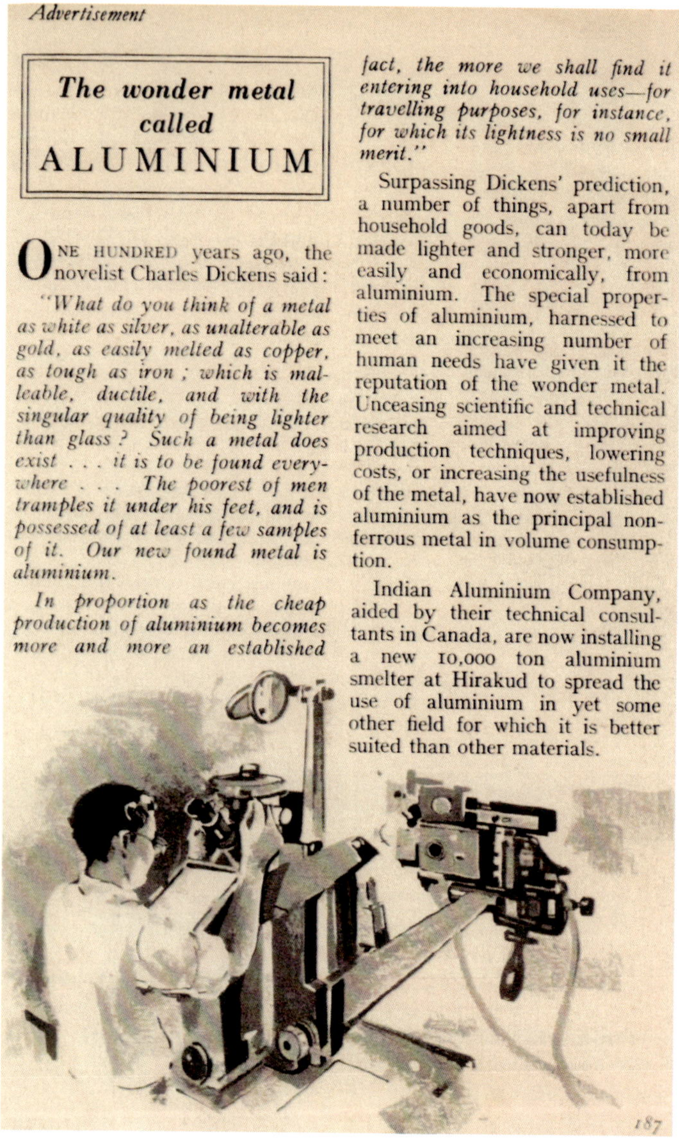

Most corporate advertisements of the 1950s educated the reader about the nature or purpose of the business. The objective was to position the company as playing a useful role in India's march towards achieving self-sufficiency. In the Indian Aluminium Company ad, the copywriter has done a lot of fact-finding. He has, surprisingly, found a piece written by the celebrated Victorian novelist Charles Dickens on aluminium. While Dickens was prolific in his writings, who would have thought he also had something to say about aluminium? Apart from the copy, what draws our attention here is the realistic illustration. It is some piece of machinery that may have been used by the industry.

Over-the-counter (OTC) products

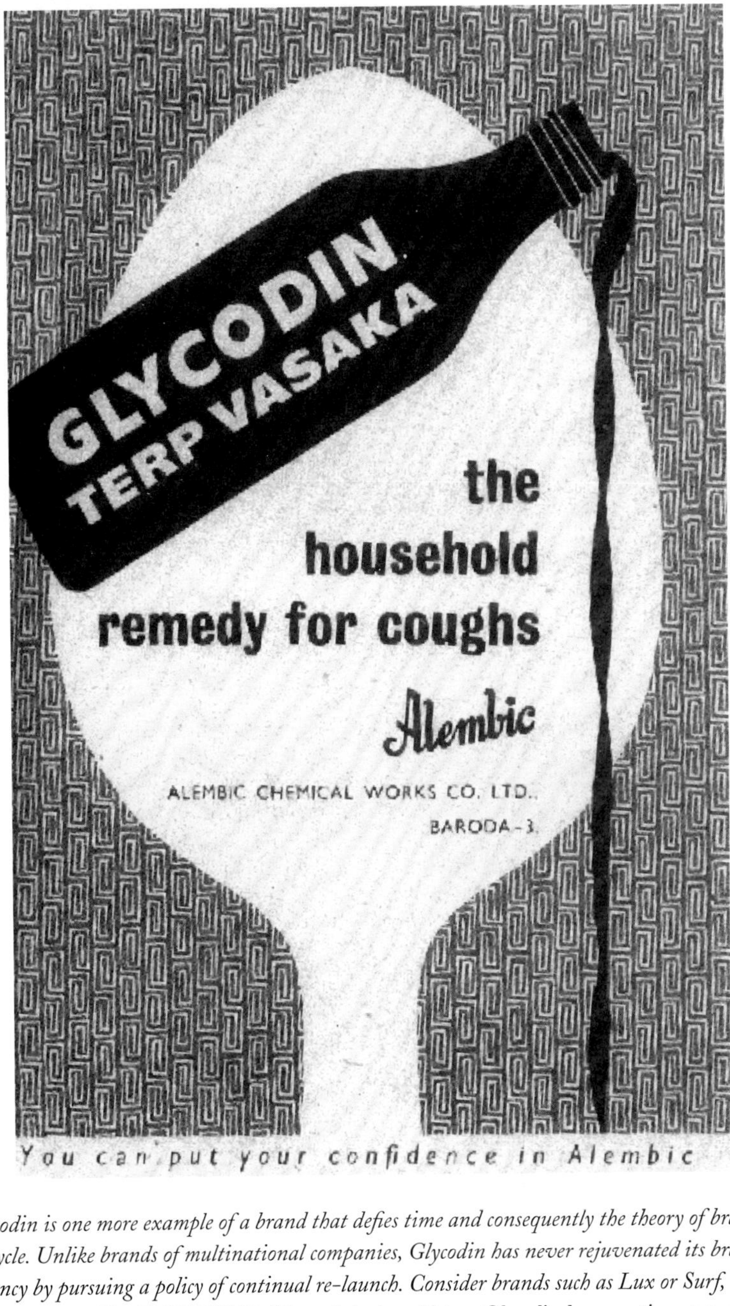

Glycodin is one more example of a brand that defies time and consequently the theory of brand lifecycle. Unlike brands of multinational companies, Glycodin has never rejuvenated its brand saliency by pursuing a policy of continual re-launch. Consider brands such as Lux or Surf, which are always NEW or IMPROVED. Through its long history Glycodin has sometimes presented a lifestyle platform in advertising, but such occasions have been infrequent.

The market of OTC cough syrups in 2013 is estimated to be in excess of Rs 500 crore. The present advertisement has everything to recommend it. A headline that addresses the reader directly; body copy that elaborates on the effectiveness of the remedy promised; and the added benefit of the brand being safe for children. In the long term Glycodin proved to be a winner while Sirolin died a natural death. In India the main cause of decay of brands has not been a lack of consumer demand; generally brand mortality may be traced to organisational decay.

The secret of brand longevity in Indian markets is efficient distribution. The cream advertised here did not have a long presence in the OTC market although when it was launched there was a latent demand for such a product in Indian homes. Burnol, a competitor, was doing well as a handy medicine for the housewife who often suffered from minor burns and cuts because she spent the greater part of her time cooking. But Borolin, which carved a sizeable market nationally in the 1970s, was to dominate the market for some time. In the 1970s and 1980s, a number of all-purpose antiseptic creams were introduced by various companies to establish a presence in this obviously lucrative segment. Distribution has played a greater role in the success or failure of brands in the country—far more than advertising.

Consumer durables (commodities)

Cement was by and large a commodity kind of product. The ACC Limited advertisement highlighted the actual use of the product for various mammoth infrastructure projects that were then coming up in various places. The ACC campaign follows a testimonial route to build brand identity.

In a single advertisement four different places are identified where the ACC brand of cement was used. Within the clutter of different visuals (all in illustrations) the layout provides prominence for the copy, which is to-the-point. For the 1950s, the ad has very little text. Perhaps the copywriter, looking at the small size of a full page in Reader's Digest, *chose economy in words. However, the ad also conveys that ACC cement is used all over India. It is an untidy ad.*

Compare this advertisement with the current campaign of Ambuja Cement where a muscular man is visualised holding a dam between his arms, flaunting the line, 'Compressive Strength'. The Ambuja campaign slams its brand positioning down the throat of the target audience.[77]

The third advertisement of the series is a conceptual one. It is obviously meant for those in the Public Works Department in Bombay. The illustration is of Marine Drive. The advantages of concreting the surface are spelt out point-wise to highlight these. ACC aimed at increasing consumption by exploring areas of public interest that would be served by using cement.

[77]A recent TV ad on another cement brand takes a comic route of a family that has separated wanting to come together once more, but a cement wall erected within the house between the two units of the same family cannot be broken down because the cement proves too tough. A storyboard like that is used to break through the clutter of ads but at this point in time I cannot recollect the brand name although I have been exposed to this advertisement many times. The ad typically assumes that the target audience is likely to make a purchase decision based on top-of-mind awareness alone, whereas it is likely that for cement a purchaser may be inclined to consider professional opinion before deciding on the brand. The decision would be influenced by his reason for purchase—whether he is buying cement for small repairs, or for building a boundary wall or for the construction of a whole building. (I am reminded by my editor that this advertisement features the well-known film personality Boman Irani. I thank my editor for this information.)

Decorative paints

The beauty of this particular advertisement lies in its simplicity. The pack is prominent as is the logo of the company. The copy is precise and the hand and paint brush are actually drawn realistically. The only negative comment about the visual is a man wearing a white shirt with the sleeves buttoned at the wrist should not be opening a can of paint. Purists of the English language may also question the correctness of 'an' before the ICI logo.

Duco is obviously a paint for surfaces other than walls. The visual attempts to set it apart with the rendering of the paint brush into a person. But the colours are drab. The art director was challenged by Reader's Digest *offering one free colour so he chose a selection of greens and shades of grey and black. JWT, and later HTA, handled ICI the longest among ad agencies. They did a memorable outdoor and print campaign with animals, which were presented in beautiful colours. The concept also combined two different animals imaginatively. ICI was Calcutta-based then; the account was handled by HTA. Subhas Ghosal took an active interest in the account and interacted on a personal level with the top management in ICI.*

There were few paint companies in India in the 1950s. ICI was a market leader in the premier price segment but smaller companies such as Addisons of Madras were active in lower price segments or in specific zones. The painter here has some slight resemblance to Gattu, the famous symbol presented as a painter in shorts with his unruly mop of hair and mischievous smile created a few years later for Asian Paints by India's most famous cartoonist R.K. Laxman. The illustration of the painter is not superlative. But it tries to carry over the impression that painting is not difficult, that it may even be fun to paint walls. The trend now is to present high-class people such as Soha Ali Khan doing her own wall, which is quite far-fetched in the Indian social context.

One of the ugliest paints ads I have seen; it includes every possible brand promise. The scarecrow figure is so poorly drawn, it may not have persuaded people to buy the paint.

Durables: Household products

Philips, a Dutch company, was the leader in radios and lighting in India. It set up a great distribution base. Radio and lighting formed two independent units and dealers handling either radio or lighting and accessories were trained. The company set up a two-tier mechanism of dealing with product complaints; first at the dealer outlet and, when he failed, at the company service centre. Each group of dealers was formed into a body supported by the company; they met regularly, shared ideas and sorted out problems with the company. Many of these problems were supply-related.[78]

[78]I was fortunate to handle the Philips advertising account in Calcutta while I was with Clarion. And then when I worked for OBM I handled the account for a period of six years in the mid-1970s uninterruptedly, making many lifelong friends.

Jhankar Radio never became a competitor to Philips. There were a number of small companies manufacturing radios, but the market was dominated by three large brands, Philips, Murphy and GEC.

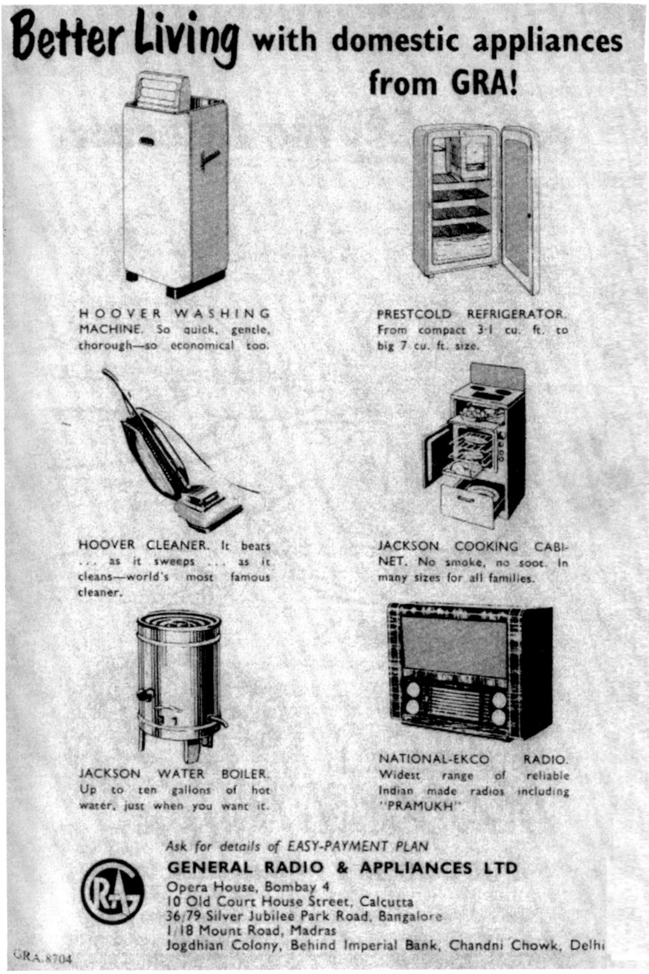

Many of the products advertised here did not penetrate into even upper-class households till well after the 1990s. For instance, the washing machine, the cooking cabinet and the Hoover cleaner.[79] *In the 1950s, even refrigerators were extremely rare. Post-1995, washing machines began to be used more commonly in middle-class households. In the twenty-first century, the need of an electrically-operated floor cleaner is still unfelt despite the fact that the domestic help is no longer an easy find. In India, cutting across demographic groups, wiping the floor with a wet cloth every day is a common phenomenon. This is called 'ponch' by the housewife. Till such time some company invents a machine for a cheaper 'ponch' than now, electric cleaners will continue to have little relevance.*

[79]I recall a funny experience in a friend's home; this was in the eighties. They had bought a vacuum cleaner, which was quite expensive at the time. Their maid dared to operate it. The whole family resented this and she was questioned why she used it without seeking permission—didn't she know how expensive it was?

Air conditioners were a luxury in the fifties; very few offices had them. Only homes of the truly rich could afford this luxury. Expatriates in multinational companies in Bombay, Madras and Calcutta enjoyed furnished accommodation. The senior executives were often given air conditioners as perks. Only the best cinema halls in metro cities had air conditioning.

People could choose between different popular makes of vehicles made in the UK or the USA. Initially, the Indian government continued to import vehicles. Later, imports were discouraged and finally stopped when cars and trucks began to be manufactured in the country. Hindustan Motors produced Ambassador cars and Hindustan trucks at its factory located at Hind Motors, near Calcutta. Tata trucks rolled out from Telco factories at Jamshedpur and Poona. Fiat cars were manufactured in Bombay. Madras was the home of Standard cars and Ashok Leyland trucks. Mahindra & Mahindra specialised in four-wheel drive vehicles, popularly called 'Jeeps', with canvas tops.

This workmanlike ad, based on the features of the 1956 Plymouth, may be regarded as copy-heavy by our standards but does a commendable job in highlighting the main features in a layout that is balanced and displays the style and look of the vehicle. Note the line drawing of the vehicle, which was necessitated by the constraints of printing half-tones.

None of the Indian motor/truck manufacturing companies had a need to advertise. There was a queue for any kind of vehicle. In fact at its worst the wait for a family car was around five years. Unlike in the USA, neither the car manufacturers nor banks forwarded loans for purchase. The whole amount had to be paid for—the manufacturers also learnt to take an interest-free advance at the time of booking. To dissuade people from buying cars, the government imposed punitive tax and excise, which accounted for as much as 40 per cent of the cost of a vehicle.

With far less copy than the Plymouth ad, this ad builds a lifestyle association with the brand. Once more the style of illustration of the car is similar to the Plymouth ad.

As we reconstruct the past we need to consider the climate prevailing in most of the multinational companies since they were the major spenders in advertising. Senior executives, who became managing directors after Independence, recall the discrimination that existed then. Whether it is P.L. Tandon,[80] who headed HLL in India or Ajit Haksar,[81] who Indianised ITC during his long tenure at the helm, they narrate similar experiences of not being treated equally with European managers and being forced to put up with an ever-present colour bar that determined admission to clubs and unequal pay for the same responsibilities shouldered.

It is in this context that we should regard the ascendance of a handful of Indians to positions of authority in what were then leading advertising agencies. D.K. Gupta, for example, was assistant manager in D.J. Keymer in its Calcutta office. A colourful personality, a rare calligraphist and a keen follower of modern Bengali literature, he formed Signet Press, a publishing concern for Bengali books, which set standards for publishing in the vernacular.[82] Satyajit Ray, the great film-maker who joined advertising as a visualiser in D.J. Keymer, was first interviewed by him. Gupta asked him to work on a few layouts to test his skill as an artist. On his recommendation Ray bagged his first job—in Keymer.

Bal Mundkur observed that he was the only Indian covenanted member on the staff of D.J. Keymer in Bombay when he joined them after quitting his job at Air India.[83] There were few Indian managers in large and medium-sized organisations in those times. Indians who made it even to the middle management level were generally exceptional in calibre. In a commemorative issue published in memory of D.K. Gupta, contributors to the issue, who had seen him at work in D.J. Keymer, universally spoke about the man's outstanding proficiency.[84]

---

[80] *Punjabi Saga*. P.L. Tandon recalls, 'I had recently begun to get tea on a tray and had a towel with my name in the managers' toilet. I had no contract, no perquisites or privileges beyond the tea and the towel.'

[81] Ajit Haksar is quoted in an article by S.L. Rao, published by *The Telegraph* on 9 October 2006: 'Socially there was generally only superficial communication between the whites and the blacks, with the former living apart in their four walls, using clubs barred to Indians; the latter condescendingly invited to a servants' ball or dinner by the boss once a year, usually at Christmas, sometimes not even then.' I recall a story of one Mr Lal who was heading the board of directors at ICI going to its explosives factory at Gomia, now in Giridih district, Jharkhand, where he had heard Europeans had cleared out the water in the swimming pool because some Indians had used the pool. This was in the early 1960s. He compelled the whites to bathe with Indians in the same pool.

[82] The books published by Signet Press in its nine years of existence have become collectors' items. Satyajit Ray, Subhas Sen, the poet Subhas Mukhopadhyay, among many others, offered their services for free. Indeed, D.K. Gupta probably spent all his savings on the project. He took up a job with Bata as the advertising manager when D.J. Keymer closed down its office in Calcutta.

[83] This was stated during an interview with the author in New Delhi in 2000.

[84] Even a perfectionist such as Satyajit Ray has commented on D.K. Gupta's outstanding proficiency in advertising, especially his meticulous eye to detail.

One of the products launched with a lot of fanfare and advertising support was Dunlopillo. The company worked hard at getting early converts across different user segments such as public transport, hospitals and theatres (the Lighthouse theatre in Calcutta had all the seats converted to Dunlopillo). Posters and press advertisements were developed. Although the advertisement that follows is in colour it was surely not carried as a colour advertisement in the dailies, which did not then print colour ads.[85] The advertisement reproduced here was printed in the in-house magazine of the company. The material was processed from a copper block, since offset printing was unknown then. But the colour processing of the block was executed with care. Note the tonal variation maintained in the cross-section drawing and the clarity of the half-tone pictures at the bottom.

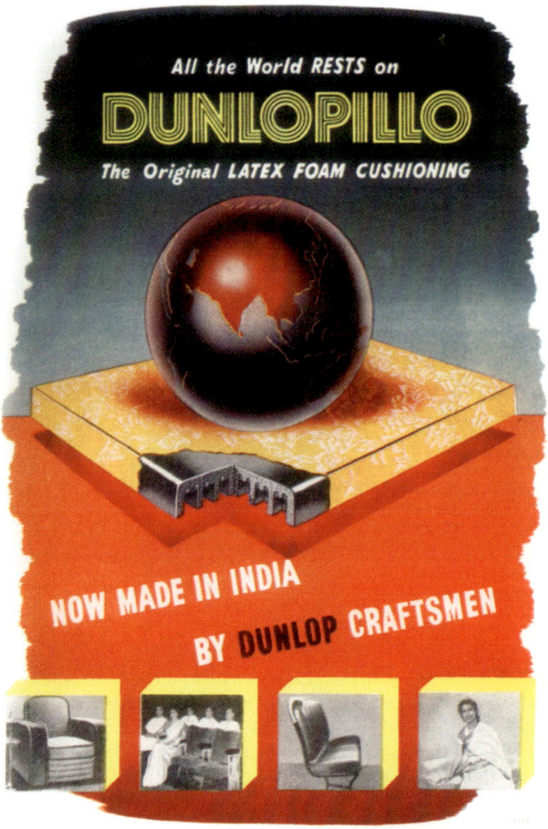

Gossain & Co. is the biggest job printing house in Kolkata in 2011. It continues to excel in high quality printing and is also the most reliable when it comes to jobs required 'yesterday'.[86] As we go to press it is sad to report that Gossain & Co. is no more a single company. In 2012, the children of N.K. Gossain decided to separate. The printing house is broken up into small segments; each segment is managed by one of the sons of the founder.

[85]Perhaps the sole exception was *The Times of India Annual*, which carried colour advertisements.

[86]I was sent to Gossain & Co. for training when I joined Clarion in the early 1970s. The founder, the late N.K. Gossain, personally oversaw the training imparted to the team of junior account executives.

This advertisement created by D.J. Keymer & Co. included a number of uses of Dunlopillo presented both aesthetically and unobtrusively. In advertising, showing cross-section drawings is generally done for industrial products. Illustrating the cross-section helps to explain its distinguishing features. Here the product cross-section is used as a base on which a globe rests, implying its worldwide popularity, and the various uses of Dunlopillo are presented through photographs. Another interesting point to note is the presentation of two different kinds of chairs—a sofa suggesting comfort at home and a seat in a public transport.

There were many hurdles for advertisers. A major issue was the increasing scarcity of quality newsprint; or in reality *any* newsprint and art paper. Newsprint and coated art papers were imported for the most part and there was a severe shortage of foreign exchange. This situation only grew worse with time.[87]

Inimitable Laxman on the subject

[87]I reproduce a news item carried by *The Times of India* of Bombay dated 10 January 1950. It was reporting on a meeting held in Calcutta. The subhead read, 'Newsprint Control Order'. 'An extraordinary general meeting of the Indian and Eastern Newspaper Society was held in Calcutta on 6 January, with the president, Deshbandhu Gupta, in the chair and 33 members. Among other matters of internal interest, current position of newsprint imports was considered and in appreciation of the present foreign exchange difficulties to which the Society's attention had been drawn by the Government of India, a resolution was passed requesting the government to re-introduce the price-page schedule which formed part of the previous Newsprint Control Order, for as short a period as may be necessary, subject to the definite provisions that there should be no restriction on additional quotas required by newspapers for genuine increases in circulation and that there should be no bar to the starting of newspapers.' People associated with the advertising or newspaper industries in the seventies would recall how newspapers were started in the 1960s and 1970s only for the purpose of obtaining a newsprint quota, which then was disposed of in the black market. We have always been ingenious as businessmen.

Multinational companies took most of the available advertising space in the more popular dailies. A few of the larger Indian companies carried on regular advertising campaigns though a number of them went in for classified display columns or released small display advertisements. Some brand advertisements, as we observed, are quite modern in their appeal.

Door-to-door promotion

In sales (marketing was still unknown), direct contact with consumers was often used as part of a company's strategy. *The Times of India* of 11 January 1950 carries this advertisement in the situations wanted column: 'Wanted Ladies For Door-To-Door Canvassing. Pay Rs 100/- plus commission and conveyance expenses. Apply Post Bag 1057, Bombay 1.' In the same paper we come across two other advertisements. One appears in the situations wanted column, where an advertising professional offers his service: 'All Round Experienced Commercial Artist seeks permanent post or freelance work. Contact Box 8772, The Times of India.' The mention of freelance work implies there was more work in agencies or in the ad departments of newspapers than could be managed by their regular staff.[88] The third advertisement in the 11 January issue was a promotion of the national flag with a film:

JAN PAECHAN
Starring NARGIS
A FREE FLAG!
For Republic Day Celebrations!

India's first Republic Day celebrations

This was a memorable occasion because it was on 26 January 1950 that the Constitution adopted by the constituent assembly on 26 November 1949 came into force. India was officially declared a union of states, and a sovereign, secular and democratic republic with a parliamentary system of government, which is governed by the Indian Constitution. *The Times of India* and all other mainline dailies carried special supplements. *The Times of India* also inserted a colour magazine within its Republic Day special issue, which included a few articles along with advertisements.[89]

[88]Later freelance work affected most large agencies as their trained hands, mainly art directors and copywriters, took up assignments privately. Their moonlighting affected the quality of work produced by the agencies. Most agency heads were aware of what was going on, but few wished to stop the practice.

[89]I have written a separate note on the special number published by *The Times of India* on the occasion of the first Republic Day celebrations in 1950. This is likely to be of interest to many readers who are interested in modern Indian history. (a) The supplement explained with illustrations the three arms of our democracy—the legislature, the judiciary and the executive. (b) It detailed out the relationship between the central and the state governments (which is not a part of this note for the sake of brevity). (c) It also has the musical score of the national anthem, which was obviously new to the newborn nation.

The occasion was treated as a marketing opportunity by *The Times of India*. The supplement that was published along with the day's paper carried many advertisements. Companies conveyed their best wishes to the new republic. A few claimed they were associated with India's freedom struggle, while most advertisers attempted to forge a connection relevant for the occasion. This section included a number of ads that are shamelessly sycophantic.[90]

Although Subhas Ghosal had commented that corporate advertising was not much in evidence in the 1950s, looking at old issues of newspapers one does come across quite a lot of corporate advertisements. For instance, the Republic Day special issue published by *The Times of India* includes more than a fair share of them—some good, a great many fair and quite a number pretty bad both in content and in execution. Let us present some of the ads that appeared in this issue.

[90]In a recent observation, if memory serves, the Supreme Court advised the central government not to waste public money by frequently advertising the exploits of various ministries where the sole purpose is to show the incumbent minister's face.

on the road to progress
Steel links India's frontiers......
Bridge over the Tista
A new metre gauge 142½ miles of Railway line through Indian territory is now open for traffic linking Assam with the rest of Indian Union. This project has been completed months ahead of schedule.
One of the many pile bridges used to expedite construction.
The first train comes through.
This achievement was made possible by 7,000 tons of Indian Steel in addition to the track rails, and by Steel in various other forms.
TATA STEEL
THE TATA IRON & STEEL COMPANY LIMITED, HEAD SALES OFFICE: CALCUTTA.

In both these advertisements the companies try to associate their business activities with the infrastructure needs of a newly-independent country. The ICI advertisement through its visual of a typical miner of the times (who, of course, looks healthier than he actually was) encapsulates the early 1950s. After the nationalisation of mines, when all mines came into the fold of Coal India Limited, miners at least had shirts on their backs, and wore trousers or shorts and were not dhoti-clad or bare-bodied as shown.[91]

The Tata Steel advertisement celebrates the railway connection with Assam, connecting the state with the rest of the country, which involved laying out railway tracks on 142.5 miles besides other interconnected jobs for which Tata Steel supplied the steel. In the following four decades, large or medium companies presented their story of contributing to nation building in most corporate campaigns. That was predictably boring and interested only those who developed the ads or spent good money releasing them. Yes, newspapers were also beneficiaries since they earned good revenue.

The quality of newsprint was so poor that advertisers in India and their agencies learnt to live with this constraint till the mid-1980s. Line illustrations reproduced better than quarter-tones, and quarter-tones with finer screens were not used. The difference in the quality of reproduction is seen if the Tata Steel advertisement is compared with the General Electric advertisement that follows.

The locomotive presented in the Tata ad, in quarter-tone, is not easy to figure out. Whereas in the General Electric ad, the locomotive presented as a line illustration stands out. Indeed, in the General Electric advertisement, all the visuals are in line illustration. The radio, the props including a flower vase, an alarm clock, a table lamp and photographs on the wall, along with the couple sitting listening to a radio programme, every visual element is in line illustration. The visuals have absolute clarity although the ad is printed on the same newsprint.

[91]A few years later, Indian Explosives Limited (IEL), a unit of ICI, started manufacturing commercial explosives for mining in Gomia, in Jharkhand. The first President of India, Dr Rajendra Prasad, inaugurated the commissioning of the plant. Obviously the unit was regarded as one of national importance.

You Benefit...
Most countries have been aided in the development of electric power by the General Electric Company. Some 200,000 G-E products have been created so that industries and homes might enjoy improved standards. The chain of benefits extends to everyone. A nation installs General Electric apparatus to convert water power and other natural resources into current. Typical examples of benefits then available are electric locomotives which transport people and goods speedily, efficiently—and appliances such as electric clocks, vacuum cleaners, radios, lamps, kitchen appliances which mean new ease and convenience in the home. However you use electricity, you can place your confidence in the leader.
GENERAL ELECTRIC
U.S.A.
The Standard of Excellence
THROUGHOUT THE WORLD...
IN INDUSTRY AND HOME
INTERNATIONAL GENERAL ELECTRIC CO. (INDIA) LTD.
Bombay Calcutta Bangalore

Saru Smelting & Refining Corp. Ltd uses the occasion to highlight its own achievements in non-ferrous metallurgy. This typifies a lot of corporate advertising that is seen in the country. Companies generally use every occasion to present their contribution to society. The current ad is unattractive in appearance and boring in substance. Most occasion-specific corporate ads are unreadable.

This jewellery company does not make a song and dance about its excellence of design or wonderful track record of serving customers. The message is direct. Visually unattractive, one must bear in mind that in the fifties the national emblem may not have been widely recognised. I will not be surprised if some of our modern legislators fail to recognise the symbol. Perhaps those who have spent time in jail would vaguely remember seeing the symbol somewhere.

The Favre-Leuba advertisement chooses to celebrate the occasion as ambassadors of Switzerland. The flags of both nations are displayed literally hanging down rather than fluttering with joy on the occasion.

Jhaveri Brothers do not believe in wasting money on advertising; the company shows a single-minded resolve to sell its ware.

The beginning of the trend in sycophancy, with photographs of national leaders in ads, started in the early 1950s. Today all political parties governing at the centre or in the states release advertisements through public sector companies extolling the virtues of these wonderful supermen and, not infrequently, women. Here are a couple of early examples of ads exploiting the image of national leaders.

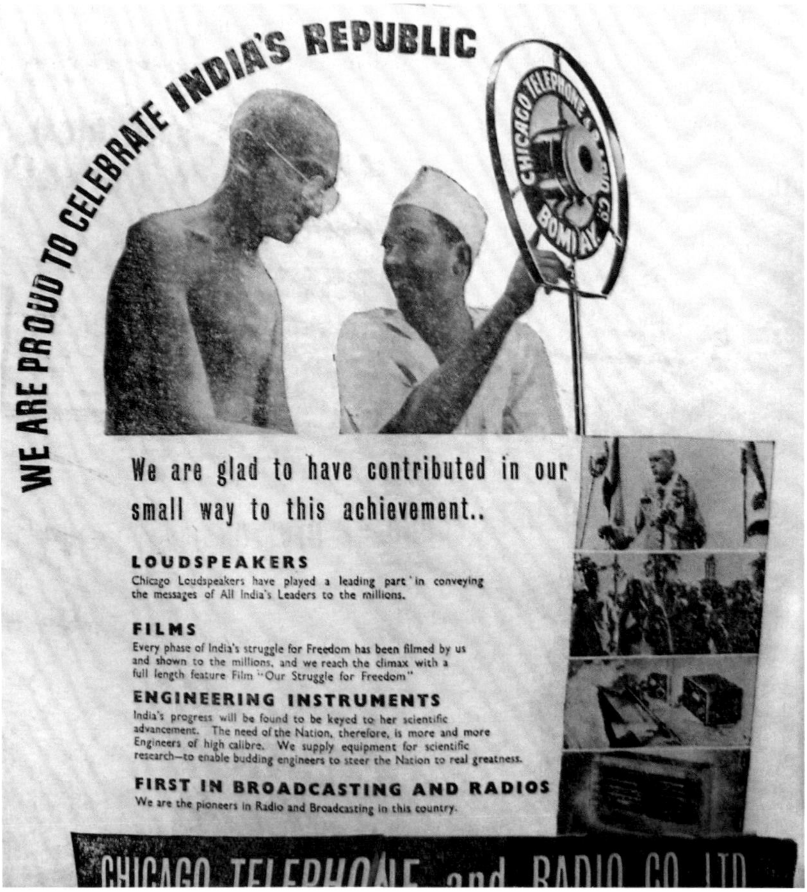

The subhead sums up the ad. Indian companies are only too willing to tom-tom their association with the winning side to gain commercial mileage. Chicago Telephone & Radio may have had as close a link with Chicago as Lahore Photo Stores in Daryaganj, Delhi, has with Lahore in 2013. Did Gandhi agree to be a model for the company? See the smile on the face of the man standing next to him, pointing at the mouthpiece. The ad supports words with pictures. Nehru and possibly Subhas Chandra Bose feature in an inset as do other leaders not clearly identifiable in a second inset. Of the last two small pictures, one shows engineering instruments and the other a radio.

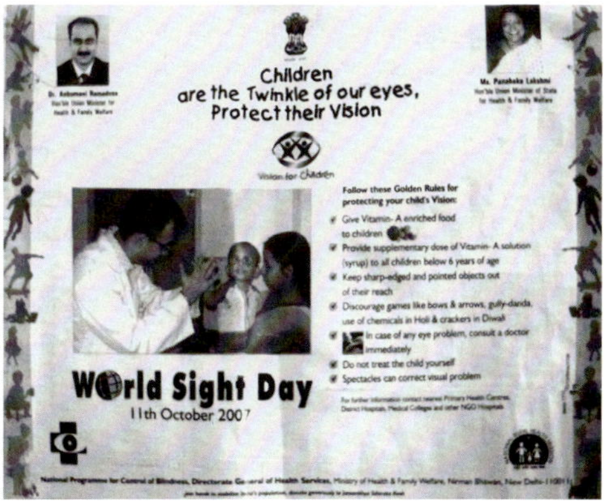

Fortunately, the Directorate of Advertising and Visual Publicity (DAVP), who designed and released this advertisement, included at least one child in the frame. Most of the visual space is taken up by officials.

Chicago Telephone & Radio took no chances. It had both Gandhi and Nehru featuring in separate ads on the same day and in the same newspaper supplement.

As is evident, India has travelled a long way down the road of sycophancy 60 years after Independence. Now, leaders big and small appear in ads at the taxpayer's expense.

Even Gandhi is used by politicians to bolster their personal image. That day is not far when we shall all laugh seeing the father of the nation in a small inset while current political greats hog the major part of an ad. Perhaps an adventurous political heavyweight will remove the picture of Gandhi on 2 October and just have his own photograph with his spouse beside him.

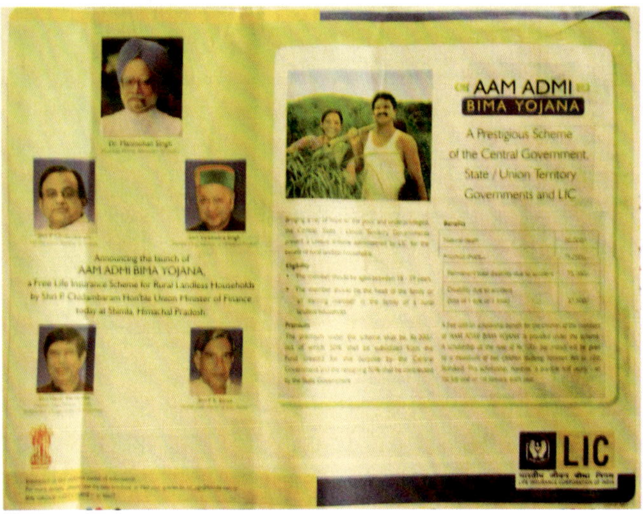

The Life Insurance Corporation (LIC) thought fit to include as many political faces as possible in one advertisement, forgetting that its 'Insurance for the Common Man' is a product like any of their other products, which may be positioned on its benefits or features, but not carried on the backs of our dear leaders.

Chicago Telephone & Radio was starting a trend that was followed without any major change for the following six decades and more.

Advertising industrial products

Advertisements for industrial products were designed with care. Apart from major mainline English dailies there were no specialised publications dedicated to specific industries that could carry such advertisements. For industrial advertisements it may be emphasised that the poor quality of newsprint made it difficult to show machines or machine parts with clarity.

A technical ad has to explain the technical facets of a product. The target audience comprises experts who understand the technical nature of the benefits presented. The emphasis in the current ad is to sell a number of different products on the strength of the company name. Every product mentioned in the copy is presented in line illustration. They reproduce with clarity. This advertisement is probably aimed at distributors of such products rather than end-users.

enough food for all the millions
who inhabit INDIA
by 1951."
The Ferguson System of Complete Farm Mechanisation
Grow More Food - More Cheaply
WITH
FERGUSON

This advertisement for tractors (facing page) is far ahead of its time. India in the early fifties was not in a position to even think about farm mechanisation when there was a surplus of farm hands and 90 per cent of the population were farmers without occupation for much of the year. The advertisement was clearly aimed at government officials who were decision-makers for the purchase of expensive equipment such as tractors, which may possibly have been engaged in government sponsored projects. The farmer was generally so poor that buying a tractor was unthinkable. Public sector banks did not then give loans as they do today for agriculture and to small and medium-scale industries.[92] Bank nationalisation was still many years away. In some ways the socialistic slant pursued by the central government from the 1950s to the end of 1980s, which saw the setting-up of large manufacturing units in the public sector, provided the base on which the private sector took off.[93]

The visual of muscular biceps (next page) reinforces the notion of the durability as well as sturdiness of the machines supplied. However, this particular visual was destined to become a cliché in industrial advertising. Another notable feature of the advertisement is the prominence given to the logo and symbol of Worthington. Further, the baseline becomes integral to the format of corporate or industrial advertising. It is a company slogan; sometimes this slogan is carried over into all corporate communication to reinforce the message.[94]

---

[92]A recent disturbing trend in Maharashtra and Andhra Pradesh is that farmers commit suicide as they are unable to repay their debts due to crop failure or not being able to get a good price for crops when faced with a bountiful harvest. This may be traced to the political reforms started by Dr Manmohan Singh, which is a total turnaround from socialism that was supported by the same Congress Party from the time of Nehru. The banks have hardened their stance in giving loans without guarantee of repayment, which makes the hapless farmers fair prey of loan sharks. Local leaders, again of the Congress Party, appear to be the main loan-givers in these regions.

[93]Dr Amartya Sen, while editing *The Economic Times* of 21 December 2006, commented: 'In public healthcare, the private sector could do a very good job if there was basic health service in the country. That is one lesson we can learn from the European experience—that the private sector is parasitic on a functional public sector.' In India this holds true for other sectors as well such as agriculture, IT, transport and services including banking and insurance.

[94]In the 1980s, Dunlop used the message, '*Dunlop is Dunlop. Always ahead.*' *The Telegraph* called itself '*The Unputdownable*'. Steel Authority of India Ltd (SAIL) continues to flog '*There is a bit of SAIL in everyone's life.*' Personally, I believe lines such as these are examples of poor communication. However, through constant use people become familiar with poor grammar or silly statements and begin to believe that these are highly creative additions to a company's corporate image.

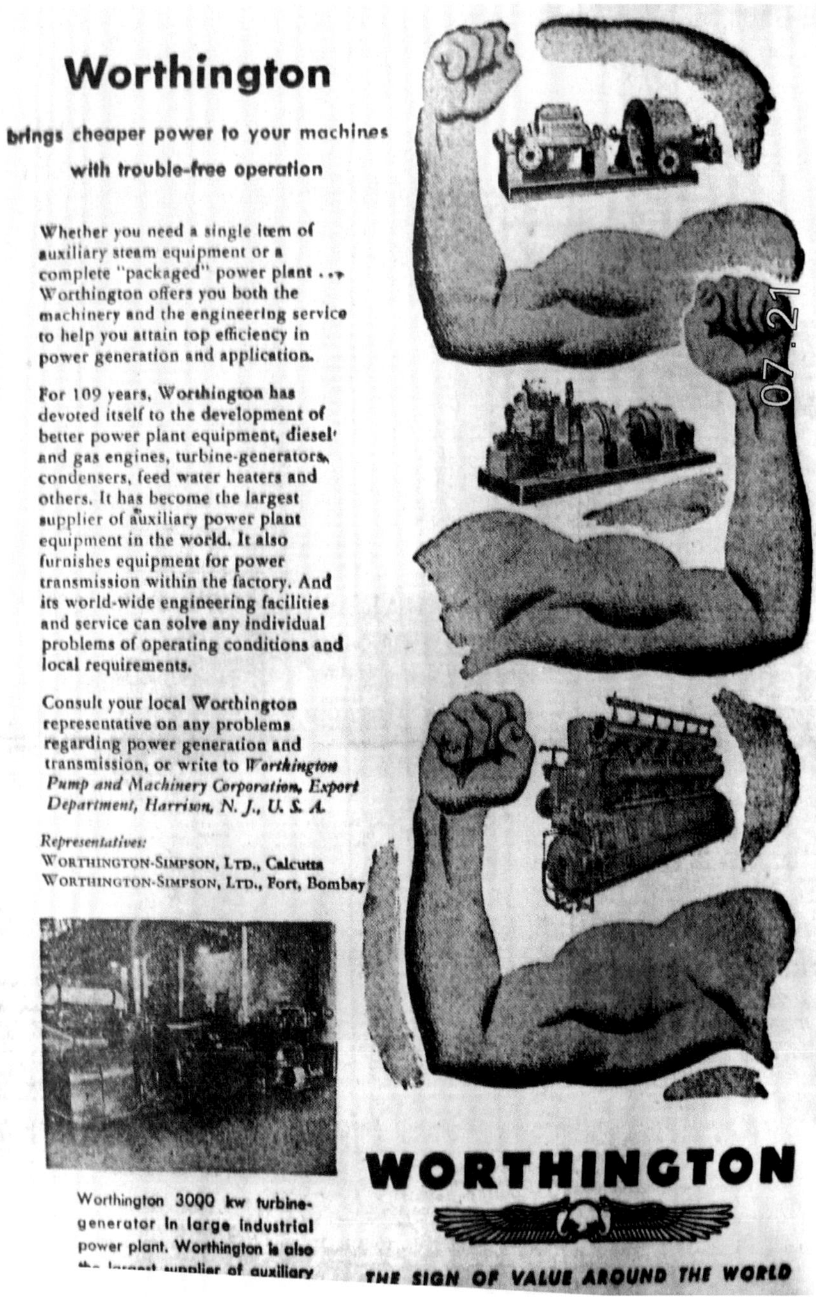
Worthington
brings cheaper power to your machines
with trouble-free operation
Whether you need a single item of auxiliary steam equipment or a complete "packaged" power plant ... Worthington offers you both the machinery and the engineering service to help you attain top efficiency in power generation and application.
For 109 years, Worthington has devoted itself to the development of better power plant equipment, diesel and gas engines, turbine-generators, condensers, feed water heaters and others. It has become the largest supplier of auxiliary power plant equipment in the world. It also furnishes equipment for power transmission within the factory. And its world-wide engineering facilities and service can solve any individual problems of operating conditions and local requirements.
Consult your local Worthington representative on any problems regarding power generation and transmission, or write to Worthington Pump and Machinery Corporation, Export Department, Harrison, N. J., U. S. A.
Representatives:
WORTHINGTON-SIMPSON, LTD., Calcutta
WORTHINGTON-SIMPSON, LTD., Fort, Bombay
Worthington 3000 kw turbine-generator in large industrial power plant. Worthington is also
WORTHINGTON
THE SIGN OF VALUE AROUND THE WORLD

Industrial advertising often had to educate as well as persuade the target audience. An engineer of the 1950s would have been aware of the application described. In a sense it was the educated non-engineer who could be a decision-maker, being informed about the involvement of the company in the country's well-being.[95]

[95]I worked on this account in 1976 when I joined Clarion as account executive. The company was then known as Indian Oxygen Limited (IOL). J.M. Kaul, a doyen of PR in India and author of *Public Relations in India*, the first textbook on PR in this country, was at the time advertising and PR manager of IOL.

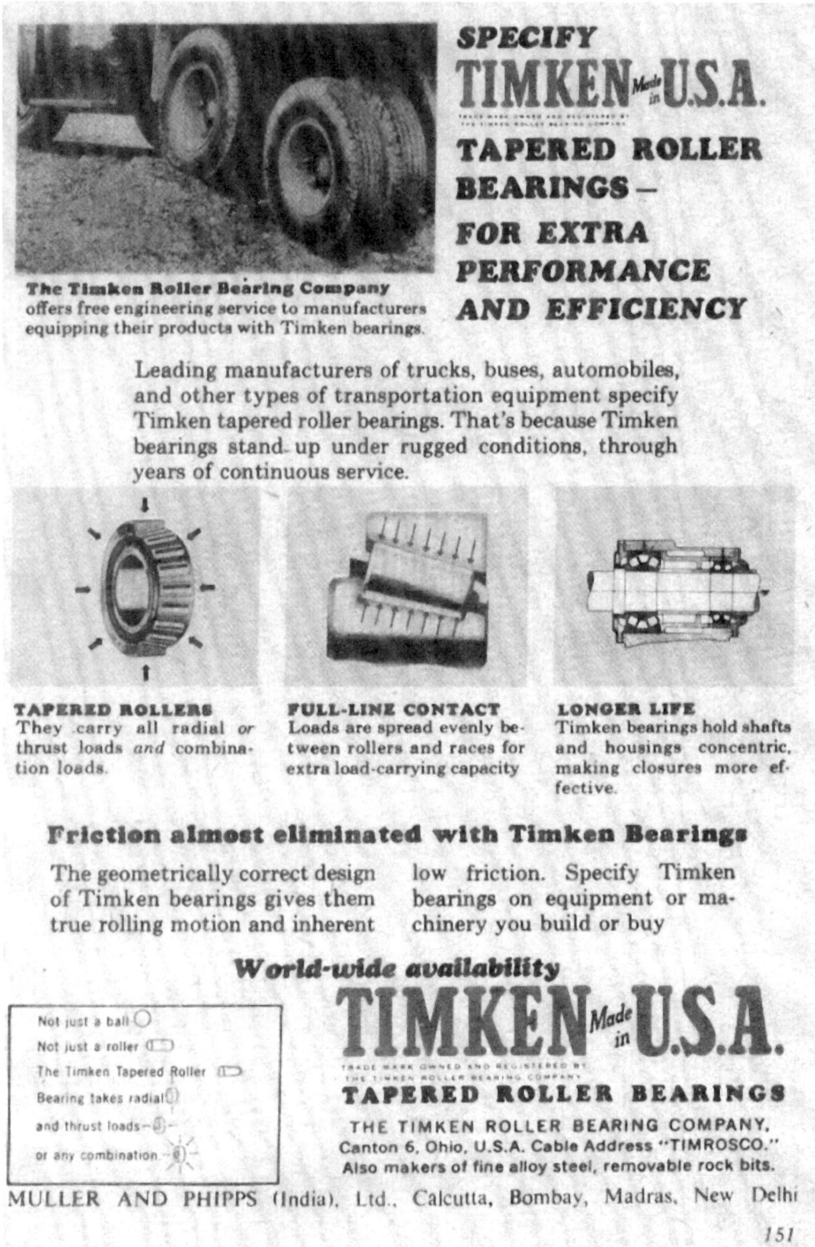

This advertisement does not load too much copy to explain things. Visuals, which are quite prominent for the size of the advertisement, support the messages that are positioned as captions underneath. A photograph is used to show the rough terrain over which vehicles move while the bearings are presented in line drawings for clarity.

The Trombay power station advertisement combines a technical story of power generation with a corporate tale. The great steam boiler that is partly visible is a complex piece of machinery that shows the company's industrial capability. Notice the drawing. The operator is drawn by hand; he is not from a photograph. Indeed, the entire visual is an illustration or a half-tone given a line treatment operating from a hard print. The baseline is unexpectedly bold for the times, if we remember that Nehru was laying the foundations of a socialist India, which was just a step away from any totalitarian communist government. Individual freedom was devalued by various Congress governments for 50 years. Unlike other large corporate groups, the Tata Group, led by J.R.D. Tata, stood for free enterprise. It paid a price for not towing the government line.[96]

---

[96]Air India, which was founded by J.R.D. Tata, was nationalised. He was the chairman of the board of directors in the initial years, but later the management of the company passed directly into government hands. While J.R.D. Tata built one of the most loved airlines during his tenure, the inevitable decline of the maharaja began when ministers and bureaucrats were appointed guardians of Air India. Tata was also denied permission to manufacture motor cars for years.

This advertisement anchors itself on a product benefit. Champion spark plugs lead to savings of 10 per cent on each tank of fuel. It reads like an ad of the twenty-first century when petroleum prices are hitting the roof and the whole world is concerned about global warming. In the 1950s, oil prices were stable because oil producing nations had not learnt the benefits of cartelisation and not a soul knew anything about global warming.

Caltex motor oil promises a three-fold benefit and closes with the claim that it doubles engine life. It would have been interesting to ask the company or the ad agency what they believed was engine life. In this country motor vehicles served owners for 40 or 50 years. Cars bought in the 1950s were running on Indian roads even in the 1990s.

The larger agencies, among them JWT, Lintas, Clarion and Ulka, produced work that established quality standards of the times. Ads were first written in English. Even after Independence a number of leading agencies had Englishmen on their staff as copywriters, account executives and managers. Designations such as account planner, vice president and human resource head were unknown. The expats left India in the late 1950s and early to mid-1960s. Indian copywriters came from English medium schools and the majority were more comfortable with English than with the vernacular.

A comparison of world advertising in the decade of the fifties shows that advertising in the USA was more advanced than in Europe. American ad agencies explored freshness of ideas in order to compete with other agencies. Technical innovations in photography, cinematography and printing created exciting possibilities for advertisers. A number of universities in the USA already offered courses in management. Initially the English looked upon management studies as a reflection of the eccentricity of Americans. Advertising formed part of the curriculum.

Advertising was always regarded as vital for business in America since the 1870s. In the post-First World War era, the country was well on its way to becoming a leading industrial power in the world. In the post-Second World War era, the USA was the most affluent country. Its economy was driven by mass consumption. Advertising naturally played a prominent role in driving mass consumption. Advertisers and universities allocated funds to advertising research; to understanding consumer psyche; and in testing the results of advertising campaigns.

While consumerism drove the US economy, a number of countries were influenced by the emergence of the Soviet Union as a major military power. The Soviet economy followed the tested path of the fascist dictatorships. Militarisation resulted in large industrial projects that provided jobs to demobbed soldiers after the war. The Soviet Union provided a model for other nations to follow. England had a large support base of pro-labour politics. Leading Indian politicians, including Nehru, were admirers of planned development even if that meant stifling the latent Indian propensity of citizens to be entrepreneurs. India faced major problems; there were simply too many mouths to feed and the economy was virtually crippled. The logistics of communication between village and town, between the government, local and central, and the governed was based upon an infrastructure that was created to rule over a subject nation. Per capita income was so low that living was nothing short of a miracle.

In such a situation advertising was regarded by the Congress Party as a tool of capitalist endeavour. Capitalism was frowned upon. The Congress Party indoctrinated the common man against capitalism. Capitalism was portrayed as the ultimate evil. It remains a wonder how Indian advertising in these trying years after Independence managed to attract talented young men and women into its fold. Without social recognition, operating on the fringe of business and rendering a service that was officially looked upon as redundant, these young people proved their mettle in the following 40 years. Though unrecognised, they turned out remarkable campaigns not only for brands but also for the government.

Media in the 1950s

In the early to mid-1950s, press advertising was far more critical to any campaign than television. This applied to India just as it held true for the USA or England. Television would take many more years to arrive on the subcontinent. In the 1950s, television was beginning to grow in importance in media plans only in the USA. Even in England, advertising in cinema was a recent development.[97] In the USA, as many as 481 commercial television stations were functioning by 1958. Over 88 per cent of all homes in the USA had a television set by January 1961. In fact, there were more homes with television sets than there were homes with bath tubs or telephones at the time, which may be as much a reflection on the general standard of personal hygiene in that country as their fascination for telly shows.[98] Surveys on viewing habits showed that 7 out of 10 persons of all ages watched television with an average viewing at around one-and-a-half hours each day. This was unthinkable in the UK; in India it would take another 30 years for black-and-white television sets to become common to a sizeable number of households in metro cities and Class 1 towns.

In the UK, while commercial TV was available by the mid-1950s, the medium did not find ready acceptance as it did across the Atlantic. The disparaging verbal description of TV as an idiot box was generally prevalent. Even a humourist such as P.G. Wodehouse, who authored brilliant farces, essayed a rather uncharacteristic vitriolic opinion when he stated, in 1955, during the launch of Britain's Independent Television, 'It is the foulest, ghastliest, loathsomest nightmare ever inflicted by science on a suffering human race.'[99]

---

[97]Leslie E. Gill in his book *Advertising and Psychology*, published in 1954, records, 'Cinema publicity is a comparatively new medium and one that is admirably suited to local as well as national publicity. Radio advertising and sponsored television are not yet available in this country.'

[98]*Principles of Advertising*, Advisory Editor: Woodrow Wirsig, Pitman Publishing Corporation, 1963. (Woodrow Wirsig was then the editor of *Printers' Ink*.)

[99]*The Economic Times*, *Brand Equity*, 31 January to 6 February 1996. I have not seen it in any Wodehouse novel.

An interesting insight into advertising allocations in the USA in the 1950s is provided in the following table, which was drawn up by the Central Research Department of McCann-Erickson Inc. and published by *Printers' Ink.*[100]

Medium	National/Regional	$ in Million	Percentage of Total
Newspapers	National	548.9	8.4
	Local	1,708.8	26.3
	Total	*2,257.7*	*34.7*
Radio	National	406.4	6.2
	Local	305.9	4.7
	Total	*712.3*	*10.9*
TV	National	296.7	4.6
	Local	91.7	1.4
	Total	*388.4*	*6*
Magazines	*Total*	*573.7*	*8.9*
Outdoor	*Total*	*149.2*	*2.4*
Direct Mail	*Total*	*923.7*	*14.2*

A point to note in the chart presented is the importance ascribed to local coverage. In totally dissimilar markets, that of India and the USA, advertising naturally followed the path of actual distribution of goods and services. Both countries were large and advertisers in both the countries faced the challenge of making brands available to customers across a vast territory. It is evident from the chart that in the USA, localised advertising was regarded as more important than national advertising. A question: Were there more localised *brands* compared to national brands in America?

- Local newspapers constitute the biggest share of advertising expenditure, and next is direct mail. Both are pointers to the importance of regional markets. Since direct mail occupies the second most important position in an advertising mix, it suggests that advertisers were alive to customer preferences and maintained a regular mailing list of prospects.
- In newspaper allocation, the ratio of local to national is three is to one. For every three dollars spent in local newspapers, one dollar is spent in national coverage.

[100]This appears in *Introduction to Advertising*, sixth edition, by Arthur Judson Brewster, Herbert Hall Palmer and Robert G. Ingrahm. McGraw-Hill Book Co. Inc. 1954. If we add the percentage of total for different media, the total comes to 77 per cent, leaving a sizeable 23 per cent unaccounted for.

- For TV allocation, which in the next 10 years would grow in importance, the allocation between national and local is 3:1, which is the reverse of the trend in newspapers. The overall expenditure over this medium is close to one-sixth that of newspapers. This may be due mainly on account of the popularity of some shows in nationally televised channels. Besides, some of the largest advertisers purchasing network time were companies with a national reach in the USA, such as Proctor and Gamble (P&G), which was the largest advertiser. In 1960, P&G spent $46,406,679.[101]
- Television viewing in the USA in the late 1950s and the beginning of the 1960s was a family affair.[102] Most families watched TV programmes together just as families in India saw soaps and the episodic presentations of Ramanand Sagar's *Ramayana* and B.R. Chopra's *Mahabharata* in the 1980s.[103]
- In the USA in the fifties and sixties, television was largely black and white, similar to the seventies in India. But in terms of choice of stations, viewers in the USA had on an average a choice of five stations,[104] unlike India where there was nothing except Doordarshan till well into the 1980s.
- 'Magazines' were given an almost equal share as national newspapers and as a separate media class claimed almost as much allocation as radio.

By and large what this reflects is an economy driven by general prosperity, where the level of literacy was high and advertising expenditure was supported by media choice. Television was beginning to change leisure habits of people; television was also making it possible for the advertiser to package his advertisement in a way that he could not do in cold print.

India, on the other hand, had to build its economy from scratch. Where per capita earning per month was as low as Rs 22 per month, hardly sufficient to keep a person alive, what consumption could such an economy trigger?[105]

---

[101]Wirsig, Woodrow, Advisory Editor. *Principles of Advertising.* Pitman Publishing Corporation. 1963.

[102]Gaw, Walter. *Advertising: Methods and Media.* San Francisco. Wadsworth Publishing Inc. 1961. He observes, 'Television, probably more than any other advertising medium, delivers the advertiser's message to the family as a unit. Television, as we have seen, has replaced radio as a focal point in the living room, where several or all of the family gather to view it together.' (p. 305)

[103]Both these shows were telecast around 10 am on Sundays. Viewership was more than 90 per cent of the total number of estimated TV viewers in India. Of course, at the time there was a single channel—the government-owned Doordarshan. I remember streets being deserted on Sunday mornings and visitors were not welcome in Indian homes as no one wanted to be disturbed while the show was on. Even public transport was scarce in cities.

[104]Gaw, Walter. *Advertising: Methods and Media.* San Francisco. Wadsworth Publishing Inc. 1961. Gaw notes: 'Only two per cent of all television homes in the United States today are limited in choice to a single television station and the average home has a choice of five.' (p. 310)

[105]K. Lahiri in *Publicity: Art & Literature,* published in 1955, observes, 'Where the average per capita income just exceeds Rs 22 per month, hardly enough to keep body and soul together, and the proportion of population paying taxes approximates to 0.2 per cent, what returns can be expected from publicity, which on final analysis depends on the purchasing capacity of customers?' (p. 171)

In hindsight it is amazing that there was any advertising at all and that for the insignificant overall expenditure on advertising there was so much variety.

Early research in advertising

P.L. Tandon may have been one of the first to be involved in consumer research.[106] He joined HLL in 1937 and began his innings by being pushed into a department that was being formed to undertake consumer studies. The chief of finance felt that a chartered accountant who had qualified in Britain was an unknown commodity best kept at bay.[107] The finance chief was not a qualified chartered accountant himself. In a way, Tandon, who was second in seniority in the department of consumer studies, pioneered market research in 1937. From this time on HLL was one of the few companies in India that regularly investigated consumer preference. Tandon's department studied consumer preference, including the preference of women consumers, at a time when a large section of women did not venture out of their homes.[108]

In the fifties, research had become quite common to advertising in the USA. A great many areas were simultaneously probed as developments in psychology manifested how this new science could be applied to advertising. What motivates consumer purchase? Whether advertisements placed on the left or the right side draw more attention? Whether magazines that charge higher rates for special positions may justifiably claim added value? Why do people buy the things they do? Are purchase decisions taken rationally or are they largely irrational? These were some of the subjects of study in leading American universities that offered management courses including advertising courses.[109]

---

[106]P.L. Tandon lived till the ripe old age of 92. He died as recently as 2004 in Poona. At the time two of his sons were also alive.

[107]P.L. Tandon, *Beyond Punjab*, Hind Books, 1971.

[108]An interesting anecdote in Tandon's book deals with a question on monthly purchase of household supplies such as toilet articles. Tandon's boss, who had done research in the UK, was puzzled when he tried to answer the question how were purchases made for items women used since men generally went shopping while women stayed at home. A team of women investigators (again an unheard-of development in the 1930s) got them the answer. They said while men buy monthly household items, women tell them what they should get for the house. Happily for the men sanitary napkins had not been invented!

[109]*Advertising Psychology and Research* by Darren Blaine Lucas, who was research consultant to BBDO and Steuart Henderson Britt, who was vice president and director of research, Needham Louis and Brorby Inc. The book was published in 1950 by McGraw-Hill. They observe: 'In the past two decades, consumer research has become more a science of eliciting accurate information by means of personal inquiry. The problems are so complex that the National Research Council and the Social Science Council have appointed a long-standing Joint Committee on Measurement of Opinion, Attitudes and Consumer Wants … One of its first projects is a study of the problems of interviewer bias.' This book provides tips on basic areas of consumer research such as (a) Most people have but scanty knowledge of their buying motives (b) The average person thinks in concrete terms (c) Unimportant details are forgotten quickly (d) Many people are indecisive (e) People follow the line of least resistance. My personal opinion, on the score, having spent 30 years in advertising, is that there are no hard and fast rules in determining consumer preference, which changes with time. Between two generations of consumers there may be a wide divide in human response to an advertising pulse. It is not uncommon to see one generation completely turning away from choices that were hugely popular with a previous generation.

In the UK, where consumer research was bemusedly regarded as an American novelty, there was a reversal of attitude by the early 1950s. Advertising professionals were veering around to the view that research in consumer lifestyle and buying habits may enable advertisers to direct their communication better towards their target audience. Initially a lot of research was focussed on content or message in an advertisement. Eminent intellectuals from various disciplines, not just psychologists, saw the relevance of consumer research in the modern world.[110]

Television

Television broadcasting began in India on 15 September 1959. TV programmes were broadcast twice a week for just one hour a day in New Delhi. There was a single transmitter with a reach of 25 km. The entire exercise characterised the political mindset at the time that went to extraordinary lengths to prove to the world that India could not be ignored. It was typically this mindset that inspired the Indian Railways to build the world's longest railway platform at Kharagpur, in West Bengal. With no importance given to the advent of an exciting new medium, TV was no one's baby at the Ministry of Information & Broadcasting till the early 1970s. There was no advertising on TV. A number of capsules were made on education and agriculture but without anyone having a television set not even the producers could say who would see them.[111]

Film

Nowhere in the world has film brought so much happiness to so many and for so long as in India. The evolution of India into an economic force has not taken place overnight; the growth of the Indian economy has been painfully slow from the 1950s to the 1990s.[112] People suffered all kinds of deprivation. The bare necessities to sustain life were conspicuous by their absence. No food. No potable water. No medical care. No education. No access to toilets. In such an environment Hindi films and other regional

[110]F.R. Leavis, an eminent critic of English literature, writing with Denys Thompson observed in *Culture and Environment*, 'It is encouraging that in America, where the progress of Western civilisation has gone furthest, there should have developed such a reaction as Consumers' Research.' Chato & Windus, London, 1960.

[111]*A&M* magazine dated 31 January 2001. The article notes, 'The programming consisted mainly of farm programmes for rural audiences, folk songs, folk music and some women-oriented programmes.' When rural people did not have radios very few villages could have possessed community TV sets at the time.

[112]The Congress governments at the centre were mainly responsible for perpetuating poverty in India as they followed a so-called political agenda called socialism that dragged the majority into woeful poverty and created a master race comprising the political class, the bureaucracy and the rich trading community, who all had a hand in the public till.

films, notably Marathi, Gujarati, Tamil, Telegu, Malayalam and Bengali, provided mass entertainment. Legendary actors and film directors made their reputations in this inhospitable environment. In the southern states of Tamil Nadu, Karnataka and Andhra Pradesh, a number of popular actors became politicians with mass following.

Hindi films produced in Bombay set very high standards in execution. Cinematography generally included shooting in exotic locations within India. In a way Hindi films familiarised viewers with beautiful places in the country which they could not visit personally. Most successful Hindi films included memorable songs which have not lost their popularity after six decades. The best talent went to Bombay where merit was the only criterion for success; the city was cosmopolitan and welcomed everybody. Lyricists, scriptwriters, musicians and vocalists, film editors and experts in lighting and photography all came to Bombay and found the competitive environment and the enormous opportunity for work stimulating.[113] Bombay provided the best back-end support facility for editing films. Investors spared no pains in upgrading technology.[114] That alone was no simple task since the government did not encourage import.

[115]

[113]Despite the presence of the Shiv Sena, a chauvinist Maratha Hindu political party that is intolerant towards people who come to Bombay from other regions of the country, Bombay continues to welcome talent in cinema, the arts and in other spheres of life.

[114]In an interview, one of the most eminent ad film-makers in India, Kailash Surendranath, told me that Manoj Kumar, the famous film actor, bought a lot of lenses and did not mind lending them if asked. Surendranath often used these lenses for experimentation. There is a profile of Surendranath and his contribution to ad film-making in the chapter that deals with the 1970s and 1980s.

[115]This picture has been scanned from *The Illustrated Weekly*. It will be evident to anyone looking at the picture reproduced here the poor quality of paper that magazines and dailies had to make do with at the time.

Hindi films were the most popular throughout India. In the southern states there was some resistance when the language problem divided India between those who welcomed Hindi as a link language in this multilingual nation and those who did not. But that did not lessen the popularity of Hindi films anywhere. For example, films starring Raj Kapoor and Nargis were box office successes. Between 1950 and 1956, the duo starred in no fewer than 12 films, which is surely a measure of popular demand.[116] In Bengal, the duo of Uttam Kumar and Suchitra Sen tugged at the heartstrings of youngsters with their roles in romantic love stories centred on middle-class Bengali families.

Advertisers and ad agencies had noted the emergence of cinema as an important medium as early as 1930s, but the technical difficulties involved in producing a film remained a constraint.[117] An edition of *Dunlop Gazette* noted that it took more than a year to make a corporate film.

[116]*The Illustrated Weekly of India*, issue dated 25 April 1971, has an article by Bunny Reuben in which the author notes the names of the films starring the two: *Pyar, Jaan Pehchan, Awaara, Amber, Bewafa, Anhonee, Ashian, Aah, Dhoon, Papi, Shree 420* and *Chori Chori*. Every title here was a hit film.

[117]See *Indian Advertising 1780 to 1950*, pp. 226–227. JWT made the first film for General Motors in 1931, which was of 20 minutes duration. Later, JWT made ad films for Horlicks, which were exhibited in a demonstration van. Similarly, HLL made films on Dalda to familiarise people with a cooking medium that was less expensive than ghee, but which could be used to fry tasty *samosas* and *jelebis*.

Ad film production in the 1950s

Few adverting films were made at the time. Like most other countries, media usage by advertisers and agencies was lopsidedly in favour of newspapers. Film had the potential of delivering the advertising message more forcefully to a very receptive audience willing to view *any film* with total attention. When film-exhibition vans went a little outside the metropolitan areas they always had an eager audience waiting for them.[118] But most ad agencies lacked infrastructure to handle film production.

Lintas advertised for a film executive now and then, and with popular brands of HLL such as Lux and Dalda they were involved in film production more than any other agency of comparable size with the exception of JWT. At the time Lintas did not strictly make the grade as an agency because it was the in-house advertising arm of HLL and that was not quite the same thing as being in the business of advertising as an agency, which meant servicing multiple clients and surviving on commissions earned from the media.

So, without a film production department, copywriters and art directors initially took faltering steps in learning the ropes of film production. The agency presented a storyboard, which was a rough outline of the film—on one side of the paper the audio portion was written down and in the adjoining space the frame of what came in the visual was drawn. After initial approval by the advertiser, estimates were obtained from film producers. The producer ultimately selected to give final shape to the storyboard actually made the film. No matter what agencies told clients to justify charging 15 per cent of the production cost, the actual involvement of agencies was minimal. Clients at the time rarely, if ever, asked agencies what their contribution was to the film to justify their commission.[119]

Generally for film production the commission amount was paid directly by the advertiser as it was directly billed to the advertiser by the agency, much like an artwork.[120] At times the film producer loaded 15 per cent on his bill, noting the agency commission amount in a transparent manner. The artwork components in a film obviously came from the agency, for which a separate bill was raised. These components generally comprised the following:

[118]I have seen in the seventies that it paid to inform villagers in advance about any film-exhibition. The place chosen would have villagers coming from near and far to watch a movie. They sat through any film, however incomprehensible to them, because it meant free entertainment.

[119]Looking back to the 1970s, I count myself lucky to have learnt from clients who took enormous pains in teaching their servicing executives. Rathin Mitra of East India Pharmaceutical Works Ltd in Calcutta was respected by the agency heads of Clarion and OBM for his role in grooming greenhorn account executives.

[120]When I first came into advertising in the early 1970s this was the practice. I assume this had been the practice in the earlier years also.

- Logo and symbol of the company.
- Brand logo where the film was brand-related. For instance, if it were a tyre film, the brand of tyre would be very much an integral component of the film. This artwork would be provided to the producer by the agency.
- For brands in the launch phase, dummies for packaging were made. These were generally supplied by the agency.

Where agencies fell short

There were very few people trained in film production. Till the early 1960s, India did not have a film institute that was later set up in Poona to impart formal education in film-making.[121] There were a few exceptional individuals who spent time and energy to be self-taught. The eminent film-maker Satyajit Ray was one such person. But while he was involved in making newspaper ads and much later, after leaving Clarion, developed a typeface called *Ray Roman,* he did not make a single ad film. Not even an ad film for feature films which he directed. However, he did make interesting posters for outdoor display for every new film that he directed. These film posters are now regarded as collectors' items. In Clarion, Chidananda Dasgupta, father of the famous film director Aparna Sen, gravitated to the production of advertising films/documentaries although he headed the servicing team on the ITC account.

Shyam Benegal and Govind Nihalani are two other eminent film-makers who began their acquaintance with films from Lintas.

Why did art directors and copywriters face problems with films?

Film as a medium combines many characteristics that are not present in a one-dimensional static medium such as print. Each frame of the storyboard drawn on paper was only a bare skeleton of what it was to become after interconnecting layers were ultimately combined. Examples of these layers:

- Sound
- Dialogue as distinct from music
- Effects and use of lights and filters
- Acting

[121]The government of India acquired the spacious grounds of Prabhat Studios in Poona along with motion picture equipment and buildings in 1960. The government established the Film and Television Institute of India (FTII) as a follow-up to the recommendation of the Film Enquiry Committee to train students in the techniques of film-making. The FTII was placed under the Ministry of Information & Broadcasting. The syllabus was developed upon the guidance of Remy Tessonneau, director of the Paris-based Institute des Hautes Etudes Cinematographiques (IDHEC), who visited Poona in 1961 and drew up an outline for the courses. Regular classes in the FTII commenced in 1961. The Television Training Wing, which was operating in New Delhi since 1971, was moved to FTII Poona in 1974.

- Emotion as conveyed through music or in acting
- Special sound effects to heighten the intensity of special scenes
- Animations and graphics
- Visual demonstrations
- Testimonials where celebrities or experts could speak in their own voice, adding to credibility

No art director or copywriter untrained in film-making could conceive the final form the storyboard would take. Clients did not ask; they knew the film producer would add values that an agency was incapable of presenting in a hand-drawn storyboard.[122] Not infrequently, the client, too, made his uninformed alterations to a storyboard submitted by his agency. In most of the bigger agencies some art director or senior copywriter managed the overall responsibility of film production. Dhritiman Chatterjee of HTA and Barun Chanda of Clarion, both of whom acted in Satyajit Ray's films as well as in films by other directors, helped their respective agencies in film production.

Most advertisers who exhibited films in theatres were manufacturers of consumer products such as soap, shampoo, cologne, hair oil or packaged hydrogenated vegetable oil, most notably Dalda of HLL. In a way, HLL was the first to use models in its advertisements as part of a well thought-out creative strategy. Lux soap followed the international brand strategy of positioning Lux as a 'beauty' soap—the soap preferred by film stars. This was the path taken from the beginning of the twentieth century. Popular film stars appeared in Lux films as well as in print ads with the claim that Lux made their skin beautiful and glowing. Lux continues to exploit the perennial advantage of an ageless strategy; just the faces of film stars change with time. The message and execution remain the same.

Lux also leveraged the strategy for regional campaigns. Local heroines featured in advertisements meant for specific states. For example, Lux ads in Madras presented popular heroines from Tamil cinema. Obviously this meant a wonderful flexibility in use of a common creative platform. The advertiser paid a fee for celebrity endorsement but even heroines did not skin the advertiser to his bones while charging a fee. Thankfully for advertisers in the 1950s, event managers and professional career management companies were non-existent. Stars did have their secretaries but they were little more than trusted aides who had no role in decision-making.

[122]Animated storyboards were not used till 40 years later. These presented a nearer approximation of what the final edited film was likely to be.

There were no modelling schools. Celebrities were sometimes roped in but, except in Bombay, it was difficult to approach women to appear in films. In Madras and Calcutta, which were important centres of advertising in the 1950s, modelling was generally 'No, No' in middle-class households.

Dubbing in regional languages

Films were dubbed in regional languages after the primary production was complete for brands that sold across different states. Hindi was not understood universally as it is today. The general acceptance of Hindi as a link language happened much later. In the fifties and sixties, whether Hindi or English should be the official link language was a contentious subject of discussion that rapidly descended to the level of angry exchange between the pro-Hindi and anti-Hindi citizens of India. That Hindi gradually became an accepted link language of the nation was due, in large measure, to the popularity of Hindi feature films, but more especially because of Hindi lyrics. As Tamils, Malyalis, Kanarese and Telegus are hard-working people ready to venture out of their home states in search of a livelihood, they began to move to the major centres of trade in the country, namely, Bombay in the west, Delhi in the north, and Kanpur and Calcutta in the east. They became proficient in Hindi, especially those who moved to Bombay, Delhi and Kanpur.[123]

In the 1950s most scripts had a traditional slice of life approach to telling a story on celluloid. An ad film generally had a beginning, a middle and a conclusion that carried the product promise or restated the benefit that a consumer would derive upon using the brand. And the advertiser had a full minute to sell his product, unless he was using static cinema slides, which were shown for a shorter duration of 30 seconds.[124]

In the 1950s and '60s, the impact of popular cinema (box office hits) had little influence on the preparation of advertisement storyboards. Ad films remained true to their course—selling product features or benefits without using themes of hit films as hooks. These became popular after *Sholay*,[125] and all kinds of products used Gabbar Singh as anchor. The agency creative wing was deemed responsible for the outcome of the final product. Later, film producers encroached upon agency territory, approaching clients directly for ideation and film production.

---

[123]The recent growth of regional parties all over India is a pointer to the fact that the linguistic divide is still prevalent.

[124]Many Calcuttans may remember Lighthouse, New Empire and Globe theatres carrying static slides of pest control for a major part of the intermission. I still remember the visual was that of a woman trying to swat a fly that was attempting to land on the tip of her nose. It said boldly 'Pest Control' and the name of the company was positioned at the bottom.

[125]The film was released in 1975; it was directed by Ramesh Sippy.

Formation of professional bodies on advertising and allied disciplines

Advertising Club in Calcutta

In 1952, the first Advertising Club in the country was set up in Calcutta. R.K. Sarkar, who was called 'Noelty' by friends, was the first president of the club. The R.K. Sarkar Memorial Lectures were instituted in his memory 10 years later, in 1963.[126]

Today most people may be surprised to learn that the Advertising Club of Bombay, which is the premier institution for the advertising profession, is indebted to S.P. Talyarkhan, a member of the Advertising Club of Calcutta. On being transferred to Bombay, he helped set up a similar club, so impressed was he by the role played by the Calcutta Advertising Club in enhancing levels of professional competence.

The Indian Society of Advertisers was formed in 1953.[127] The objective of the society was to create a national platform for advertisers to deliberate upon common problems and issues and to also act as a forum for interacting with the media. The society was interested in the development of the Indian press, particularly the vernacular press. It was keen to enlarge the scope of publicity in language print media and to study the rate structure for advertising prevailing in various parts of the country. Most of the leading advertisers were represented by their advertising managers or publicity chiefs. P.G. Rose, publicity manager of Burmah Shell and A.D. Shroff, director, Tata Sons Limited, were chairmen of the society at different times.

The Advertising Agencies Association was formed around this time. The objective of creating such an association was to start a forum for advertising agents where they could discuss professional issues and problems. Membership was later expanded to include advertising agents, advertisers, publishers, printers and process engravers. Enlarging membership diluted the original purpose of starting such a forum. Ad agencies remained at the receiving end of all the other groups that became part of this association. When clients did not pay on time the agency could do nothing about that; when newspapers blacklisted the agency, refusing to extend credit because of their own error (sometimes deliberate), the agency could not do anything about that; when process engravers stopped work or threatened legal action for long overdue payments, the agency could only plead helplessness but had to ensure that the job was processed somehow. The poor agency was always between a rock and a hard place.

---

[126] *Ad-Missive, Journal of Advertising Club Calcutta*, issue dated May 1988. From Urmimala Chaudhuri's personal collection.

[127] *Publicity: Art & Literature* by K. Lahiri. This book is available in the National Library, Kolkata. It is likely to be the first book on publicity/advertising written in India after Independence. The book was published in 1955. Unfortunately, I do not have the name of the publisher.

India sent a delegation to the International Advertising Conference in Great Britain. A.M. Patel spoke on the role played by advertising in raising the standard of living in South-east Asia.[128]

The Art in Industry Exhibition in 1948, held in Calcutta, stimulated graphic art in publicity. The government of India, through the Ministry of Information & Broadcasting, instituted annual state awards for excellence in printing and designing. The entries were judged purely on the production values.

Publicity material included posters (offset and letterpress), folders (offset), single-page or multi-sheet calendars and general purpose or presentation diaries. Besides cash awards, certificates of merit were given to the winners. These were valued by the recipients and framed and exhibited in the offices of printers, advertisers and agents. While the intention of the annual competitions was to help raise standards of printing, the problems of lack of good quality paper and ageing printing machinery were to dog the industry and advertising for the following three decades. The disincentive to import—including new printing technology—hardened in the 1960s and 1970s, as the country faced some of the harshest years in its recent history.

Around this time, although the volume of research work on publicity was negligible, the International Chamber of Commerce is said to have promoted research in the country.

[128]It would be interesting to discover what he said. South-east Asia was almost entirely under colonial rule. Standard of living for Asians in Asia was woeful; starvation was rampant and endemic. In such an environment advertising could do precious little to alleviate suffering or help improve quality of life.

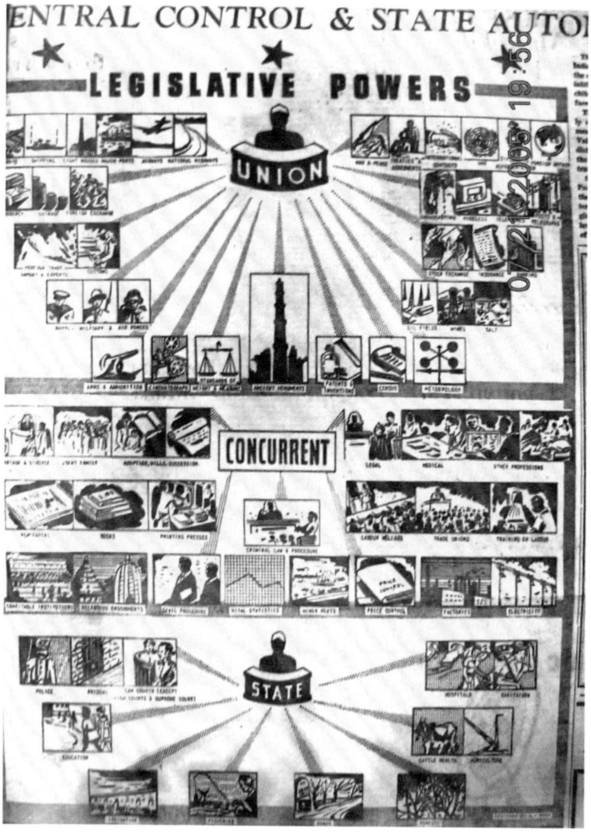
ENTRAL CONTROL & STATE AUTO
LEGISLATIVE POWERS
UNION
CONCURRENT
STATE

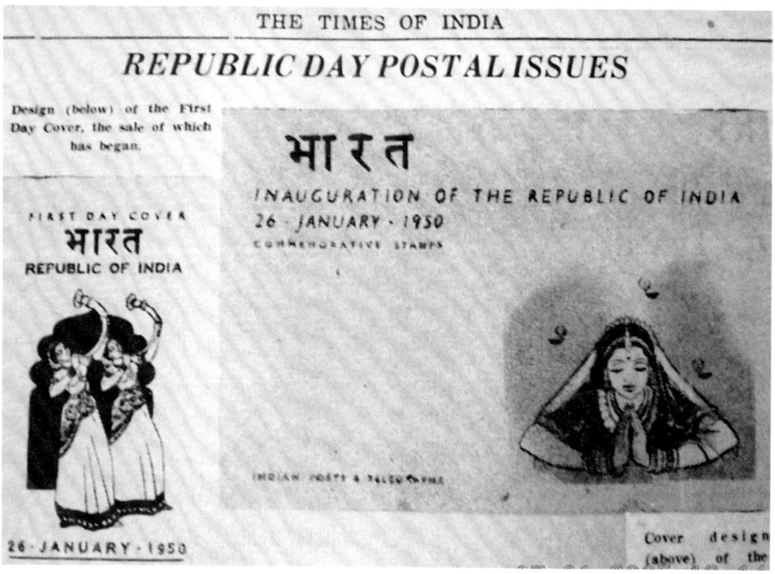
THE TIMES OF INDIA
REPUBLIC DAY POSTAL ISSUES
Design (below) of the First Day Cover, the sale of which has began.
FIRST DAY COVER
भारत
REPUBLIC OF INDIA
26 · JANUARY · 1950
भारत
INAUGURATION OF THE REPUBLIC OF INDIA
26 · JANUARY · 1950
COMMEMORATIVE STAMPS
INDIAN POSTS & TELEGRAPHS
Cover design (above) of the

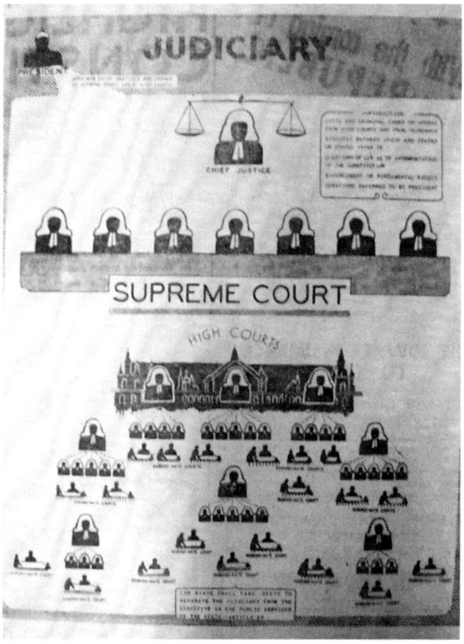
JUDICIARY
PRESIDENT
CHIEF JUSTICE
SUPREME COURT
HIGH COURTS

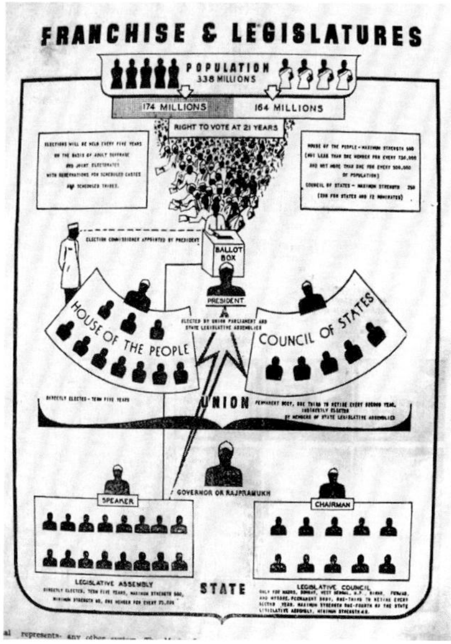
FRANCHISE & LEGISLATURES
POPULATION
338 MILLIONS
174 MILLIONS
164 MILLIONS
RIGHT TO VOTE AT 21 YEARS
BALLOT BOX
PRESIDENT
HOUSE OF THE PEOPLE
COUNCIL OF STATES
UNION
GOVERNOR OR RAJPRAMUKH
SPEAKER
CHAIRMAN
LEGISLATIVE ASSEMBLY
STATE
LEGISLATIVE COUNCIL

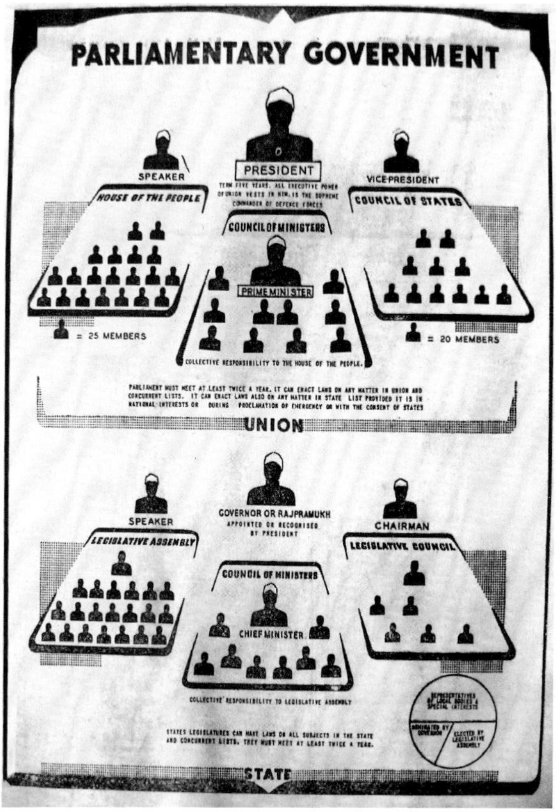
PARLIAMENTARY GOVERNMENT
SPEAKER
PRESIDENT
TERM FIVE YEARS. ALL EXECUTIVE POWER OF UNION VESTS IN HIM. IS THE SUPREME COMMANDER OF DEFENCE FORCES
VICE PRESIDENT
HOUSE OF THE PEOPLE
COUNCIL OF MINISTERS
COUNCIL OF STATES
PRIME MINISTER
= 25 MEMBERS
= 20 MEMBERS
COLLECTIVE RESPONSIBILITY TO THE HOUSE OF THE PEOPLE.
PARLIAMENT MUST MEET AT LEAST TWICE A YEAR. IT CAN ENACT LAWS ON ANY MATTER IN UNION AND CONCURRENT LISTS. IT CAN ENACT LAWS ALSO ON ANY MATTER IN STATE LIST PROVIDED IT IS IN NATIONAL INTERESTS OR DURING PROCLAMATION OF EMERGENCY OR WITH THE CONSENT OF STATES
UNION
SPEAKER
GOVERNOR OR RAJPRAMUKH
APPOINTED OR RECOGNISED BY PRESIDENT
CHAIRMAN
LEGISLATIVE ASSEMBLY
LEGISLATIVE COUNCIL
COUNCIL OF MINISTERS
CHIEF MINISTER
COLLECTIVE RESPONSIBILITY TO LEGISLATIVE ASSEMBLY
STATES LEGISLATURES CAN MAKE LAWS ON ALL SUBJECTS IN THE STATE AND CONCURRENT LISTS. THEY MUST MEET AT LEAST TWICE A YEAR.
STATE

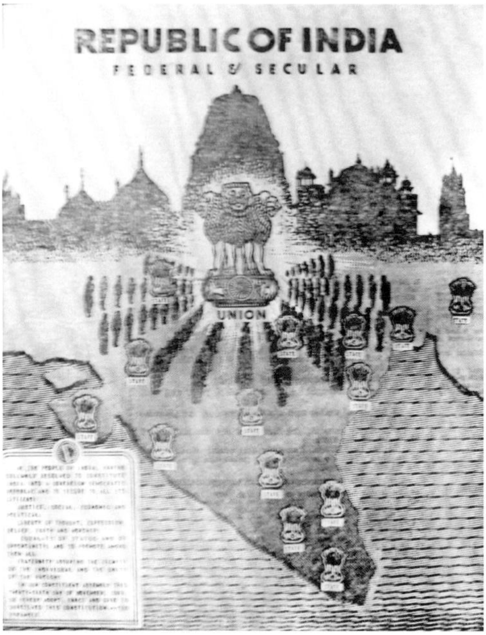
REPUBLIC OF INDIA
FEDERAL & SECULAR
UNION

THE TIMES OF INDIA
JANA GANA MANA
JANA GANA MANA ADHINAYAKA JAYA HE BHARAT BHAGYA VIDHATA
KAMRUP--PUNJAB MARATHA GURJAR DRAVID VANGA UTKAL VINDYA HI-
-MACHAL JUMNA GANGA JALADHI TARANGA TABA SHUBA NAAME JAAGE
TABASHUBA ASISH MANGE GAYE TAV JAYA GATHA JANAGANAMANGAL
DAYAK JAYA HE BHARAT BHAGYA VIDHATA JAYA HE JAYA
HE JAYA HE JAYA JAYA JAYA JAYA HE

2

1960–1970

Transition

The border war with the People's Republic of China in 1962 and the aggression unleashed by Pakistan in 1965 determined the course of the history of the decade. The death of two prime ministers of whom the first, Nehru, set India's political agenda post-Independence and the second, Lal Bahadur Shastri, despite holding office for barely 19 months, brought back a sense of pride among the citizens of the country. This was after the disastrous debacle against the Chinese.[1]

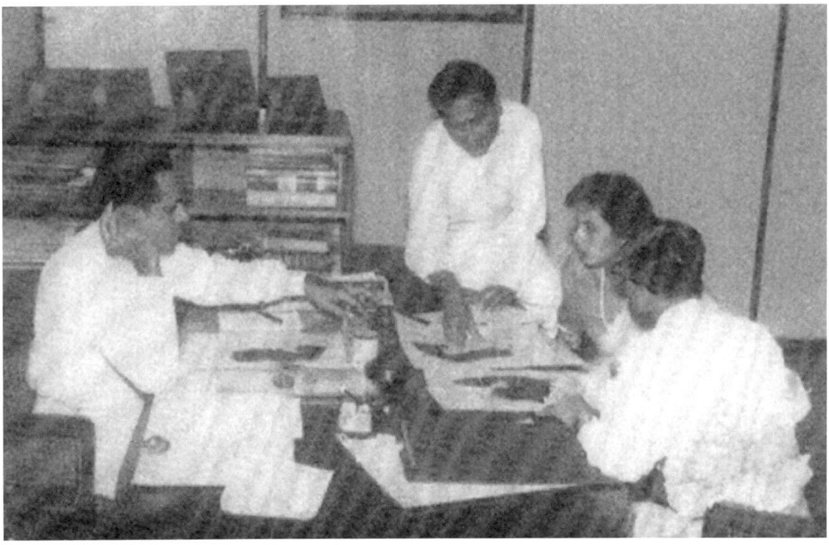

A rare group photograph from the early 1960s. Souvendu (Kanu) Basu, chief art director, Clarion, perched on the table, explains the creative approach to a campaign. In the frame are (from left to right) Subhas Sen, Tara Sinha and Subrata Sengupta who were all directors of Clarion.

[1]We are not counting Gulzarilal Nanda who stepped in as the interim prime minister for a few days.

However, it was during Shastri's early tenure as prime minister in October 1964 that the Central Government sent a circular to the states in which they were asked to report on the progress made in the use of Hindi. The Central Government offices were directed to begin communicating officially in Hindi with non-Hindi speaking states. However, the non-Hindi speaking states, especially the southern states, objected strongly to this.[2] There were violent reactions across many parts of the country. The Central Government had managed to create an emotional divide between the citizens of India, which sparked protests sporadically for over 15 years.[3]

The sixties will go down in history as a decade of hunger. The government had to wage a continual war to feed millions who did not earn enough for one full meal a day. Ministers went around the world with a begging bowl asking for aid. The minister of food, C. Subramaniam, went to the USA for immediate relief in 1964. With few products available in the market, advertising was unimportant. Advertising agencies worked on small budgets and with the government leaning heavily towards socialism, multinational companies dithered in setting medium- or long-term goals, expecting that they would be asked to leave suddenly. Even Indian companies in the private sector were regarded with suspicion. Taxation for business was punitive, it encouraged nurturing a parallel black economy.

Important advertising events in the sixties

- Bal Mundkur quits Bomas and starts Ulka in 1961.
- Nargis Wadia quits Lintas and starts Interpub in 1963.
- Kersey Katrak leaves L.P.E. Aiyars and sets up MCM in 1965.
- Ayaz Peerbhoy leaves Everest and starts Marketing & Advertising Associates (MAA) in 1966.
- Nari Hira starts Creative Unit in 1968.
- Sylvester daCunha leaves Advertising and Sales Promotion (ASP) to start daCunha Associates in 1969.

[2]The chagrin of non-Hindi speaking people is understandable. A year earlier, in 1963, the Official Languages Act was passed and that allowed for the continuation of English as a medium of official communication.

[3]Only in 1990, that is, almost 30 years later, V.P. Singh as prime minister managed to create such a divide between people in the country when he put into practice the recommendation of the commission led by B.P. Mandal, reserving 27 per cent of jobs in government services for backward classes. The limit of reserved seats in colleges and schools and vacancies in government jobs has been raised over the years by various state governments and by different Central Governments, raising a new class of Brahmins among the backward castes. In Tamil Nadu, over 60 per cent of all vacancies, whether in educational institutions or in government jobs, are reserved for the backward castes. Careers are no longer dependent on talent. Being born into a backward caste family opens doors to the best schools, colleges and universities and even leads to quicker promotions in government jobs. Whereas the founding fathers of the Indian Constitution wanted to root out the evil of the caste system from society, V.P. Singh and after him the cohorts of self-serving politicians have succeeded in reversing the process.

First advertising convention

The decade of the sixties transited through pain, wars, food scarcity and rampant black marketing in everything that was available and an inadequacy among the political class to come to grips with the fundamentals of the economy. However, for the advertising profession what was noteworthy was the advertising convention that was held at the India Exchange Hall in Calcutta over three days from 29 to 31 March 1960. Three hundred and fifty delegates attended the convention. They came from all over the country.

Sookamal Ghose, director of Amrita Bazar Patrika Private Limited, delivered the welcome address:

> As far back as July 1959 a few of us met at the Calcutta Club with the idea of organising an advertising convention in Calcutta. Shri Sachindra Nath Banerjee of Clarion Advertising Services, Shri Jugal Srimal of Progressive Publicity Service and Shri Samar Dutt of Everest Advertising were with me at the time of this small beginning. We did not know then that our discussion around a tea table would be able to create an atmosphere that would bring down to Calcutta even Dr B.V. Keskar. We also did not know that the idea of holding a regional convention would expand into a project of an all-India convention. Slowly, we gathered courage and convened a formal meeting, at which we took the decision to hold the first all-India convention on advertising.
>
> In course of time we earned the support of all the professional bodies, such as the Indian and Eastern Newspaper Society, the Audit Bureau of Circulation and the Advertising Agencies Association of India …
>
> In my tours abroad, I have observed the tremendous role that advertising plays. They proved to me that advertising leads to bigger sales, which means lower prices, quality products, more employment. A competitive economy not only helps to make the economy stronger, but offers people a better and more comfortable way of living.
>
> In my opinion people are slowly beginning to realise the value of advertising and visual publicity. They are becoming convinced that advertising is nothing but an art of informing people. This art, or technique, is needed by businessmen, whether they sell or buy; by public bodies and by the general public.
>
> I am here to thank, on my personal behalf and on behalf of the reception committee, in particular Dr Keskar, Mr Chinubhai Kilchand, Mr J.V. Lund, deputy director, United States Information Service in India, and Mr S.K. Kooka, commercial director, Air India International, for coming and encouraging us with helpful advice.
>
> I also fail to find proper words to thank our chairman of the steering committee, Mr R.K. Sirkar, who took great pains to conceive and organise the details of the convention. It is rather sad that Mr Sirkar is laid up with a knee injury. Mr T. Gupta,

> deputy chairman of the steering committee, has filled the gap and we all know that he will steer all of us very ably with his experience and progressive outlook.
>
> I dare not forget our secretaries, group leaders, other officials and members without whom this very difficult task of organising the first advertising convention would have been an impossibility.

A number of speeches were delivered on the occasion. These focus on different subjects of importance to the advertising profession and—combined—present a wonderful perspective of the times and its challenges.

S.K. Kooka (Bobby)

S.K. Kooka (Bobby) was educated in England, where he spent most of his formative years. He joined Air India under J.R.D. Tata. He appointed JWT as Air India's agency because, unlike other agencies, it did not on its own pitch for his business. The Air India maharaja soon became the most recognised mascot in the world.

Kooka was an exacting taskmaster, setting difficult deadlines for his agency. He looked for offbeat advertising. He made his agency deliver advertisements that became a hallmark for excellence. They are comparable with the best advertisements produced anywhere in the world at any time. His advertising was contemporaneous; inexpensive, because he chose a few hoardings along with mainline English newspapers as his principal media; often quite controversial. He was not afraid to make fun of politicians or the venerable J.R.D., his boss in Air India. Not surprisingly he was asked to remove his hoardings at times by politicians whom he riled with his humour.

Writing his obituary, Subhas Ghosal mentioned that Bobby Kooka wrote his own copy. Therefore, one surmises that the great Air India campaigns were a collaborative effort between Kooka and JWT's art director for Air India. Ghosal also mentioned that he lived alone in his old age with his favourite German Shepherd. At home he was surrounded by books, for he read voraciously on diverse subjects.

Umesh Rao

Umesh Rao, who began as an artist in JWT, is credited with what remains one of the finest symbols in modern business: the maharaja of Air India. Umesh Rao became the chief art director of JWT/HTA in course of time. Alyque Padamsee, in his autobiography, *A Double Life*, calls Rao the art chief of his agency. Although much of the credit of the appearance and style of the Air India symbol is given to Kooka, the fact is that without Rao the maharaja would never have been conceived. More than 60 years after making his first appearance, the Air India maharaja still appears so refreshingly original, a tribute to the genius of Rao.

Subhas Sen

1923–1972

Subhas Sen began work at D.J. Keymer as an apprentice. Prior to joining Keymer he was teaching English in Santiniketan. In 1956, when Keymer closed shop in Calcutta, Sen joined Sachindranath Banerjee, Subroto Banerjee and Subrata Sengupta to form Clarion. He was one of the founder directors of the company and later, at the time of his death, he was heading the Calcutta branch of his agency.

He believed in the importance of advertising in Indian languages. A proficient writer in Bengali and English, he encouraged translators to think in vernacular instead of being restricted within the strict confines of the English copy. Almost all advertising was conceived in English and translated into Indian languages. Translators walked in and out of agencies delivering their work as a lower class of writers. Subhash Mukhopadhyay, the famous Bengali poet who supplemented his income from poetry by taking up translation work from the two leading agencies, Clarion and JWT, narrated in an interview with the author that he received considerable encouragement from the two 'burra sahibs', Subhas Sen of Clarion and Subhas Ghosal of JWT.

Looking at the advertisements in the kennel & livestock column of 2 April 1960 in *The Statesman*, who would think that the country was passing through very difficult times?

For Immediate sale Black Panther, rare specimen. Delivery ex-Calcutta. Sale, Cocker Pup and Siamese Kitten, Fantail Pigeons, Chickens of Different Breed; and Aquariums. 11 Braunfeld Row, Calcutta 27.

The beauty and diversity of animal life and plants had not been destroyed although men were continually encroaching on forest land since the turn of the century. A special breed of human beings called 'Promoters' was still not born, which perhaps explains why the country had such a diversity of flora and fauna.

Some of the other advertisements under different columns in the same issue of *The Statesman* seem to reinforce the image of India being a very happening country in the sixties, where people had a lot of disposable income. This is unreal! India continues to remain a world of make-believe. A recent government announcement in 2013 would have people know that poverty has declined by 26 per cent; a meal can be purchased for Rs 15, which is far from true.

DINE AND DANCE
VOLGA
NEW DELHI
FAMOUS FOR DELICIOUS
CHINESE AND CONTINENTAL FOOD
Dance till 1 am tonight

Three other Delhi hotels, namely, Gaylord, Tavern and Imperial, advertised along with Volga. With few connecting flights between the metros it was unlikely that any guest could travel the distance for a jolly evening stretching into the wee hours. But it is hard to imagine that those who spent money buying space in Calcutta's number one English daily were wasting their advertising budget. For these ads appear quite often in the pages of *The Statesman*.

If Delhi restaurants advertised in Calcutta, surely Calcutta restaurants could not be far behind. Here is an advertisement of Skyroom, a place that the generation born between 1945 and 1955 may still fondly remember and miss. They served on silverware and pampered guests with excellent food. They did not serve liquor. Yet, till the time the owners decided to close it for good, not being able to cope with aggressive trade union activity so characteristic of the 1970s, there were long queues outside this restaurant.

This advertisement was in size 5 cm x 1 column.

You will love the sophisticated
atmosphere of

SKYROOM

Where excellent food and courteous service awaits you. Phone 23-1323

In the sixties, Park Street was known for high-class eateries; lights and fun. There were discotheques; the ageless Usha had not then made her mark, but Trincas drew a number of celebrities from Bombay as the next ad testifies.

AIR-CONDITIONED
TRINCAS
First Appearance of
JESICA JAMES
BOMBAY'S CUTEST CROONER

Mocambo, which like Trincas is still open to business though its character is much altered, solicited business from morning till night.

MORNING COFFEE
IN THE
DISTINCTIVE GRANDEUR
OF
MOCAMBO
Calcutta's Society Rendezvous
Dinner-Dance from 8 pm

A couple of ads under Ballroom Dancing:

ASK PETER DEY (London, Paris) for correct step. Style, poise. Practice Thursdays. Silverstar School.

AT THE EASTER DANCE there's sure to be fun. Brush up your steps before it has begun. Vicky insists that you must dance. Make up your mind here's a golden chance! 239 Karnani Mansions, Park Street, Calcutta.

For motorcycles and cars there was a fairly brisk second-hand market, if we read the column specified in different issues of the paper. The edition of 2 April carries the following offers for sale:

- **B.S.A. Motor Cycle 2.5 h.p.1952 Model for Sale.**
- **For Sale, Purchase and Exchange of your car, visit Barman & Co. 5A, Royd St, Calcutta 44-3957**
- **Humber Supersnipe Model 1948 and Hawk Model 1947 for sale. Phone Rajan Motors ...**
- **Rover '48, Rs 4,250 from respectable owner.**

Indians have always been fascinated with jewellery. In the weekly or fortnightly papers of the nineteenth century, we come across regular advertisers who invited customers into their shops to purchase or pawn ornaments.[4]

[4]See my book *Indian Advertising 1780-1950*, which covers this period.

The ads published in 1960 read quite like the ads carried by papers in the nineteenth century.

The Statesman *dated 2 April 1960 had this advertisement:*

JEWELLERY AUCTION
Under instructions from Sri S.N. De, of Messrs. Manual Agarwala & Co., Solicitors

VICTOR BROTHERS
WILL SELL BY PUBLIC AUCTION
At 59-B Park Street, Calcutta -16
(Next to Park Street Post Office), on Sunday, the 3rd April, 1960 at 10.30 a.m.

VALUABLE JEWELLERY
Diamond Necklaces, Rings, Earrings, Eartops, Bracelets, Buttons, Nose Pins, Pearl Malas, Bangles, Churies, Full Sets etc. Also Emerald and Ruby Ornaments.

On View
Today, Saturday, from 12 noon to 5 pm

Imports

The Central Government was steadily curbing imports of what were regarded as non-essential luxury products. A ban on import of watches came into force in July 1957. The 'Group of Watch Importers' released a front page solus 30 cm x 2 column advertisement in the New Delhi daily *Hindustan Times* on 5 January 1960. The ad is interesting as it quotes figures indicating balance of trade position for India in the decade of the fifties. Besides, the tone of the ad shows that people were not cowed down by the government. This changed in subsequent years as bureaucrats and politicians between them removed all vestiges of freedom from the common psyche.

DOES SHORTAGE OF FOREIGN EXCHANGE
EXIST FOR WATCH IMPORT ONLY?

Body copy: In justification of banning watch import, we hear frequently of shortage of foreign exchange. What does this shortage mean? A favourable balance is when we can import within the total value of our export. If our exports fall from an amount and imports remain over that, we call it shortage of foreign exchange.

Did we import watches previously only when we had a surplus balance from our export? No. Here are the figures:

Year	Import	Export	Deficit
1950–51	650 crore	601 crore	49 crore
1951–52	970 crore	733 crore	237 crore
1952–53	671 crore	577 crore	94 crore
1953–54	576 crore	531 crore	45 crore
1954–55	656 crore	594 crore	62 crore
1955–56	706 crore	609 crore	97 crore
1956–57	832 crore	612 crore	220 crore
1957–58	927 crore	637 crore	290 crore
1958–59	863 crore	578 crore	285 crore

(Source: Statistical outline of India published by Tata Industries)

We have been running at a deficit on foreign trade for over a decade. If over 4 crore worth of import licences could be given in 1955–56 on total import of 706 crore, why is no licence given for watches in 1958–59, when our import is 863 crore? Why has the import been banned since July 1957?

Is a watch such a non-essential item? Would it make much difference if an additional crore or two were spent on our total import of 863 crore for the livelihood of 50,000 watch dealers and their 300,000 dependents?

Issued in the interest of fair trade by a group of watch importers. Post Box 8926, Calcutta-13.[5]

There is an interesting ad on the socially critical subject of body odour. Long back in the late 1930s and early 1940s, P.L. Tandon of HLL had faced the problem of body odour when he had tried to explain to his British boss that in India body odour is not a concept that is likely to work as a platform in advertising, as people sweat in the heat and are not bothered by body odour. However, advertising helps to create consumer demand by presenting new products that have not been seen before. It is difficult to judge so far back in time how successful an advertisement on underarm hair was—the ad was targeted at a female audience. The paper in which the ad was inserted was *Hindustan Times* and the place New Delhi, where Punjabi and other North Indian women with their sturdy good sense are in a majority.[6] After all, no

[5]It is not surprising that the group of watch importers selected *Hindustan Times* for this release as New Delhi mandarins determined policy, but what is intriguing is the use of a box number. Did the officebearers think it more prudent to remain incognito? The group was Calcutta-based. Today any group representing a trade body would certainly be headquartered in New Delhi.

[6]The ad asks customers to 'beware of spurious imitations', suggesting the product enjoyed a good share of the market.

one has as yet said that North Indian women have stronger body odour than other women in the world or that they do not share the common female trait of delicacy that might prevent them from asking for a product that is positioned for underarm hair.

Never risk your charm with
UNDER ARM
HAIR

In a hot climate like ours it is natural to perspire profusely. However, if the perspiration is allowed to accumulate in the arm-pit due to under arm hair, an offensive body odour will mar our social success. Depil dissolves away the hair easily and pleasantly.

DEPIL
PERFUMED HAIR REMOVER
PEARLINE-PARIS PRIVATE LTD.
P.O. BOX 493 BOMBAY 1

In a box in reverse: CONTAINS A GIFT COUPON
Beware of spurious imitations. Buy genuine Depil with the blue metal Pilfer Proof Cap.

The quality of print advertising in general was of a fairly high standard.

Examples of fast moving consumer brands:[7]

The body copy which may not be very legible in the advertisement (facing page) here reads: *You'll sing for joy when you bathe with LIFEBUOY! What a lively, bracing feeling of freshness! And that rich LIFEBUOY lather protects your health. It washes away the germs in dirt—every dirt that you cannot avoid picking up. The whole family stays healthy with LIFEBUOY!*

A HINDUSTAN LEVER PRODUCT

[7]I am including the ads in sizes which are smaller than the actual sizes they appeared in newspapers but as large as the page format of the book will allow. This gives a truer reflection of the merit of these ads and whether they could force a reader's attention. Indeed, the quality of these ads may even be tested on a panel of people now, if they are pasted on actual paper and prints taken of the paper and circulated among the panel. They may be asked to see the page without being specifically told to watch ads and then asked to recount the ads they remember after seeing the paper for 10 minutes. This is an old method used by researchers in the USA in the 1930s or even earlier.

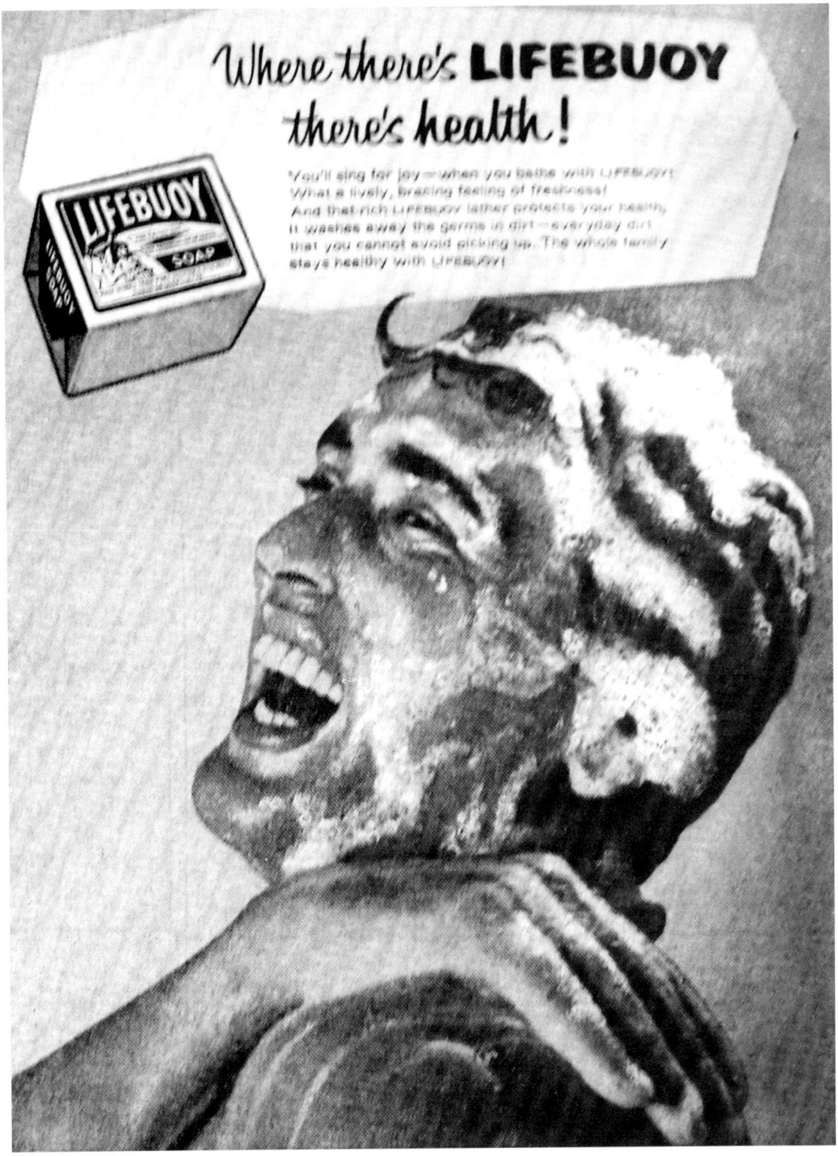

The expression on the model's face—the sheer joy of a cool refreshing bath—was only rivalled many years later by the brilliant Liril film produced by Kailash Surendranath for Lintas where the model Karen's face in a waterfall became the symbol of India's new age advertising.

While on the subject of germicidal action that has been a favourite hobby-horse for advertising professionals, here is a Savlon advertisement that talks of killing germs. The interesting point to note is that the product is not positioned against the popular antiseptic Dettol but as a brand for cuts, burns and nappy-rash. This is a small ad tucked away in one corner of *The Statesman*, with poor selection of typeface, although there is some merit in the illustration. The brand is especially positioned for paediatric use, as the visual suggests.

The body copy reads:

'Savlon' Liquid Antiseptic contains 'Hibitane' which kills more germs and more kinds of germs. Does not sting. Cleans as it disinfects. 'Savlon' Antiseptic Cream is for minor cuts, burns and common skin complaints. Prevents nappie-rash.[8] Helps nature heal.

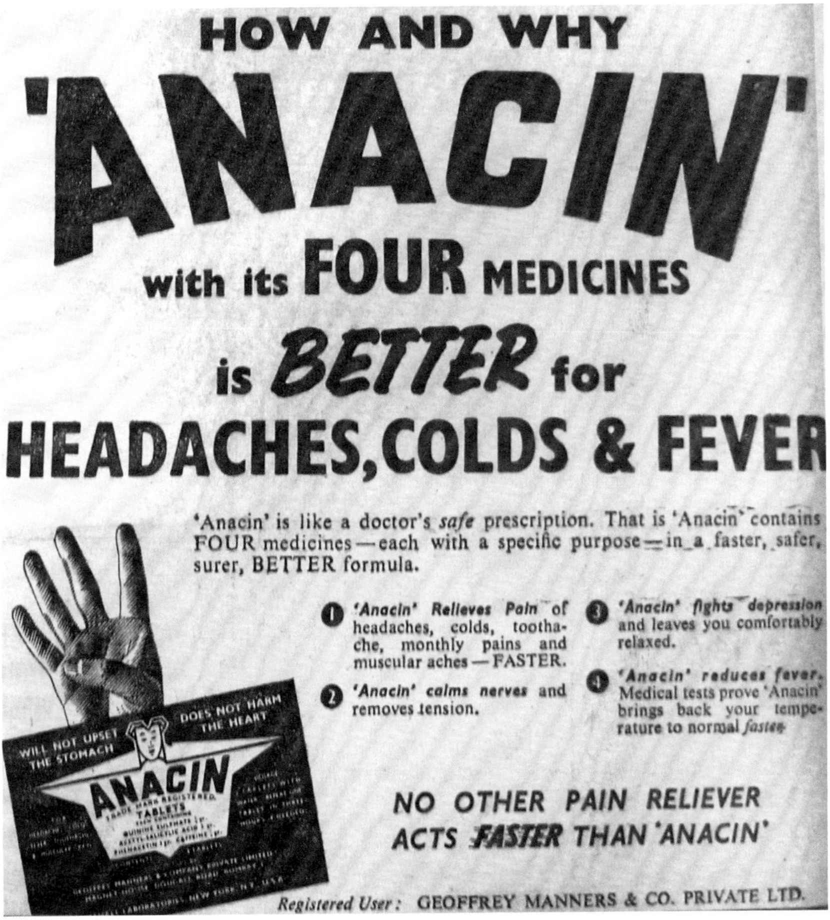

Anacin ran this campaign for a long time. The four fingers beside the pack has become one visual element over time; etched in the memory of those who suffer from headaches. In comparison, the Saridon advertisement appearing in the same paper (*The Statesman*, Calcutta), is an unpretentious 10 cm x 1 column advertisement that does not do justice to the strength of the brand in medicine shops. The visual is clumsy.

---

[8]Nappy is misspelt.

Though children do face many problems, they do not suffer from headaches. In the 1960s, the concept of product positioning was unknown. However, the role of advertising in branding was not unknown.[9]

[9]A committee on advertising with Woodrow Wirsig, editor of Printers' Ink as advisory editor, published a book titled *Principles of Advertising* in 1963 (Publisher: Pitman Publishing Corporation) where the authors note: 'Branding has increased even more rapidly since 1900 because of the increase in types of products and because of the changes in marketing conditions. The great increase in the number of packaged goods naturally increased the use and importance of trademarks or brands.' This book is available in the National Library, Calcutta.

In the context of branding, Bobby Kooka's speech at the advertising congress covers all the salient aspects for his times and ours. It is a delightful speech as he dwells on his own brand, for which he certainly may take part credit for its creation. In his inimitable way he also takes a dig at the state of politics in India. With a captive minister of Information & Broadcasting gracing the occasion, he just could not let the opportunity slip.

Selling differently (title of Kooka's speech)

Ladies and gentlemen: this is the first convention that has taken place in our country and so, as the prime minister would say, we are in the presence of history. The fact that 350 distinguished ladies and gentlemen are present here just shows what a beginning we have made; because advertising is after all the show window of industry.

When Mr T. Gupta asked me to speak on 'Selling Differently', I am not sure whether he didn't also imply that I could sell discreetly! Working for an airline, we are today in the throes of a revolution, which is taking place in our midst, with the creation of the Jet, with the fact that an aeroplane can fly from London to India in eight hours and as was done recently from Zurich to Bombay in seven hours. I had the privilege and pleasure of taking the Boeing on a proving flight to Europe and back. We took this beautiful creature to Cairo where the Egyptians looked around it, the tremendous apparition, but unfortunately in the end they were disappointed when the aeroplane did not have the loudest horn in the world! We took it to Rome where the Romans, who love beauty in any form whether it is on 16 wheels or two legs, gazed nostalgically at this beautiful creature on the tarmac, walked round it, whistled, patted and even pinched it when nobody was looking! We took the ship to England—and the English with their rare reticence (it's bad manners to stare), turned away. Ours was the first ship with a Rolls-Royce engine to go to England ahead of BOAC's, but I must not rub that in now that we are pool partners. And so, we took a plane-load to Paris on that aircraft—a plane-load of Englishmen and English women—and it was a la mode as far as Paris was concerned, because the same ship had never been there.

Ladies and gentlemen, that brings us to today, when we have got the Boeing and we have got transportation that run at 600 miles an hour. But going back to 1932 when air transportation was in its infancy, in those days we had small planes, we had a pilot but were never privileged to have passengers on board! They were a luxury; we had no headaches in those days; we only carried mail! And it is a true story, when the skipper (who is flying for Indian Airlines today—a big burly Punjabi)—was delighted to find that in his chicken box he had two huge chickens instead of the usual one, he made short work of both. He was hungry and he kept throwing the pieces behind his shoulder, as he demolished each one in turn, to find suddenly that there was a passenger behind him all the time (his very first passenger)! That was a true story to show how much progress we have made in this country.

We carried mail, we carried no passenger. We could not advertise, we didn't have the money to advertise in those days. So, what could we do? We had to issue timetables and have arrival notices in the newspapers—Tata Airlines: Departure Karachi … Arrival Bombay …! That's all the advertising we could afford. Then the war came. There was a great upsurge throughout the country—and we were carrying passengers. It was a delightful experience! But we were small, we were insignificant. We didn't have a lot of money to spend. We couldn't match our big competitors all over the world. So we thought we would have to do something different. We thought we would like to suggest a corporate image—as our American friends would say—which would be the emblem of our company. He is supposed to depict hospitality and, I should say, service. So we chose a man, who, unfortunately, looks like a maharaja. He became popular and unpopular. People told us that here we're doing away with the princely caste system in our country and here was Air India encouraging it! But we would explain that he is not a maharaja. He is a little emblem, he is a little ridiculous, he is slightly bogus. We make him look awfully foolish at times and rather pathetic, but we would like to think that he is lovable all the time.

Trying to be different in our advertising, ladies and gentlemen, has created a number of problems for us. We have, for instance, a flight information card on which we have the description of flight illustrated by our little man chasing a lady, a lady dressed in a 'sarong'. We got into trouble because an important minister complained and said that we were not paying due attention to the womanhood of India. So we scrapped that.

We had a 'seat occupied' card on board which you placed on your seat when you got off at an intermediate station. We had the maharaja sitting there with a pretty little girl sitting on his lap in a salwar-kameez and another irate female looking on. And the maharaja was saying, 'I am sorry this seat is occupied.' This didn't go down too well with a lady MP who complained to our minister, who gave orders that every card must be withdrawn forthwith. So we did that as well.

We had an advertisement in London recently where we talked about Georgy Porgy and how he kissed the hostess and made her cry. We had trouble with that—there were questions asked in the house, 'Were our hostesses being badly treated by our passengers these days and what were we doing about it?' Another ad was scrapped.

We once talked about distrusting Nick the Greek when he bought gifts (those who did Latin will remember that). We got complaints from the Greek embassy in New Delhi saying this was no way to talk of Greeks who were always great friends of India and had done a great deal for us.

We have always found that the straight story is always a bit of a bore. We have never had the money to splash banner headlines and have large advertisements bludgeoning their story, forcing you into acceptance day after day and week after week. So we have had to try a different approach, ladies and gentlemen. We had to talk about other things. We had to ridicule ourselves and, if I may say so, with the great sense of humour that does exist amongst our people we have reasonably well succeeded and we are awfully grateful to you for bearing with us. The fact that film stars are paid fortunes for advertising their faces and talking about a particular soap or a particular toothpaste, shows how much there is in advertising. I think the time will come and I hope it will come, when an advertisement would be like a book or a poem which you would love to read and read again, not because it talks about toothpaste but because somebody like Hemingway has written the copy for the toothpaste.

Well, I am sure some of you will remember the old, famous advertisement in the London tube, in the old days where they said, 'No smoking, not even Abdullas'.

… All of you who have seen American magazine advertising, I am sure, will agree that the illustrations are often much superior than the copy. When they depict food your mouth waters and when you see an advertisement on perfumes, you can almost get a whiff of that beautiful and exotic perfume in the room. Very often advertising is better than the product. And that is how it should be. Advertising should take men out of the rut. It should make him dream when he reads copy; it should make him go ecstatic when he sees the drawings and the photographs. It's like travel pictures—they paint Hawaii and Tahiti as wonderful places to go to for your holiday. The fact that once you have been there, you'll never want to go again makes no difference—as I say, it is supposed to make the reader gaze longingly at something which he would like to possess. Then the copywriter and the owner of that particular product has sold the goods.

Our prime minister and the hon'ble minister are in the fortunate position of making announcements in our country to our people for which they do not pay. Had they to pay for every word they speak, they would soon be in the advertising business! And so, I think that our cabinet from PM downwards, all of them are as much as any of us—hucksters from Madison Avenue!

We have seen Air India advertisements appear in large sizes in most national English dailies in India in the fifties and sixties. Despite Kooka's assertion that Air India was too poor to advertise, like other major airlines of the world, he had the privilege of being in the public eye all the time. Indeed, it was to Air India's credit that they crafted advertisements, which were gems to be appreciated in whichever medium they appeared.[10]

The fundamental principle in media planning today is to saturate a medium with repeated releases. This means that the advertiser has to have a large war chest. Unless an advertisement is seen frequently it is unlikely that the target audience will recall the brand or be driven by the brand message. The easiest way to beat forced presence in media is to make a memorable advertisement that can be done when the idea packs *inspiration.*

Kooka underlines the basic principle of both these approaches in his talk. He pushed his agency JWT to churn out brilliant concepts all the time. He was fearless enough to take controversy in his stride. He must have faced the great J.R.D. Tata on a number of occasions, looking quizzically at him with his eyebrows raised as if to ask, 'Now, what have you done *this time*?'

Going through the speech, we participate in the business of account management in the sixties. The manner in which a knowledgeable client draws the outline of a creative brief and a media brief for the agency is given here.

For the creative team the client suggests a strategy that has the potential of continuity. Contemporaneous happenings in society, politics, sport, as we now know with the benefit of hindsight, were grist to the mill. The client was also willing to cover up for the agency in case the actual topic that anchored the advertisement was regarded as inappropriate or even offensive by the high and mighty.

For the media planner, the watchword was to follow a plan that was not simply designed to ride roughshod over competition, sinking them in waves of insertion. The strategy was to conserve ad-spend, relying on the creative merit with which the client hoped to capture the share of mind of the target audience. Therefore, the media mix comprised newspapers and hoardings. Mainline English dailies, with a sizeable circulation among the core target audience (those who travelled abroad), brought the brand home. Hoardings in the best locations in the four metros gave each ad a larger than life presence, more so because they were always topical.

---

[10]Here is an obituary, written by Subhas Ghosal, who at the time was the chairman of HTA. This was carried by *Business India* in its issue dated 29 July-11 August 1996. This obituary unfolds the life and times of the extraordinary man 'Bobby' Kooka.

'The little fellow'

The day after Bobby Kooka died, the Air India ad had the maharaja saying, 'I have lost my voice'. But read the voice once more: *'My first contact with J Walter Thompson was in early 1939 on the second floor of Bombay*

House, home of the aviation department of Tata Sons. Peter de Peterson of JWT called on me. He had corn-blue eyes and a tie to match. He was clad in an immaculate suit of white linen and spoke very superior English. We had nothing to advertise because all we carried was mail, with the odd passenger when load was available. So Peterson's visit was social, joy for both non-client and Bombay's leading agency.

JWT had class; they were choosy when they selected a client. And we were Tata's, so we were 'in', the fact that we didn't advertise didn't matter." (JWT/HT's 50th anniversary)

Those few lines reveal the man; his freshness of approach, turning a routine business solicitation into an amusing anecdote. It was not in Kooka's nature to be pompous; he said it was a congenital disability. His most favoured description of the maharaja, for instance, was 'the little fellow'. A self-image?

As an apprentice with JWT over 50 years ago, it was given to me to serve as an errand boy between Kooka and the late, great art director Umesh Rao of JWT. Together, they created the Air India maharaja. But it took time. Rao had to draw dozens of sketches before one would fit Kooka's fastidious ideal of the maharaja. It was to be the template for the future. The most important feature was the eyes, which are forever lowered, in humility, promising service, not servility. Only once, and this after Kooka's retirement from Air India, did someone have the gratuitous creativity to open them. The eyes looked dead. And were promptly shut.

When I first met Kooka, Air India's commercial department was housed in the mezzanine floor of the Army and Navy building. The mezzanine just about cleared Kooka's height of a little over five feet; as I watched him at work, he seemed like an eagle in its eyrie. He was all stillness and action and energy and intuition, and with it all, a commanding eye for detail. Clad in a silk shirt and French cuffs and collar, always a Windsor knot on his tie, he spoke very superior English.

At that time, when Tata Airlines was evolving into Air India, with all the cares and pressures that went with the turf of the No. 2 in the organisation, Kooka still found time to write all the advertising and publicity material. Among his many original ideas was the pocket-size booklet given out to passengers on board Air India. The first edition was swept up before you could say, 'getting acquainted'. All to the good. Kooka had begun to chafe at the banality of the two words. He re-named the edition 'Foolishly yours'. Much more to the point. Via the maharaja he made fun of his airline, his passengers and even of his chairman! The man could carry off his irreverence and irony because he did it with panache. Criticism he brushed aside like a wayward speck on his pin-striped jacket.

Educated in England at public school and Oxford, he was more English than the British. Yet he did not speak as if he had the Elgin Marbles in his mouth. And so his audacity in creating a hitherto unknown kind of advertising baffled the establishment in a British Raj environment.

'Everything I did was "just not done", and when kind and generous folk applauded my eccentricities, Kooka was to J Walter Thompson's white brass, like the scorpions, the cobras, the heat and the mosquitoes of India, a pestilence to be endured,' Kooka said years later.

In 1974—when HTA had fallen on hard times—we invited Kooka to take on the chairmanship of the agency. He recalled the meeting thus: 'When Subhas Ghosal and his predecessor Morris Mathias asked me if I would accept the chairmanship of HTA I did not wait for an answer. Subhas is certain I said "Aye" because I was not told the bailiff was at the door. Wrong! If HTA were on the skids—and they were—and had I been forewarned, I would have said, "Aye. Aye" with greater alacrity.'

People in our trade think of Bobby Kooka as a pioneer in Indian advertising. Perhaps they fail to realise that he broke fresh ground in advertising, no matter where. No one before him had used the wit of idea and the charm of language to elevate advertising from simple commercial communication to a world of self-effacing enticement.

As the years mellowed him, he became even more kind and, towards some blessed individuals, affectionate. But there was always the possibility of a gentle dig. Once when at a party HTA was hosting, I got him a drink he said, 'Subhas, you'll never make a barman, your whiskies are too large. Never mind, our ambassador to the USA has the same failing, I'm told.'

The last time I saw Kooka was almost a year ago. He was surrounded by books. His beloved dog, Ludvig, the boxer, was long dead, and Kooka was very alone; except for his books, hillocks of them all round, and the previous day's issue of *The Times*, London, by his side.

One does not mourn the death of a man who was so true to himself, so giving of civilising influences and yet who had to suffer the cruelty of so much illness. One mourns the realisation that we shall not see his like again.

Sui Generis.

Cigarette advertising was important both to agencies and to the media in the 1960s. Packs did not carry any statutory warning. There were no skull and cross bones on display or images of withered lungs. Those were happy days when doctors did not associate smoking with cancer or heart disease.

ITC was a major client for the leading agencies such as JWT, Clarion and Ulka, because cigarettes were advertised heavily. There were many brands—vernacular newspapers not only in metro towns but equally in smaller towns earned revenues from cigarette advertising. There were a few national brands, while there were many regional brands that had to be supported with local advertisements. Since ITC made substantial profits from year-to-year, they could initiate support to agencies to study consumer behaviour. IMRB, an offshoot of JWT, was born because of ITC. Clarion, too, started its in-house market research company named Core, relying mainly upon ITC for business.

It was not just newspapers and magazines that received a continuous windfall through cigarette advertisements; cigarette brands also appeared in films, providing work to film producers.

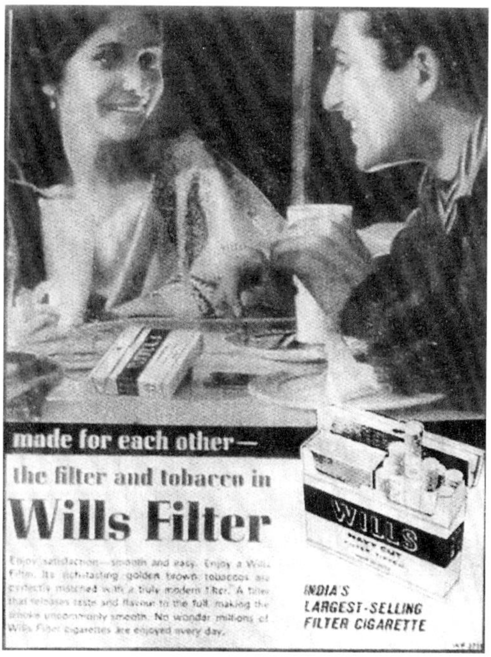

This advertisement was one of the most memorable ads crafted by JWT. People familiar with the times claim that the concept originated with Subhas Ghosal. When I interviewed A.N. Haksar at his residence in Delhi, he recalled that Ghosal came to him with the concept. Haksar was the chairman of ITC over a long period of time.

It is possible that Johnson & Johnson were as worried about population explosion as the government of India. Great minds in the government were spending sleepless nights to coin a catchy slogan that appealed to all Indians to cease or desist from conjugal relationships. They were on the threshold of coining the memorable campaign, 'Hum Do Hamara Do'. But the beauty of the advertisement lies in its effect; where the emotion reflected on the lady's face makes a black and white ad come alive. Indeed, a lot of campaigns in the 1960s depicting individuals or groups successfully portrayed emotions to support the brand promise.

This was the time when a number of memorable films were produced by four eminent film directors of the country—Ritwik Ghatak, Satyajit Ray, Tapan Sinha and Mrinal Sen. In fact, Ghatak's film and Ray's *Debi* were released almost simultaneously. Both the film ads are distinguished for attractive typography. Ghatak's film ad dramatises the film with a frame of the film.

Some Hindi films dealt with major social issues combining entertainment even as they focussed on social themes. Memorable playback songs became popular throughout India. The film page in *The Statesman* in the early 1960s captures some of these films.

IT STARTED WITH A KISS

METRO

"TEN THOUSAND BEDROOMS"

E-L-I-T-E

JOURNEY TO THE CENTER OF THE EARTH

APRIL LOVE

MINERVA

MONEY, WOMEN and GUNS

THE KING'S THIEF

"THE SHAGGY DOG" IS COMING

MENOKA

AWAL YAR?

42nd COMBINED WEEK

Maya Mriga

RADHA . PURNA . PRACHI

FIFTH WEEK!

A POWERFUL MUSICAL ROMANCE WITH A THOUGHT-PROVOKING SOCIAL STORY

DEV ANAND • WAHEEDA REHMAN

Kala Bazar

PARADISE

PEOPLES FAVOURITE

5th WEEK!

SREE . INDIRA & Others

MINAR . BIJOLI . CHHABIGHAR

A FAMILY FILM TO SUIT ALL TASTES!

FASHIONABLE WIFE

JAYMALA

ROXY

KRISHNA . PURNASREE

RUPALI

MENOKA

PARAMOUNT

ALAKA

PICCADILLY

KAMAL

REGENT

SRILAXMI

NOW RUNNING

Nav-Ketan's

BAAZI

DEV ANAND . GEETA BALI

K. N. SINGH . JOHNNY WALKER, ETC.

SOCIETY

A STIRRING TALE OF LOVE WITH SWEET SONGS & DANCES!

FILMISTAN'S

MAINE JEENA SEEKH LIYA

ORIENT . LIBERTY

—NOW SHOWING—

FILMISTAN'S

ANARKALI

BINA ROY — PRADEEP KUMAR

JANATA

—NOW SHOWING—

FILMISTAN'S

NAGIN

VYJANTIMALA—PRADEEP KUMAR

KHANNA . BHAWANI

—NOW SHOWING—

SHANTARAM'S

JHANAK JHANAK PAYAL BAAJE

ANGAR

at Minerva Theatre

STAR THEATRE

INDIA'S ONLY AIR-CONDITIONED LUXURY THEATRE FOR STAGE SHOWS

Paramaradhya

SRI SRI RAMKRISHNA

SISIR KUMAR BHADURI

TALKIE OF TALKIES

BASUSREE & BINA

13th SENSATIONAL WEEK!

Dhool Ka Phool

OPERA

NU PARK

CALCUTTA'S CHOICE SPOT FOR DRINKS & SNACKS

MUSIC NIGHTLY

55, Park Street, Calcutta.

DINE AND DANCE IN THE CONTINENTAL ATMOSPHERE OF

MOCAMBO

Calcutta's Gay Rendezvous

GLAMOROUS

SWEET LORRAINE

THE CROONER WITH THAT "SOMETHING"

PURNA

THE INSPECTOR GENERAL

BASUSREE

"GIANT"

Gufa

THE ONLY RESTAURANT

(NIRULA'S, NEW DELHI).

At Air-conditioned

TRINCAS

Calcutta

DINNER-DANCE

JESSICA JAMES

H.M.V. TROPHY

DARJEELING CENTRAL HOTEL

The Best Food Known from place to place Served in a dignified, Relaxed atmosphere

SKYROOM

THE WHOLE CITY IS AGOG OVER THE PRESENCE OF THE MYSTERIOUS BUS CONDUCTOR . . . INTRIGUES! MURDER!! ROMANCE!!! SONGS!!!!

BUS CONDUCTOR

PREMNATH

SHYAMA

PRABHAT . DARPANA . KALIKA

A RESTAURANT FOR FAMILIES

Hotel Marina

WANTED

WORKS MANAGER-CUM-PRODUCTION ENGINEER

with at least 10 years' experience in first-rate factory for foundry and engineering concern of repute in Punjab. Bright prospects for really competent man. Write stating qualifications, experience and salary acceptable to:—

Box No 7754, The Statesman, New Delhi.

COLD STORAGE PLANTS

LLOYD

DINE AND DANCE AT

VOLGA

New Delhi

THE MIDNIGHT RENDEZVOUS FAMOUS FOR DELICIOUS CHINESE AND CONTINENTAL FOOD

DINE AND DANCE at GAYLORD

NEW DELHI

TAVERN

HOTEL IMPERIAL

NEW DELHI

TONIGHT

Britannia marketed assorted biscuits in beautiful tin containers. These tins were a special attraction for mothers.

There were brands which were positioned on quasi-medical claims, such as Clinic Special Shampoo, which was meant to rid hair of dandruff. It was a product that continued unchanged for quite some time; a sticky-blue solution with not even an attractive odour.[11]

[11]A recent TV commercial of Garnier Fructis shampoo carries a sequence that is absurd. It presents a young foreigner pulling a ton of bricks with her hair. Thanks to Garnier her hair is as tough as the hair on an ass's tail and not a single strand breaks after this exploit.

A large number of advertisements on cosmetics were conceived without any human element. The preponderance of celebrities endorsing brands, as they do today, was non-existent.[12]

Max Factor was a premium brand priced higher than popular talcum powders and soaps. Naturelle herbal shampoos were also premium in price. Yet both brands depended on words alone to inspire purchase. Around this time or perhaps a little earlier, Ogilvy was building the Hathaway brand with the man wearing an eye-patch to add distinctiveness. We should remember that at the time there was no euphoria regarding the use of herbal products. In fact, many a brand derived from various chemical processes were sold to consumers as wonderful discoveries of modern science. In India no product was subjected to rigorous testing in government laboratories before being marketed. Perhaps the only exceptions were medical products.

---

[12]The government is likely to introduce a new law that makes endorsers liable to face penal action if the brands they endorse do not actually have the benefits promised by them. Such a law will be welcome for buyers of products and services in the country.

The Naturelle ad is ahead of the times, it flogs natural products as opposed to synthetic products.

Here is an example of the general trust reposed on packaged and branded products. Marketers regarded consumers rather casually. The baseline sums up what the brand differentiator is: 'a sky-blue mouth purifier'. The ad does not explain what this might be in the body copy, which has more blah than content.

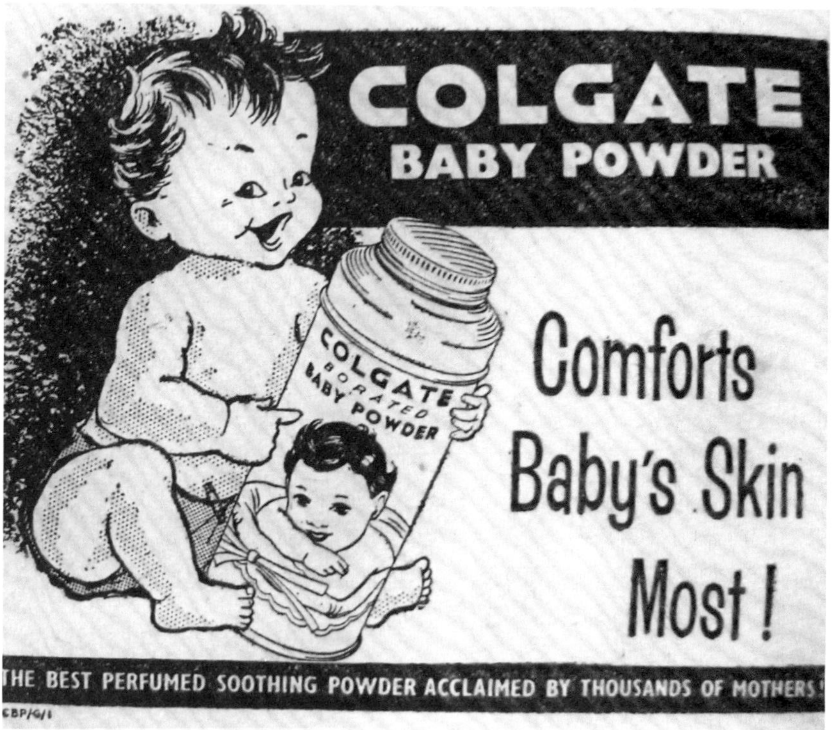

Babies always create visual appeal in advertising, no matter how they are presented, in line illustration or half-tone.

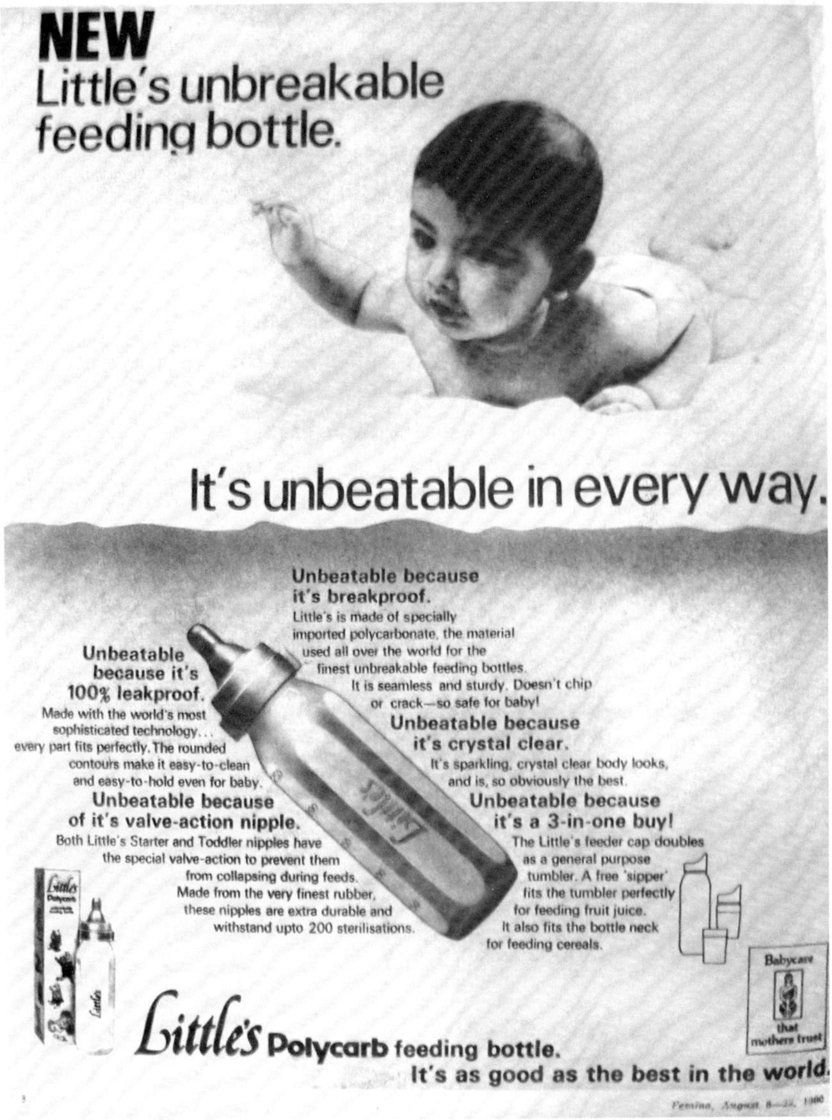

The feeding bottle ad draws our attention as it is obvious that polycarbonate feeding bottles were a fairly recent introduction in the sixties. Children born in the fifties and sixties were sometimes introduced to feeding bottles in the more well-to-do-homes, but they were expected to hold on to large and rather heavy glass bottles. In ordinary homes in West Bengal 'jheenuk-bati' was more prevalent. This enabled the mother to force milk down a child's throat with deft use of her thumb to prise open his mouth, as she forced him to swallow.

Indian art directors were generally poor in English. Anglo Indians and writers who came from the Goa-Konkan belt in the west of the country were exceptions. The more eminent art directors who expressed their views on Indian advertising in the first advertising congress were mainly expatriates. Among the Indian stalwarts was P.N. Sarma who was an art director of national repute. He later became the managing director of Bomas. His speech in the congress was an analytical appraisal of commercial art and art directors in ad agencies.

Wolff Olins

Wolff Olins was the managing director of S.H. Benson, as reported in a recent article in *Brand Equity*. He was appointed head of the agency at an early age and steered the company for a few years before leaving India in 1965, handing over charge to P.N. Sarma. His appointment typifies the era immediately after Independence. Foreigners, by virtue of being foreigners—that is European, American or Australian—were regarded as more acceptable to the Europeans, who still headed a number of important multinational companies in India. It is not difficult to understand why Indian political parties (not only the Congress but all the others as well) and Indian public opinion were opposed to companies being governed in a way that placed Indians in subservient roles. Olins picked up a great deal about branding, a nascent and evolving concept at the time, during his tenure in India and marketed this new knowledge through a long career span that ultimately brought him back to India, and to Bombay, where some of his children were born. He generously maintained that Sarma was the obvious choice as leader and his own appointment was an embarrassment.

P.N. Sarma

Sarma was the joint managing director of Bomas when he delivered this speech in 1966. He was an art director himself and was well-known throughout India. Olins, his predecessor as managing director in Bomas, who was appointed over the head of Sarma in the early 1960s, said in a recent interview, 'Sarma should have been the head and not me.'[13]

[13]See Vikram Doctor's article in *Brand Equity* of 4 August 2008. He says that Wolff Olins headed S.H. Benson, which took over Bomas. But I find from the souvenir published during the advertising congress in the mid-1960s in Calcutta, where Sarma delivered the speech reproduced here, that Sarma was then the joint managing director of Bomas. There is obviously a confusion of chronology here. When did Bomas become S.H. Benson?

The role of an art director: P.N. Sarma

Perhaps it would be better, before I start my remarks on the role of an art director, to make it clear that I shall speak about the art director in India rather than his counterpart abroad. This differentiation is necessary, because the art side of advertising differs considerably in India and the role of the art director, with it.

For example, not many of the agencies in India have art directors working exclusively on certain accounts and where they do, they do not have the wide variety of freelance artists from whom they can commission the artwork. This is one of the reasons why in India most, if not all, the art directors have been outstanding illustrators. In the UK the same people would have turned freelancers, where there's more money.

I do not for a moment doubt that the system as it exists abroad, of commissioning artwork from freelance studios is an excellent one—it gives the advertisers the use of a wide variety of techniques and styles. And it saves the agency overhead cost in that they do not have to employ specialists on their payroll. But the studio in India has grown up side by side with the agency, forced by necessity rather than by choice.

The demand for really good artists has not been met by the art schools, as the potential of commercial art training as a career has not been fully understood. Second, the teaching of applied art has suffered owing to the lack of trained teachers. In some cases the teachers themselves have fallen behind the times in their outlook, which has to be contemporary always.

Agencies have, therefore, been forced to train artists wherever they can and keep a vast army of artists to be of service to the clients. This situation is fast changing, however, but I would confine my remarks to things as they exist today.

From my foregoing remarks, you will observe that the art director in India works within certain limitations. Not that this should be considered a serious handicap, since the applied artist trains himself to accept these limitations to his creative abilities and should be quite used to working within these limits.

It might be easier perhaps to understand the role of an art director if I were to divide the role into broad categories. The art director is responsible for:

a) Planning a campaign, working in close collaboration with the copy group, market research and account executive.
b) Commissioning photographs and artwork wherever necessary.
c) Liaising between artists and account executives.
d) Looking into the administration of the studio.
e) Recruiting and training artists.

It is not difficult to understand the role of the art director insofar as the first category is concerned; that is the most obvious one. What is not so clear perhaps is how creative the art director can allow himself to be in these initial discussions.

It is often not realised that a campaign can go on the rocks even at the early stage owing to faulty thinking on the part of the art director. The aim of every campaign is to be bold, distinctive and original. But at every stage it is for the art director to ask himself whether he has got the artists or photographers to interpret the campaign the right way, whether the budget set apart for production is adequate to do justice to the campaign and whether the time available is sufficient to allow for experiments.

For example, to decide on an extensive hoarding campaign might look all right as a coloured rough and an impressive list of towns but the art director has to ask himself the question whether, in the absence of lithographed 16 sheet posters, is there any organisation capable of painting the hoarding all over India to a deadline date and still keep faithfulness to the specimen hoarding layout. It is at this stage that the art director should simplify his thoughts to suit the particular media.

Take another example. A campaign with an insertion schedule of, say, 12 insertions—a different advertisement every week—sounds bold and exciting. But to decide on a theme that involves commissioning of photographs and turning them into scrapper-boards means you have a real problem on your hands to catch the deadline dates; unless you are planning for the year after.

Then there are pitfalls which an art director must avoid ... I refer to the growing importance of market research. As an artist, it is annoying to constantly hear what the consumers would like to see in an advertisement ... The art director tends to feel that his territory as the torchbearer of the best traditions of applied art is being encroached by these newcomers who claim to know the pulse of the people ...

... I must admit there are very few art directors in India today who can effectively contribute towards arriving at a theme or a basic approach to a campaign. This is due, as I mentioned earlier, to the fact that art directors in India have reached their present position by being illustrators. This in itself is not a bad thing; but an art director should be much more than an illustrator; he should have good general knowledge of the habits and customs of the people; of places and things; of art and religion; of music and theatre.

All this sounds as if the art director should be an all-round genius. No—all I ask is that the art director should come down from his ivory tower and treat the subject of applied art as affecting people of varying levels of social, economic and cultural groups.

Observations on P.N. Sarma's speech

It will be in order to make a note of the salient points in Sarma's speech as they pertain to the state of commercial art in advertising in the fifties and sixties.

- The person who became an art director in an agency was likely to have been an illustrator. His proficiency as an illustrator may have disposed him towards adopting a style which was illustration-oriented.[14]
- The art director in India faced constraints in conceiving a campaign because of technical reasons—the quality of newsprint in newspapers, which was the primary medium; the practice of hand painting of hoardings; and the limited reach of cinema and radio.
- An art director who read little and knew even less of social and cultural aspects of life circumscribed his creative contribution.
- The growing importance of market research aroused suspicion in art directors and copywriters since research gave them directions as to what they could say, do, or present in their advertisement.[15]

A number of speeches delivered at the Indian Advertising Convention in 1966 also deliberated upon the creative side of advertising. In all of them there was the obvious compartmentalisation of the creative process as copy and art. These are presented as mutually exclusive, which has been the trend in advertising insofar as it pertains to the development of the creative platform for a campaign. Since there is not a huge corpus of writing on the creative disciplines in Indian advertising, we should consider some of these discourses, as these talks help to develop a perspective of advertising 40 years ago.

C.H.G. Moorhouse, director at JWT, a versatile cartoonist and a leading visualiser in Indian advertising in the sixties, spoke on 'Commercial art and photography':

> The primary object of any advertisement is the communication of ideas. In advertising, as we all know, we do not sell products or goods as such, but rather the services and benefits those products and goods bestow on the user. So it is not toothpaste we sell, but the idea of attractive, healthy teeth which come from the use of toothpaste; it is not just soap, but its cleansing action and the cleanliness it gives; it is not just cold cream we sell, but the beauty it brings to its user.

---

[14]When I entered advertising in the early seventies, every reputed art director had an individual style. For example, O.C. Ganguli, Raghunath Goswami, Ronen Ayan Dutta, Samir Sarkar, all from Calcutta, were well-known for their distinctive styles as illustrators.

[15]In the first Indian advertising congress multiple speakers deliberated upon research. In the inauguration speech even Minister Keskar touched upon the subject. E.J. Fielden's speech was entirely on market research. Tara Sinha, C.H.G. Moorhouse (director of JWT) and, as we see here, Sarma—all spoke about the growing importance of research. Perhaps an important point not covered during the congress was, 'How to understand market research and how to apply research in the creative process'.

This idea of inferred benefit holds good not only with regard to such consumer products as I have mentioned, but is equally true when we set out to 'sell' such ideas as civic sensibility, thriftiness, social justice; the idea of insurance and protection against unknown hazards and risks, the idea of social equality and so on.

Here are the imponderables; the non-material concepts which typify even more clearly our projection of ideas as against the selling of products. To accomplish this task of communication in advertising we use a combination of pictures and words, or rather a visual impact plus an elaboration of the argument in 'copy'. The illustrative argument may be confined to a typographical effect, but this visual appeal is always present. You are all very well aware how, in a purely typeset advertisement, atmosphere can be created by the choice of types and by the general format of the advertisement.

Let us never forget that each of these components—the picture and the words—has its own job to do. Effective advertising results from a merging and balancing of these elements. Yet, though they are complementary, their action on the observer is distinct, each has a specific task to accomplish.

A clever writer can create mental pictures just as effectively as an artist can draw a visual sketch; but where the writer needs time and the cooperative attention of the reader, the artist can establish almost instantaneous visual communication.

Visual impact is immediate. The eye registers at a glance before a single word has been read, or its meaning absorbed. A picture creates an impression, builds a mood and from this point words take over and must fill in the picture-mood, swelling the first quick visual tones to the full dimension of the message argument and theme. The reason for this quick emotional reaction to illustrative content is due to the fact that much of our thinking, our deductive and memory process, is almost entirely a matter of mental polarisation. Because of varying conditioning factors among the observers, which may include education, social training and past experience, a picture beyond a certain basic point may mean different things to different people. An artist, in short, can never be entirely certain of the mood-reaction he is going to create and obtain.

The only thing he can be sure of is that he will obtain an emotional reaction and that he will get a different response from different people.

With the increase of literacy our audience is becoming wider and wider, with an increasing variation in taste preferences, standards of life, perceptions and sophistication.

Advertising, as we do in India to a public where levels of perception and receptivity vary so tremendously, and where norms of taste and habit also show great divergences, the question of the illustrative content and response becomes many times more important. There is no single art idiom so widely and generally accepted at the present time that it may be used to convey our ideas with any certainty at all levels.

The use of traditional art has been suggested. The development of the Indian advertising style is inevitable with the fine creative art direction now evident in Indian advertising. But the art director will use the most effective means—if some of these have been used abroad it is incidental. The emergence of an Indian style in advertising is a natural development.

I speak, of course, of techniques as well as of general conceptual projections. Here, on the one hand, our illustration will raise enthusiastic comment, while there it is received with rancour and derision. How far may we stylise? How far should we restrict the presentation to absolute realism?

The illustration has to do its job in presenting what we see—either with the material eye, or in the mental vision of our sensibilities. The form and manner of art projection in view of the points I have mentioned is, therefore, a source of controversy and dissension—and from my own experience—acrimonious debate!

Is there a way whereby we can come nearer to a clear understanding of how this task should be tackled; nearer to a proper solution of the problem, which is constantly posed in the creation of the illustrative content? If we keep before us constantly the fact that our chief aim is to communicate, then we can come closer to a proper and reasonable solution in regard to illustrative projection. Art in advertising is not merely decorative—it must serve a purpose—that is a guiding principle.

To begin with, what are the factors we are dealing with? An advertisement, no matter whether it is selling products or imponderables, can serve no purpose unless it is readily and completely understood by the reader. It becomes pointless and dumb when it says something in a manner which is not comprehended.

Your good copywriter strives to use language which is clear, impressive and unambiguous. He avoids using words which may be misunderstood, or which are not in the vocabulary of the average person. He never uses a difficult word if a simple word is ready to hand, and he is careful to direct the reader's thinking in a direction where he can be convinced that he has need of the product or service.

The illustrative element to do its part of the job effectively has to project the same concept idea and the picturisation has to be planned as carefully and as much without complication as the copy. It must lead the mind directly to the idea. Otherwise, the illustrative element becomes entirely incidental and merely an illustration to the text. In that case, it has no job of its own to do and falls outside the scope of this discussion. Let me repeat—advertising art in an advertisement always should have a specific task. It cannot be incidental.

I would suggest that the communicative art element has much more to do than 'look pretty', otherwise it becomes absurd and redundant in an advertisement. A better course then would be to confine the illustrative element merely to pictures of the pack of product and a secondary amplification of how it should be used.

What then should the illustrative element aim to accomplish in order to communicate its idea? I think we may agree that it cannot be described merely as an adjunct to the copy, as it has highly important functions of its own to perform. These functions can be defined as—to bring the reader to a point in space and time where the copy commences and will elaborate the impact; to provide an emotional background against which the copy will gain in conviction; to how, when and where the product touches the reader's life and how it may be obtained; to show what the product looks like and to give the product and the advertising a personality.

These functions are inter-related. There may be call for one or more of them, or for all of them in toto or in part. We may safely say that there is no useful application of the illustrative element which does not fall from within them.

Now, whether it is to secure attention, or to create an emotional background, or to show the product in desirable surroundings, it is necessary for the artist to use art techniques, conventions and symbols which are familiar to the reader. If he does not he will fail to make himself understood, and so will fail to achieve anything at all.

One of his first objectives is for the artist to understand what language of visual convention, art idiom and symbols is understood and accepted by the reader, and what are the contact points which arouse a response?

Can we define Mr Average Reader?

It is possible from available statistics, from the same sources of market research and consumer research used as a basis of copy, to obtain a statistical picture of an average newspaper reader ...

The creative art director instinctively understands that a sale is not based on logic alone, but that emotions are the real motivating force, and while keeping his art idiom intelligible to the consumer, he uses any and every device possible to stir the reader to an emotional response.

It is the product personality which he places in the consumer's mind, which obtain his emotional reaction, and not just the virtues of the product alone, that clinches the sale ...

... There are wide variations in the receptivity in our public and gaps still exist in the literacy pattern in India, so much so, that not one of us concerned in advertising can ever overlook this fundamental educative obligation. Our advertisements are a powerful factor in forming a pattern of life in this country, of formulating standards of taste and appreciation and in spreading culture.

It, therefore, becomes incumbent on your visualiser to try and lodge in the mind of the recipient an ever higher ideal, an ever higher norm, an ever-increasing awareness of the better things of life. If the illustrative content is to help in performing this task—and I am sure we all sincerely believe that it has to—then it must speak in terms, in techniques and in symbolism, in format and designs which will draw the reader's mind and awareness always away from the mediocre and the lowest denominator towards a higher, more informed and cultured awareness, a higher standard of concept and appreciation. And let it be repeated that the more the visualiser knows about his task by way of consumer research, the more opportunities will he have of exchanging views and experiences intelligibly.[16]

In the years before us there is going to be an ever-widening scope, an ever-increasing demand, as never before in India, for the exercise of skill and creative ingenuity; there will be opportunities for advertising.

Observations

Moorhouse speaks in the same vein as Sarma. Like him, he emphasises the importance of using research tools to get a surer feel of the target audience (*in his words, 'newspaper readers'*) in order to communicate effectively. In summation of this important speech, we note the following:

1) The art director concentrated on the newspaper advertisement. The national daily was his primary medium, which gave maximum visibility to his advertisement. Cinema, radio or even other forms of print media such as POP items are not mentioned.
2) His concern for the development of advertising in India with its Indian content in illustration is genuine. While there may have been a few issues that raised the hackles of European advertising professionals in India, the contribution of the likes of Moorhouse and Fielden was considerable.
3) Moorhouse is already talking about advertising driving the consumer by exciting his psychological need more than his physical need for products.
4) He observes that the picture of an advertisement is seen first by the reader before he reads the selling proposition found in the copy. He may choose not to read the copy if he is not excited or intrigued by the picture. Therefore, the art element has to do much more than 'look pretty'. Art, he argues, engages the reader first—before the written text.

[16]He introduces in his speech a much larger social ambit for advertising. While most advertisers and agencies are content to judge advertising on its impact, we should think about what the speaker says here.

5) Moorhouse, Fielden, Sinha and senior personnel in the leading advertising agencies such as JWT, Clarion, Lintas and Bomas thought deeply about their work because they were in fact regularly training newcomers to the profession. No professional course on advertising was conducted in India.

Research was the big thing in advertising. Fielden devoted his entire speech to research. He dwelt on topics such as sampling, drawing up the questionnaire and deriving valuable insights into what could be communicated in advertising, based on an understanding of what the prospective customer was looking for in the market or from a brand.

Since it is difficult to access speeches/articles regarding the creative disciplines in advertising, let us hear what John Walton had to say on the subject. Walton was the deputy manager of Lintas and for a period was the chief copywriter of the agency. Unlike today, when deputy manager denotes a menial level in an organisation, it was then considered a very senior position in an agency. His speech was titled, 'What makes an advertising idea click?'[17]

> What do we mean by an advertising idea? We are not going to discuss the kind of idea that pleases some creative people—the sort that wins cries of praise from other advertising men but sales from nobody. Nor even the sort that wins CAG awards and gets into the art director's annual.
>
> I think a discussion of this kind should cover all kinds of advertising ideas and not just the clever ones and bright ones. Our range should extend from plain announcements such as 'Finlays for Gloster Cables' to the latest antics of Mr Tata and Mr Fison, from a Jenson & Nicholson cinema slide to the latest and most glamorous film poster.
>
> Again, I don't think we should limit ourselves to press advertising—we advertising people are perhaps all too press-minded when, as we have already heard, the main mass media of this country are perhaps the film and outdoor advertising. So in discussing advertising ideas let us discuss all media available.
>
> ... What I mean by an advertising idea that clicks is quite simply one that gets results ... an idea that effectively communicates the advertiser's message to the audience at which it is aimed.
>
> ... I want to clear out of the way three extraneous questions which have a bearing on the effectiveness of an advertising idea.
>
> 1. Does the product or service advertised really fulfil the promise of the advertising being considered?
>
> Advertising should never be called in, like a fire brigade, to rescue a product from its shortcomings ...

[17]In 1960, when he delivered the speech, he was the creative head of his agency.

2. Is the social and economic climate basically favourable to the proposed advertising? In other words, can the market understand our idea and can they respond to it?
3. Is the advertising idea right for the media for which it is to be used?

... Two ingredients, I think, are essential to any good creative idea. First, it should possess the power to evoke the product or service in the consumer's mind ... Second, a good creative idea should add something to life and enrich the experience of those who see it ...

... The basic need of every advertiser is to make himself and his product or service known. He must be easily recognisable the instant he is seen in the press, the cinema or outdoor advertising.

The means by which he can achieve his call-signs are obviously such devices as logo types—for example, B.O.A.C., Anacin, Glaxo, Amul; figures and characters—for example, Air India's maharaja, Mr Tata and Mr Fison, I am Tea; slogans and phrases—for example, Fly the Finest, B.O.A.C. takes good care of you, 4 medicines in one; distinctive styles and designs—for example, Handloom, Pears Soap, Savlon. It is surprising, but few advertisers use this kind of call-sign.[18]

Call-signs like these help to make an advertiser a part of the general knowledge of the people in his market. They can play a vital role in building a product's brand image or personality.

Sometimes I think we change them too often, forgetting the value of the goodwill they build for us. Too soon we begin to think our public is tired of them because we are. We change them so often—or omit to use them altogether, so that in the end our advertising has no recognisable call-sign—and, therefore, our communication system breaks down.

It is, of course, not enough for an advertiser to establish his identity; he must make contact with his public. For this he needs to know and use the receiver's call-sign ... How can it do this?

Most obviously, by addressing its audience directly:

For example, 'Stuffed up Nose?' say the FENOX ads. 'Headache?' say the Aspro ads.

Then something about the advertising must suggest the audience intended. Perhaps a situation, or problem, within the reader's range of experience. Perhaps a style or language that prompts a response from the audience. Very often, it calls for the employment of an enrolment appeal—vanity, emulating pride in the home, or security. The difficulty facing most creative people is that often they do not know what appeals to people. Often in India they have never had any direct

[18]The last sentence will not stand up to scrutiny. Advertisers in India have been using call-signs since the nineteenth century. Patent medicine not only had distinctive packaging but also symbols which they reminded customers to check out before purchase in order to ensure they were buying the genuine product.

contact with the people they are trying to persuade. Hence the need for study, research and touring…[19]

…We need copywriters in Indian languages. Somehow advertising must sell itself to Indian language writers as an interesting and worthwhile profession. When Indian writers begin thinking about advertising then we can expect that advertising will really reach and appeal to Indian markets …

… Most of us live and work in Bombay, Calcutta, or Madras and most Indian advertising ideas are, I suppose, produced in either of these cities.[20] It pays occasionally to take a look at these through the eyes of, say, Nagpur or Trivandrum, or even much smaller towns, or even through a villager's eyes. We are, I submit, too often operating on a Bombay or Calcutta wavelength.

Not only this. We are too often working on an urban, literate wavelength, when we ought to be on an Indian one.

True, advertising is a western development and came to India from the West, but it seems to me—although I must say it diffidently—that it is time Indian advertising began making use of purely Indian ideas, Indian situations, Indian designs and colour combinations. We are still translating copy, most of us, and we are still translating intrinsically western ideas and situations into Indian terms. This, I am sure, is not enough, Indian advertising needs to start growing from Indian roots.

I remember a long evening with Subhash Mukhopadhyay, Gyanpith award-winning Bengali poet and one of the best among modern poets in Bengal after Tagore, who was forced to supplement his income with translation work given by his friends in leading ad agencies. He told me that he faced an impenetrable wall in agencies if he tried to do something original. The agencies wanted translation that remained true to the English original; I can appreciate Walton's anguish.[21]

---

[19]John Walton was clearly an expat. The average Indian art director, whether in Bombay or Calcutta, was from a middle-class home. He went to the market to buy vegetables, eggs, meat and fish. In those days of scarcity he often had to find out where his favourite brand of cooking oil was available. Lesser men in professions other than advertising suffered paralysis or even death sometimes since they bought spurious mustard oil at cheaper than market rates from rascally traders. The art director took considerable pains to even know where fine quality of rice or a necessity such as baby food was being sold in the black market. If he planned to see the latest Hindi, Tamil or Bengali movie, just released, with his wife (it was a male-dominated world) he had to know the going black market rate for a ticket. So it is unthinkable that an art director or copywriter knew little about the real world outside the agency.

[20]A reviewer of my first volume of Indian advertising history, covering the period 1780 to 1950, has wisely commented that 'the book is Calcutta-centric with some references to Bombay'. Walton's comment explains the point why modern Indian advertising has centred around the cities of Bombay, Madras and Calcutta—till about the mid-1980s when Calcutta started slipping and Delhi began to occupy more space in Indian advertising.

[21]I also recall Subhash Mukhopadhyay saying that two persons had genuine concern for Indian language advertising. They were Subhas Sen of Clarion and Subhas Ghosal of JWT.

It was not till the mid-1990s that Indian advertising transited to the vernacular. Visuals based on experiences in daily life with its colourful tapestry of diversity began to impact Indian advertising. For example, take the wonderful Fevicol commercials. One is based on life in Rajasthan—with rural people travelling by bus clinging on to every inch of available space (with Fevicol to keep them glued, lest they fall off). Another equally memorable TV spot is that of the south Indian angler getting his catch, which he does by applying Fevicol to his fishing tackle while his urban friend looks at him with disgust, having failed to hook a single fish. But, the 'Indianness' of advertising in the country happened only after a clutch of talented copywriters and art directors arrived from small towns.

Copywriters writing in the vernacular were looked upon more as translators than original writers in the fifties, sixties and seventies. They were not given a brief on which to work. After a copywriter wrote in English, and more often than not after an advertisement or a campaign had been approved by the advertiser, language copy was written. This was an afterthought and was initiated because the advertiser or, on his behalf, the media planner in the agency included some vernacular dailies or magazines to reach a wider target audience.

What was the Indian market like at the time of the first Indian advertising convention? P.L. Tandon, who was then the vice chairman of HLL and also the president of the Advertising Club of Bombay, covered this important topic in his speech at the convention, with wonderful clarity of vision and an incisive perception of the market realities in India:

Prakash Lal Tandon

We do not often think of it, but India today combines all the stages of marketing evolution. We still have barter in some of the remote hill and jungle areas, which at the same time receive some manufactured products such as kerosene, tea, matches, tools, cloth, vanaspati and soap, brought there by means of modern complex marketing. Thus one sees in these villages, which have barely reached the monetisation of economy, barter and sophisticated marketing side by side. Like our Indian society, the economy contains extremes of evolution, the bullock cart and the jet plane; the cow dung and the atomic reactor; barter and advanced marketing. And there is nothing wrong in this. Because we employ some old methods, it does not mean that we should not, at the same time, look ahead and learn to use even the most modern techniques. In fact, in any form of planning, we must look ahead and make sure that even if it is on a pilot scale, the latest techniques are being studied and adopted.

It has unfortunately been the case in India that our entrepreneurs, private or public, while accepting the latest in plant and equipment, have ignored or left marketing to chance. It has been suggested that they sometimes install equipment, which is perhaps more advanced than our present needs, but when it comes to marketing, the number of companies that have employed the latest methods is indeed very few. One cannot think of many that have a first rate modern marketing set-up, though one can think of many who have the most modern plant and equipment. The emphasis has been on productivity and increasing output. But production is of no use without consumption, even though it may not be possible to realise the desire for greater consumption until per capita consumption rises—but the desire should be there.

I wonder why this should be so, because as a nation, we have a good business sense. We are the only country in the world where business became a caste. Modern marketing should, therefore, have come quicker to us than modern industry. However, it is never too late and there are signs that it is probably on the way. The very fact that we are holding the advertising convention in Calcutta and discussing marketing is an indication of the growing interest in this field.

I do not wish to discuss the principles of marketing ... instead, I should like to discuss a single aspect of it, 'Decision-making in marketing management'.

Marketing management in the past has relied largely upon its experience and empiricism. In the traditional approach to marketing decisions, emphasis was placed almost entirely on personal judgement. This is gradually changing. Hunches are giving way to a deeper study and evaluation. Hunches and pragmatism are highly useful, but they can have shortcomings. The most profitable or workable course in the short term may not always be the most acceptable in the long term. And in a developing economy, decisions have necessarily to be a well-thought-out combination of the ideal and the practical.

As the size, speed and the impact of decisions grow, modern marketing management is being aided and guided by a growing body of specialised services and advice. Some of these are relatively new and cannot perhaps claim much credit at this stage; others, while they have been in existence for a considerable time, are re-orienting their outlook. There is, thus, a growing realisation of the role of these services, such as marketing research, econometrics, operations research and management accounting.

Conventional research has been used as an aid to marketing for many years. It collects information about the markets and products in such terms as what people use, how much they use, how often they buy, their likes and dislikes and preferences. This is straightforward charting of consumer habits to give us surface bearings on both urban and rural markets. But there has been developed quantitative research, such as brand barometers, which tell us the state of our brands and those of other manufacturers; retailer sample surveys, to show off-take from the retailer's shelves; and consumer panels, to indicate household consumption of certain articles. They attempt to provide a quantification of the habits of the people.[22]

Yet another field which is beginning to be explored is qualitative research, which goes below the surface and asks the reason WHY and what lies behind WHY. Motivation research, as it is called, probes deeper into the expressed preferences, likes and dislikes of people. It attempts to build brand images to help marketing people to see their products as the consumers see them.

Marketing research, in addition to the quantitative and qualitative research, which looks into the past and the present by telling management what people's habits and likes and dislikes have been in the past and are at present, also looks forward into the future. It will study what people's habits might be tomorrow. As an example, the middle-class Indian society in the urban area is undergoing a change, the joint family is breaking down; women are taking to work and domestic servants are becoming difficult to engage. Will this have an effect on our Indian cooking, which has been a product of the joint family, cheap labour and much leisure? Will the new housewife turn to toast and bread instead of chapatis; to packaged cereals for breakfast instead of a cooked dish; a pre-prepared and packaged masala instead of having to grind it for hours? Upon an assessment of such change will depend marketing management's actions in the future and the products they may launch …

---

[22]In the advertising convention, Fielden delivered a speech on market research. But it was very elementary in context, more suitable for people at the time who may have been totally unaware of this new-fangled field that was so often mentioned by sales and advertising people. Tandon certainly had a far better insight into market research because HLL used research continuously. Therefore, I thought it expedient to present Tandon's speech where he mentions the various kinds of research tools with easy familiarity and not as esoteric subjects.

> … In recent years advertising budgets have been increasing and this has led management to seek methods of determining the actual effect of their advertising money in creating sales. Since advertising is an investment like plant and machinery, one should be able to determine the return management is going to get on its money and how the advertising budget will be allocated over media. The newly-developing answer to this old problem is measurability of advertising. Like motivation research, it is still in its infancy, but it is a field in which experimentation is going on and may soon provide an answer to the question, '*How much should we spend on advertising?*'

The major problems confronting clients, agencies and the media in the 1960s pertained to three main areas:

1. Newspaper was the obvious first choice in media selection. It is curious because people were largely unread. Understandably, advertising was concentrated in and around the four major metros. Smaller towns were hardly covered by the major Indian languages or English dailies. Papers published from smaller towns had very little advertising traffic. They depended on personal contacts in ad agencies or with advertisers to get some advertising flowing to them.[23]
2. Because of poor quality of newsprint, art directors relied heavily upon line drawings.

K.V. Matthew, manager, department of information services, Burmah-Shell, mentioned in his speech in the advertising congress:

> Any client who expects any standard of reproduction these days thinks twice before using a photograph in his advertisement and I personally consider it very necessary for advertisers of consumer products to be able to use photographs with ease and felicity. I do not think that the line drawings and other techniques to which clients are compelled to resort to provide the same authenticity, motivation and verisimilitude that photographs give you … I somehow feel that in spite of the low quality of newsprint which is available to our papers, there must be a way out of this impasse … In this and other matters of technological improvement, I hope the city which leads India in quality of printing could play a vital role ….[24]

[23]I recollect how owners of small publications repeatedly visited my agency for inclusion of the publications in a campaign. The media manager in Clarion Calcutta, Biswanath Majumdar, treated them with respect and generally included smaller publications in a campaign. He had a phenomenal memory for publication rates.

[24]For a Calcuttan it is wonderful hearing someone as important as Matthew saying that Calcutta was a centre of printing excellence in the country. Burmah-Shell, being one of the major advertisers, required many leaflets and brochures every year.

S.N. Banerjee

S.N. Banerjee (who was called 'Ban') was the founding managing director of Clarion. He successfully led a team of highly talented individuals each with an ego bigger than a football field. He shaped the agency so well that every employee believed that he was a member of India's best ad agency. Soon Clarion became the number two agency next only to JWT. Ban had a mercurial temper. He was also a stickler for detail. Having worked in every department in the agency, he knew when things did not fall in place. Ban was also scrupulously honest. There were many stories about him. It was reported that on a visit to Delhi he was received by the company's manager and vehicle at the airport. Because he intended to make a personal visit he returned the company vehicle and took a taxi. It was also said that if he posted personal letters he always paid for postage and did not use company envelopes. He was the only managing director in Clarion who planned the succession on his own retirement.

However, he had to assume the responsibilities of Clarion in 1980 when the company went through its first internal sedition with a large number of senior and junior executives deciding to leave. He was appointed managing director by the Calcutta High Court. Despite the ensuing negative publicity, he still managed to hold on to Clarion's biggest clients. So long as he remained managing director, the bad boys of Clarion did not have a free rein. He was already in his seventies and stepped down because of failing health.

3. Media planning was a specious name given to what was really scheduling of advertisements. Few figures on circulation and readership were available. Whatever was provided by the Audit Bureau of Circulation (ABC) was confined to only member publications. ABC reports did not cover all publications. The reports furnished relied a great deal upon unauthenticated numbers given by member publications, based on goodwill and accompanied by entertainment of the audit team.

Tara Sinha, who was then a director of Clarion, chided the press for only looking at the profits they earned without making any effort to support ad agencies and advertisers with authentic figures on their circulation and readership. Excerpts from the speech delivered in the advertising convention make interesting reading.

> ... Our knowledge of press, as a medium, is not all it should be. Apart from circulation figures and broad regional classification of these figures little else is known. Experience and inspired guesswork guide the space buyer in media selection. But how much more effective would the use of media be if more information were

> available to aid the agency space buyer? A few years ago some publishers conducted small research projects on their readership. But since then no similar studies appear to have been undertaken. Why is this? Has the press reached a stage of complacency with advertising revenue growing to new records—and some publications even turning down advertising? The answer may be that publishers are so busy keeping pace with rising circulation and increased advertising that there is hardly any time left for them to consider other problems.

The basic problem with Indian advertising in the period from the 1960s to the mid-1980s was that advertising agencies did not have media options. Every campaign was so newspaper-centred that the other media hardly received a second look. Only a very brave account executive—and that too at a senior level—could contemplate taking an innovative media approach for a campaign. It must also be said that Air India and Amul showed the way in being visible on hoardings rather than in newspapers or magazines, though both these brands did buy quite a bit of space in frontline newspapers and in the more popular magazines. Sinha's chagrin indicates a degree of professionalism in Indian advertising. Advertising professionals were aware of their shortcomings in their respective disciplines. Most of them were familiar with developments in the West, especially in the USA. And they all wished to provide better service to their clients. Sinha in her speech outlines the importance of reaching out to those who formed, as a consumer group, a 'mass market' as distinct from a market dominated by the wealthy consumers. She is ahead of the times in predicting the growth of a mass market in India.

> … It is important to remember that we are not always interested in the so-called 'class market'. It sometimes seems that certain popular papers appealing to the mass market are almost ashamed of this fact. In reality, however, their strength lies in this. For it is this popular market, that is, the mass market, to whom most of the products of the future will be sold.

In the twenty-first century, advertisers and advertising professionals in agencies are debating on what the ideal structure of an agency should be. In a fairly recent interview even Sir Martin Sorrell, who owns the WPP Group of Agencies and also a number of first-line media companies, wondered whether divorcing the creative and media functions is the best thing for advertisers.

Since the 1990s, the trend has been to separate media operations from the creative functions of the agency. This was initially tried out by P&G and every big budget account followed suit first in the USA and then elsewhere in the world including India. In the first Indian advertising congress, Subhas Ghosal focussed on the subject of the commission earned by the agency—and whether this was justified. The debate has not ended. His speech is important because it gives a breakdown of an agency's operational costs.

His speech was titled 'Where the 15 per cent goes'. Why did he deliver a speech on the subject of an agency's earnings? Were clients questioning the justification of an agency to pocket 15 per cent? Did they feel that this 15 per cent came not from the media but was borne by them? Later big spenders such as HLL and others tallied their brand profits and asked why should the agency share no risk of a brand's performance in the market and walk away with 15 per cent commission.[25]

> On the opening day of the convention, while putting forward 'The case for advertising', Toto Gupta remarked how extraordinary it was that a speech in defence of advertising had to be made at all at a convention in which the participants are either actively engaged or vitally interested in advertising.
>
> Basically the reason why Mr Gupta stated the case for advertising is also the reason why I am here today to try and investigate where the 15 per cent goes. This is because in our first convention we have perforce to deal with some of the fundamental albeit obvious questions of advertising ... if only to promote greater understanding and more relevant discussion of these subjects among the practitioners and users of advertising.
>
> This is why I can stand here today and be bold enough to talk about where the 15 per cent goes, even though I know that to most people in this hall what I am going to say is well-known.
>
> Also, to many of you it is probably not as important to recapitulate where the 15 per cent goes as it is to spread the realisation that almost all of it does go![26]
>
> Which brings me to the question ... who in heaven's name fixed this 15 per cent? I know that many advertisers consider this figure outrageous ... and yet to the agency managers, almost universally, it adds up to no more than a pittance.[27]

---

[25]I recollect R.K. Swamy was tireless in explaining to his account executives why 15 per cent is barely sufficient to keep an agency running. If it were so, I would not know how he made the fortune he earned. He was not a frugal Tamil Brahmin.

[26]This continues to be the bone of contention. Advertisers believe it is much too much in a business environment where their earnings are never assured.

[27]Jeremy Tunstall comments on the 15 per cent commission earned by agencies in *The Advertising Man in London Advertising Agencies* published by Chapman & Hall Ltd (1964). This differs considerably from Ghosal's view and hence I note Tunstall's comments here for comparison. 'During the 2nd World War, when most advertising was placed by agencies for government departments, the standard commission received from media was 10 per cent. After the War the agencies and their Institute of Practitioners in advertising pushed hard to raise this to the American standard of 15 per cent. The big breakthrough came when the commercial television companies all decided to offer the full 15 per cent—no doubt as an incentive to encourage agencies to introduce television departments. This put the television companies at an advantage when competing with the press and other media still only offering agencies 10 per cent or 12.5 per cent. Slowly the newspapers followed ... Some agencies have now adapted a practice of charging the clients the difference for any advertising placed in media not giving the full 15 per cent level of commission. This means that agencies such as the London Press Exchange and JWT automatically receive 15 per cent on all advertisements they release. In America, where 15 per cent commission has been much longer established, there have been frequent reports that it was doomed. In the 1930s, the Hasse Report forecast the eclipse of the system; Roger Burton said in 1956 that the 15 per cent commission would not last more than a decade ... Again in 1958, Professor Albert Frey ... foresaw the weakening of the 15 per cent system, although he did not predict what would take its place.'

... the principle of fixed compensation paid on established rates—the stabilisation of the figure of 15 per cent—did not take place even in the United States and Great Britain until the 1930s. What did happen during this period was that an increasingly large number of publishers recognised that by allowing a standardised commission to advertising agencies they were creating a situation whereby the agencies were forced to compete on the basis of service. Publishers welcomed the development because they were relieved of the responsibility of preparing copy and layout, for which they were in any case ill-equipped ...

From the advertiser's point of view this system made it possible for him to draw upon specialised services which the agencies offered free. It meant that the advertiser could take advantage of the objective point of view that the agency provided—a point of view so essential for the effective promotion of sales in an increasingly competitive market. The wise advertiser realised that the agency had the gift of seeing his product as the consumer saw it ...

But, whereas the first advertising agency's work was fairly simple, today the advertising agency is a complex business unit which must continually offer more and more advice and aid the manufacturer in the selling of his product or service.[28]

And that is precisely the reason why the 15 per cent commission system is under fire both as a method and as an amount of agency compensation ...

... More people, more minds, more talents are being devoted to the spending of the advertising rupee than were employed a decade ago. And certainly a decade from now even greater variety, as well as size of effort will be called for in order that the returns from advertising are more demonstrably related to expenditures on it ...[29]

I shall quote to you block figures of agency expenditures that I have here, given to me in confidence, from three advertising agencies.

Salaries	Other Expenditures	Profit before Tax
Rs	Rs	Rs
A 10.70	**2.53**	**1.77**
B 10.90	**3.50**	**0.60**
C 8.70	**4.80**	**1.50**

[28]This is a major area of constraint for all agencies, irrespective of size or affiliation to large foreign agencies. Besides advertising, the strength of a brand depends on its distribution muscle. No agency man takes the trouble of visiting hole-in-the-corner shops such as Subhas Ghosal used to. To be honest, even advertisers' sales or marketing personnel are complacent if a brand is doing well. When it is not all these pros are taken by surprise!

[29]I have never really understood why agencies have always been shy of being accountable for the actual benefit obtained through advertising a product or service. They have been quick to point out that since advertising is a part of the marketing mix it is not possible to isolate the benefits solely derived from advertising or to quantify such gain in rupees. I believe it can be done. I have seen it happen many times in my career spanning over 35 years with respect to reply coupons and promotion-related campaigns where the clients' expenses have been directly related to sales. Marwari companies, in particular, are very hard-nosed in this regard. Rightly so!

Against every Rs 15 earned, agency A spent Rs 10.70 on salaries, agency B spent Rs. 10.90 and agency C spent Rs 8.70.

All other items of expenditures have been lumped together in the second column, under which head you see agency A spent Rs 2.53, agency B spent Rs 3.50 and agency C spent Rs 4.80.

These respective expenditures left agency A with a profit before tax of Rs 1.77, agency B with a profit of 60 paise and agency C with Rs 1.50.

I should like to point out that the figures relate to what could be considered medium- and large-sized agencies billing, say, Rs 40 lakh and above.

As Agency A made the largest profit I will use its figures as the norm in this discussion ... precisely because I want to focus attention on the status of agency profits ...

... The overwhelming bulk of the expenditure of an agency is on personnel but it is of interest to analyse why this should be so.

Certainly to those critics of the advertising agency business who feel that agency management is extravagant, it should be pointed out that one of our greatest problems is the low rate of utilisation of productivity. When I say this, I am referring almost exclusively to the work of the creative people in the agency—copywriters and visualisers—who are also the more highly paid.[30]

The difficulty with the work of such creative people is that because their output is not mechanical it cannot be controlled in point of time.

... One may say reasonably that with such a man only 30 to 40 per cent of his time is really productive for the agency in the sense that it results in work which is eventually presented to the advertiser. At this stage, again, a fairly high percentage of rejection or revision is customary, so that ultimately only a small percentage of the total effort made is translated into 15 per cent commission for the agency.

... having operated the business in the most tight-fisted manner, the agency winds up at the end of the year with a profit before tax of 1.77 per cent and an after-tax figure of 0.81 per cent.[31]

---

[30]In my experience, I have seen copywriters and visualisers so loaded with work—always with an impossible deadline for submission—that I have wondered how they managed to switch from one subject to another and then on to a third in a single day. I have very fond memories of our wonderful studio in Clarion in Free School Street, Calcutta. I also have wonderful memories of the studio at R.K. Swamy Associates with Arunava Chakraborty at the helm and with Surojoy Banerjee combining the twin roles of the branch manager and the resident copywriter. I have no hesitation in saying Banerjee was the best and unfortunately the most underrated copywriter in R.K. Swamy then. However, I have also had the misfortune of working with a bunch of overrated and underperforming art directors in OBM, propped up by a director who placed them on a pedestal.

[31]No intelligent person would get into a business with such poor return on investment combined with back-breaking labour. However, in the 1960s, we were seeing the beginnings of an accounting system that obfuscated real earning and presented a picture of near-penury. This was foisted on business by the misplaced Congress political belief that making an honest profit was immoral and against Gandhi's views on simple living.

> Since we have assumed that these figures could be expected to apply to agencies with billings of Rs 40 lakh and over, the qualifying agency would, on this basis, make a profit of Rs 70,800 before tax and Rs 32,400 after tax. And in order to make this profit it will have carried on its staff approximately 80 people—for experience shows that you require one employee for approximately every Rs 50,000 in billings.

Business in any country is governed by economic compulsions, which are in turn influenced by the current socio-political environment. The Indian business history is a tale of overt and covert government control—the empowerment of a bureaucracy that became progressively debased and lost its very *raison d'etre*. The government began to encroach on every aspect of social life. Commerce and industry that always play a critical role in the economy naturally became a focal point in the government's perspective. By controlling the levers here the government could control and manipulate the lives of citizens.

The government in choosing a socialistic pattern of development decided to directly own and manage infrastructure industries, all of which soon became white elephants with mounting debts. The government also controlled private industry by setting in place what is today described as the licence raj.[32] With this in mind it would be appropriate to read the speech made by the minister at the advertising convention. Dr Keskar did not have a fan following. People who knew him or interacted with him recall his hatred for Hindi film songs. Some said he was rigid in his views.[33]

Any political party that holds the reins of power for a long time shows inflexibility with regard to its political philosophy and begins to coerce other organs of the state and ultimately the common citizen to follow its dictates.

Dr Keskar's speech

> When I was invited to inaugurate the first All India Advertising Convention in Calcutta I readily accepted, as I felt the convention was indicative of the new developments and trends in the growth of Indian advertising. I am glad to find here representatives of different interests associated with advertising, advertisers,

[32]Licences were granted by an ever-vigilant bureaucracy. They soon realised the money-making potential of this exercise. Till this day the common citizen of independent India hasn't been able to win his freedom from bureaucrats and politicians.

[33]I covered this aspect in the section on radio in *Indian Advertising 1780 to 1950.*

advertising agents, printers and publishers, all gathered together to take stock of the past progress and plan for the future.

Although in its restricted sense advertising stands for the promotion of sales of a product and for making things known, in the modern age its scope has tremendously expanded—the drive for a cleaner city, the sales promotion for a new product, the popularisation of a new idea, are all helped by advertising through different media.

I am glad that advertising has been growing in India. In fact, during the past few years, the growth has been very marked, but we do not have any statistics regarding the volume of advertising in the country. A few years ago, I understand, a rough estimate was made of total press advertising in the country, but the estimate, like most other estimates, was vague. I wish some organisation would take up the task of giving us correct statistics, regarding the volume and growth of advertising in the country. The fact that it has grown cannot be denied and it is the sign of a progressive economy. I have always felt that advertising has a very important role to play towards raising living standards in India. Our Five Year Plans have increased economic wealth, which in turn has made available greater purchasing power among the masses. Advertising can play a very effective role in harnessing the purchasing power for the good of the people and increasing production. In this connection I would like to stress the fact that advertising has also got to make known our development activities to the masses. Completion of our development plans is a stupendous task and the government alone can hardly achieve the widespread publicity which is needed in this field. It would be helpful if prestige advertising of some of our main commercial houses, which are associated with development activities, is correlated to publicising development activities. Some beginning has already been made in this sphere and I hope this convention would give a lead in the matter. Public service advertising has contributed a good deal to the welfare of the communities in the West and I do not find any reason why we should lag behind.

I do not agree that free enterprise as it is defined in the USA is essential for prosperity, even in the advertising industry. India's choice of a mixed economy of public and private sectors is based upon urgent national necessity—a desire to attain higher standards and prosperity as soon as possible. There is full scope for the advertising industry in a mixed economy as ours.

Although advertising in its modern sense has grown in India considerably during the past 50 or 100 years, there has not been much development of indigenous traditions in advertising. It started and has been modelled mostly on the lines of western advertising. A stage has now been reached in its growth when various advertising interests in the country should put their heads together to see that advertising in India is Indian, both in idiom and expression. It can only be effective if it talks the language of the people, if it utilises their vision and culture.

I would, therefore, emphasise the necessity of utilising the tradition of Indian art and culture in the case of Indian advertising. Something is already being done and I am sure in due course different schools of Indian art would contribute to the success and growth of this industry.

I am sorry to note that Indian industry is not very advertisement conscious. The important role that advertising can play in popularising goods is not yet sufficiently realised by the industrialists in the country. Even today, the bulk of advertising in our country is either that of the important foreign concerns or their Indian equivalents. They fully realise the importance of making themselves known to the people. The major part of the purely Indian industry still appears to be conservative regarding this matter.

The development of Indian advertising on healthy and effective lines obviously demands trained personnel. I was rather surprised to find that we still do not have any training institute in the country that could give effective training in advertising. I hope your convention would give thought to the matter and plan to establish some training institute in India.

A few years ago, the Press Commission examined at length the role played in the economy of Indian newspapers by advertisements and suggested certain measures to improve advertising standards in the country. They stressed the need for market research, greater use of Indian language papers and recommended the setting up of an organisation to deal with objectionable advertisements. I am happy to find that a certain amount of market research has already been done but there is an urgent need of readership surveys in the country.

Regarding the use of Indian language papers, I feel that their value as media appears to have been underestimated by both advertisers and the advertising agencies. I believe it has been wrongly estimated that the Indian language papers have less pulling power than the English papers. I wonder if this assumption has ever been substantiated by any readership survey or other authentic information. I would always advocate that greater attention should be paid to the claims of the Indian language and district papers, keeping in view the effect of multiple readership. I would also suggest that the Indian language papers—especially smaller papers—should pay greater attention to the layout of the advertisements appearing in them. It is necessary that the district newspapers should furnish sufficient information to the advertisers so that their utility as effective media could be fully realised.

It appears obvious that if advertisers aim to reach the largest possible mass of the people in the country and if advertising is not meant simply to be a patronage for showing the goodwill of the advertisers towards particular papers or people, the languages of India and the language papers will have to be utilised to the fullest possible measure. No amount of advertising or publicity in English will ever reach the bulk of the people, however much might be spent on it. That advertisers are not yet utilising the languages very much can only indicate that they are not geared for mass publicity campaigns for their goods. Even with the limited literacy in this country, the people who will buy goods can only be reached through the languages. The immense potentiality of this has probably not yet been realised by the advertising world.

On account of the rapid growth of advertising, there have been complaints of some objectionable advertising in certain spheres. In this connection I am glad to know that the plan to set up an Advertising Council of India is nearly completed and a tentative code of ethics is ready which, if effectively implemented, should be helpful in dealing with the problem. I hope the council will come into being soon.

Literacy in India has made considerable progress, but it is still only 40 per cent—a figure which has an important bearing on schemes of mass communication. The most remarkable feature of Indian history is that the development of thought, spread of ideas and information, has been very little through the written word. Culture has always been transmitted through audio-visual means ... Films of entertainment and instruction are undoubtedly the biggest single means of mass publicity today and do fall in line with the traditional preference for audio-visual communication.

... In a developing economy, advertising has a good deal to contribute. It is a happy sign to find that advertising interests are becoming conscious of their responsibility. I have great pleasure in inaugurating this convention and wish your deliberations all success.

Advertising agencies in the sixties

Advertising in the sixties was mainly focussed in Bombay, Calcutta and Madras.[34] Delhi at the time did not have a concentration of business as it does now. Advertising was confined to local businesses, which were like cottage industries. But it was the nation's capital; all the ministries were headquartered in the city. Every ministry released statutory advertisements. The consolidated billing of advertisements released by the government was sizeable. Besides, with Nehru's socialism, the government started floating companies in core sector industries that required large capital outlays. These companies also released statutory advertisements and the bureaucrats and ministers controlling them were based in Delhi. For many years after Independence, foreign-owned advertising agencies were not allowed to handle companies in the public sector or advertisements

[34] I hope critics who review this book will note the reasons why the history does not cover other cities. As mentioned earlier, I was roundly criticised by a number of eminent critics for writing a Calcutta-centric book with some coverage on Bombay. The book covering the earliest phase of Indian advertising featured Bombay, Calcutta and Madras simply because Indian advertising was confined wholly or mainly to these cities.

released by government departments. Nonetheless, Delhi was beginning to have a much greater impact on all business activities as Prasanta Sanyal observed in his historic speech on public relations that he delivered in the advertising congress.[35]

Full service ad agencies did not have a separate PR wing, but in the larger agencies such as JWT, Clarion, Ulka and Everest, to mention the big ones alone, with L.R. Swamy, a Madras-based agency, every account executive handling a national account had to undertake a number of jobs that were essentially PR-related. These jobs required the creative support of the agency; they were regular, not one-off exercises, earning good revenue for them.

If corporate PR is divided into 'Internal PR', covering target publics within the organisation and 'External PR', covering target publics outside the organisation, who yet exerted influence upon the functions of the organisation, the common things that were regularly prepared by the agency for PR included:

For internal PR:

1. House journal.
2. Bulletins for notice boards, which had a designed masthead and format.
3. Banners and other display items during internal functions.
4. Company stationery; letterheads, visiting cards, envelopes.
5. Developing a company house style, standardising use of the chosen corporate colour scheme.
6. Developing a roster of annual events shared by company employees in which the corporate logo was prominently displayed. For large manufacturing companies these events generally meant an annual play, annual sports, founder's day, Holi, Diwali and Christmas parties.

For external PR:

1. Annual report.
2. The annual general meeting, which was the most notable event—the hall was done up in corporate colours with banners announcing the occasion.
3. Corporate press campaigns.

[35]PR was then very much a part of an ad agency's repertoire of services. The specialised PR agency was still many years away from materialising in India. We shall of course include a few campaigns which are PR-oriented up to the late 1980s since PR and advertising were regarded as two sides of the same coin and many companies had a PR manager looking after advertising. Three of the top PR experts in the country at the time were heading advertising functions—Jolly Mohan Kaul, who wrote the first Indian textbook on PR, headed IOL's advertising department in the 1970s; Sanat Lahiri, the first Asian to be elected president of the International Public Relations Association, and was the advertising and PR manager of Dunlop; and Prasanta Sanyal, the managing director of Clarion in the 1970s.

Bal Mundkur

Anne Mukherjee

4. Press releases.
5. Exhibitions centred round the corporate story.
6. Tender notices, which were the most visible advertisements for public sector companies.
7. Appointment advertisements that, for private sector firms, had a preamble giving a brief history and the reasons why it was doing so well and why it was a much sought after company for promising candidates.
8. Dealer boards that normally made sufficient provision to feature the logo and symbol of the company—the dealer's name generally occupied a much smaller area. This was especially true for tyre dealers; cigarette and pan shops; outlets supplying fizzy drinks; and general provision stores.
9. Standardisation in use of mastheads and slogans for appointment advertisements and tender notice advertisements.

The big agencies were JWT, Bomas, Clarion, L.R. Swamy and Grant Advertising. But this decade saw exciting developments in a slack advertising market as a number of advertising professionals decided to leave their agencies and explore the uncertain prospect of starting on their own.

Bal Mundkur quit Bomas in 1961 to set up Ulka. His agency soon made a mark with a number of outstanding campaigns for clients such as Ceat tyres. Mundkur was uncompromising on quality. He was ably supported by his wife Anne who believed in seeing things for herself. She travelled extensively to see where Ceat hoardings had been displayed or followed up on research on comprehension of the ad message in a campaign to combat malaria.[36]

[36]The population of working women was quite small. Travel was not easy. Though overall the law and order situation was much better than now and nobody had heard of the 'War on Terror'. Perhaps the most difficult aspect of travel was lack of proper accommodation and toilets. For any lady travelling to remote locations it must have been very difficult. Even Indira Gandhi as prime minister devised makeshift toilets in different places she had to visit.

In 1963, Nargis Wadia left Lintas to set up Interpub. While there should be no gender bias, we should still note that this was the first agency started by a woman.[37] The decade of the sixties saw the setting up of many agencies that made their mark producing memorable campaigns. The total advertising spend in India at the time was very small. All India expenditure for press advertising was Rs 10 crore while the total expenditure on screening ad films was Rs 80 lakh.[38] Yet, new agencies were started and quite a few survived for a number of years. They must have made profits to keep going. Like Mundkur, people who set up ad agencies did not follow a frugal lifestyle. So the profits made in the business must have been good. Among the agency heads, Kersey Katrak, who lived like a prince, managed to destroy himself and his agency within a few years; but not before he blazed a trail, like a meteor disappearing after burning himself out.

Kersy Katrak

Kersy Katrak set up MCM in 1965 after a four-year stint with Lintas. MCM was unlike any other agency. Breaking the conventional mindset of not chasing accounts, Katrak respected no agency-client relationship and angled for every business he saw as worthwhile having. He began his foray with a memorable campaign for WIMCO—a match manufacturer—releasing a series of nine half-page ads in *The Times of India* on successive days. The colour black was predominant, which dramatised the action of hands striking matches to light various things such as a candle, a diya and so on. This was unheard-of at the time and the campaign won the first ad club award of the Bombay Advertising Club.

Katrak was the typical flamboyant advertising man who spent fabulous sums on partying. Soon prospective clients lined up to be invited to his parties. He forgot that MCM had to be managed within the 15 per cent of its earnings. Kersey and MCM were responsible for creating a false aura of glamour surrounding the advertising profession, which persists till this day because advertising professionals after him have continued to stoke this image.[39]

[37]In an article, again published by *Brand Equity*, dated 18 February 2009, Vikram Doctor mentions: 'Interpub was the first agency run by a woman and which employed a lot of women and it was an instant hit.'
[38]These were the figures quoted by Irshad Farooqui, media and research controller of Lintas, in the speech he delivered in the first Indian convention on advertising in 1961.
[39]Source: Vikram Doctor's article in *Brand Equity* dated 9 January 2008, 'Remembering Kersy Katrak'.

In 1966, Ayaz Peerbhoy set up MAA after leaving Everest. Another advertising great of yesteryears, Sylvester daCunha, quit Stronach's and joined ASP, a Birla agency, which he headed till 1969. He started his own agency subsequently as he felt stifled at ASP.

Sylvester daCunha[40]

Sylvester daCunha strolled into advertising not in India but in London. This was in 1951; he was 21 years old. India had won her Independence just four years ago; the Second World War had ended six years before. A lot of young men were going to Britain at the time, especially fresh medical and engineering graduates who helped rebuild Britain's war-ravaged economy and society.

daCunha got a job in the London office of a Bombay-headquartered agency, which then was among the largest in India. It was called L.A. Stronach. Stronach was a pucca sahib, but as Subhas Ghosal mentioned once, he was a tight-fisted person who paid his people poorly.

As daCunha recollected in an interview, 'I told them I knew nothing about advertising. And they said that was fine. I just had to know about India.' He worked in London for three years, picking up first hand his knowledge of advertising. But unlike most other Indians who arrived in England to settle down, daCunha did not like being treated like a second-class citizen. He returned to India.

On his return he could not find a place in any of the foreign-owned agencies. It was certainly possible that the people he met were scared of his British training and perceived him as a threat. However, on the ship back to India he met John Kurrien who was then the manager of ASP. He offered daCunha a job in an agency that was dowdy compared to most other Indian agencies.

daCunha's return to India was one good thing that happened in Indian advertising. His association with ASP improved the image of the company. The Life Insurance Corporation (LIC) came on board and ASP designed its logo and daCunha remained with ASP for a long time. When he changed, it was because the agency refused to move with the times. He began his third innings with the setting up of daCunha Associates.

In 1967, daCunha bagged the Amul account and, along with Bharat Dabholkar, gave an identity to this brand. 'Amul butter' became a brand, which later was worth one billion dollars. The campaign was always topical and little money was spent compared to the results obtained through its

[40]I spell his name the way I see it spelt by *The Economic Times* dated 3 October 2007.

The Amul girl

presence in outdoor media. The Amul girl featured in all the ads, as did the memorable line, 'Utterly butterly delicious Amul'. Like the Air India ads, the Amul ads were topical, tongue-in-cheek, but unlike Air India, the Amul ads were never cheeky. They had a friendly tone in whatever they said. The Amul ads were destined to run longer than the Air India ones where the only thing that was partially retained or partially resurrected was the maharaja, after the disastrous nationalisation of the airline.

daCunha is also remembered for his writings on advertising. In the 1980s, under the pseudonym Esdee, he published a popular column in *The Economic Times*. In an age when advertising meant all the services that a full service agency was expected to provide to a client, his essays covered all aspects pertaining to the profession—creative, including copy and art, research and marketing-related subjects that were allied to or derived from advertising. In recent issues *The Economic Times* has been publishing some of these writings of the 1980s as a column.[41]

Something old, something new

Marketers frequently ignore one of the most fundamental laws in marketing

> A new brand must be seen to possess some features superior to the brand leader. Me-toos, and there have been dozens recently, come a cropper precisely for ignoring this commandment.
>
> We have recently seen the introduction of some soft drink brands which could not claim perceivable superiority over the existing leader. They foundered. Taste-alike toothpastes have tried to challenge Colgate on its own ground and failed. Twin butters attempted to dislodge Amul without success. Copy-cat shampoos have been badly bitten when confronting Halo and Sunsilk.
>
> The rule book tells us that a new brand must offer some new and attractive feature that the leader does not possess. Promise toothpaste held up a clove and took a slice off Colgate. Clinic shampoo claimed a unique ingredient to fight dandruff.
>
> Two new products recently announced deserve mention for having the good sense not to follow the leader. Hot Shot is a new camera that positions itself for the beginner. Apparently its makers have gauged that 'what people don't like are the complicated instructions they associate with photography. The mumbo-jumbo that photographers use'.
>
> The Hot Shot is a boon to all of us who are grannies at heart when it comes to handling photographic equipment. This particular apparatus does the trick without fuss—just press a button, they say. 'There's no complicated loading and unloading. No focussing. No setting exposures. No readings. No timings.'

[41] *The Economic Times* dated 18 November 2009 re-printed the article titled 'Something old, something new'. Readers will understand how well he wrote and how informative his articles were.

Rooster Mosquito Coil has decided to tilt with the brand leader. The new coil claims to handle easier, not break easily (suggesting its established competitor does) and not to exude heavy smoke (implying number one fills up the room). This is a worthy example of how to introduce a new brand in a product category already controlled by others. More often than not credit for second generation successes must go to the R&D department of the new entrant. Alas, one sees such few instances of innovative thinking in new product launches. Marketers erroneously expect that heavy advertising and sales effort will compensate for lack of new product ideas. That is not the way it works, as a trail of long deceased brands will attest.

Food for thought

The ads around us portray Bombay as the city-state of gluttons. A large proportion of messages are aimed at the 'inner man'. First come the parade of restaurants—Outrigger, Samarkhand, Rangoli, Supper Club, Sampan, TukTuks, Chin-Kai, Centaur Pool, Village, Café Royal, Delhi Darbar, Kabab Korner …

Then the kitchen aids—Sunflame grill, Rotomat oven, Navjyoti, Nutan stove, Hawkins and Prestige pressure cookers, Rico and Sumeet mixers ... And the new foods and drinks—Bakeman biscuits, Samant and Sneha butters, MacDowell soda, Rush orangeade … Now and then food stands out for marketing attention. Gits is a new instant mix that reduces fatiguing run-up to dosas, vadas, uttapams and so on. It is winning a lot of friends because the end results match homemade varieties.

Labour saving culinary products confront the housewife with a subtle dilemma. If the product totally eliminates her participation (like pre-cooked TV meals), she will feel guilty of abandoning her role as a home provider. This is what happened in the USA, when instant cake-mix was introduced in the fifties. It failed to win acceptance until the brand Sara-Lee presented a cake-mix that required the housewife to break a raw egg into it before setting it in the oven.

Vance Packard in his Hidden Persuaders narrates the experience of Jell-O. The psychological barriers that this brand encountered with the US housewife of the forties may not apply to her contemporary lib-minded sister. But it does have lessons to draw for her Indian equivalent today.

Where guilt feelings on a large scale presented a challenge to marketers was with the easy-does-it, step-saving products devised for the modern housewife. The wives, instead of being grateful for these wonderful boons, reacted in many cases by viewing them as threat to their feelings of creativeness and usefulness. Working wives (numbering about 10,00,000) could welcome these shortcut products, such as appliances, but regular housewives, in large numbers, showed unexpected resistance.

The 'creative' research director of an ad agency sadly summed up the situation in these words: 'If you tell the housewife that by using your washing machine, drier, or dishwasher she can be free to play bridge, you are dead! The housewife today, to a certain extent, is disenfranchised; she is already feeling guilty about the fact that she is not working as hard as her mother. You are just rubbing her the wrong way when you offer her more freedom. Instead you should emphasise that the appliances free her to have more time with her children and to be a better mother.'

Our small fears and anxieties like our guilt feelings, offered many openings for the depth manipulators to map successful campaigns for enterprising merchandisers. It was found, for example, that some products repelled us in a small but measurable way because they filled us with a mild uneasiness. The trouble that befell Jell-O is an example. Over the years Jell-O was a familiar sight in millions of households because it was established in the public mind as a simple, easy-to-make, shirt-sleeve type of dessert. Then in the early fifties its mentors, ambitious for it to look nice in ads, began showing it in beautiful, layered, multicolour creations with elaborate decorative touches. The ads were spectacular but did not produce the expected sales. Jell-O was in trouble without knowing why. Dr Ernest Dichter was asked to depth probe the situation; his investigators, in talking at length with wives, soon pin-pointed the trouble. The wives felt a vague sense of inferiority when they saw the beautiful creations advertised. They wondered if they would fail if they tried to duplicate it and they vaguely resented the idea of someone watching over their shoulders and saying, 'It's got to look like this.' So, many started saying to themselves when they see a Jell-O ad, 'Well if I've got to take all that trouble I might as well make my own dessert.'

After Dr Dichter made his diagnosis, Jell-O went back to being a simple, relaxed, shirt-sleeve dessert without fancy trimmings. In 1956, for example, it was typically shown in a simple, one-colour mound, amusing fairytale drawings, that created widespread comment and admiration for the dessert.

In a study published in 1976, the sixties stand out as the decade with the largest number of new ad agencies:[42]

PERIOD-WISE ESTABLISHMENT OF REPORTING AD AGENCIES

Period	No. of Agencies
1920s	3
1930s	1
1940s	6
1950s	4
1960s	14
1970s	1

Another interesting point that this research study throws up is the decline of Calcutta as a major centre of advertising and the fact that Delhi was going neck and neck with the advertising capital of India—Bombay—in terms of the locations of the head offices of major agencies. As far as the volume of business was concerned, Delhi was placed third after Bombay and Madras, but the difference between Delhi and Madras was marginal.

DISTRIBUTION OF LOCATION OF REPORTING AGENCIES' HQS

Place	No of Agencies having HQs
Bombay	12
Delhi	11
Madras	6
Calcutta	3
Ahmedabad	1

[42]*Advertising in India-selected Research Studies.* Edited by Singh D.R., R.K. Tandon, K.M. Upadhyay and N.K. Das. Department of Business Management, Punjab Agricultural University, Ludhiana, 1976. The observation following the table reproduced above goes: 'There could be several reasons for this large growth in the 1960s. One of these could be that increased industrial and business activities, as a result of various development plans, resulted in increased demand for advertising activities. Further, the appreciation of the role of mass communication techniques was growing in the government sector as well.'

VOLUME OF BUSINESS AT VARIOUS CENTRES OF REPORTING AD AGENCIES

Location	Volume of Business (in lakhs)
Bombay	1,702.50
Madras	325.47
Delhi	315.50
Calcutta	108.75
Ahmedabad	15.33

The report clearly states that Bombay had twice the number of head offices of agencies compared to Delhi, while Madras and Calcutta do not come anywhere close. Obviously Bombay was the centre of the advertising business in India.[43]

The Punjab University study also classified agencies by billing. This classification seems to be quite similar to the one made by Subhas Ghosal in the speech he delivered in the 1960s in the first Indian advertising congress in Calcutta.

Category	Number of Agencies
Small (billing Rs 0-49 lakh)	18 (65 per cent)
Medium (billing Rs 50-99 lakh)	3 (11 per cent)
Large (billing Rs 100 lakh and above)	7 (25 per cent)

This is a sad reflection on the state of the Indian economy, which for a long time had stopped growing appreciably. Advertising business, which is dependent on other business for growth, slowed down. The government was suspicious of the word 'profit' without which no business may prosper and the advertising business remained static. The Hindu rate of growth was what every kind of business had to be content with and there was no incentive to manage a business profitably. Despite the gloomy business climate, a new generation of professionals began coming into advertising with diplomas from business schools.

[43]To quote the study: 'This scrutiny clearly showed that Bombay (with head offices of as many as 69 agencies) was way ahead of Delhi (with head offices of 31 agencies). Thus, Bombay with practically double the number of head offices as compared with Delhi can definitely be considered to be the main centre of ad agency business. On a further scrutiny, we found that Calcutta and Madras with 11 and 8 head offices, respectively, still lagged behind Bombay and Delhi as far as concentration of ad agencies business was concerned.' *(Advertising In India—Selected Research Studies.* 1976. From the collection at the National Library, Kolkata.*)*

The full service agency

From the early 1950s most advertisers spending large sums in media desired their agencies to provide *full service*—creative, media, public relations and event management. When an agency appointed a vendor to undertake a project such as an exhibition or film production, the client played a passive role in the selection of the most suitable vendor. The agency designed the exhibition pavilion and made a storyboard for the film to be produced.

An advertisement released by Blaze, the only exhibitor of ad films, shows that there was no increase in the number of cinemas in India compared to the early 1960s.

In his speech at the first Indian advertising congress in Calcutta, Irshad Farooqui, who at the time was the media and research controller of Lintas, mentioned that there were 4,000-odd cinemas distributed over 2,000 towns and that 80 per cent were concentrated in towns with a population of less than one lakh and over 50 per cent of the total were in towns with a population of less than 50,000.

Blaze had a monopoly on film exhibition in India. It aggressively fought off competition, burning down offices of another organisation that dared to offer an alternative to advertisers. It actually covered far less than the total universe of 4,000 theatres and did not pay the hall owners on time. After many months, when Blaze paid the hall owner, it generally paid short and hence old disputes were never settled. Hall owners often did not screen ad films because they had not been paid for past screening. Blaze generally offered a discount to advertisers for non-screening and was raking in the bucks because of its monopoly at the cost of agencies and their clients. The situation came to such a pass that a consortium of leading agencies decided to form a separate body to ensure better screening of films by the theatres; that too failed to break Blaze's control on cinema. It was only after Doordarshan began accepting ads that the inevitable happened and Blaze lost much of its hold upon advertisers.

Social historians may research the reasons for the number of theatres in India not going up substantially over a period of 15 years between 1961 and 1976, when the Blaze ad was released in *Admissive*, the journal printed by the Advertising Club of Calcutta. Not only were Hindi films very popular, but so was regional cinema in the states of Andhra Pradesh, Madras (now Tamil Nadu), Kerala and West Bengal. Vividh Bharati popularised Hindi film songs all over the country.

Hall owners made good money and cinema halls ran to full houses quite frequently in an environment that was socially dull with few options of entertainment. For media planners, film remained a second choice after newspaper ads possibly because (a) reach through cinema was limited (b) the high initial cost of film production and (c) the uncertainty of maintaining a planned screening schedule.[44] Film production was expensive. The government kept a tight control on raw stock, which was imported.

Research, selling and overkill in advertising

Advertising research was beginning to make an appearance in India. The country did not have sufficient media reach across the entire subcontinent. But in the five metros and other large suburban centres the top layers among the socio-economic classes (though small) were wooed by competing brands in the FMCG categories. Though competition in consumer durables was limited, except for ceiling and table fans, marketers of consumer durables still sought media space and time to address consumers.

[44]In 1961, Irshad Farooqui mentioned in his speech in the advertising congress, 'The total gross turnover on film advertising is estimated to be in the vicinity of Rs 80 lakh as against the press turnover, which is estimated between Rs 7 and 10 crore … At the moment, a meagre sum of Rs 80 lakh distributed among 4,000 cinemas is not sufficient inducement to the industry and, therefore, their attitude to film advertising has remained casual.'

In the advertising congress in Calcutta in 1961, Edward J. Fielden, who was heading JWT, chose 'Market research in advertising' for the subject of his speech.[45] He dealt more closely on research in advertising, such as the usefulness of conducting copy tests, than on consumer research. The fact is, money was being spent on research. The leading agencies, namely, JWT and somewhat later, Clarion, not only began their research wings, which operated as separate entities, somewhat later as independent companies, the agencies spent what may be regarded as small fortunes on primary research, considering that total advertising billing did not amount to more than Rs 10 crore per annum for the whole country.

Research initiated by the agencies helped professionalise media planning. Media planners found the census reports, published by the government in every decade, a useful tool in their planning process. ABC provided circulation figures of member publications and media experts hazarded knowledgeable guesses in determining gross and net readership of individual newspapers in specific geographic zones.

Advertising around the world

In western countries, advertising was beginning to be regarded as too intrusive. Agencies, on their part, were concerned about getting their advertisement noticed since media space was crowded with too many ads. Clients spent larger sums on marketing research to understand whether their advertising budget was being spent intelligently. Agencies earned their commission and more from research agencies; these studies were generally mentioned to show the client that the agency was correct in its creative approach; if the campaign failed it must have been for reasons other than advertising.

Advertising professionals were coming round to the opinion that in order to be effective, a campaign had to be engaging; to be 'fun'; that a direct sales pitch was not enough. In the USA, media space was far more crowded than in Europe because the USA was already the leading world economy and there were numerous brands fighting to carve out their separate space in the consumer psyche in order to survive.

By the late sixties and early seventies, many sociologists and church officials were expressing their concern on the glut of advertisements in every waking medium. Children, it was feared, were being targeted by

[45]He mentioned in his speech, 'The market research man in advertising is also expected to keep abreast of the changing trends in the economic affairs of the country. He must know the meanings, uses and limitations of data, and be able to interpret them in relation to individual business.'

unscrupulous marketers.[46] In India cigarettes comprised a very rich source of advertising revenue for all media—press, film and outdoor—and ad agencies considered themselves fortunate if they bagged a cigarette account. In the USA, questions were being asked as early as the 1950s on whether cigarette smoking was injurious to health. Despite a powerful pro-cigarette lobby working behind the scenes and influencing senators to stymie studies connecting smoking to ill health, particularly cancer and heart disease, slowly but surely legislation was on the way that would impact the marketing of cigarettes significantly.[47]

Around this time some of the most powerful cigarette brands were being built in India. Among them perhaps the most memorable was Wills filter (of ITC) with the slogan, 'Made for each other', always depicting a modern young and up-market couple with the slogan, '*Filter and tobacco perfectly matched*'. It proved such a success that various stalwarts in ITC and its agency HTA (now JWT) claimed credit for the line.[48] The company thought it fit to institute a yearly contest to select a *Made for each other couple* in every metro city. Newspapers covered these events and the couples selected were sent to an all-expenses paid holiday. In a way we could call the 'Made for each other' annual event one of the first event management exercises in marketing. Today, when marketing whiz kids and their professors talk about 360 degree connect with the consumer they may have more media in mind, such as digital and social media, but they tread the same worn path of Wills filter in the sixties.

---

[46]Ron Goulart in *The Assault on Childhood* (Victor Gollancz Ltd, London, 1960) writes, 'Kids are spending more time with the kid business advertisers than they are with us, they get more education from them than they get from school. Though cigarettes are not supposed to be a children's product, a considerable amount of cigarette advertising is still aired during prime hours of child viewing. Complete with cowboys. The whole tobacco industry spent $1,94,079,300 on television advertising in 1966, and our kids saw most of it.'

[47]Arthur Kroeger, Francisco M. Nicosia and Charles J. Dirksen in 'Advertising Principles, Problems and Cases' (published by Richard D. Irwin Inc. Homewood, Illinois, 1960) cover the subject admirably. They note: 'As far as cigarettes were concerned few significant changes occurred up until the 1950s ... The state of affairs changed in the early years of the 1950s as medical researchers began to correlate a relationship between smoking and health. These reports dramatically changed the working environment or conditions of the industry, constituting a threat to the successful merchandising of the products ... An important development in this context was the appointment of 10 scientists in 1962 to a committee on tobacco and health by the US surgeon general. The above report (published in January 1964) was followed by studies by Congress, the Federal Trade Commission and the Federal Communications Commission. As a result of these studies, such requirements as placing a warning on cigarette packages (1966 and 1970), the permission to include contents of tar and nicotine in advertising (1966) and the banning of cigarette commercials on TV (1970) were adopted. Moreover, a rule was issued in 1967 that TV channels broadcasting advertising for cigarettes had to give free time for anti-smoking messages.'

[48]A.N. Haksar, who was chairman of the board of directors, in his autobiographical tome *Bite the Bullet* said it was his line. He repeated the same thing when I met him in his Delhi residence in the mid-1990s to present a copy of my book *ITC versus BAT: A Case in Indian Corporate PR* (Wheeler Publishing, Delhi).

Let us look at press ads of 1960s vintage:

JWT was the biggest agency in the country in capitalised billing. A sample of ads from the JWT archives will indicate the standard of advertising in India and also present some national brands.

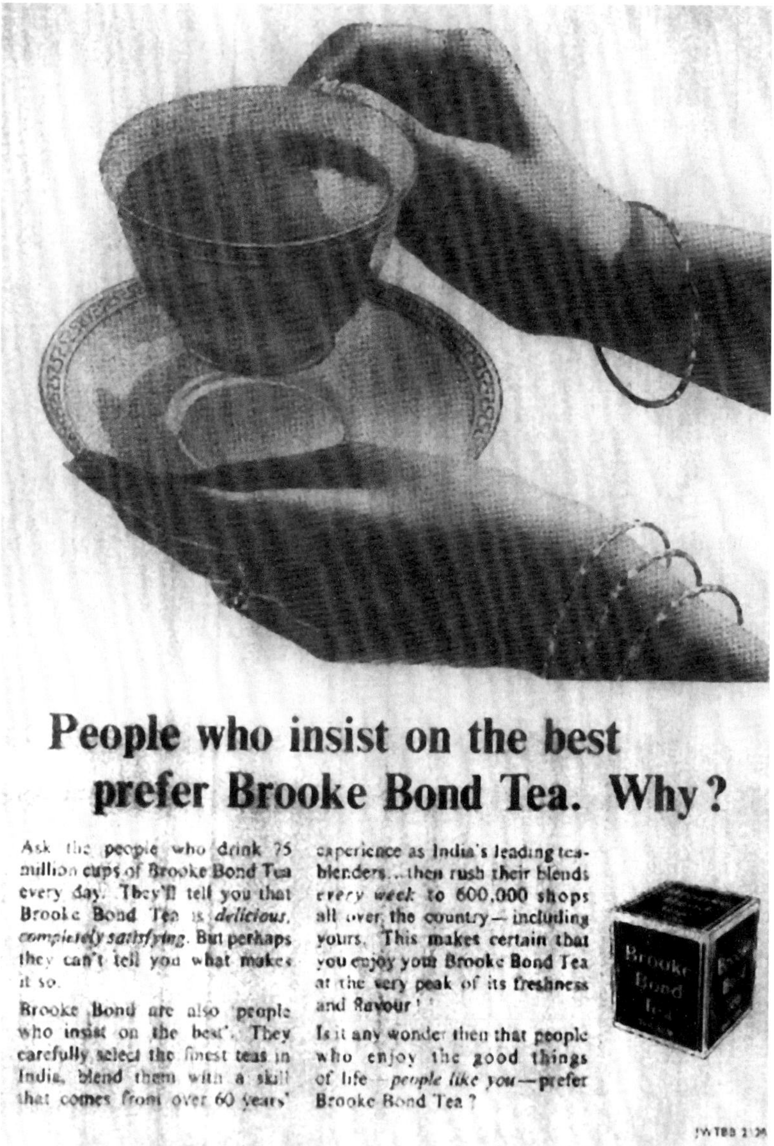

Brooke Bond was a Calcutta-based account; one of the blue-chip clients of JWT. Most tea companies were Calcutta-based. Clarion handled Lipton.

A simple ad that uses the Air India symbol beautifully—the list of places Air India flies to from Bombay establishes a worldwide network.

This was a notable piece of promotional item developed by the great modern painter Salvador Dali for Air India. I am not sure whether approaching Dali was inspired by JWT. A limited number of ash trays were made. The lucky few who received one have handed down priceless property to their children.

JWT ads were neat in their execution. Since black and white ads were in a majority as colour options were far fewer than now and more expensive, art directors were proficient in making the best use of the poor quality of paper on which their ads were finally printed.

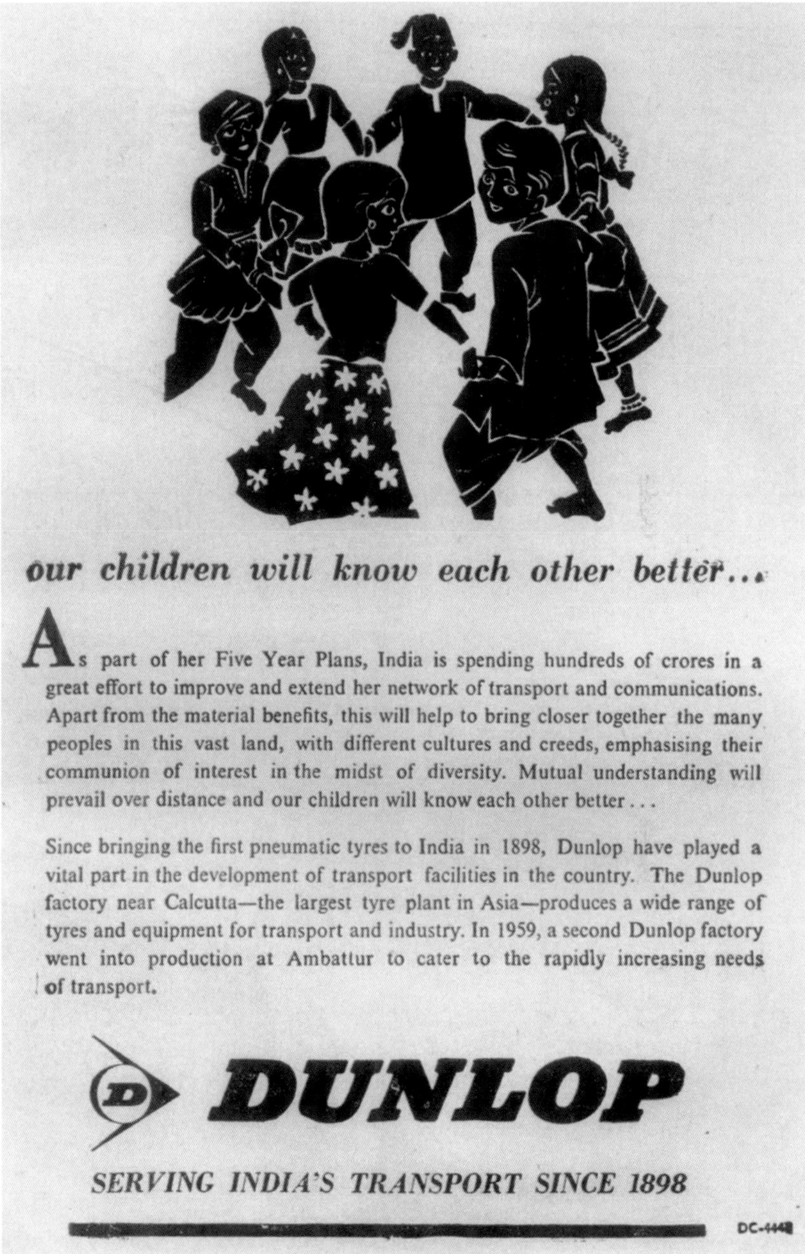

A Dunlop corporate advertisement reproduced from an old Dunlop Gazette *demonstrates the skill of the copywriter as he wrote long copy. Although the subject—national goals—was flogged by every company, the ads had to link the respective businesses with these national goals. Not all companies had a strong platform on which they could mount their stories.*

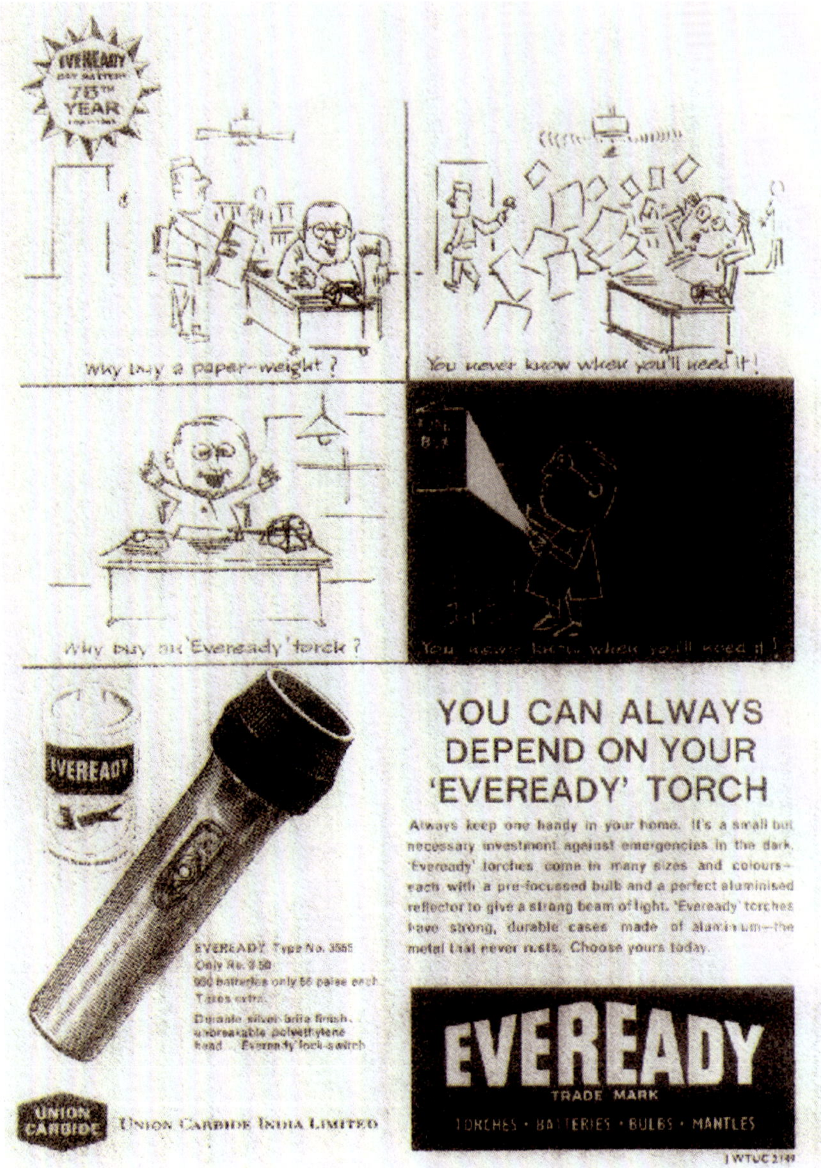

JWT had most of the so-called blue-chip accounts. All its offices were well-staffed and the agency employed the best art directors, copywriters and account executives. It also trained copywriters and account directors after a fashion since there were no vocational training centres for advertising.

Another brilliant tongue-in-cheek advertisement for Air India. The creative combines Hindi (probably because of the language movement that rocked India through the fifties and sixties) with English.

The range and flair of JWT campaigns can be seen from these ads. Just as O&M is the flavour of the season today, seeing advertisers flocking to it with business, it was JWT that remained the top-notch agency for a span of 50 years after Independence. The copy is in telegraphic mode. An unusual ad for the times! A copywriter in 2013 would probably write such copy.

How many airlines did JWT handle? I have seen a TWA ad with the JWT key number. It is surprising that Air India allowed JWT to handle rival airlines. In the genteel years of advertising prior to the rough and tumble of the post-1990 economic liberalisation, when agencies expressed reservation about handling competing accounts, JWT faced no problem.

The print advertisements of the twenty-first century should be studied in comparison with the ads now seen in magazines and newspapers. Very often we are left wondering how is it that with the passage of 30 or 40 or even 50 years there is hardly any difference in the techniques and styles of print advertising between then and now. Perhaps copywriters write less today. With television becoming the main medium, copywriters learnt the art of writing differently for television.

MCM

MCM was both a blessing and a curse in the history of Indian advertising. We have already covered Kersey Katrak elsewhere in the book; the ads shown here demonstrate the raw power of MCM campaigns. Some of the most famous names in Indian advertising spent their early years in MCM.

Ajit Balakrishnan and Arun Nanda who set up Rediffusion; Ravi Gupta who started Trikaya; Mohammad Khan, Panna Jain, Arun Kale, Arun Kolatkar, Kiran Nagarkar, Anil Kapoor, Sudarshan Dheer and Veeru Hiremath cut their teeth on advertising at MCM. While some of them started their own agencies they created very different styles. But perhaps the underlying unity of all these campaigns was in thinking big, in terms of dominating the memory space of the target audience (a) visually by engaging the reader's attention with eye-catching visuals and bold messages and (b) spatially by releasing large advertisements.

The larger established agencies tried to figure out whether MCM was a menace to the whole industry. I do not know what Subhas Ghosal's opinion might have been, but he was known to be a person who detected creative flair earlier than most of his contemporaries. I broached the subject once with the late Subrata Sengupta of Clarion who said in his caustic understated way, 'Well, MCM was a flash in the pan'. I read Mani Ayer's views on MCM, he was highly critical. I detect professional jealousy in most of this criticism.

3

1970–1980

Growth

The political and economic events that defined the decade of the seventies began evolving from the mid-1960s. The most significant event that was to shape the history of independent India was the break-up of the old Congress Party. The process started in 1967 and ended in 1969 when Indira Gandhi, who was the prime minister and the leader of the party in Parliament, was expelled from the party by Congress President Nijalingappa. She successfully gathered support among Members of Parliament and defied him. This set in motion a number of events. Indira Gandhi's government announced a slew of populist programmes. The declared objective was 'garibi hatao'; but the real purpose was to neutralise party mandarins who wished to exercise control over the prime minister. Banks were nationalised as were other important core sector industries.

Developments in neighbouring Pakistan led to the Indo-Pak war of the early seventies. On 17 December 1971, Bangladesh became an independent nation after the Indian army routed the Pakistani army in what till then was East Pakistan. This victory renewed national pride among Indian citizens, which was badly bruised after the Indo-China conflict in the early sixties. But the country continued to face the harsh reality of grinding poverty compounded by a lack of economic growth. In the decade of the seventies, two Five Year Plans were implemented. The Fourth Plan, from 1969 to 1974, had the twin objectives of growth and self-reliance. During this plan period, expenditure on family planning was raised to Rs 278 crore from Rs 25 crore in the Third Plan.

For advertising, family planning became an important and visible part of campaigns in press, radio and cinema. In terms of reach the government endeavoured to cover the whole of India, towns and villages, and hence campaigns ran in all Indian languages. A consortium of leading ad agencies was roped in to improve upon the delivery of the campaign. In the ultimate analysis, the Fourth Plan ended without achieving targeted growth. National income rose by only 3.3 per cent against the target set of 5.5 per cent, while increase in the production of food grains was marginal, at only 2.7 per cent, where the increase was discernible more in the production of wheat than rice with pulses, oil seeds, cotton and jute not registering any growth.[1]

The Fifth Five Year Plan (1974–1979) set its basic objective as the eradication of poverty; it was also felt that a decrease in the rate of growth of the population was an important corollary. The average growth rate during the Fifth Plan period was only 3.9 per cent, against a revised target set of 4.4 per cent. India was getting used to what was derisively called the Hindu rate of growth. In the meanwhile India's neighbours in South-east Asia were beginning to prosper. The prosperity of these nations was compared to the lack of progress in India. The Fifth Plan period was different from all other Five Year Plans that preceded it because it was implemented at a time of great political turmoil.

India's Five Year Plans are a reflection of the immediate and medium-term political compulsions of the ruling party in New Delhi. These plans are an offshoot of social anomalies. Grandiose plans have generally remained plans on paper because they were unrealistic. Five Year Plans, except for the First Plan, were never meant to deliver what they set out to do. The entire exercise was an eyewash. It is now perhaps too late to ask those entrusted with this important function how they could be blind to the problems faced by the common man. Did they never ask their wives? (Presuming they were married and male.)

Since India's Independence, this was the first plan period that had a non-Congress government at the Centre under a diehard Congressman, Morarji Desai, who despite his many years in politics was extraordinarily pig-headed. The Janata Party government at the Centre was destined to go down with its bandwagon of political heavyweights led by a humourless moralist who only knew that he was always right. For the first time a plan period was reduced by a year. Thus the Fifth Plan period was from 1974 to 1979.

Advertising in any era reflects the general socio-economic condition of people living at the time; their hopes and aspirations. Lifestyle is reflected through visuals and words; in press, in film or over TV shows. Film and TV are especially powerful determinants of lifestyle aspirations in India because these media influence lives so directly.

The decade of the seventies was not merely a continuation of the period that went before it in terms of products available or brands sold; advertising of the seventies reflects the great social disruption that happened with the promulgation of Emergency late on that fateful evening of 25 June 1975.

[1] A student of history looking at the various Five Year Plans will see how the core objectives changed between plans and where every Five Year Plan, except the First Five Year Plan, never met the basic objectives set.

Newspapers and magazines lost their freedom to present news the way they wanted. Leaders of all Opposition parties were imprisoned. Companies—starting with public sector units—began printing corporate advertisements in newspapers which were undistinguished in their limitless praise of Indira Gandhi and her government.

However, it must be said in favour of the Emergency that for the first time irresponsible trade unionism, which had spread like a cancer through industry, was checked. For the first time also the performance of all public sector units, especially the Indian Railways, improved remarkably. Even government officials were forced to attend office on time. Trains, surprisingly, reached their destinations as scheduled.

However, the concentration of power in a single person inevitably led to social excesses such as Indian society had never experienced after Independence. Her younger son Sanjay became the vortex of power within her government. He was young, intemperate and impatient. He began a population control programme which set targets for the bureaucrats. They merrily went about fulfilling these targets through forced vasectomies of the indigent. Very soon the high-handedness of Indira Gandhi's rule led to social dissent. Her party was thrown out of power in the general elections and she was sent to prison for a short time by her opponents. They wanted her to face the treatment meted out to so many leaders of the Opposition during the Emergency.

The volume of advertising went up substantially between the start and end of the decade. Gross billing rose from Rs 650 million in 1971 to Rs 1,600 million in 1978.[2]

---

[2]Chunawalla, S.A. and K.C. Sethia. *Foundations of Advertising Theory & Practice*. Himalaya Publishing House, 1985. Authors note: 'In India, the advertising industry has seen phenomenal growth, increasing in its outlay in less than a decade from Rs 650 million in 1971 to Rs 1,600 million in 1978. The gross billing of advertising in the press alone has risen in India in less than a quarter of a century from Rs 70 million in 1954 to Rs 985 million in 1978 (p. 1).'

In the seventies, HTA was the largest agency in Indian advertising. It had a dominant presence in all the metro cities; the branch offices were fully staffed and equipped to provide the facilities expected of a full service agency. HTA showcased the biggest brand names in business and its key numbers generally denoted a high level of creative output. However, there were changes in the management structure of HTA. With the Indian government's deep distrust of the West, especially the USA, expatriate managers probably found themselves unwanted. Subhas Ghosal who, despite his brilliance, had to wait in the wings for a long time even after Peter Fielden stepped down in 1966 was finally invited to become the chief executive in 1975.

E.J. (Peter) Fielden

Peter Fielden joined JWT India after a stint in the Middle East. In a way he built up JWT to being the premier ad agency in India. He is credited with creating the basic infrastructure for advertising in all the metros where the agency had its offices. He advocated research. He also began a process of training executives in his agency.

Alyque Padamsee, who began his career in advertising in JWT, reminiscing about Fielden said he believed in the policy of divide and rule within his agency, setting up one executive against another. In a biographical sketch on Fielden in an HTA in-house journal, he is credited with most of the collateral developments in advertising, which is an encomium that should be carefully balanced. After all, Indian advertising developed because of the contribution of a large number of professionals.

Being managing director of India's biggest agency, he certainly wielded clout within the profession. When he handed over his regency of HTA in 1966, India had become socialist leaning; he may not have enjoyed the same success that he had with members of the British-Indian government prior to Independence.

Fielden's tenure as MD lasted 35 years. Greg Bathon, John Gaynor and Morris Mathias completed their turns as managing director before Ghosal began his long spell. He became chief executive in 1975 and retired in 1985, handing over the reins to Mike Khanna, his handpicked successor. From

1985 till his death in 1998, he set up HTA's second agency, Contract and managed it so well that it became one of the top 10 agencies in the country.[3] From the year he started as an apprentice in 1945, his advertising career spanned 53 uninterrupted years.

In the seventies, the agency business was changing. Indian agencies were now managed entirely by Indians; they did not do a bad job despite the disincentives. Blue-chip companies such as ITC, Bata, ICI, Shaw Wallace, GKW, Metal Box, India Foils, McNeil & Barry, Andrew Yule and Balmer Lawrie found it expedient to induct Indians at the board level. HTA, like ITC, gradually loosened the controls of its foreign promoters although these companies acknowledged their nominal affiliation to the mother unit, which in the case of HTA was JWT in New York, while for ITC it was BAT in London. That both HTA and ITC successfully managed to operate as independent companies was due entirely to the capability of the two men who headed these companies—Subhas Ghosal in HTA and Ajit Haksar in ITC. Both were trusted by their international associates and encouraged to operate as they thought fit in a challenging business environment.

Although HTA was a dominant force in advertising in the seventies and eighties, it did not actively pursue the business of large Indian companies, as some other prominent agencies were doing. Big Indian companies assigned their diverse businesses often to in-house agencies or felt more comfortable interacting with medium or smaller ad agencies. The Birlas had more than one agency in its collective fold, which included ASP, one of the leading agencies nationally and Communication Consultants (commonly called CC); the Sarabhai Group went to its own in-house set-up, Pratibha. HLL had Lintas as a captive agency. By now Lintas was looking around to add to its roster of clients so that it received due recognition as a large professional agency on a par with the best in the country.

Dunlop, which dominated the tyre market, divided its brands between HTA and Clarion, giving its extensive range of industrial products (that did not see a lot of advertising activity) to OBM. The Tata Group, which, like the Birlas, dominated manufacturing in the private sector supported many agencies including HTA, Ulka and Clarion. Getting into the agency business did not require a great deal of capital; there was room for anyone with talent and entrepreneurial flair. For the advertising business Bombay and Delhi were especially promising. While Bombay was the home of most large groups, Delhi was closing the gap with Bombay as entrepreneurs increasingly shifted base to the capital from all over India. Calcutta lost ground.

[3] *Solus* (a publication of the Advertising Club of Bombay), Vol. 35, Nos. 6 and 7, June–July 1998.

In an interesting article titled 'India' published in the *International Handbook of Advertising* in 1964, Subrata Banerjee, who was associated with the formation of Clarion, analysed the overall market and advertising dynamics in India in the early sixties.[4] His brief clear presentation of markets and advertising gives a wonderful perspective.

- According to the census of 1961, the number of cities and towns had doubled compared to the previous census of 1951. *(Is urbanisation a definite indicator of progress? Perhaps not in the Indian context.)*
- Clarion had published *Market Rating Indices for Towns,* one of the early attempts at combining research with advertising. In this study, which was based on the 1961 census, only 108 towns were covered with a population of 1,00,000 and above. The top 10 towns in order of merit *(which probably implies purchasing power)* were:
  1) Greater Calcutta 2) Greater Bombay 3) Delhi 4) Madras 5) Hyderabad 6) Ahmedabad 7) Kanpur 8) Bangalore 9) Poona and 10) Nagpur.
  Banerjee made a tabular summary with respect to Class 1 cities (numbering 108), which together had a population of 36 million people.

Group	Clarion Index of Market Fertility	Number of Cities	Percentage of Population	Percentage of Market
A	50 and above	4	30.9	43.3
B	10 to 50	10	21.9	17.4
C	5 to 10	21	18.3	15.5
D	Below 5	73	28.9	23.8
Total		108	100	100

With purchasing power being so city-centric, it was not surprising that in the absence of radio and television as advertising media, advertisers and agencies had to depend mainly on newspapers.[5] Banerjee also observes that major media have trade associations. Newspapers had their association in IENS; the printers who did a commendable job in printing leaflets and

[4]Subrata Banerjee is credited with having suggested the name 'Clarion'. He was a copywriter. But he left the agency after a short while. I met him a few weeks before his death in 2002, if my memory serves, and even then he felt bitter about his parting of ways with Clarion.

[5]Banerjee comments, 'According to Report No. 2 of the National Sample Survey of the government, the distribution of purchasing power gradually improves from the rural areas through the small, medium-sized and larger towns to the four largest cities, Calcutta, Delhi, Bombay and Madras. In the rural areas, 55.6 per cent of the population is below the expenditure level of Rs 15 per head per month, and in the urban areas 37.5 per cent. Only 3.6 per cent of the rural population is above the level of Rs 43 per head per month and no more than 11.4 per cent in urban areas. In the major cities 13 per cent is below the Rs 15 level, and 35.7 per cent is above the Rs 43 level.'

posters, danglers and diaries had their own Federation of Master Printers.[6] However, there was nobody representing hoarding contractors.[7] Ad agencies and advertisers had their own associations in the Advertising Agencies' Association of India and Indian Society of Advertisers, respectively. ABC, an independent body with members from publications, agencies and advertisers, provided essential inputs to media planning.

What kind of reach did the press, that is, the newspapers have? Here again Subrata Banerjee throws some light in his article, as the following chart shows:

LEADING INDIAN DAILIES

Newspaper	Circulation	Rate per '000 Paise	Number of Centres from where Published
Indian Express	2,49,462	8	5
The Times of India	1,75,350	10	2
Thanti (Tamil)	1,59,837	11	3
Navbharat Times (Hindi)	1,38,556	8	2
Hindu	1,20,197	10	

LEADING INDIAN PERIODICALS

Periodical	Circulation	Rate per '000 Paise	Frequency and Language
Kumudam	2,44,889	15	Weekly/Tamil
Ananda Vikatan	1,88,188	15	Weekly/Tamil
Blitz	1,63,538	10	Weekly/English
Filmfare	1,08,513	22	Fortnightly/English
Kalki	1,06,035	18	Weekly/Tamil

In another interesting table, Banerjee highlights the abysmal penetration of the print media, although it happened to be the main medium of communication. Advertisers must have had modest expectations about unleashing campaigns on a sparse target audience. Or they may not have faced stiff market competition because most things were scarce. And hence whatever was seen in advertisements was good enough to keep a brand visible for buyers or potential buyers.

[6]The printers did a wonderful job for agencies despite having large arrears on payment. In most cases the agencies received payments for print jobs very late and they had to first pay the IENS or lose their accreditation.
[7]The hoarding contractors were often at each others' throats. They were generally unsocial fellows—thugs—and coming together in a federation to support their combined interest had to wait till the mid-nineties.

Language	Population	Circulation of Daily Newspapers per 1,000 People
Malayalam	13,400, 000	4.0
Gujarati	16,300,000	2.1
Tamil	26,500,000	2.2
Telegu	32,900,000	1.8
Marathi	27,000,000	1.5
Urdu and Hindustani	21,700,000	1.0
Kannada	14,500,000	1.0
Bengali	25,100,000	0.8
Hindi	1,08,700,000	0.5
Oriya	13,000,000	0.4
Assamese	5,000,000	0.1

Of the five most highly circulated magazines, three are Tamil magazines. This is somewhat of an anomaly, considering that Malayalam has almost double the circulation of newspapers per 1,000 persons compared to Tamil.[8] Kerala had the highest rate of literacy. It is surprising that no Malayalam magazine features in the list. But the future trend of regional magazines overtaking English magazines in leisure reading is indicated. As with most other countries, women constitute a large segment of committed readers of magazines. Since a large proportion of women were housewives, largely confined to their homes, they obviously had more time to read magazines.

The following table provides a quick glance of the relative importance of the media, based on actual spend, in the 1970s.[9] The table indicates the dominance of newspapers over all other media selected in media plans. An interesting point to note is the relative strength of out-of-home (hoarding) and radio as other important mediums that attracted advertising expenditure.

Cinema was fourth in terms of budget allocated. Cinema screening was rather uncertain as the entire business of screening was in the hands of Blaze. This company enjoyed a monopoly over screening nationally. Blaze was tough and not squeamish about employing questionable methods to completely smother competition. Companies which regularly used cinema knew too well what was happening and were cautious in screening films. They ensured that

[8]In 2009, *Malayala Manorama*, with a circulation of 6.15 lakh and *Vanitha* (circulation of over 5 lakh), both in the Malayalam language, are first and second in circulation among all magazines in the country. I really do not have an explanation as to why or how three Tamil magazines feature in the list of five in 1970.
[9]*Foundations of Advertising, Theory and Practice* by S.A. Chunawalla and K.C. Sethia. In their book they mention that the source of the chart was *The Economic Times* dated 21 July 1981, in an article titled 'Marketing and advertising' authored by Zachery.

their travelling salesmen had free passes to check whether a film was screened as per schedule. They were reimbursed the cost of a cinema ticket if they decided to go on their own or had no free pass. But in a big country such as India, Blaze was the ultimate winner; who could check actual screening across 5,000 theatres on a daily or weekly basis? A film was expensive to produce and it was a shame that Blaze never allowed a film to get full coverage as planned because of deliberate non-screening.[10]

Radio features third after press and hoarding. All India Radio had a long list of products it would not permit to advertise; cigarettes and tobacco-based products and liquor featured in the list. All India Radio did not permit advertising of jewellery for reasons difficult to fathom since none of the stalwarts of India's freedom movement had ever said anything adverse about wearing jewellery. Indeed, on a number of occasions when Gandhi needed funds, Indian women gave their jewellery and he accepted all of that with gratitude. It is possible that radio also includes Radio Ceylon, which was a highly popular station that played Hindi film songs and had big sponsors such as Binaca, supported by Ameen Sayani, unquestionably the most notable producer of radio programmes in the world.[11]

DISTRIBUTION OF TOTAL ADVERTISING EXPENDITURE BY MEDIA (PER CENT OF TOTAL)

Year	Press	TV	Radio	Cinema	Outdoor/ Transport
1970	79.5	-	7.1	5.5	7.9
1971	77.9	-	7	6.4	8.7
1972	74.9	-	7.6	7.3	10.2
1973	72.5	-	7.5	8.5	11.5
1974	67.6	-	7.6	8.3	16.5
1975	67.9	-	8.6	8.7	14.8
1976	69.8	1.2	8.1	8.1	12.8
1977	70.1	2.7	7.5	8.0	11.7
1978	70	4.1	7.6	7.1	11.2
1979	68.9	4.7	8	7.1	11.3

[10]At the cost of repeating myself, I note that I have attended many meetings with Blaze at Clarion, where we debated exhibition weeks based on reports sent by the client and the agency's own spot checking. On a number of occasions, when Blaze could not deny these reports, it deducted as much as 50 per cent from the bill raised. At the agency account executives often joked that Blaze was into a great business of non-exhibition. Whatever it earned meant profit for the company.

[11]I have covered radio in *Indian Advertising 1780 to 1950.*

A note added to the table states: 'A study of the index of media rates since 1970 and of the total advertising expenditure at constant prices reveals the interesting fact that up to the year 1979, India's advertising volume was consistently below the 1971 level.'

The table also shows that TV was not a sought-after medium till about 1976 when it began drawing advertisers' attention. And then between 1977 and 1978 there was a significant jump in advertising spend over TV. When newspapers took notice of this trend the leading national dailies started a more aggressive campaign; their advertising executives visited agencies and advertisers to explain the advantage of newspapers over TV.[12]

The media market in India is unique. Where else in the world do we see a single company enjoying complete monopoly over television, dominating all other media, but because the government owns Doordarshan the company is allowed to drift? A number of politicians, both from the Congress Party as well from anti-Congress coalition governments, who were in charge of Doordarshan, being Ministers of Information & Broadcasting, did not upgrade technology or studios, thus allowing private TV channels to marginalise Doordarshan after these became functional.

Initially the programmes on TV were uninteresting. These were telecast in black and white. It is a wonder viewers watched TV programmes patiently for years. Foreign programmes shown were generally sourced from socialist countries. Russian circus shows were a lot better than Doordarshan programmes. It was not until Ramanand Sagar's *Ramayana* was telecast did Indian television penetrate into Indian homes. With B.R. Chopra and Ravi Chopra's *Mahabharata*, Doordarshan was established as the most powerful channel that could reach homes across this vast country, riding on the back of India's most loved epic.

[12]S.A. Chunawalla and K.C. Sethia in *Foundations of Advertising—Theory & Practice* (Himalaya Publishing House, 1985) observe: 'In India, advertising business was worth Rs 160 crore in 1978, out of which Rs 98.5 crore alone was in the press media ... The oldest and largest advertisement agency in India is HTA, which had a gross billing of Rs 13.50 crore in 1978–79 and employed 450 persons. The second largest advertisement agency is Clarion, which had a billing of Rs 8.15 crore and employed 420 persons in the same year. The top 10 advertising agencies put together had a share of Rs 60 crore advertising business in 1978–79, which is more than one-third of the total.'

Research on effects of advertising

In Europe the 1970s saw sociologists scanning the effects of advertising on people. Their approach brought in a fresh element that weighed advertising in terms of social impact. Sut Jhally in a probing coverage of the advertising industry presented a viewpoint that put advertising, media, industry and popular culture in a melting pot where all of them combined to mould social behavioural trends.[13] Although this book was published in 1987, the work of social anthropologists from the 1950s through to the 1970s indicated that advertising and the media were powerful initiators of change. In 1977, Dallas Smythe in his seminal article argued that (a) mass media produce audiences as commodities for sale to advertisers and (b) that advertisers engage this audience power to work by getting audiences to self-market commodities to themselves.

As early as the 1950s Thorstein Veblen coined the phrase 'conspicuous consumption'. He viewed consumption not as a private affair but more as a social activity and postulated that consumption is socially based and judged. Satisfaction is measured against a social scale, which denotes an average standard. As a society gets richer and more goods become available to a larger number of people, the average standard also rises and the 'level' of satisfaction remains stable.[14]

Sociologists were also beginning to be curious on the man-woman relationship as seen in advertisements. Erving Goffman in his book *Gender Advertisements* argues that the man-woman relationship depicted is similar to a parent-child relationship—man takes the role of parent while the woman is like the child. He cites examples from common visuals in ads. A woman's hands is commonly shown as caressing, whereas a male hand is shown firmly grasping an object. It is as if a woman, like a child, is not in full control of her environment unlike the man. Goffman's book was published in 1979.

In the 1980s, Sut Jhally took the argument further. He hypothesised that in the twentieth century there were two significant parallel developments in advertising. (1) There was a shift from explicit statement of values to implicit values and lifestyle images. (2) A decline in textual material with collective increase in 'visualised images in well-being'. Jhally contends that

---

[13] *The Codes of Advertising: Fetishism and Political Economy of Meaning in the Consumer Society*. St. Martin's Press by arrangement with Printer Publishing Limited. 1987.

[14] This seems to suggest that the standard of living rises proportionately for the whole society. In India today we cannot agree to this view. While there is a definite improvement in the standard of living of a great number of people, for a much larger majority there isn't a similar improvement in lifestyle. The social scale—if there is one—shows a very disproportionate improvement in the living standards of a minority. However, this minority in terms of actual numbers is so huge that it is being recognised globally as a large segment of consumers for all kinds of products.

the dominance of image-based advertising draws greater attention, retaining at the same time a significant degree of ambiguity.[15]

Sociologists pointed out that goods are simultaneously communicators about social ideas and power and satisfiers of human needs. Though with constant improvement in living standards human needs tend to change in character; moving up from basic needs of food-clothing-shelter-health-sex to *psychological needs* when society arrives at a stage when basic needs are met. Eminent sociologists such as Sahlins and Baudrillard agreed that consumption is largely a business of manipulating signs in advanced capitalism. Objects lose the vital connection with their practical utility and instead become the signifier of constantly changing abstract qualities. This is achieved through control of the symbolic code given to commodities. Control over demand and symbolism rather than the physical production of goods becomes the important focus for companies.

More and more needs are brought within the ambit of sign consumption. Individuals are so constantly exposed to these signs across time and space in the media that they lose autonomous control and surrender to the code. Baudrillard maintained that the system no longer needs universal production—it requires only that everyone plays the game. The market is the central institution in this new monopoly of the code.[16]

Indian advertising professionals were also debating over various issues pertaining to the influence of advertising in society. Some of them were concerned about criticism that regarded advertising as an irresponsible catalyst for social change. Leading ad professionals stoutly defended their profession, saying that advertising merely *reflected social trends.* Advertising presented what was already accepted in society as normal or acceptable social behaviour for a group of people who influence as well as initiate social change.

The debate continues and is likely to continue forever. Unlike any other form of mass communication, advertising derives sustenance from repeat exposures in the media. Even ordinary ads are so heavily flogged across TV channels, and for good measure, also exposed in other media to synergise impact through continual presence that the target audience are compelled to notice. This does not happen with any other form of communication, not even

---

[15] I am not sure what he means. Associational links built into an advertisement draw certain groups of people who aspire to a similar lifestyle whereas ambiguity is likely to repel these groups if in the process other groups lower in the social scale were equally attracted by these associational links.

[16] Considering brand marketing as it has evolved over time I find a lot of truth in this observation. Young people today are given acronymic names such as GX (Generation X) to slot them into preference groups indicating purchase behaviour for various categories of consumer consumables—both durables and perishables. Sometimes articles published in *Brand Equity* are so full of acronyms (writers obviously feel the whole world understands what they wish to convey) that readers are left to solve the puzzle (presuming they have the patience to carry on reading).

with news unless it is a calamity of unspeakable horror such as the Bhopal gas tragedy at the Union Carbide factory.

Alyque Padamsee

Alyque Padamsee has remained the most recognisable face in Indian advertising for close to 50 years. He started his career in JWT on a salary of Rs 300 per month, which was princely for the times. However, he personally felt it was a social climb-down as he recalls having to travel by bus, which was unthinkable while he stayed with his family. He worked with JWT for 10 years and then joined Lintas.

He headed Lintas in the 1970s and 1980s where he was called 'God'. He engaged in a running battle with India's biggest agency, HTA, by claiming that his agency Lintas had overtaken HTA in billing. This kind of contest, like the perennial fight between cola brands, keeps the pot boiling; many vain advertisers who are the clients of big agencies puff up their chests by engaging one or the other of India's top 10 agencies.[17]

Padamsee reached the top of the agency he worked for; he was regarded as one among the best in his job, on a par with Subhas Ghosal and Subrata Sengupta. He also emerged as a reputed actor on the English stage and happened to bag important roles in award-winning films. He played Jinnah in Attenborough's film on Gandhi.

In Lintas he led a team of dedicated professionals in all departments of advertising—creative and account servicing. The fact that he was a successful business leader was proved after his retirement. His successor lacked both his charisma and his ability. In most professionally managed companies the efficiency of a super leader gets reflected after his departure when the world sees the successor is falling woefully short of the standards set.

During his tenure as the CEO of Lintas he attracted talent from the leading agencies. Padamsee should be credited for much path-breaking work that was developed in the 1970s and 1980s. The Liril film was breathtakingly beautiful. It would not have been possible but for his presence. This fact was repeatedly stressed by Kailash Surendranath who produced the film.

[17]I remember the MD of a Calcutta-based FMCG company, which happens to be the only one currently making news with brands and endorsements on an all-India basis from eastern India, say with obvious pride that he had kept the great Alyque Padamsee as a retainer or ombudsman for his advertising. What exactly he was supposed to do he was not too clear about when we had this discussion.

Lintas had all along been under the shadow of HLL. It was in the Padamsee era that the agency actually became a force in the advertising world by aggressively increasing its client roster.

What were advertisements like in the seventies—in their structure (copy and visual); in the range of products and services covered and the impact that successful campaigns had? Textile ads outnumbered ads of most other products.[18] This was because textiles progressed rapidly in a competitive market environment. A number of brands became popular household names and were advertised heavily in all forms of media available to advertisers—print, cinema, point of sale, outdoor and TV. Retail showrooms were set up by the leading textile-makers.

The Madura Mills advertisement on the facing page appeared in *The Illustrated Weekly of India*, a Times of India Group publication, in January 1971. The agency that created and released the ad was Bensons, which became Ogilvy Benson & Mather shortly after.

Executives who were hired by OBM were expected to run through Ogilvy's Magic Lanterns. These provided useful and detailed directives on how to go about advertising different products and services. Ads prepared by OBM were generally of a pattern. They were neat in execution, with more text than most other advertisements in the category and anchored the brand very strongly. They also came with long headlines. Ogilvy maintained that the headline may consist of as many as 24 words. A headline had to encapsulate the total message of the ad so that if a prospect did not feel like going through the body copy he would have all the content just reading the headline.

In the present context there is no headline. The sensuousness of the experience is conveyed by the woman in the ad in different poses with a suggestion of sexuality.

[18]Indubala H. Pandya observed in her book *English Language in Advertising* (Ajanta Publications, Delhi, 1977), 'The number of samples from textile advertising is, of necessity, far greater than the number of samples from cosmetics and pharmaceuticals because the average number of textile advertisements in a magazine is about three times as many as cosmetics advertisements and about 10 times as many as pharmaceutical advertisements.' In a sense her book is a path-breaking exercise for the 1970s. Few advertising professionals in India wrote anything on their profession. Although the number of books written on advertising today has increased it is still far short of what should have been produced, given that the national advertising outlay is in the region of Rs 40,000 crore now.

Madura Mills advertisement, The Illustrated Weekly of India.

S.R. Ayer (Mani)

S.R. Ayer (Mani) became the managing director of OBM in 1974 when he was only 39 years old. He came into advertising at the comparatively young age of 23 in 1958. By the time he became managing director he had already been in advertising for 16 years. OBM was among the top 10 agencies in India, but was nowhere close to the leading agencies in billing.

Ayer may be credited for building the creative powerhouse that OBM turned into with his penchant for nurturing talent. He quickly selected a team of individuals and moulded them into a team fitting into a *gharana* that they were proud to belong to. During Ayer's tenure, OBM branches in Delhi, Madras and Calcutta began winning new clients in the face of competition from the old established agencies as well as from the new set of creative hot-shops such as Rediffusion.

As managing director, Ayer kept a close watch upon the financial performance of his agency. He also gave the branch managers sufficient liberty to manage their show.

OBM was an agency biased towards people in the creative departments. Those actually in contact with clients came a poor second.[19]

Ayer was selfless when it was a question of preparing for the future. He groomed Ranjan Kapur as his successor. In Roda Mehta he discovered one of the most competent media planners in the country. Ayer also selected Piyush Pandey, who was destined to take over the reins from Ranjan Kapur when he retired.

The agency had suffered because of repeated change in ownership. From D.J. Keymer it became Bomas then S.H. Benson and finally, after David Ogilvy acquired S.H. Benson, the agency became Ogilvy, Benson & Mather. Despite the frequent change of ownership, all credit must go to the Indian

---

[19] I worked for four years with OBM in Calcutta. They were the unhappiest years in my life. The director-in-charge ensured every executive remained miserable. There was too much of repetitive work of an unproductive kind. Studio hands and account executives spent many nights every month preparing for pitches or just doing normal work because art directors and copywriters only worked when they felt like working. Workdays stretched from 9.30 in the morning till about 9 pm at night on an average. After office hours art directors stayed back to drink whisky, while account executives bought the booze so that they could face their clients the following day with the work, as promised. On most occasions this did not happen and the account executives received an earful from irate clients.

managing directors who retained a good image of the agency—especially the perception that it produced consistently good creative work. In recent times there have been attempts to minimise the contribution of P.N. Sarma who was the managing director before Mani Ayer. While Ayer in his long tenure of around 20 years prepared the ground for OBM to grow into the number one agency in India, it would only be fair to acknowledge that, without Sarma, Ayer may not have received the support of a strong creative-cum-servicing team, which is the basic structure of an ad agency.

Media and the concept of a full service agency

In the 1970s and 1980s, as in the preceding decades, clients looked for a composite package of services from an advertising agency. These included media planning and media execution. The structure of the advertising agency changed after the 1990s. First, P&G decided to abort the age-old remuneration structure prevalent in the advertising business and accepted universally. The agency earned 15 per cent commission from the media for the advertisements released through them. P&G reasoned an agency earning this commission was assured an income, which was unfair because this commission earning had no link with the performance of the advertising among target consumers. P&G, therefore, told the ad agencies working for it that it wanted a more accountable system.

This new position rejected the age-old argument by agencies that it was impractical and unfair to ask them to justify advertising expenditure incurred against sale. Agencies argued that advertising was only one of the components of a marketing mix and therefore how can advertising alone among all other components be entirely responsible for a brand's market share? However, given P&G's enormous ad budget, agencies fell in line. Now, the other big spenders who were watching all this from the sidelines jumped into the fray. If P&G was the first to question agency remuneration, could HLL be far behind? The company was a bigger advertiser than P&G in India and it asked its agencies to pass on some of their agency earning to it.

A new development took root. Media buying became the most important element in media services. For clients the focus shifted; the emphasis was now on what bonus was the advertiser earning from the media for this campaign? It seemed as if the business of advertising strapped itself into a seat on a time machine that took the profession back to the days of Volney B. Palmer in America, when media buying was the only service provided to advertisers by individuals who acted as go-between with the media on one side and advertisers on the other.

However, in the 1970s and 1980s, the full service agency was in its heydays despite the fact that the value of the total advertising expenditure in India was nothing compared to the volume and value in the USA, Japan or South Korea. India, we ought to remember, was passing through a constricting political environment that was choking the economy and that almost led to the collapse of the nation's economy by the beginning of the 1990s.

Sushen Saha of HTA, Indrani Sen, who worked in different spells in Clarion and HTA, Roda Mehta of OBM, and Tapan Pal who flitted in and out of media planning, marketing and research gave shape to media planning in agencies in the 1980s. In the process they developed a healthy working relationship with the media. TV was in the government domain; it was a monopoly. Doordarshan did not care whether agencies bought television time. But newspapers and magazines, especially the latter, were eager participants when new campaigns broke. Media planners managed to do an efficient job with insufficient tools in terms of readership or viewership figures which could be relied upon. They shared a healthy distrust of the figures available and were not afraid to venture out on their own, often travelling to different places to audit for themselves the circulation/distribution of magazines or newspapers and the screening of films in cinemas across smaller towns.

For clients with limited budgets, media planners often managed great deals to ensure that the campaign resulted in the desired level of visibility. The media also lent support; this included not only smaller newspapers or magazines, but also the national press.[20] Almost every media planner was self-taught. In fact, in larger and medium-sized agencies, media planners played an active role in hiring prospective media executives to assist them and they devoted a lot of attention in training their juniors. Sushen Saha, who was media director in both Clarion and HTA at different times, trained a lot of successful media professionals in both agencies. When Mudra set up the Mudra Institute of Communications (MICA) in Ahmedabad, India had its first institute for formal training in media planning.

Roda Mehta came from a background of research and hence was a natural choice for the media. Most media managers came with backgrounds in statistics or research. Like Mehta, most strayed into advertising and had little idea of what they were getting into. Answering questions mailed to her, Mehta opens many windows that current managers in agencies and in marketing

[20]Some of the leading newspapers such as *The Statesman* in Calcutta and New Delhi and the Times of India Group went out of their way to support small or start-up ad agencies. I personally benefitted from both these papers when I set up my own agency in Calcutta. *The Statesman* released the first campaign on credit though the credit given was for 30 days because my agency did not have INS accreditation. On another occasion, Pradip Guha, who was then director in the Times of India Group, very kindly overlooked a slip-up on the part of the agency with regard to the release of a Dunlop corporate campaign comprising five ads. He ensured the campaign got a second insertion for free.

companies such as P&G and HLL would do well to study. I reproduce the entire mailed interview in a footnote.[21]

---

[21] *1) How did you get into advertising?* After completing my Masters in Management Studies with specialisation in Operations Research from Jamnalal Bajaj Institute of Management Studies, University of Bombay, in 1971, job recruitment interviews were being held on campus. HTA, then India's largest advertising agency, was looking to hire a person to computerise the first-ever National Readership Study, 1970, undertaken by ORG. I got selected with a salary offer of Rs 750 per month. Also by ICICI Ltd for Rs 1,100 per month. Not knowing anything about advertising, I sought the advice of Dr (Mrs) Patil, Head of the OR department at the Institute. Her assessment was that working for HTA would mean treading uncharted territory with the opportunity to contribute; ICICI would offer a well-defined career prospect. My personal ambition was to contribute and grow, and so I took up the HTA offer. As I have said, I strayed into advertising.

2) Were you always in media? Or did you come to the media from servicing? No, I started in the media as media research executive and grew from there finally into agency management and leading profit centres.

3) The agencies you worked for—or was OBM the only place? I started with HTA in April 1971 and moved to OBM in June 1975 where I continued till I left the profession in June 1998.

4) Did you go through any professional course on advertising/media? No.

5) I'm informed that you taught in a number of management institutes? If so, the names. Primarily J. Bajaj Institute (1972–74) and IIM Ahmedabad (1986–89). I was invited to other institutes like XLRI, etc but for short-term workshops or as a guest lecturer.

6) In your time at O&M what were the major issues in media planning? It started with getting clients to accept media planning as a discipline! Then to get them to appreciate the need to integrate marketing strategy and planning to media strategy and planning for maximum brand impact and ad spend/creative execution value. By the late seventies this had been accomplished at OBM. Getting the media to accept that media planning was about impartial and well-educated choices in media selection, vehicle selection and advertising placement and scheduling. That the best partnership came from well-balanced teams on both sides of the selling and buying media. This placed a lot of pressure on the existing sales people and their managements to reinvent themselves.

7) Did you in the early 1990s foresee the emergence of media buying as an activity that would be more important to clients than planning? I witnessed the emergence of innovative and cost-effective media buying from the mid-1980s to enhance media planning effectiveness. However, I never foresaw that media buying or rather media rates would overtake all other considerations for clients.

8) Your comments please on the advantages/disadvantages of a full service agency vis-à-vis now when media and creative are separated? Does the client gain or lose in the process? There is no doubt that once HLL set out to create a centralised media purchase system in the early 1990s, the start of the decline of integrated brand solutions came to be. All clients wanted to join the bandwagon to get the lowest negotiated rates, based upon which agency hiring as well media choices became the cornerstone of brand decisions. Clients soon thereafter came to believe they were better 'purchase managers' and negotiators and soon that led them to direct media buying, creating a competitive environment with their own agencies. Media owners took natural advantage of this phenomenon. In short, the 1990s was one of the most disastrous phases for the industry. Traditional account management-led agency managements were slow to react and respond to these changes. Inevitably, the West, having preceded India in these developments, set the framework for the response mechanism to meet clients' new demands through media planning and buying houses.

Unequivocally, the separation of creative and media was the worst thing that happened to brands. The teaming of a multi-disciplinary set of great minds to define brand issues in the marketplace, brand strategy and positioning in the consumers' mind, communication objective and strategy, creative and media strategy and objectives, creative and media big ideas, consumer feedback, client integration, leading into final execution—in short, a complete 360 degree brand campaign—was lost forever. What the client and the brand got were creative messages or advertisements (by and large), media plans and media deals, and new media experimentation.

I have no doubt that HLL lost its place as the pre-eminent marketing company with highly valued professionals and brands in the Indian firmament of companies by the mid-2000s. It did not take too long! But in the process, agencies lost their brightest minds and new recruits today say they have 'no role models to look up to'. In sum, the entire marketing and communications industry has been the loser.

9) How did you help your smaller clients to get a better deal from the media? Largely through innovation and creative use of the media. Contrary to normal belief, the media used to work harder for every rupee spent by smaller clients as their only aim was to get their brands the best possible media opportunities.

Indrani Sen

Indrani Sen worked for both the leading agencies, HTA and Clarion, ending her agency career with JWT as media director. She then worked for a few years with the Calcutta-based FMCG company Emami. Like Roda Mehta, she grew up in a media environment that provided meagre statistical support in planning. She was also actively involved in training young media aspirants in both Clarion and JWT. She is now associated with MICA as visiting faculty.

Tapan Pal

Tapan Pal began his career in advertising as a media planner in Clarion. He was one of the early recruits from management institutes. He completed his post-graduate diploma in management from XLRI Jamshedpur. Prior to that he earned an MSc degree in mathematics from Jadavpur University, Calcutta. Pal worked in various companies, sometimes in marketing, sometimes in research and at other times in media. He was the founder CEO of Zenith in India; he worked for a spell in Discovery Channel and was also the CEO of AdMar, a research organisation that was an offshoot of Tara Sinha McCann. He keeps himself abreast of the latest developments in the media. Now he heads a new-age organisation that tracks a client's media buy and provides inputs on the efficiency of a media plan post-implementation. This gives him the opportunity to interact with advertisers and with media agencies very closely, providing valuable inputs to both.

I do not believe advertising has grown more complex with the years—the number of services offered has definitely increased, building an aura of professionalism among receivers of services and providers of services.

This advertisement was also carried in the 10 January 1971 issue of The Illustrated Weekly of India. *Created by Madison, the advertisement flogs the brand name in the headline itself. Because print was the main medium in the media mix, every agency tried to include action in the visual to make the ad interesting. However, 'fabrics' as a product group was quite cluttered, with many brands competing for market share.*

The perennial problem that agencies face in highly competitive product categories is that they all end up producing me-too campaigns. When agencies pitch for new accounts these same humdrum layouts are presented as highly inspired efforts by the agency's think-tank. Most clients prefer to

The Poddar Textiles ad includes all the masala. Most ads have fewer visual props. The top left half of the cover was torn. As a result, the advertisement on the following page is visible.

remain silent and suffer through an unending afternoon or morning. Ads in every competitive product category look-read-feel exactly alike because agencies do not make the effort to think differently. The worst offenders are advertisers with the biggest budgets and their agencies.

Looking at the 'fabric' segment, we see almost every ad is built around a man and a woman—generally both. To denote lifestyle, props are used, such as a motorcycle, a pair of binoculars, a plush office seat, a camera and so on. Place one beside the other, interchange the brand names, and nothing is lost and nothing gained.

The merit of the DCM ad lies in the simplicity of its message. Terene is obviously a new kind of fabric. DCM combines terene in its chiffon saris. The saris are colourful and, as the model in the ad demonstrates, terene saris are comfortable to wear outdoors. The agency behind this ad was ACIL (Advertising Consultants of India Ltd).

ACIL began as the second agency of Clarion. It became an independent agency when a number of senior executives took it over during the first battle for management control of Clarion. They literally walked out with ACIL and got a number of national accounts. However, this agency did not last long as the leaders quarrelled with each other. Professionals who joined them from Clarion left soon enough. A number of them headed other agencies in due course. Madhukar Kamath, who heads Mudra now, returned to Clarion representing Bates and arranged a takeover by Bates. After a renewed stint in Clarion he returned to Mudra.

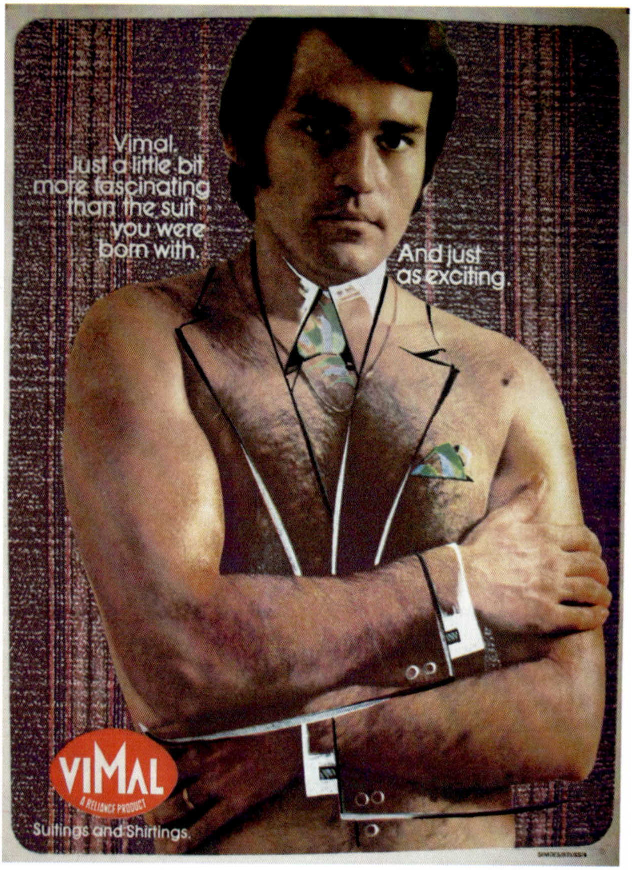

Frank Simoes tries a bold experiment of breaking through the clutter—building an ad with a nude model. Note even though the model is wearing nothing he appears to be clothed. There is no headline and the copy, which features like blurbs in a comic strip, says nothing about why Vimal is exciting. This ad appeared before Mudra was born. Mudra was the agency founded by the owners of Vimal that naturally took over the advertising of Vimal and other sister organisations owned by Dhirubhai Ambani.

At times we come across instances of the same agency handling different brands of textile. This is unusual because in the seventies clients and agencies felt very strongly that an agency should not handle any competitive brand. Of course a major exception was India's largest advertiser, HLL, which alone had multiple brands in competitive situations of which all or a large number of them were handled by their in-house agency Lintas.

Talking of textile, here are two advertisements that appeared for competing brands in the same issue of *The Illustrated Weekly of India*. Both ads carry the key number of Everest.

This advertisement of Mafatlal carried the key number of Everest as did the following ad of Elpar. In the Mafatlal ad, the creative experiment with copy display; notice the subhead which is placed at the bottom in the manner of reflection. I am not sure whether the water at the base of the ad makes it more appealing.

This ad is remarkably ugly both in terms of the models selected, the way they present themselves in the ad, as well as the general layout. The models look like bad characters with poor dress sense as in the Hindi films of the seventies. Everest had a reputation of being a well-managed agency financially and professionally. How this ad went past the agency's scrutiny and was sold to the client is an issue ad people should reflect on. Ugly ads do make money, but they also mar an agency's reputation and spoil the image of the brand sold.

Here is an ad refreshingly different from the normal look of advertisements. Not surprisingly this came from Lintas. Alyque Padamsee, who was one of the prime movers in the agency by the time, may have influenced breaking away from prudery in the presentation of women in Indian advertising. The Lux ad revels in the freshness of a woman's skin in the visual, supporting the sensuousness of the copy of the ad.

The fabrics market was challenging. To survive competition not only did every brand invest in media space and time but Indian fabrics developed a worldwide reputation for excellent quality. Besides, they were cheaper than stuff produced in Europe and the USA. There were plenty of stories about Indian visitors to the exotic West (so few had the money or connection to get that far) returning home with towels bought in London only to discover after unpacking that they carried the familiar DCM label.

The 1970s was a decade of change. Some of the most combative and capable advertising professionals came into the top management rung of leading agencies; besides a number of new agencies were started by talented young men who worked for MCM, after MCM folded up due to the inability of the owner to appreciate the economic fundamentals of the business of advertising.

Ravi Gupta, who turned Trikaya into a creative powerhouse.

Ravi Gupta,[22] like a lot of advertising professionals, drifted into the profession and left it richer by his association. After graduating from St. Xavier's College, Bombay, he studied mining geology in Cardiff. He joined a flock of highly talented individuals at MCM after a stint in Ulka and Inter Publicity. He started Trikaya in 1978. When asked how he arrived at this name for his agency, Gupta replied that he was looking for a Latin word that signified three; to stand for marketing, communication and media. Someone pointed out to him that a Sanskrit word would fit perfectly—'Trikaya' or three forms.

No agency can really flourish without a creative flavour. In Christopher D'Rozario and Vikas Gaitonde he found two great creative persons in his team. No agency can achieve recognition without supportive clients. Initially Ravi Gupta was blessed with a number of them. Managing director of Real Value, Pheroze Engineer, was one who 'pre-bounced ideas' on Gupta.

Narottam Seksaria, managing director, Gujarat Ambuja Cement, regarded Trikaya as an honest agency and gave it all the company's work. Suresh

[22]I am indebted to *The Economic Times* for some of the facts on Ravi Gupta. An article published on 26 September 1990, written by Vidhu Khanna, gave an interesting profile of Gupta. It seemed to be based on an interview. Gupta expired prematurely sometime after this and his position in Trikaya was taken by Nirvik Singh who had headed the agency's operations in Calcutta.

Subrahmanyan, the ad manager of Dunlop, handed the account to Gupta on a platter. He pulled out Nirvik Singh from HTA to handle the account when after a contentious takeover of Dunlop by Manu Chhabria the company decided to part ways with HTA, as the agency was regarded as being close to the RPG Group.

One of the negatives of multinational agencies taking over ongoing Indian concerns is the loss of beautiful Indian names. Trikaya has already become Grey; it will not be long before DDB Needham erases the Mudra name. R.K. Swamy may not have the poetic ring of Trikaya or an artistic name such as Mudra, but it is an Indian name with the memory of an untiring man who built one of the strongest agencies in the country. On the nameplate today BBDO precedes R.K. Swamy although BBDO built on the strong foundation that R.K. Swamy gave them. Clarion's eventful history is already forgotten under the enveloping cover of Bates, a new untried agency in India despite what it may be in the USA. Similarly, in Ulka, FCB comes before Ulka. How much longer will it be before Ulka is erased?

Suresh Subrahmanyan

Suresh Subrahmanyan began his advertising career with Clarion in Calcutta. He subsequently worked in HTA and Grant Advertising before joining Dunlop where he became the advertising manager.

Like Bobby Kooka in Air India, Subrahmanyan had a phenomenal feel for good advertising. With his easy-going style he inspired his agencies to develop path-breaking campaigns. Trikaya presented Dunlop scooter tyre Spectra Wide to the world very dramatically. In fact, the brand was initially named Spectra. Trikaya reasoned that since it was the widest scooter tyre in India, the name should be Spectra Wide. The campaign, which broke in film, showed a whole range of common things in the 'wide' angle such as a girl playing tennis with a very wide racquet. The theme of wide was expanded to include other everyday items.

Clients such as Kooka and Subrahmanyan are indeed rare in Indian advertising. They share some common traits; these may be itemised as:

- The ability to see and distil the strengths of their own organisations.
- The ability to inspire agencies to deliver above average creative work at all times without stressing out the individuals working with them.
- To inspire account servicing executives to interact with experts from within their organisation at all times.
- The ability to reward good work with a sincere 'thank you'.
- To support the agency when in need, which was often the case with the INS breathing down its neck.
- To protect the agency against general or unfair criticism by any individual in the company other than themselves.
- The ability to judge creative work and sometimes allow the agency to go ahead with work that many others in the organisation were likely to disapprove.
- To expect the agency to *deliver* even when deadlines looked impossible.
- Above all, the ability to disregard small failures on the part of the agency and to reassure it that it could do better.

The young man sandwiched between Subhas Ghosal on the left and Prasanta Sanyal on the right is Gautam Ghosal. He came to ITC from Grant Advertising and became the advertising manager of ITC within a short time. He had to juggle with brands and agencies. Three of India's leading agencies were working for ITC—HTA, Clarion and Ulka. Ghosal was a leading figure in advertising circles in Calcutta and had a pan-India presence because his company was one of the biggest spenders in advertising. He died when he was in his forties. His death came as a shock. Advertising, people realised, was a tension-prone business that led to heart attacks. Lethality was added to the glamour of the profession. Not that ad men and women were thereafter seen to lead sensible lives—drinking less, smoking fewer cigarettes, not worrying about deadlines and avoiding late night parties. The Advertising Club of Calcutta annually gives the Gautam Ghosal Award for Advertising Excellence in his memory.

Arun Nanda, Ajit Balakrishnan and Muhammed Khan started an agency called Rediffusion. Khan later broke away to start Enterprise. They did brilliant work for their clients—work that was fresh in approach, bold in execution, and memorable.

Advertising from the 1950s till about the mid-1970s attracted very unusual persons. They came into the profession untrained and were generally misfits in other professions till they got to an ad agency where they found other people like themselves. They came in two forms—as builders of organisations or as persons who delivered memorable ideas in advertising. The first group excelled in doing different things for different people, all on the same day. Such people loved to face the odds. Briefing the creative team; sitting down with media planners; cajoling newspapers to give a solus position without extra; seeing the printing of posters and danglers; and ensuring clients paid on time was all in a day's work. The second group comprised copywriters and art directors who earned recognition for their companies by the brilliance of their ideas.

Muhammed Khan

Muhammed Khan was a rare person. He built not one company but was associated with the start-up of three agencies that left their mark upon Indian advertising. He was one of the co-founders of Rediffusion in 1973; in 1978, he started Contract with Subhas Ghosal; in 1983, he set up his own agency, Enterprise. In all three the brilliance of creative work set the agencies on to a growth path. His name is associated with the historic Charms campaign. In this he gave a new image dimension to a popularly priced cigarette. He took the common name Charms from everyday usage; students who generally smoked the Charminar brand (mainly because it was the cheapest brand going at the time), referred to the brand as 'Charms'.

Khan gave a new look to a popularly priced brand. The pack came in denim shades. The advertising was fresh and celebrated youth in outdoor situations. Like all great copywriters of the time, Khan believed in the importance of copy in advertising. In an interview with *The Economic Times* he said, 'The copy is important in bringing out brand attributes. How can a photograph possibly convey that?'

In the final phase of his advertising career, his agency, then called Enterprise-Nexus, created a memorable campaign for the 'National Egg Coordination Committee' with the simple headline, 'The best square meal in the world', with the visual of an egg and a baseline that asked, 'Have you had

The historic Charms advertisement, which gave a new image dimension to a popularly priced cigarette.

an egg today?'. The Hindi campaign, which was seen on television, was even more memorable with the Hinglish line, 'Sunday *ya* Monday *roj khao annde*'.

Khan, like other well-known men and women in advertising, was a character around whom stories were woven. He was credited with a short temper, which may not have been a true reflection of the man. Those who worked with him said he was 'cool' and that he only lost his temper when he saw work low on creative merit. But it is because of people such as Muhammed Khan, Roda Mehta, Alyque Padamsee, Umesh Rao, Vikas Gaitonde, Kanu Basu, Tara Sinha, Ram Ray and R.K. Swamy that a profession such as advertising begins to be talked about socially, and finds recognition as an interesting career path to pursue, attracting new talent into the profession.

R.K. Swamy

R.K. Swamy began his advertising career in 1940 as an assistant in the editorial department of JWT. It is more than likely that the term 'assistant' denoted a junior clerk. We know foreign agencies in the pre-Independence era and till about the early 1970s did not welcome Indians with open arms into the officer cadre. It is also certain that R.K. Swamy came from a lower middle-class family with school-level education.

He made his mark in JWT by the dint of his own considerable merit. He finally broke away from the agency, which he had served for 33 years, to found his own in 1973. He must have been middle-aged by then. His parting was not amicable. He believed that the elevation of Subhas Ghosal to the position of managing director of HTA had been unfair. He thought Ghosal was preferred because he was 'more Western' and so more liked by the superiors who found Swamy too 'Indian'. He carried this bitterness in his heart throughout his life.[23]

However, Swamy built his agency quickly. When he quit HTA he was the branch manager in Madras. Therefore, he had considerable influence over many clients. He left with some of the bigger clients handled by HTA in Madras. He also left with a few talented copywriters and art directors from the branch, promising them a brighter future if they came with him.

[23]I worked in R.K. Swamy Associates for four years and on at least three occasions spent whole days and nights with the chief. I recollect Swamy talking about his leaving HTA on more than one occasion.

Swamy exploited the gap that existed in servicing 'public sector' clients. These were owned by the government of India, often mismanaged, most were deep in the red and existed only because they were financed with taxpayers' money. Many of the bigger units often had officers from the Indian Administrative Service (IAS) foisted upon the board as managing directors. Such people were untrained to manage businesses and bided their time till they moved to the next posting.

Who would have thought that public sector organisations could do an image makeover? R.K. Swamy got into the act. A number of organisations such as BHEL and MECON, which were exceptions to the rule of inefficient public sector undertakings, provided an opportunity to the team at R.K. Swamy to showcase its creative work.[24] Copywriters such as Sumit Chatterjee, who was initially the creative chief at R.K. Swamy, Siben Datta (who had an excellent track record while with JWT before joining Swamy), Surojoy Banerjee and art director Arunava Chakravorty produced some of the most visible campaigns for public sector companies.[25]

Credit must also be given to Swamy for investing in research. Like HTA and Clarion, he set up an independent company. Hansa Research was headed by Dr Vasumathi, who brought both knowledge and experience to the agency. It did significant work in compiling data related to the media, consumer buying trends and rural market trends.

However, before Swamy died he probably realised that if his agency had to be on the growth path it would have to tie-up with some international agency of repute. Swamy diluted his family's shareholding in the agency and hitched up with BBDO, which later went on to acquire an equal stake in the company.

For a man who started his company when he was over 50 years old, his achievement in setting up a company, ensuring continuous growth and leaving footprints with memorable creative work must surely stand out in a profession that is characterised by shooting stars and dying meteors.[26]

---

[24]In my interaction with R.K. Swamy I observed that he played the Tamil card if he met a Tamil officer in government service anywhere.

[25]Surojoy Banerjee as copywriter and Arunava Chakravorty, the art director, also produced a memorable campaign for Regent Special Filter cigarettes marketed by National Tobacco Company. This was featured among the most memorable campaigns seen in the country in the 150th anniversary special issue published by *The Times of India*.

[26]In recent times, especially after R.K. Swamy's death, his company (now called BBDO–R.K. Swamy) has not produced path-breaking work.

The Regent Special Filter campaign was a re-launch exercise and proved very successful. The campaign came as a three-ad teaser series. When the material of the first ad was presented to The Statesman *in Calcutta, the ad manager wished to know what would be the following ads. They had to be given a sneak preview of the entire series before they consented to carry them in their daily. The copywriter for the campaign was Surojoy Banerjee and the art director was Arunava Chakravorty. The brand manager in National Tobacco Company was Rashid Kidwai, a flamboyant and aggressive challenger to ITC's supremacy in cigarettes. This team worked on many memorable campaigns, some being highly controversial such as the present one. In Patna, hoardings were pulled down. The image of R.K. Swamy Associates received a makeover from that of a 'steady-conventional' agency to a creative agency that was not scared of doing eye-catching, if controversial, campaigns. But none of this would have been possible without Kidwai.*

Arun Nanda

Like R.K. Swamy Associates, another successful agency had its beginnings in 1973. It had an unusual name—Rediffusion. What the word meant few understood. Many clients were so confounded by this unusual name that they often mispronounced the name. Diwan Arun Nanda with his associates from MCM, Ajit Balakrishnan, Arun Kale and Muhammed Khan, set up a small office in a dilapidated building in Worli. They each invested Rs 33,000 and managed a capital of Rs 1 lakh, a princely sum in the 1970s.[27] Like any start-up, these young men knew they had no chance of bagging any prestigious account.

Nanda, in a recent interview, revealed that Rediffusion made its breakthrough with two accounts. Both of these were located in Calcutta. In a competitive pitch, it won the Eveready battery account. Senior managers in Eveready were impressed with their presentation and sought clearance from their head office in the USA to work with an unknown new agency. Nanda observed that they were already handling the Geep battery account. They had done some interesting work, which had been noticed at Eveready. It is not clear why they wished to give up the Geep account. Was it only because Eveready was number one in the dry cell market?

After this they got the Jenson & Nicholson account, which again was a Calcutta-based organisation. The campaign, which used outdoor as a primary medium, was one of the most visually arresting campaigns in the annals of advertising history. The line, 'Whenever you see colour think of us', with the Jenson & Nicholson logo, enabled them to spin new visuals through the years. With Eveready and Jenson & Nicholson, Rediffusion announced that it had to be noticed among the most creative ad agencies in the country.

Arun Nehru was the marketing director of Jenson & Nicholson when Rediffusion bagged the account. When Rajiv Gandhi decided to enter politics, Nehru became a trusted aide. He introduced Rediffusion to the Congress Party. Generally speaking Indian ad agencies have not had much success with political campaigns. If the records are searched it may be seen that whenever any big agency has worked for a political party, that party has invariably lost the elections. The Congress Party has been the worst sufferer. It fared badly first when Indira Gandhi turned to Clarion

[27] Arunava Chakravorty and I started an agency in Calcutta in 1984 with an initial capital outlay of Rs 50,000 given by a client in Bhilai. The premises comprised a single room and thankfully a toilet rented out by Major Tapan Ghose. In Bombay, as Nanda recounts, in those days rented accommodation was impossible to get as all the laws were in favour of the tenant. It was the same in Calcutta.

to work on its campaign and then again when Rediffusion worked for the Congress.

The Bharatiya Janata Party (BJP) fared no better with Trikaya Grey. Its 'India shining' campaign cost Atal Bihari Vajpayee his prime minister's chair and his party went into a long period of hibernation.

As a matter of fact, Indian agencies have little understanding of common aspirations, particularly in the uncharted, little-known and neglected village communities. Together these communities comprise the majority of the electorate in India. Whereas even the meanest rascal who enters the political arena has a feel of the popular political pulse and keeps changing his colours accordingly, no ad executive manages to read what they see, much less what simmers beneath the surface. The 'India shining' campaign is an example of professionals making a hash of what they attempted to achieve. When figures from research are tabulated, interpreted and given to the copywriter and the art director, they are just not equipped to read the basic facts. They do not go out into the field and, if in case they do, they do not speak the common language.

Rediffusion built upon the strength of its visibly exciting creative fare of the 1970s and early 1980s. It continued to prosper as an agency, but reading the trend of the times, Nanda decided to tie up with foreign partners after the liberalisation of the economy in the middle of 1990s. He seems to indicate in a recent interview that his company gained by this move.

The seventies was also the decade when a clutch of professional ad film-makers appeared on the scene. They made films for a living; some of them set up companies. They scouted agencies for assignments. Since few films were made, they were highly competitive in their bidding. Unlike today, making an advertising film was regarded to be the function of the ad agency.

Ad agencies such as Lintas, Clarion and HTA appointed film production executives. For the big agencies there was ongoing work. For the second tier agencies, films were far fewer and they did not require a full-time film executive. Shyam Benegal and Govind Nihalani went on to achieve fame as great film directors in their own right after they quit Lintas. Barun Chanda of Clarion, who started as a copywriter, later concentrated on film production for his agency as the creative director. He also achieved fame as an actor in one of Satyajit Ray's memorable movies. Dhritiman Chatterjee, who was creative director of HTA, pursued a second career as a cinema actor. Prasoon Joshi was yet to arrive on the scene, striding across a varied universe comprising advertising, popular music and Bollywood films.

Zafar Hai, a Bombay-based producer, was among the most sought-after film producers from the mid-70s till about the early '90s. He did all the films for Nescafe coffee and other brands from the same stable. Whether the Nescafe films were a replica of films made elsewhere with only Indian faces replacing the faces of foreign models is not easy to tell. But Hai brought into his films a feeling of upmarket lifestyle. His films had class. The music and environment was more Western than Indian. Brand was dominant. And, quite like David Ogilvy's known approach to film-making, Hai introduced the brand within the first few frames. And in the last frame he had a dramatic pack shot to remind his audience that they could not possibly disregard such a wonderful product.

Kailash Surendranath was the first among equals. In an interview in 2002, he recounted his early interest in films. Without any formal training in the art and science of film-making, he waded into the medium and learnt the job the hard way. It is important to bear in mind that in the seventies editing films was a physical process, there were no computers. The effects used in films had to be carefully thought out. The entire process was time-consuming and expensive. For a young man beginning a career in film production it meant doing everything himself.

Kailash Surendranath

Kailash Surendranath was born in 1952. That perhaps makes him the first ad film-maker of the post-Independence generation who decided to carve out his career in the uncertain world of advertising film production. At the time film storyboards were drawn by hand and each frame was briefly described by a copywriter who was trained to write copy for the print media. The copywriter wrote press advertisements most of the time and was not well versed in film-making. This was a problem with all ad agencies, big and small. The big agencies sometimes carried one or two persons in the copy or art departments who had some exposure to film-making on the job. But ad men are notoriously fickle in their disposition and they change agencies faster than they change their shirts. So clients heard when they finally decided to shoot a film that so-and-so who knew all about film-making has moved on. Lintas worked on more films than other agencies and had bankable agency expertise in film-making. Most agency film experts generally knew no more than their clients.

Brand positioning had not become the jargon of every brand manager. Management graduates were just about waking up to the exciting career opportunities that advertising offered. Some were doubtful. Many left after a few months or after a couple of years, realising that the hard grind involved was incommensurate with the peanuts earned as salary. Agency salaries then were lower than what a good mill hand in Worli earned in a month. Over time the mill hand earned perhaps two or three times as much as an account executive. HTA and Clarion paid their account executives a monthly salary of around Rs 800 in 1975 when the Liril film was made. Art directors and copywriters, always a pampered lot in advertising, may have earned a trifle more, but they were adept at moonlighting. They earned envious sums from all the work they did after office hours for smaller agencies. Illustrators, in particular, had a good market going for them.

Surendranath often explored an idea. He would shoot a few sequences at his own expense and then present these to one of the leading agencies to see whether the idea would excite them too. The Liril film broke new ground in India. Today everyone associated with the film takes credit for the idea, the storyboard, the model, the setting and the music. But in the final reckoning more credit should go to Surendranath than to anyone else. Most of his films show him as a film-maker who could easily transcend the shortcomings of a storyboard and add value by exploring the wonderful moments of life—with the product thrown in—where the woman or man is supremely happy in a hedonistic fling of self-indulgence. Very often the real contribution towards making a good advertising film goes to the agency. Producers who contribute so much are forgotten.

Karen Lunel in the first Liril film

If he had done nothing else in life except the memorable film, *Mile Sur*, on national integration, he would still have earned his place as a remarkable ad film-maker. Suresh Mullick of OBM, the chief creative director of the agency at the time, has been credited with the idea. He, too, was highly talented, but in the final rendition of the storyboard Surendranath deserves credit for delivering a truly memorable film.

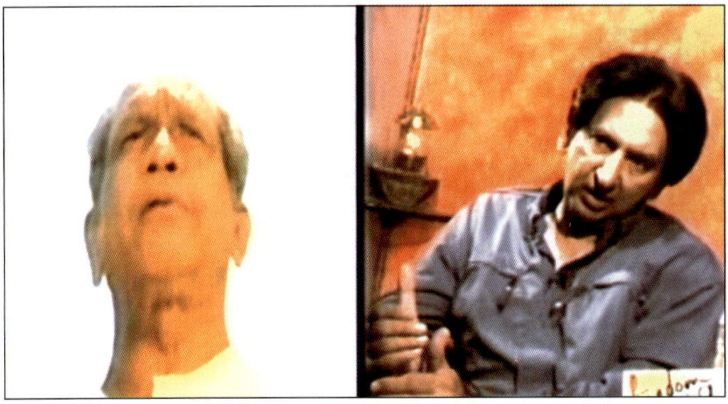

This photograph was given to the author by Kailash Surendranath. He is to the right of the frame seeing a frame featuring the maestro Bhimsen Joshi who appeared at the beginning of the film Mile Sur.

One cannot forget that those were terrible days. In West Bengal, the Naxalite movement of the '70s resulted in unremitting violence. The Communist Party of India (Marxist)—CPI (M)—assumed the reigns of local government and ruled the state for over 30 years, suppressing dissent, stifling the spirit of democracy and attacking the backbone of industry that forced all big and medium businesses to go elsewhere. There was the fallout in Punjab after the storming of the Golden Temple in 1984. Young men and women were dying for their beliefs. In the north-east there was trouble in Mizoram and Nagaland since Independence. Assam entered an era of uncertainty. India seemed to be falling apart. It was a tattered mosaic of old cloth that the leaders were unable to stitch into a whole fabric. Given the overall situation, making a film that evoked a sense of oneness with conviction was no easy task. This film alone achieved what the political leaders could not. It dramatised unity in diversity. It was through music that the film connected with people living in a vast country—it brought home the spirit that enabled a great subcontinent comprising different societies to live as one family.

Surendranath received encouragement and support from Manoj Kumar who had already achieved fame both as an actor and a director of films that focussed on nationalism. He is called Mr India. He tirelessly experimented with effects and bought expensive lenses. Surendranath would borrow a lot of the hardware and use them for his ad films.[28]

[28]This was told to me when I interviewed Kailash Surendranath at his office in Bombay in 2007. I was amazed by his memory. He recollected having seen me in Clarion and mentioned the name of my boss at the time. This was in the mid-1970s.

Ravi Chopra

Another major film production unit that forayed into ad films was B.R. Ads. B.R. Films was an important producer of Hindi commercial cinema. The late B.R. Chopra, a recipient of the Dadasaheb Phalke award, was a leading director who had to his credit a number of highly popular films. He was different from other Hindi film directors in that while he produced films that ran to full houses, his films invariably carried a social message or were anchored around social themes. His son Ravi Chopra, who had an avid interest in advertising films, did a lot of path-breaking work in ad films that they produced in the '70s and '80s. B.R. Ads was probably the first ad film production company that sourced celebrity stars for advertising films. Truth to tell, film stars did not realise the amount that their celebrity status could command. Chopra was eminently reasonable in his estimation to agencies.[29]

Chopra was never content with mediocrity. He did not spare his resources to back every ad film he took up. There were difficulties in sourcing raw stock. With a feature film producer such as B.R. Films this was not a major constraint. Whereas a smaller producer shooting a 100 feet of film would start quibbling for every retake, especially if the length went over 150 feet, for Chopra nothing mattered but excellence. Even when his assistant repeatedly warned him regarding the number of retakes he remained unfazed. It was with B.R. Ads that the fairytale jaunts to tulip farms in Holland, to London and Big Ben, to South Africa and safaris, began to feature in ad films. For Four Square cigarettes the storyboard included a sport till then unknown in India—hang-gliding. They shot the sequences in Europe with a hang-gliding champion. These films were shown across theatres in India for a number of years.

Coke and Pepsi wars became a regular part of every summer marketing cycle. From the campaign, 'There's nothing official about it', the two major soft drink companies slugged it out on television. However, neither of the two colas won Indian hearts. It was 'Thums Up' all the way. These films were different as the positioning sought to capture a specific niche of a macho adventurer who dared to break his own neck with every single adventure.

[29]I have worked closely with B.R. Ads on a number of projects and can verify how reasonable their charges were despite giving them film storyboards that demanded a lot out of them.

Whether these campaigns kept Thums Up as India's favourite cola drink or whether it was the inherent quality of the product that people loved, the fact remains that till date Thums Up continues to reign while Pepsi and Coke stay behind what was to begin with an Indian brand. Neither Pepsi nor Coke ever faced a competitor so superior in their worldwide market.

In the ensuing decade agencies began to lose their place as the best people to go to when making an ad film. Clients normally follow a trend, which is set by one or two big spenders. In the 1950s and 1960s, the major trends would begin either with the leading cigarette companies or with the leading tyre companies or with HLL, which had the largest portfolio of popular FMCG brands. Later, from the end-1980s through to the 1990s, the mantle of initiating change in trends passed into the hands of the two foreign cola giants, Coke and Pepsi. The following trends were major in film-making:

- Films were first made of 30-second duration as the exhibition format changed for films screened at the theatre to films for TV. This again underwent further change when clients who spent huge sums in production decided to revert to a longer one minute TV commercial from 30 seconds at least for the initial burst.
- The route of celebrity endorsement became the norm. A few celebrities began to endorse all kinds of brands without any thought as to whether their endorsement increased brand equity or the fees they charged merely pushed companies into bankruptcy quicker.
- When film stars began endorsing big brands such as Pepsi or Coke, they opened their own production companies. Agencies gradually lost ad film production jobs.
- Specialist ad film-makers such as Prahlad Kakkar dictated terms to clients. They jacked up the base price for TV commercials to a level where only very large companies had resources to engage them. No one repeated the question that David Ogilvy had asked in the 1950s: 'Why should the cost of producing a film be so high?' In India, advertisers generally feel that the most expensive film producers make the best films. How else can they charge such rates?
- Technical improvements in TV film production and editing made films sleeker and more entertaining. Advertising was rapidly being geared to weave entertainment into the brand experience.
- The spiral increase in production cost may be attributed to: (a) elaborate sets (b) foreign locales (c) the inclusion of film stars or cricket players who priced themselves high (d) the advent of professional career management companies that entered into expensive deals with the stars in their fold and therefore raised their price to ensure maximisation of profit from each brand endorsement.

Public relations

The business of a full-service agency has disintegrated in the new millennium. But from the 1950s till about the mid-1980s, full service ad agencies supported their clients with both PR-related services and advertising.

In the 1960s and 1970s, many large corporate houses had a PR manager overseeing both advertising and PR activities. Many eminent professionals worked for organisations who were big media buyers such as Dunlop, Shaw Wallace, ITC, Tisco and Telco and a host of paint companies in Bombay and Calcutta. Some of these people included Sanat Lahiri of Dunlop and Prasanta Sanyal of IOL, S. Viswanathan, advertising manager of Lipton; J.M. Kaul of IOL the first to author a textbook on PR in India; R.P. Gupta of Tata Steel; Gautam Ghosal and Aditi Shyam of ITC. And Manishankar Mukherjee of CESC, who is one of the most celebrated modern Bengali novelists, and a master in his chosen profession—public relations—that he has seen from a nascent stage and still continues to serve, giving excellent PR support to the RPG Group of Companies.[30]

Unlike now, the PR agenda of any big company included as a routine exercise a corporate campaign that broke in the press either every year or every other year. This was an important assignment for the agency. Since major national dailies and magazines were selected to run such ads, the agencies got a platform to showcase their creative strength. The clients benefitted by telling their 'core' public important news pertaining to themselves. The agency handling the PR side of a corporate house also worked on a number of other related items that gave it a steady source of billing. For example, all big companies published an in-house newsletter. Some companies such as ITC published more than one. One of the major assignments of a PR manager was to ensure that the house magazine appeared on time. This meant coordinating with various departments to get newsworthy material, which could then be edited and given to the agency to polish up. The PR manager walked a tight rope ensuring that the in-house magazine did not turn into a litany of praise of the managing director and his engaging spouse. It is also important to remember that in the '50s,'60s and '70s there were no computers. Typewriters were used. Mistakes could not be avoided altogether; nor could mistakes be easily corrected like today. Printing was done by letterpress. Somewhat later, offset printing was used by companies that wanted a quality house magazine. Guest Keen Williams, with Pritish Nandy as ad manager, printed a high quality house magazine.

[30]The high profile PR professionals of the twenty-first century may still learn the fundamentals of public relations from Manishankar Mukherjee. He plans publicity meticulously and is never in the limelight. PR professionals today such as Niira Radia probably miss the basic point of PR when they build their personal images and then use this clout for short-term gains. In the process they lose sight of ethics in business, they land themselves in trouble and cause worse trouble for the clients they are supposed to be working for. I am afraid we have not heard the last of Radia.

All the big companies produced an annual calendar and diary. The calendar was theme-based. Sometimes the theme pertained to the core business activity of the company; at other times it was one that included a strong visual appeal. For example, for Chloride India (manufacturers of Exide car battery), OBM developed a 12-sheet calendar with creatures of the deep seas.[31]

The diary was no simple day and date compilation. It started with a company profile, replete with pictures of the managing director, his wife, other senior officials facing the camera with dour faces since the MD happened to be the centre of attraction, and a few photographs of plant or machinery. When the company exported some item, it was given its due place of importance since Indian exports did not amount to much those days.

The PR manager was also expected to entertain the high and mighty as well as keep the press happy. The members of the press were content if they were not forgotten for dinner invitations and were given a few gifts now and then. Nothing expensive but things such as pen sets, diaries, ties and cuff links with the company logo on them.

The annual report was another major item that passed through the agency ritually for 'doing up' the figures. The creative team in the agency spent long hours preparing suitable alternatives for the cover design. No company in India was making waves. They all plodded along from year to year. There was nothing to look forward to since the people who were at the helm of the government of India regarded 'profit' as a dirty word and their licence raj was hard to beat. The PR manager advised his agency to prepare a plan for despatching direct mail to important government functionaries. These were designed and arty letters in arty envelopes carrying special embossed seals of the managing director duly arrived at the addresses of the 'influential people' in various government departments. How many were read and how many were acted upon is difficult to tell without any evidence of research.

The first PR practitioners were actually wearing two hats by our standards today. They were in PR as well as in advertising. The most well-known practitioners were somehow located in Calcutta, not Bombay. The genesis of the Public Relations Society of India (PRSI) may be traced back to 1965, when Sanat Lahiri, Sankar Mitra, R.P. Gupta, Prasanta Sanyal and J.M. Kaul, along with a few others, formed the Public Relations Circle. In 1968, at the first All India Conference, it merged with the national body.[32]

At the time public relations and publicity were often used interchangeably. In Dunlop, for example, Sanat Lahiri was the publicity manager. He was

---

[31]Ayesha, the copywriter who slaved on the calendar, was a marine biologist who had earned her degree in the UK. I worked for OBM at the time.

[32]Handout published by PRSI in 1994 when it reprinted an old paper authored by Sanat Lahiri in 1976 titled, 'Public Relations in India', which earned him the Shriram Award of the Delhi Management Association in 1976.

Sanat Lahiri (left) with U. Nyun.

already making his mark in the international arena in his discipline although India was a poor country with little infrastructure. Central ministers routinely travelled with a begging bowl to secure food grains for people. Apart from a few specialist disciplines Indians did not feature on international panels.

Large agencies, namely HTA and Clarion, retained the services of a senior executive who was adept at handling corporate jobs. Prasanta Sanyal, for instance, was chief of PR in Clarion before he was elected to become the managing director of the company. Normally they did not have to undertake activities that lobbyists handle nowadays, but they were beginning to develop a holistic perspective of PR.[33] Prasanta Sanyal presented a paper at the first advertising congress in Calcutta titled, 'Making your case heard in Delhi', which drew immediate attention to the fast-changing power structure in the country, leading to the need to re-assess business policies in the light of the unfolding new environment.

Sanat Lahiri

Sanat Lahiri came from a distinguished family. He was the great grandson of Ramtanu Lahiri, who was a prominent figure of the Bengal Renaissance. He was a tall man, very fair, heavily built, with an impressive double chin. In the early 1970s, he had already become the publicity manager of Dunlop. He spoke well and he spoke with authority. By the mid-1970s, he had a team of fairly senior executives handling PR and advertising functions reporting to him. Among them was the famous Bengali novelist Manishankar Mukherjee.

Lahiri was for a time the president of the Advertising Club of Calcutta. He initiated training programmes conducted by the club. In these programmes all important subjects pertaining to PR and advertising were covered by senior members of the profession working for ad agencies or advertisers. Lahiri addressed many gatherings and wrote on PR-related subjects or on advertising quite often.[34] He was the first Asian to be elected president of the

[33]In May 2010, *Hindustan Times* picked up the story of Niira Radia, who runs a slew of PR firms. She not only helps renegade politicians get plum postings but her long arm seems to stretch to the PM's office. This is a dangerous portent for national security and calls for laws to restrict the scope of functioning of lobbyists and PR firms.

[34]I attended the second training course of the club. Sanat Lahiri spoke on 'Briefing the agency'.

International Public Relations Association. He was also the communication consultant to the United Nations Economic Commission for Asia and the Far East. He was for a time the chairman of the Audit Bureau of Circulation. His monograph on PR, a pioneering work, won him the Shriram Award of the Delhi Management Association in 1976.

Prasanta Sanyal

Prasanta Sanyal

Prasanta Sanyal was one of those gentlemen comrades who spent their green years in the service of the undivided Communist Party of India (CPI). Subrata Sengupta and J.M. Kaul were comrades-in-arms, hiding from the police before they realised it was best to surface and enjoy the sun. They probably drifted into advertising, a profession led by social deviants and therefore a profession that regarded with disdain any career path that was predictably boring.

All his friends, associates and critics agreed that Sanyal was extraordinarily gifted in his handling of people. He heard everyone; he helped whoever came for assistance;[35] he read avidly, remembering and storing much of what he read and heard, which turned him into an engaging conversationalist. In this time of 'sms' messages, Facebook and Twitter, it is impossible to recreate another age to explain the advantages a conversationalist enjoyed in various social circles. Sanyal naturally gravitated towards PR.

His career was eventful. He was general secretary of the All India Students Federation. He was a staff writer for his party's weekly paper. He spent five years as the general manager of People's Publishing House (PPH) in Bombay. He put an ailing concern on its feet. He added a new dimension by setting out to discover new writers. He was the first to draw up a perspective plan for his organisation; PPH continued to benefit from this plan long after he left. He worked for a short while in the Indian Statistical Institute where the famous Professor Prasanta Mahalanabis accommodated him.

Then Sanyal joined JWT as a copywriter. This is where his career in PR and advertising formally began. After a short while he went to Clarion, but left it to join IOL as its PR manager. It was around this time that his services were requisitioned by Indira Gandhi, who was then the Minister for Information & Broadcasting.

[35] I was privileged to work in Clarion when Prasanta Sanyal was the managing director. Every payday various people turned up at Clarion. We were told PS (that is how we referred to him) shared his own salary with them. Ritwik Ghatak, the famous film-maker, was perennially short of cash and came quite frequently. I can well imagine how difficult it must have been for him to meet his own expenses. The leading agencies then did not pay their chief executives in lakhs.

In 1967, he left IOL and took up an assignment with *The Times of India* as its bureau chief in London. He returned to India in 1969 and joined Clarion as the director, PR. He became the managing director of the company, which he led for 10 years, a period that marked the peak in Clarion's long and tumultuous history.

In 1975, he was elected president of the Advertising Agencies Association of India. He served on the National Committee of the Audit Bureau of Circulation, representing the ad agencies. After his retirement from Clarion in 1979, he worked as member of the senior management group in Calcutta's leading newspaper publishing house, the Ananda Bazar Group of Publications.[36]

J.M. Kaul

A short fair man with a welcoming smile, J.M. Kaul, who was the PR manager of IOL, is an important personality in Indian PR. He is generally self-effacing in personal interactions, but is no pushover when debating an issue. Like his friend and mentor, Prasanta Sanyal, he devoted some of his best years in the service of the CPI. His early education in St. Xavier's Calcutta taught him to speak and write English well. He was a keen participant in debating. His book, *Public Relations in India*, was the first textbook on PR in the country.

It was from the middle of the 1980s, when pioneers such as J.M. Kaul retired from their jobs, that a new breed of PR experts began to make their presence felt. By then the importance of Calcutta as a centre of advertising and PR had lessened. This was inevitable because businesses in the eastern metropolis were finding it impossible to co-exist with violence unleashed by militant trade unions.

A new breed of PR professionals emerged. They generally came from newspapers. Journalists with a few years of work experience saw the business opportunity of PR, they could use their contacts in the press. It took very little to set up a company. With perseverance it was possible for an entrepreneur to consolidate a PR set-up. Companies with names such as Good Relations and Perfect Relations cropped up in Delhi. They serviced their clients with diligence and professionalism. Soon they established offices in the other metros where business was growing.

[36] I have sourced much of the material from a small book published after his death, *Remembering Prasanta Sanyal*, printed at Laurens & Co. (Printers), 9 Crooked Lane, Calcutta.

4

1980–1990

Learning

The decade of the seventies ended ominously for India in more ways than one. In 1977, General Zia-ul-Haq headed a coup and dislodged the elected government of Pakistan. In 1979, he had former Prime Minister Bhutto hanged. Zia-ul-Haq started a clandestine exercise to bleed India. China became a close ally of Pakistan and leveraged the continuing tension between the neighbours to its own advantage.

The eighties was a decade of blood-letting. In Punjab, J.S. Bhindranwale, who was initially propped up by the Congress Party to break the stranglehold of the Akalis in Punjab politics, became a centre of political power. His brand of extremist Akali politics led to demands of a free state in Punjab. Indira Gandhi decided to rein in Bhindranwale in 1984. It led to the storming of the Golden Temple, the most hallowed place of worship for the Sikhs.

Punjab went through a terrible period of rebellion. The common people suffered. The revolt received support from the government of Pakistan. The eastern states were also restive. The Mizo and Naga insurrections were long-standing festering wounds that the Central Governments were trying to contain. Assam, which was seeing a change to its population mix because of continuous migration from Bangladesh, also broke into rebellion. The new military rulers of Bangladesh were no friends of India. Bangladesh provided a safe haven for the rebels. China gave them arms and trained their soldiers who were disaffected youth in search of a better future, which they believed they could not get in India. Manipur, which like the rest of the North-east was undeveloped and had very little Central assistance, was waiting to turn into yet another state in revolt.

Economically, there was hardly any movement forward over the years. The following table show the standstill position of the Indian economy between the seventies and the eighties. The economy was ruined by the Congress Party ruling in Delhi. Socialism was the flavour of the seasons that followed Independence. Lifestyle-related goods and services were regarded with suspicion. The table reflects this position.

PRODUCTION OF AUTOMOBILES IN INDIA (in '000s)[1]

	Cars and Jeeps	Commercial Vehicles	Two-Wheelers	Total Motor Vehicles	Tractors	Total Vehicles
1970–71	45.8	42.3	108.6	203	20	221.3
1980–81	47	74.1	440.3	558	70.3	658.6

The eighties also marked a watershed in changing taste and food habits. Maggi Noodles achieved this with a remarkable campaign that was initially aimed at families in the higher socio-economic groups where lifestyle changes were likely to face fewer hurdles of rejection; the campaign then percolated down to the lower economic strata. Nestle carried on a relentless TV barrage for years. It cornered for itself 90 per cent of the market share of the Rs 1,000 crore instant noodle market by 2010.[2]

The 1980s brought about a considerable change in media exposure among Indians. Television grew in importance and replaced newspapers as the primary medium for all major campaigns. There were major technical changes in producing films for television. Initially ad agencies and film producers used the usual 35 mm film format in colour. Later, cameras for television production were freely available. And editing a movie became far more flexible with computers replacing the age-old manual process. There were major improvements in effects and in sound recording. Recording studios were digitised by the end of the eighties and early 1990s.

Subrata Sengupta

Subrata Sengupta died in March 2004. In the obituary published by *The Economic Times* he was said to be 85 years old. We therefore assume he was born around 1919.

It is difficult to place men such as Subrata Sengupta and Subhas Ghosal, who were friends, in a time grid. Sengupta's biography may have been included in the earlier chapters or 1990s because from the mid-1950s he was a well-known ad personality. Like Ghosal, he had a very long and

[1]I have taken these figures from 'India at 50', published by Express Publications (Madurai) Ltd, 1997.
[2]*Brand Equity*, 23 June 2010.

productive life and died in harness, working till the end. The only reason for placing him in the 1980s was the unimportant fact of his retirement from Clarion as executive vice chairman and CEO in 1983. He did not retire from advertising. Ghosal requested him to be the advisor at Contract Advertising, where Ghosal was into his second innings, doing exceedingly well.

When D.J. Keymer closed down operations in Calcutta in 1956, Sengupta along with Sachindranath Banerjee and Subhas Sen went to Keymer clients, requesting them to support a new agency that they proposed to set up. The agency would be formed as a cooperative of employees. Dunlop, which had seen the talent in Sengupta and the team that he led, agreed to nurture and support the new venture.

Sengupta soon became the visible face of Clarion. He built up a reputation for strategic thinking that was based on the realities of the marketplace. He was later posted in Bombay where he helped Clarion become one of the leading agencies. He handled some of its key accounts. Geoffrey Manners' Kolynos toothpaste, Philips audio systems and Farex from Glaxo were brands he helped to establish. His clients held him in awe.

He was a formidable opponent for agencies when it was a matter of competitive presentations in winning accounts. Ghosal, quoted in the obit, is supposed to have said, 'We do our business by our gift for the gab. Subrata is a thinker, who brings in intellectual rigour or brainpower into advertising'. Sengupta taught at the leading business institutes in India and was associated with IIM Ahmedabad between 1970 and1974 and then with IIM Calcutta. He was also one of the first professionals who wrote books on advertising and marketing. *Brand Positioning*, a well-researched work based on his brand experience, is a textbook for students of advertising.

However, Clarion, the agency he founded, began to flounder as senior managers running the business started quarrelling among themselves for a share of the fish and loaves. The union proved to be the kingmaker. After Sengupta, CEOs were appointed and sacked in a theatre of the absurd. The union boss could not determine whether he should rule over the kingdom as chief or allow a dummy chief to sit on the high chair while he pulled strings from behind. Sengupta was party to all these unsavoury happenings; he could be held culpable in inciting the union to destroy the agency which he founded.

Changes in media that influenced advertising

The decade of the eighties was a period of new learning for advertising professionals. In the mid-1970s, TV began to find its place in homes. This despite the fact that the entire medium was under government control, which meant that programmes were immeasurably dull. Youngsters born after the mid-1980s would hardly believe that to watch TV families visited homes of those fortunate few who owned black and white TV sets.

TV showtime was restricted to five or six hours. What did TV present? Talk shows pertaining to subjects such as health, culture, agriculture, industry, India's export earnings, education and other absorbing subjects; some dance and musical programmes; circus shows borrowed from foreign channels; sports programmes including sports that nobody had heard of in the country such as skiing, hang-gliding, surfboard skating and so on.

Colour TV became popular after 1982, the year that Asiad was held in New Delhi. Indira Gandhi sanctioned funds for around 300 low power transmitters (LPTs) across towns. Tariffs on local and imported sets were reduced, giving a boost to the purchase of TV sets. By 1985, there were 4.5 million TV sets in the country; by the end of the decade about 60 per cent of the population was covered by LPTs.

From the 1970s till the early eighties, the mindset of film producers and ad agencies was glued to the past. They edited 100 foot ad films to the requirements of TV time booked. But from around the middle of the 1980s, commercials were made for the shorter duration capsules required by TV. From 1983, Doordarshan enabled telecasting of commercial programmes across the entire national network.

Pandit Vinod Sharma

Videos became very popular and video parlours provided cassettes of the latest pirated films. Bollywood films were copied even before they could be shown in theatres. This spurious business became so serious that producers began to exert pressure on local governments to act against the culprits.

A significant development along with the spread of television was the development of commercials in the vernacular. The Vicks' *'gala me khich khich'* commercial starring Jayant Kripalani and scripted by

Pandit Vinod Sharma was a memorable one.[3] This was in 1983–84. Vicks set the trend of using TV with many repeat insertions to peg the brand in the consumers' psyche.

Pandit Vinod Sharma is a renowned scholar in Hindi and Sanskrit. He began his career with All India Radio and was involved in the production of radio plays.[4] Blessed with a rich voice, he became a favourite of many who regularly tuned into his programmes. Sharma, like most other eminent language writers of the period, was sought by agencies to translate scripts or write jingles for radio and television. He fretted when he worked for agencies because he rarely got an opportunity to do anything by himself.[5] The original idea and even the words were written in English. He only translated these words from English to Hindi.

However, he tried to persuade agencies to give the language copywriters a chance to think in Hindi. It was much later in the 1990s that a crop of small-town boys who were educated in the vernacular entered advertising and began to change the way things were done in ad agencies. But it was Sharma's pioneering work in thinking in the vernacular that broke the traditional system of making Hindi ads from English copy.

Early TV ads were far more interesting than those seen in primetime today. For example, children who grew up in the 1980s danced to the Nirma jingle every time the ad was shown on TV. Nirma demonstrated the benefit of channel saturation. There was nothing extraordinary in the storyboard; it showed an attractive model with swirls of multi-coloured cloth. But the constant repetition of the spot and accompanying jingle, 'Washing powder Nirma, washing powder Nirma', built a strong recall of the brand. Nirma became the number one brand in its segment. HLL, which had long dominated the washing segment, wore a frown.

Lintas and HLL came out with their hard-hitting Lalitaji campaign that tried to sell the concept of 'the better detergent' as opposed to a 'cheap detergent', a niche Nirma dominated. Concept-wise the Lalitaji ad was not remarkable. It was simple. The character part was played to perfection. Lalitaji epitomised an aggressive no-nonsense housewife; in some ways a person most people

---

[3]Jayant Kripalani was an ad professional who later went on to become an actor.

[4]In a small booklet published on the occasion of Pandit Vinod Sharma completing 50 years of association with All India Radio, Ranjan Kapur, who was then managing director of O&M, writes, erroneously, 'One who pioneered the concept of radio plays; and made them a part of people's lives.'

[5]I interviewed Pandit Vinod Sharma in his Bombay home in 2000 when he spoke about his anguish in generally being forced to work from English scripts.

Lalitaji explaining to the housewife why Surf gives the best value for money.

would regard as opinionated. HLL had the advantage of being a company with deep pockets. Therefore, the Lalitaji ad, like its competitor Nirma, was repeatedly shown to gain top-of-mind recall.

In a write-up on Alyque Padamsee, which appeared in *The Times of India*, the author attributed the characterisation of Lalitaji on Padamsee's mother.[6] However, this may be regarded as storytelling; advertising personalities, like film personalities, have myths or fables built around them or their lives as it enables writers or videographers to project them as colourful characters.

Advertisers found good avenues of mass appeal with programmes such as *Chhaya Geet* and the Sunday evening Hindi film shown by Doordarshan. Companies and brands were allowed to sponsor soap operas beginning with *Hum Log* in 1983. In 1984, *Yeh Jo Hai Zindagi* was sponsored by Vicco. Ramesh Sippy's *Buniyaad,* the first of the mega soaps, was telecast in 1986.[7] Nirma and Richardson Hindustan Limited (RHL) booked heavily into time slots available. Apart from HLL, Nestle, Nirma and RHL, Videocon and Godrej with its Cinthol lime rode this route with success. Sales of these brands doubled in TV towns as opposed to non-TV towns.

Television officials in Doordarshan, New Delhi, were quick to see the potential of lining their pockets by making the availability of time slots an opaque business. The bigger advertisers and their agencies recruited touts who were based in Delhi to ensure that they managed the time slots required by their media departments. The time for specialist media agencies had not come; but the function of the specialist media expert was already being performed by the tout.

Nestle's Maggi Noodles became one of the first successful TV brands. The brand reported Rs 7 crore turnover in the first year itself. It was advertised heavily on TV and positioned as a convenient in-between meals snack, especially targeted at hungry children. Nestle changed for good the snacking

[6]Alyque Padamsee recounts in his autobiography *A Double Life* that the Lalitaji film was shot down when it was first presented. Subsequently, after re-dubbing, it took a person of Shunu Sen's stature to permit screening. Sen told Padamsee that in case there was criticism after the first screening they would take it off the air.

[7]*Business Today*, anniversary issue, 2002, article by Shailesh Dobhal.

habit of families across the country. Around 1987, Nescafe was the first Indian spot to use only music and no voiceover.

Agencies soon learnt to pull at heart strings through clever use of emotions. Bajaj crystallised everything that was beautiful in an Indian home with their 'Hamara Bajaj' campaign.

A frame from the Bajaj ad film.

Expressing emotions with Cadburys chocolate.

O&M made a series of delightful films for Cadburys and claimed with conviction that for young hearts you could express emotions better than words with Cadburys chocolate. The selection of models was so good that a number of them went on to become famous Bollywood stars. One film showed a cricket match being played. A girl invades the pitch and dances in joy. In the seventies and eighties, cricket and football fans often ran onto the playing arena when a game was in progress. It was also common to see, especially in televised matches played in the UK, spectators discarding their clothes and running onto the pitch chased by policemen. The Cadburys storyboard is based on this theme.

Initially spots such as Liril, with the girl in the waterfalls, were spliced from a 75-footer cinema film; the 35 mm cinema film was run via Tele-Cine or transferred to tape and then projected. But viewers soon got used to short 30-second films on TV as opposed to longer one minute films that were generally screened in cinema halls. With rapid induction of new technology, TV commercials made by ad agencies or producers became less concept or idea-driven and more technology-oriented. Fast cuts, morphing, zipper-editing and effects—current computer-based technology makes it easy to work on effects.

Some of the other notable campaigns on TV need to be mentioned. Onida did a reverse positioning. The film brought in the devil with two horns and revolved around the idea of 'envy'. The Onida brand of television was the neighbour's envy and the owner's pride. In a subsequent film, a child devil, with two horns and a tail, was also featured.

The Onida devil was created by Avenues Advertising.

This Raymonds ad was made by Enterprise-Nexus at a later date. The slogan, 'The complete man', which Raymond still uses, owes its origin to Nexus.

Raymond was yet another brand that turned to celebrate a warm father-son relationship. The concept had a lot of possibilities of extension. Later they celebrated a teacher-student relationship, much like the father-son relationship, where both the men were well dressed, in unmistakable Raymond suiting.

In the late eighties, Shammi Kapoor and Jalal Agha, perhaps not being aware that pan masala is injurious to health, made Pan Parag a huge success with their TV spot. In so doing they also turned the nasty habit of 'chewing pan masala' and spitting in public places a national trait.

No history of television in India can be complete without recounting the impact the serials of Ramanand Sagar's *Ramayana* and B.R. Chopra and Ravi Chopra's *Mahabharata* had upon the many millions of people in India. Doordarshan was the only channel—it had a huge captive audience. Today, with so many stations, TRPs are counted in single digit. It is hard to imagine streets across towns and cities becoming empty while *Mahabharata* was telecast on Sunday mornings. People stopped visiting friends or ringing up people unless there was a crisis. Viewership of the serials was many times more than the number of TV sets because those who did not possess sets visited neighbours so as not to miss an episode.

A number of new producers made their mark in the eighties. Film stars who had high popularity ratings modelled for the big brands such as Coke and Pepsi, Bajaj, Titan, Tata Tea and various products from Dabur's extensive portfolio of brands. Brand managers were quick to spot that it made more sense if they went to the film stars directly instead of going through their ad agency. They merely wanted the brands to ride piggyback on the popularity of the film stars. Film stars started their own production units; advertisers and film stars were both happy with the new arrangement. Film production ad agencies became redundant.

Print

As far back as 1961, *The Times of India* showed that there was a ready market for specialist publications when it first launched *The Economic Times* in Bombay. The city provided the best environment for a specialist newspaper. It was the financial capital of India. Big and medium industries were located there in far bigger numbers than in any other metro city; senior managers who ran these businesses and the owners of companies needed a daily newspaper that concentrated on business news.

In the mid-1970s, Delhi and Calcutta editions of *The Economic Times* were published. In the mid-1980s, the Bangalore edition was added while, in 1990, the Ahmedabad edition appeared. The main competitor to *The Economic Times* was *The Financial Express,* which was also first published in 1961. *The Financial Express* belonged to the other big newspaper chain in India, The Indian Express Group.

Besides newspapers that were focussed on trade news, there were magazines such as *Industrial Products Finder*, which was a compilation of technical advertisements. Purchase managers of organisations found this a useful magazine to look over when they were in the market for technical products. It was first published in 1972. In 1961, *Electrical India* appeared;

it got INS membership in 1975. *Industrial Equipment News*, published in 1984, received INS membership the same year.

One of the oldest technical magazines was the *Indian Textile Journal* that was published in 1890. It received INS membership in 1965, which was about the longest any publication waited for registration with INS. *Electronics For You* appeared in 1969 and *Elektor India*, another electronics magazine, first appeared in 1983, receiving INS membership in 1985. Electronics was the new mantra of high technology in the 1970s and 1980s as TV sets and new music systems began to appear in the market. However, in India the pace of development of industrial advertising was tardy. Agencies gave little encouragement to such magazines and only included them as a reminder medium, preferring to stick to mainline dailies in English even for technical products.

The big name to be mentioned among the new magazines in the seventies was *India Today*, published from Delhi. The inaugural issue appeared on 15 December 1975. *India Today* received membership of the INS in 1978.

Previously magazines were printed on newsprint. These could not reproduce colour advertisements well. In the making of colour ads, agencies had restrictions in using fine screens. The new magazines, printed on better quality paper, allowed art directors to experiment with photographs.

India Today was modelled on *Time* magazine. It printed a great many photographs of events and happenings both political and social. The magazine quickly became popular among the younger and upwardly mobile set in metro cities. Advertising followed the growth of circulation. Very soon *India Today* introduced strict norms on receipt of ad material.[8] This was necessary for it to maintain its publishing schedule. Agencies realised that here was another publication such as *Reader's Digest* that would not wait to receive material.

India was beginning to change socially. Otherwise it would not have seen the birth of a magazine such as *Debonair* in 1972, which was permitted 'soft porn' in the country. It printed poetry and prose that no one read and readers turned the pages to see the girls on show. They were all bikini-clad but then in those days that was titillation enough for the sex-starved young Indian male. Did *Debonair* get a lot of advertising support from agencies? Not really. The problem probably lay with the advertisers. They may have felt coy using a bold medium to carry the brand message.

---

[8]I remember Meera Paul in Calcutta sweeping in like royalty at Clarion and OBM, asking for material and reminding account executives that if they did not ensure she received positives and progressives on time the ad would not be printed. Except for her professional strictness she was otherwise a very helpful soul.

Tara Sinha

Tara Sinha joined Clarion in the mid-1950s. She received training in the UK in advertising and was one of the early professionals in the field with what may today be called a marketable diploma. She was an eminently capable person and soon established her credentials as a leader within Clarion. It is also said that she did not suffer fools easily and she normally tended to be somewhat aggressive—true to the image of the American ad professional.

In the first advertising congress, held in Calcutta, Sinha delivered a speech in which she expressed in her forthright manner the unsatisfactory level of support being given to the agencies by the print media. She was scathing in her criticism of major newspapers and demanded true figures on readership. She postulated that the newspapers were making sufficient profit from their advertising inflow and advertisers and agencies had a right to demand that they invest in research so that the advertisers and their agencies could plan releases in the most suitable newspapers not on hunch but based on data.

Sinha left Clarion to join Coca Cola. She may well have been among the few Indians who had the managerial competence to do justice to a senior management position in an American company. In the late 1980s, after the retirement of Subrata Sengupta as CEO, Sinha was invited to head Clarion by the fickle 'majority' of shareholders who incidentally were also members of the notorious Clarion union. Why Sinha took charge of Clarion remains a mystery. She did not have a political bent of mind. As a professional she was only too ready to take hard decisions to put the floundering Clarion on an even keel. She was not inclined to bow before the union leaders. The parting was inevitable. She left Clarion to set up Tara Sinha McCann. In the process she walked away with some prize accounts of Clarion, such as Nestle.

As Clarion continued to flounder in their union-related trouble, and chief executives came in and left faster than anyone could count, Tara Sinha Associates flourished. Sinha set up branches in all the main metros. She started a research company and had a meaningful relationship with McCann Ericsson. In the 1990s, when economic liberalisation became a reality and it seemed none of the large agencies could survive without a foreign affiliate, Tara Sinha sold her majority stake to McCann. She leads a retired life in Delhi.

In the eighties an agency called Mudra commenced operation. Like Ulka and Trikaya, it had an Indian name and, like both these agencies, it was destined to make waves in advertising. It was headquartered in Ahmedabad, not Bombay. It came loaded with money as the company was promoted by Dhirubhai Ambani.

A.G. Krishnamurthy

The fact that Mudra belonged to a larger group with deep pockets was a departure from the normal agency start-ups where ambitious creative personnel or account servicing people with little to support them besides hope start an operation. Ambani appointed A.G. Krishnamurthy as the head of the new agency with a mandate to make it a leading ad agency in the country. Krishnamurthy proved relentless in fulfilling this objective.

Like MCM in the mid-1960s, Mudra was not afraid to ruffle a few feathers. It pursued clients aggressively and even informed clients that it would not charge for artwork. This caused much heartburn in other agencies. After establishing itself, Mudra refuted these charges as 'allegations' without any basis.[9]

A.G. Krishnamurthy also went on an aggressive hiring spree. He inducted professionals from leading agencies in creative, servicing and media and ensured they had a congenial atmosphere for doing good work. Although Mudra has never been placed alongside the known creative agencies such as Rediffusion, Trikaya and O&M, it always enjoyed considerable media presence thanks to Vimal. Vimal fabrics gave it an opportunity to be present in TV and print media in a big way.

Krishnamurthy persuaded Dhirubhai to start a school of advertising. This too was located in Ahmedabad. Krishnamurthy was designated chairman of the governing body of MICA. He encouraged the dean to invite professionals from all the leading agencies. Over a period of time MICA became the best known brand in advertising training in the country. Initially boys and girls who passed out were absorbed by Mudra. Today, a diploma from the institute ensures a sure passage to a rewarding career in advertising as agencies compete to get the best talent from MICA.

---

[9]I was intimated by a client in Calcutta, a leading pharmaceutical company, that Mudra had approached it on its own and offered to provide artworks for free. This particular company did not accept the offer because it thought the agency should charge for artworks otherwise it would not be able to pay a good salary to employees and retain competent people.

Krishnamurthy left Mudra at a time when the world of Reliance was going through a period of strife as the two sons of Dhirubhai Ambani fought a bitter war to stake their claim to the corporate booty after the death of their famous father. Like every senior employee in the group, Krishnamurthy had to choose the side he wished to serve, but in doing so he ensured that the legacy he had built up at Mudra continued in very good hands. Madhukar Kamath had been groomed by him for some years before he left to join Bates India as the chief executive.

Bates bought Clarion—a deal that was struck and sealed by Kamath. Clarion had almost closed down by the end of the eighties with constant unrest, thanks to its union bosses who refused to see the inevitable outcome of their militant trade unionism. Kamath successfully amalgamated Clarion with Bates and decided to call the agency Bates, blotting out the old name of the agency forever. As seems to be the norm in most foreign-owned agencies, a CEO loses his position in three to five years, when his overseas bosses perceive he has nothing more to contribute. At times regular interaction between the Indian CEO and his immediate superior leads to friction. In any case, Kamath like many others saw himself out of Bates soon enough.

When he rejoined Mudra as the chief executive, it was a natural succession. He was familiar with the working environment of the agency, having been employed there for a considerable period of time. His stint at Bates built his reputation as a capable leader. All credit should go to Krishnamurthy who ensured a smooth succession upon his departure. In this respect Krishnamurthy was like Subhas Ghosal and Mani Ayer both of whom ended their association with their agencies ensuring smooth succession by capable leaders.

Outdoor advertising

Outdoor advertising in various forms has been an integral part of the advertising mix in India since the late nineteenth century.[10] Outdoor did not mean only hoardings although hoardings were the most visible face of outdoor advertising. The sandwich man with a board on his chest and another on his back walked the streets of Bombay. But he had to follow the guidelines given by the police. He could not walk on the footpath; he had to keep close to the kerb, ringing a bell every now and then to warn other traffic passing by that he was around.

In the early part of the book we have seen pictures of kiosks and outdoor exhibitions. Advertising messages were put on the sides of public transport in Bombay, Madras and Calcutta. A number of companies operated in the outdoor business in all the major metro towns.

[10] I have covered early outdoor advertising in India and the UK in *Indian Advertising 1780 to 1950.*

A gentleman called Mr Nicholson ran a company in Bombay called Selvel. It was the biggest hoarding company in the western metropolis. It is likely that he employed a young Parsee gentleman named Russi B. Gimi who later went to Calcutta where he started another Selvel outfit. Long before Gimi set foot in Calcutta, a company called Karukrit traded in hoardings.

Russi B. Gimi, 1923-1993

Gimi deserves special mention in outdoor advertising. Starting his life as a poor migrant in Calcutta, he set up a business which became the biggest outdoor company in the country. He brought to the business of outdoor a touch of respectability, despite the fact that the tough men who ran other outdoor companies were regarded more as thugs than gentlemen. Gimi, with his charities and his untiring support to any cause that benefitted others, established both himself and the profession from which he earned millions on a platform of respect. He was elected president of the Advertising Club of Calcutta. He was also the mayor of the city of Calcutta.

Gimi professionalised outdoor advertising. His hoardings had a border around them. The name of his company was prominently displayed on vacant sites. He ensured excellent relations with landlords who rented their premises for hoardings. Gimi realised that the business of hoardings was largely technology-driven. He needed engineers to put up sites that would stand up to pre-monsoon gales in various parts of the country and knew that a site lit up at night gave the client exclusive visibility. Gimi charged more for premium lit sites and employed electricians to light up and maintain such sites.

He also realised the importance of building a pan-India network and opened offices in most of the state capitals in eastern and northern India. There was some understanding with the Selvel of Nicholson that the two Selvels would not tread on each other's toes. This tacit agreement prevented Gimi from going west or south where Bombay Selvel was present.

The outdoor business was highly competitive. Like in the West, the people who managed the business were not squeamish about the methods they used to bag sites, get clients and break every municipal law to ensure they earned a good profit. From the 1950s to the 1980s, corruption in public life first turned into a practical art form and then became a necessary part of existence. Municipalities, the police and whoever else was supposed to look after city amenities found a steady source of unaccountable income from 'hoarding-wallahs'. It was this sleazy underbelly of the outdoor business that led the profession to look for tough men.

There were a few who continued to professionalise outdoor. After Gimi's death in 1993, Noomi Mehta assumed control of Selvel. He initiated research in outdoor. Research studies were conducted in Delhi, Bombay and Calcutta to find out the pattern of in-city vehicular traffic flow by type of vehicle and arrive at figures that gave clients an approximation of the visibility of individual sites at different places within the city. Here was an attempt to study the OTS—opportunity to see—of an outdoor campaign and compare the average OTS with other media. Selvel also conducted studies to examine whether accidents are caused by hoardings or whether past accident statistics indicate any association between hoarding displays and accidents. For the study, Selvel engaged the Department of Transport Management of the Indian Institute of Social Welfare and Business Management, affiliated to the Calcutta University. At the time, a ruling by the Supreme Court, which banned hoardings in the Delhi municipal area and led to a national debate on the subject, made these studies very relevant.

Noomi Mehta

A chartered accountant by qualification, Noomi Mehta has been at the helm of affairs in Selvel since the death of Russi B. Gimi in 1993. Mehta is a past president of the Advertising Club of Calcutta. He speaks on issues connected to outdoor. Under his leadership, Selvel invests on a continuing basis on training of employees. Professors from IIM Calcutta and from IISWBM have conducted various training courses for Selvel executives. He takes a keen interest in social welfare, just like Gimi before him. He is also a patron of the arts—he owns an art gallery that displays the works of promising artists.

The outdoor media world has seen plenty of action after the 1990s, especially after foreign agencies began acquiring leading Indian ad companies. The WPP Group agencies such as O&M and JWT started their outdoor wing. They bought Out-Of-Home (O-O-H) media from companies such as Selvel and packaged outdoor for their clients. The so-called hoarding companies became even more marginalised because they lacked the marketing face of a large ad agency. Companies such as Selvel provided a rich resource base for O&M and JWT, who picked up professionals trained by the outdoor concessionaires. Most of those who head the outdoor arms of the leading advertising agencies trace their origin to Selvel or other traditional hoarding companies.

Subhash Dey Niyogi

Subhash Dey Niyogi joined the outdoor advertising field in 1968. If the hoarding scene then was as disorganised as it is now, it was technically far more challenging as putting up sites in distant places and getting painters to hand paint hoardings on time for a campaign was not a job meant for armchair professionals.

Niyogi trained and sharpened the management skills of almost every senior executive in the employment of O-O-H media companies in India. He also trained a large contingent of semi-skilled and unskilled workmen to undertake civil and electrical structural work and on-site maintenance.

By the early 1980s, the main centres of advertising were Bombay, Delhi, Madras and Bangalore. The major part of national advertising expenditure took place from Bombay and Delhi. Most of the leading agencies were headquartered in these cities; most national advertisers were also based in these cities. Madras and Bangalore began to see capital inflow as new businesses related to engineering and high technology services were set up.

Calcutta, which till the mid-1970s remained a major industrial metro in the country, lost its sheen as businesses owned by the richest business community in eastern India, the Marwaris, shifted their production base from West Bengal to Delhi, Bombay and the southern metropolitan cities. Advertising volumes fell sharply. But even in the 1980s the major ad agencies retained their presence in the city because a number of large multinational companies such as ITC, Dunlop and the two major packaged tea companies—Brooke Bond and Lipton—remained there, forking out sufficient work for their agencies. All this was destined to change—and change rapidly!

With the Asiad of 1982, Delhi opened up great opportunities for advertising and business. Entrepreneurs learnt to live with and exploit the political and bureaucratic establishments. As businesses flocked to Delhi, corruption became the norm. Advertising businesses took off and flourished where bribing individuals became the standard practice. Once a senior manager of a public sector or private company was netted, he ensured a smooth flow of orders as it generated earnings for him.

The quality of advertising, especially in the electronic media, improved dramatically in the 1980s. The importance of TV in media plans went up significantly. National dailies tried their utmost to hold on to their share of the pie. In the process they began to publish magazines which were part of the newspapers on Sundays and national holidays. Just as Hindi movies was a passion with Indians in the decades before the advent of television, in the 1980s Doordarshan kept the middle-classes engrossed with its teleserials. Advertising readily grabbed all that was popular for use in commercials. *Hum Log* in 1984, *Yeh Jo Hai Zindagi* in 1984 and *Buniyaad* in 1986 provided lots of leads to copywriters and art directors when they scripted storyboards.

COMPARATIVE STUDY OF RADIO AND TV IN INDIA[11]

Particulars	Radio	TV
1982		
No. of stations	86	11
No. of transmitters	162	41
Area covered	78.83%	6.74%
No. of sets	1,22,00,725	21,90,957
Total programme hours	5,72,329	46,000
1987		
No. of stations	92	11
No. of transmitters	170	225
Population covered	95%	52%
1990		
No. of stations	102	11
No. of transmitters	172	425
Population covered	96%	72%
Area covered	87%	50%
No. of sets	9,50,00,000	2,00,00,000

Press advertisements of the 1980s were a carry-over from the kind of advertisements usually preferred by clients and prepared by agencies in the previous decade or even earlier. But as the challenge of market competition between brands became more intense, there was a greater stridency in the approach and messages. 'I am the best', 'I am the prettiest', 'I am the cheapest and best' were often conveyed through ads. We assume the target audience believed everything that was said because the agencies and clients released ongoing campaigns without much change. Here are examples of advertising in the 1980s.

[11]The table was presented in a lecture delivered by Sunil Mishra, director, audience research, on 23 January 1990 in New Delhi. I have taken it from *India at 50*, published by Express Publications (Madurai) Ltd.

Fabrics

A Clarion advertisement—the lady, even if she is young and attractive, is rather like a mother or school teacher. What she is wearing does not stand out as any different from other fabrics. The baseline reinforces beauty with Binny. The dress the lady wears does not stand out for its 'prints'. The body copy is not outstanding.

The brand name was well-known in the 1980s. The ad is stupid and sexist. The concept may have been inspired by James Bond films, which were popular among the youth at the time.

Gwalior Suiting carried many advertisements in print. Like other leading brands, Gwalior also ran ads in cinema halls, particularly around festival times such as Diwali and Ganesh Puja. In black and white, the ad cost almost half of what a colour ad would cost. Credibility in the Dornfab claim is zero. Indian advertising often goes overboard with unsupportable claims.

Crafted by India's first ad agency, Dattarams, the ad is quite similar to the campaign being run by Raymonds over the last few years. Notice the opening sentence of the body copy, 'The choice of elegant families everywhere'. I wonder whether the Raymonds TV commercials were inspired by this campaign.

Celebrity endorsement of brands by India's most loved sportsmen—cricket players—was not unknown, though the trend was not a vogue with every leading brand. After the Indian cricket team won the One Day World Cup in England, other faces such as Kapil Dev, the captain of the team, Roger Binny and Mohinder Amarnath also featured as brand endorsers. They were paid a pittance. Perhaps youngsters now should be informed that the man in Dinesh is Sunil Gavaskar.

The headline connects with the World Cup. The BSA SLR brand rode on Kapil for a long time. It presented him in films, in TV commercials and in press advertising. What is interesting here is the treatment. Kapil in cartoon form is both appealing and novel. When we consider the numerous profiles of Amitabh Bachchan and Sachin Tendulkar happily endorsing so many different brands—in the same predictable way—we begin to wonder whether our art directors are really doing a creative job. Or are clients too complacent?

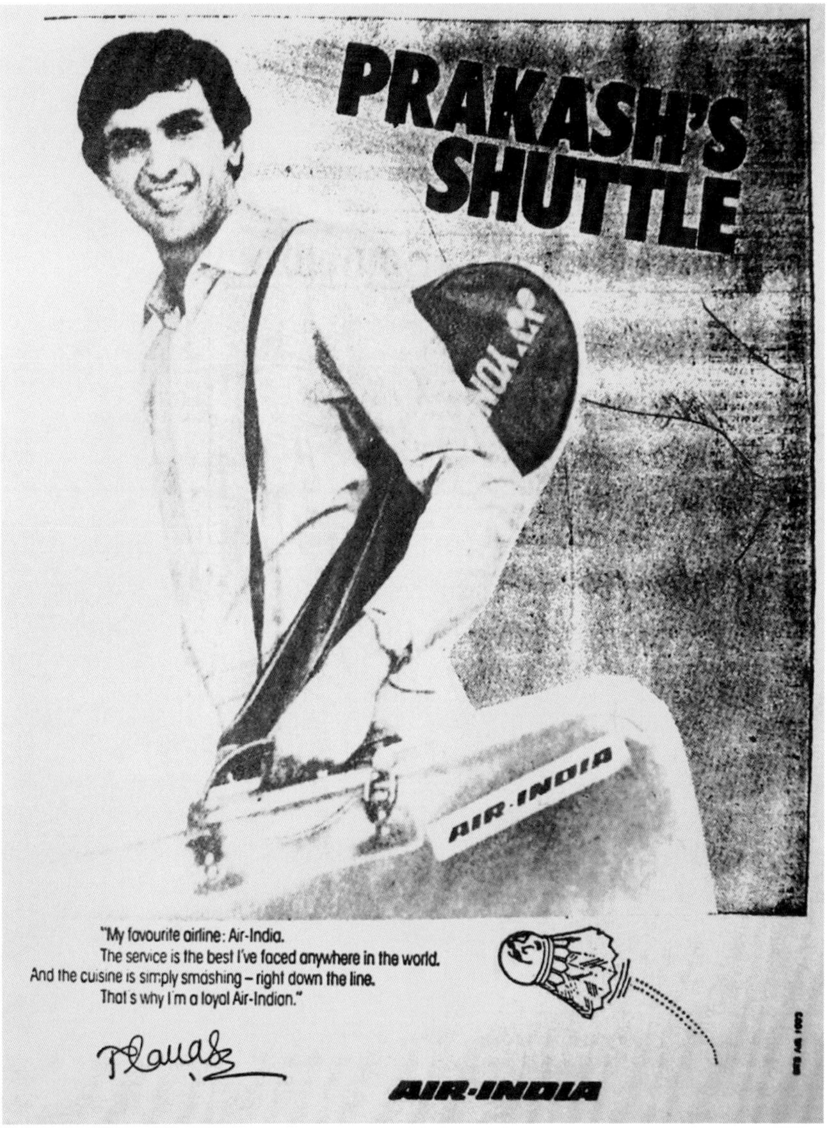

Prakash Padukone forced himself into public view in the sports arena by winning a number of prestigious international badminton tournaments including the All England Tournament. Air India, which always earned recognition for excellence in the eighties, naturally used Padukone for a testimonial advertisement.

This campaign, created by Ulka, ran for years and years featuring the same model—Dhanji Rana, who was the senior art director of Ulka until his retirement. He designed the Zodiac ads. He also trained a number of art directors who made their mark in advertising. Arunava Chakravorty, who moved to R.K. Swamy Associates and eventually started Campaign Advertising, was the foremost among them. He is still Calcutta-based and continues to work for the Zodiac brand, which he helped to establish.

Corporate campaigns

Corporate campaigns were important in the PR efforts of large and medium companies. For public sector companies, as reproduced in the Bhilai steel plant ad, a corporate campaign not only addressed the lay public but actually tried to catch the attention of bureaucrats and ministers in New Delhi. Smaller ad agencies generally designed the corporate communications of public sector companies. Continental Advertising released the Bhilai steel plant advertisement at the time of the inauguration of the Calcutta metro railway.

Another advertisement released by Continental Advertising for MECON, a Government of India company, highlights MECON's capability in environment engineering consultancy. R.K. Swamy also worked for MECON and released memorable corporate campaigns, as it did for Ranchi-based Heavy Engineering Corporation (HEC). HEC never showed a profit since its commencement. The socialists and communists in India's parliament kept giving doles to bail out the company. They believed it was in the fitness of things that taxpayers are penalised for the non-performance of worthless men and women in the company.

Most companies released corporate advertisements with the objective of informing the government that they had the nation's interest at heart; that their business helped the country save foreign exchange or earn foreign exchange, provide employment, or the company did something or the other for India's defence. The other ads that follow this one have been selected at random. Similar tiring and hackneyed themes run through all of them.

This is a chest-beating corporate ad, built along the lines of Muhammad Ali's boxing cry, 'I'm the greatest!' Although the ad is a testimonial, Lintas wisely used the names of government organisations prominently. The list of companies in this ad shows that there are eight companies in the government fold as opposed to four in the private sector. Ad agencies and advertisers have not matured enough to realise that shouting to the world, 'I am the best' carries no credibility. It may take another 50 years for a tonal change in advertising in India when ads will hopefully be understated in the message conveyed and so carry more conviction.

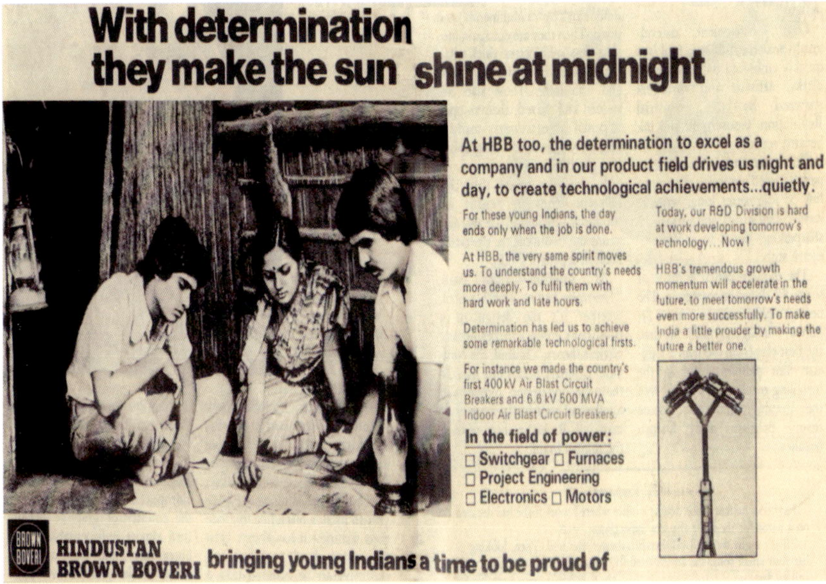

But, for Hindustan Brown Boveri, young Indians would never look forward to times they could be proud of! Other manufacturers could make the same claim without being challenged. This is the kind of hyperbole that Indian advertising could do without.

Philips was strong in branding in the eighties. It had HTA, Clarion and OBM working for it. The fun and excitement of lifestyle products is conveyed so well here. Philips took pains to connect with consumers all over India. Like Bata, it spent on retail outlets with cut-outs and motifs determined by local offices but approved centrally in Bombay. Philips was the leader in a number of consumer segments. Then the company somehow lost out. When the Korean and Japanese FMCG majors entered India, Philips alone held sway. Besides, it was generally regarded as an Indian company having farmed its markets over so many decades. Nobody spoke of Philips as being a Dutch multinational. Philips remains a case study for brand erosion. Complacency within the company was responsible for the decay. Philips exemplifies the danger of replicating brand ideas globally without analysing the impact of ideas in local markets. It came out with the stupid line, 'Let's make things better'. Nobody understood the significance of the line. Philips must have spent many millions of dollars across the globe. The moral of the story for advertisers is never get taken by your agency. Agencies are not staffed by geniuses. A successful campaign is generally understood by people. Avoid philosophic statements.

Greater options

In the 1980s, agencies had more option to use colour. New magazines were coming into circulation with greater frequency. Magazines in Indian languages were growing in popularity with the spread of education in the vernacular.

Better quality of printing paper, including art paper, was more widely available. Art directors and illustrators who still employed manual methods to draw and paint could use colour ads more often and hope to see them printed well. Besides, there was constant modernisation of offset printing in Delhi, Bombay and Madras. Printers such as Thomson Press and Ajanta Offset in Delhi, Tata Press in Bombay and Prasad Process in Madras supported clients and agencies printing high quality leaflets, posters, show-cards and other in-shop display items.

Despite the restrictive government regulations regarding imports, printers showed their entrepreneurial flair in successfully breaching the minefield of regulations unfailingly when they wanted to augment their printing capability.

Calcutta, which was the centre of printing excellence in India up to the seventies, lost its sheen. Eagle Litho fell upon bad days with fractious owners fighting with each other; Sree Saraswathy Press, which had grown big, lost out because of internal dissent. The company was taken over by the West Bengal government and that led to the inevitable end to that story. Only N.K. Gossain carried on—in 2012, the company broke up, each atomised section serving one owner. Founders of large businesses should ensure they restrict the number of offspring they have.

Computer-aided illustrations were still a decade away. Illustrators were highly-prized animals in the agency set-up.[12] The leading agencies such as HTA, Clarion, Ulka and Lintas always had a number of top art directors and illustrators in their major branch offices.

[12]In Calcutta all the well-known illustrators earned substantial income through freelance work. Their agencies did not mind. Samir Sarkar did numerous illustrations for the Puja numbers, which were routinely published by all Bengali dailies. These were popular as the most notable novelists, poets and playwrights published specially commissioned work. Most of them were later published as novels or plays or as poems in books of verse. People such as Sarkar must have been told the contents of these writings without which no illustration would have relevance. I cannot imagine that he read all these works.

Samir Sarkar

Samir Sarkar worked for both Clarion and HTA. His illustrations are easy and free-flowing. He was especially good at capturing the emotional or sensual content of an advertisement. His illustrations embellished the best national brands such as Dunlop, HMV, Philips and ITC. Sarkar was extraordinarily quick in execution and naturally loved by account executives who often had to fight with art directors and studio managers to get layouts and artworks on time. Sarkar was incomparable with the female form in her nubile sensuousness. He died in 2013.

Souvendu Basu

Known universally as Kanu Basu and addressed as 'Saheb' in Clarion, he left his stamp upon advertising not only in the agency he worked for, but across the country. Basu was chief art director of Clarion and was engaged as a core member of the agency's national resource. Subrata Sengupta making pitches in Bombay, Sudhir Lal in Delhi or Manmohan Banerjee in Madras roped in Basu to spearhead the agency's creative work. Calcutta had the best of Basu because he was based in the city. ITC, Dunlop, Lipton, Indian Oxygen, East India Pharmaceutical Works Ltd and Bata saw some of Basu's most inspired creative work.

In print ads, effect photography, elaborate tabletop shots for consumer products and increasing use of colour photography for industrial products and corporate advertising were the new trends. Fashion photography with an accent on the latest styles in wear and hairdo became part of ads that were focussed towards the youth.

Photographers, film producers, composers of jingles and studios of different kinds slotted their skills and competencies (in advertising parlance, 'positioned' themselves) for ready recognition. Adrian Stevens had a large clientele for tabletop photography. He could conjure up effects with what were new lenses and lighting that he constantly added to his magic treasure

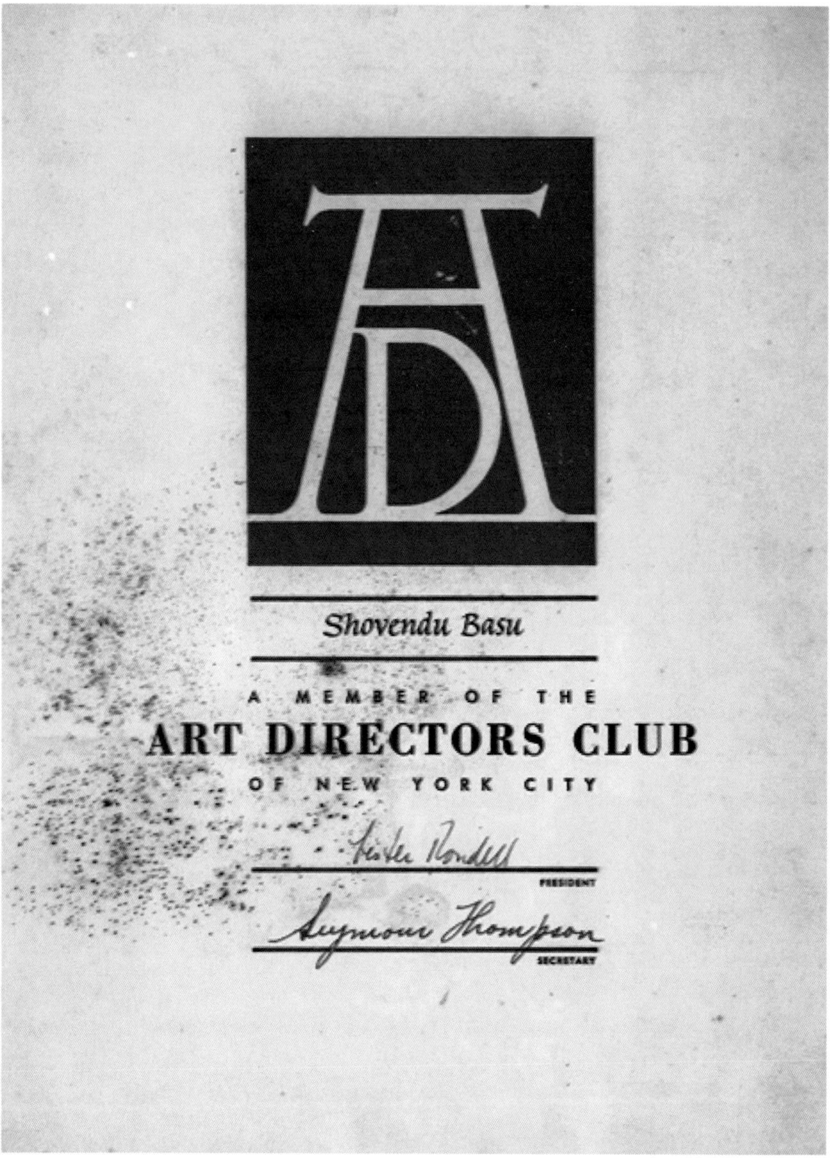

Basu may not have gone to any art college for a formal degree, but he was good enough to have obtained recognition from art directors in New York as this certificate testifies. He was fanatical about the semi-professional football league in Calcutta. Account executives knew if a match of the East Bengal Club was scheduled he would not be in his chamber, but watching his favourite team play on the Calcutta maidan.

Pradip Gupta

trove in his studio. He was pricey but then he satisfied the finicky art directors who chose to work with him. Pradip Gupta, who has his studio tucked away in one of the by-lanes in the Fort area, made his reputation as a photographer of factories, machines and people at work. There were many choices for art directors and in most metro cities there was steady work for all.

Post-Independence, the biggest name in commercial photography was that of Mitter Bedi. He had a national reputation for industrial photography. He travelled a lot and covered various types of industry. He started when photography meant colour or black and white film rolls, a light meter and standard studio lights. The more sophisticated electronic lights were far into the future. His photographs were rich in detail and he always learnt about machines and processes minutely before an assignment.[13] In fact, because industrial advertising meant the daily English newspaper as the primary medium, photographers had to take both black and white and colour photographs separately, ensuring that in both sets all angles and details had been covered. Colour photographs were used for corporate and product brochures that were printed in offset and for exhibition blow-ups. Photographers preferred larger film formats such as 120 mm films; 35 mm films for still photographs was generally not preferred.

Wilas Bhende is another name that has to feature here among the best in Bombay. He excels in tabletop and large format photography. Like all great photographers, each frame tells a story.

Ram and R.R. Prabhu earned a reputation for live modelling and ad photography that is studio dependent. These require intricate planning. Most times photography of this nature is experimental and the photographers work closely with art directors to create the aura or atmosphere around which an ad or a campaign is developed.

[13]I had the privilege of going with him to Guest Keen Williams' Howrah Works in the early 1980s.

Vivek Das

In Calcutta, Vivek Das acquired the reputation of being an excellent photographer, which he maintains till date. He built a professional studio and brought into his work the kind of professionalism that is the standard in Bombay, but sadly absent in Calcutta. He was supported by the Ananda Bazaar Group.

A later development in the functioning of the ad agency was the introduction of the computer in the studio. In the bigger agencies, computers began to enter the hallowed precincts of the studio by the middle of the eighties to the early nineties. It took away the pain of churning out layouts and artworks and carrying out revisions in the text manually. It enabled the account executive to meet the client with the job rather than an excuse as to why he could not deliver the artwork or layout when needed. Although clients were too polite to say it, an account executive often carried the reputation of being a Slick Joe who had a ready lie up his sleeve.

Summing up

The 1980s witnessed very disturbed times. Politically, the decade marked the end of the long era under Indira Gandhi, with her assassination on 31 October 1984. Her death was followed by a Congress Party contrived vendetta against the Sikh community, which was at its most brutal in New Delhi, where around 3,000 innocent Sikhs of all ages, men and women, were killed. 1984 also happened to be the year of the Bhopal gas tragedy. Over 15,000 people died on the night of 4 December, as poisonous gas seeped out of the Union Carbide factory in Bhopal.

The manner in which the Bhopal gas tragedy was tackled by Union Carbide, to avoid culpability for the mishap, proved beyond doubt the role of strategic communication in modern business. The company, facing worldwide condemnation, used its resources to launch and engineer a combined PR-advertising exercise that enabled it to escape the consequence of this tragedy in India. The Bhopal tragedy is a stark reminder that the Indian society remains vulnerable to the combined greed of businessmen, politicians and bureaucrats—the last willing to serve the interests of those who are willing to pay a price for service rendered.

On the brighter side, the 1980s saw the rise and decline of Rajiv Gandhi. He tried to initiate programmes to modernise India and to touch the lives of the common people. He inspired technocrats such as Sam Pitroda to leave their cosy lives in the West and build the infrastructure for growth. Pitroda's

Telecommunication Mission brought about a revolution in connectivity in the country.[14]

From the end of the 1980s till the beginning of the 1990s, India went through a period of utmost political unrest. There was the revival of Mandal, which set caste against caste; then there was the 'bundle' of worthless prime ministers—V.P. Singh, Devi Lal and Chandrasekhar—all with vaunting ambitions, but small merit to show. Then there was the Indian Peacekeeping Force, which went into Sri Lanka to ensure peace but ended up losing good soldiers because there was no clear mandate. And, finally, all this led to the assassination of Rajiv Gandhi in 1991. But Rajiv Gandhi's legacy as prime minister had two serious negatives. The first pertained to the Shah Bano case where he initially fought hard to bring about a uniform civil code for Muslims and Hindus alike, but succumbed to political pressure and went back to the existing system. The second pertained to the Babri Masjid where he opened the doors of an abandoned mosque for Hindus to offer their prayers to Ram Lala in a makeshift temple. The Hindus claimed that it was the birthplace of Ram and rightfully belonged to them. The Muslims felt aggrieved that a mosque was being converted into a temple. The communities were polarised. It ultimately led to the destruction of the mosque and caused a rift between the two communities, which has still not healed.

While so many events cluttered newspaper headlines, the economy remained stagnant. The maximum blame for this moribund state of affairs goes to the Congress Party, which ruled in Delhi for far greater number of years than the Opposition. No business house showed an honest face because the politicians and bureaucrats would not allow them to make an honest profit. So, private wealth was created and it was widely believed that Swiss banks had a roll of honour of the biggest names in Indian business who kept their unaccounted wealth in their safekeeping.

The decades of the 1990s opened on a sombre note. Rajiv Gandhi's assassination brought a wily Telegu Brahmin to head the Congress Party in parliament after the election results were announced in June 1991. The Congress Party won the race with the thinnest of margins, riding on a sympathy wave after Rajiv Gandhi's untimely death. When P.V. Narasimha Rao became prime minister, India was facing a critical financial position; the country had come close to defaulting on loans. The way ahead looked

[14]Young people today who speak on their cell phones almost every minute of their waking hours will not believe if they are told that before Pitroda changed everything, it was a nightmare trying to get a trunk call through. Even in-city telephone services were mired by corruption and apathy. Telephone linesmen had large incomes from keeping connections working for businessmen. They were paid a monthly retainer; on Diwali and other festivals they received 'gifts'.

bleak. Narasimha Rao took the hardest decision of all—he threw the age-old Congress Party dogma of socialism into the wastepaper basket. He gave the reins of conducting fiscal reforms to Dr Manmohan Singh, an economist, appointing him his finance minister.

The 1990s saw the emergence of India as a rising economic power. With the opening up of the economy, the business perspective changed entirely. Companies with foreign shareholding, which had steadily lost interest in their business operation in India over the years, became more assertive. A number of takeover conflicts lit up the business horizon. Indian companies at times felt neglected by their own government as MNC brands with large dollar budgets tried to capture Indian markets with their savvy and high-pitched advertising and below-the-line initiatives.

The 1990s witnessed a transformation in Indian advertising never before experienced in the twentieth century. The change was profound in terms of ownership of agencies, the appointment of agencies and the splitting up of the creative and media functions in advertising.

5

1990–2000
New Age

The decade of the '90s, leading to the new millennium, will remain one of the most discussed and debated in modern Indian history. The decade saw the rise of BJP as a national political party. The party based its political ideology on 'Hindutva', which loosely implies a party that supports all causes favoured by the Hindus as a community.

The political rhetoric of a rising BJP aroused pent-up passions among millions of jobless Hindu youth. This ultimately resulted in the destruction of the Babri Masjid in Ayodhya in December 1992. Narasimha Rao, who was the prime minister, could have stopped the mob from taking over; he did not. When Indira Gandhi was shot by her bodyguards and the Sikhs were selectively killed in Delhi and elsewhere, Narasimha Rao was the home minister, in charge of internal order and security. At the time he inexplicably remained a mute spectator and allowed the mobs to rampage through the streets of the capital city, killing defenceless Sikh men and women for a number of days.

The polarisation of Hindus and Muslims after the Babri mosque event led to riots in many cities including Bombay and Ahmedabad. Hundreds lost their lives. It was alleged that in Bombay the police failed to protect the minority community. But the story did not end here. Some powerful criminals who ran national and international crime syndicates decided to avenge Muslim deaths in Bombay. They arranged bomb blasts throughout Bombay city, killing and maiming innocent citizens.

The political situation was depressing in many parts of India. Assam was facing a violent upsurge of the United Liberation Front of Assam (ULFA); the organisation was regularly abducting officials from the oil industry and tea companies for ransom. Punjab saw renewed violence as Siddharth Shankar Ray took over as governor and decided to end Sikh extremism and their hopes of establishing Khalistan. In Kashmir, militants aided by Pakistan became active.

At the time perhaps the biggest problem faced by the Narasimha Rao government was the financial crisis. Foreign exchange reserves had touched rock bottom. Domestic and foreign debts had multiplied; India came perilously close to defaulting on re-payment of debts. Narasimha Rao appointed eight expert committees to work out the details on reforms, which included:

- Removing several controls over trade and industry;
- Initiating reforms in the public sector;
- Allowing the private sector to own major companies;
- Removing restrictions that prevented foreign companies from doing business in India; and
- Encouraging the inflow of foreign capital.

The economic reforms initiated and executed by Dr Manmohan Singh led to an overall growth in the economy. The rate of growth, which was five per cent in 1992–93, rose to six per cent in 1994 and to seven per cent in 1995. The most important aspect of these reforms was that the change was controlled; it did not hurt the common man. Besides the economic reform programme during Narasimha Rao's tenure as prime minister, a number of major laws were passed, including the Panchayati Raj Bill and the Nagar Palika Bill. These laws ensured that elections to municipalities and panchayats would be held regularly in the future.

The opening up of the economy had an immediate impact upon business. Initially the economic reforms tended to support the view that the dice was loaded in favour of foreign companies. The Indian rupee was extremely weak against the dollar. Foreign companies investing in India could pick up reputed companies and popular brands for a song. Indian businessmen felt disadvantaged. Rahul Bajaj, Ramesh Chauhan and others were vocal in expressing their misgivings about the 'new' economy in the press. Then a terrible thing happened in Indian business.

Chauhan, who despite the presence of the world's leading cola brands maintained his dominant market share in the soft drinks segment through Thums Up, sold this winning brand cheaply.[1] More than 18 years after the sale of Thums Up, the brand continues to be the most preferred cola in the country. Neither Pepsi nor Coke has ever managed to nudge it to second place. Yet in the years following the sale of Thums Up to Coca Cola Company, the brand was subjected to a de-marketing exercise. In summer, when cola sales peak, thirsty seekers of the brand would be offered Coke because Thums Up was not available.[2]

[1] I think Chauhan sold the brand for only Rs 200 crore.

[2] I have experienced this in Patna, Ranchi, Raipur and in some parts of Calcutta in the late 1990s.

With the sale of Thums Up, the Narasimha Rao government sat up and took notice. The finance minister, in taking the first steps to a global economy, had to build in checks to prevent a complete takeover wave killing indigenous enterprise. No change is absolutely painless. While globalisation meant welcoming foreign participation in the Indian economy, it had to begin with industries that were regarded as marginal in the Indian economy. And what could be more marginal than advertising?

Advertising conglomerates with offices in almost every rich country started looking at India. Though the value of advertising in rupee terms was not high or the state of the economy very robust, the promise of a new economic slant attracted some global ad companies. The early believers in India such as Sir Martin Sorrell of the WPP Group felt that this was only the beginning of a big story. WPP was quick to seize the opportunity and tied up with Tara Sinha. Who could find a better partner? The other international ad conglomerates such as the True North Group, Havas and Young & Rubicam-Dentsu preferred to wait and watch before committing themselves.

In the meanwhile other major changes were in the offing. Companies such as Coke, Pepsi, P&G, Philips and the Korean and Japanese organisations that had entered the market desired to be serviced by agencies already empanelled in New York, Chicago, Seoul and Tokyo. Only international agencies could, therefore, service such clients. Large Indian agencies began to seriously consider forging tie-ups with international ad conglomerates.

The 1990s also saw the development of new media. The rapid increase in the use of computers introduced the worldwide web into every office and later into every home. Companies realised the importance of using e-mails both for communication as well as for propaganda. Then the phenomenal access to mobile telephony got a whole new generation yapping all the time. Time got stretched as people continued to talk no matter what the hour. The world would never again be what it was when telephones were immobile.

In this chapter we will also cover the greater impact of media noise on lives, on the values and morals of society. We will observe the development of new age advertising rooted in the Indian experience. We will see how Indian advertising moves away from a verbal/vocal foundation with rational appeal to a visual foundation with sensuous appeal.

Ad industry in India: Return of the East India Company

As with every decade, the beginning of one is linked to happenings in the previous one. Not infrequently happenings that take place thousands of miles away in some distant country bear an impact upon what transpires in India. Indian advertising in the 1990s was impacted by events in the UK and the USA. Martin Sorrell took over JWT in 1987. After this he actively pursued other agencies and turned his holding company, which was called WPP, into one of the biggest ad agency groups in the world.

HTA, the Indian arm of JWT, was the largest ad agency in the country in the end-1980s. The shareholding of JWT had been diluted over the years. Indeed, HTA had a large shareholding base comprising employees of the company. Initially the WPP Group taking over JWT had little impact on HTA's India operation. But with the change in the economic climate in the early 1990s, Sorrell considered laying a claim upon HTA as WPP was the owner of JWT. He was prepared to compensate existing shareholders adequately. He went about influencing the managing director, Mike Khanna, who was Subhas Ghosal's handpicked successor[3] and utilised him as his change-agent.

The manner in which Sorrell consolidated his Indian ad empire is a lesson for takeover tycoons. Manu Chhabria faced endless conflict in many large companies such as Shaw Wallace and Gammon India. The tussle between S.P. Acharya, the incumbent managing director of Shaw Wallace and Manu Chhabria, the takeover tycoon, was long and bitter and played out in the media for the whole world to share. Generally managing directors were opposed to change, believing that a takeover would clip their wings or even drive them out of the company. The contest for ITC in the mid-1990s remains fresh in corporate memory. Even in a strongly bonded group such as the Tata Group of Companies, the elevation of Ratan Tata to the position of chairman resulted in conflict of interest in Tata Steel, where Russi Modi had to be almost physically removed from his position of managing director.

Sorrell in his consolidation of his Indian ad empire utilised the managing directors of the companies he was buying out as his instruments of change. Having taken them into his fold, he faced no difficulty in buying out other shareholders. He ensured continuity of management; he rewarded those who sold their shareholding handsomely. He deftly brought different companies with very different management practices under the overall WPP family roof; but he left each ad agency sufficient space to carve out its own identity. Differentiation is the hallmark of advertising and he realised that

---

[3]It is conceivable that Ghosal may have played a role in influencing the takeover.

every agency has to be specifically positioned for certain strengths, and every agency has to compete with other agencies, even those within the WPP Group, to flourish.

After the WPP Group persuaded the great David Ogilvy to sell his stake in O&M in 1989, Sorrell had another leading agency for the picking in India where he upped his stake in O&M to 40 per cent for the WPP Group and 11 per cent through WPP Mauritius. In fact, OBM in India was derived from S.H. Benson, which commenced operation in 1928 and was one of the oldest agencies in the country. It may have helped that Ranjan Kapur, who was the chosen successor of Mani Ayer, was related to Mike Khanna. Kapur became the change agent within O&M.

Like politicians, business leaders are quick to make deft statements when it suits them. In *A&M* magazine, issue dated 31 December 1999, Khanna stated that the name 'Hindustan' has been retained despite the fact that it was no longer Indian majority-owned since 1998 when WPP raised its stake from 40 to 60 per cent. To shore up the feel-good factor about the current turn of events, he mentioned the freedom that they enjoyed in running the company.[4] In the same issue of *A&M*, only a page later, Kapur expresses the same sentiment in different words.[5]

Sir Martin Sorrell

Sir Martin Sorrell worked as the finance director of Saatchi & Saatchi, one of the most talked about agencies in the UK in the 1970s and 1980s. He was bad-mouthed by David Ogilvy who once said that he would have nothing to do with a man who had never written an ad. Yet not too many years later Sorrell talked the language that Ogilvy understood—money. He bought out Ogilvy and even retained him as a sounding-board to keep an eye on the creative standards of his erstwhile agency.

After his unceremonious exit from Saatchi & Saatchi, he became associated with WPP—originally Wire & Plastic Products—a most unlikely name for a group that owns a large number of ad agencies, below-the-line companies, media companies, companies that specialise in PR as well as event management

[4]He is quoted saying, 'We report our financial figures to London, as listed companies do to stock markets, but we operate independently.'

[5]Ranjan Kapur said, 'They're not buying us out, they're buying in. They're investing, that's all. We run the agency.'

companies. Sorrell earned a reputation for being a tough no-nonsense profit-driven chief executive. His ambition and his capability in finance enabled him to become one of the most powerful men in advertising and related disciplines in the world. He received a knighthood in 2000 for his leadership in the industry.

For now the future of Indian advertising rests with Sorrell. He owns the leading agencies and employs the big names in Indian advertising, whose faces we see with monotonous regularity in the pages of *Brand Equity*. Sorrell himself is rarely seen in the media. But there is no doubt that he runs an empire very proficiently and outlines the functioning of his companies within a frame that is result-oriented and profit-driven.

Sorrell thinks deeply about the disciplines that constitute his business. In an interview, asked whether the separation of media from creative was a good thing for clients he answered with the client's perspective in mind, saying that many a client now feels the lack of a 'total' service package. He also observed that the two remain interlinked and cannot really be looked upon as independent functions.

Other than Peter Fielden no other person has had as much impact upon Indian advertising as Sorrell. The difference is that he remains behind the curtains but directs the play. His influence over Indian advertising will continue to be substantial because of the following reasons:

1. He has bought out the largest ad agencies. This has given him access to a roster of clients who are among the big spenders in advertising. Agencies in the WPP Group will have the advantage of experimenting with creative approaches that clients having modest budgets cannot try.
2. Ownership of some of the biggest media agencies such as Mindshare has made WPP a leading group in the media arena where the ability to scheme best buys in media is possible only when a company or group manages a large purse.
3. WPP has further shored up its '360 degree' status by either buying or starting companies that specialise in evolving or new media. WPP companies can help such group companies to consolidate since they will have ready access to their existing clients who already provide a large captive base.

There only remains the age-old truth that nothing is permanent in life. It is possible that after Sir Martin Sorrell the WPP Group may not find another individual who can hold on to the ad empire.

'The wild decade of foreign agency marriages'[6]

A graphical representation of the WPP Group as on 31 December 1999:[7]

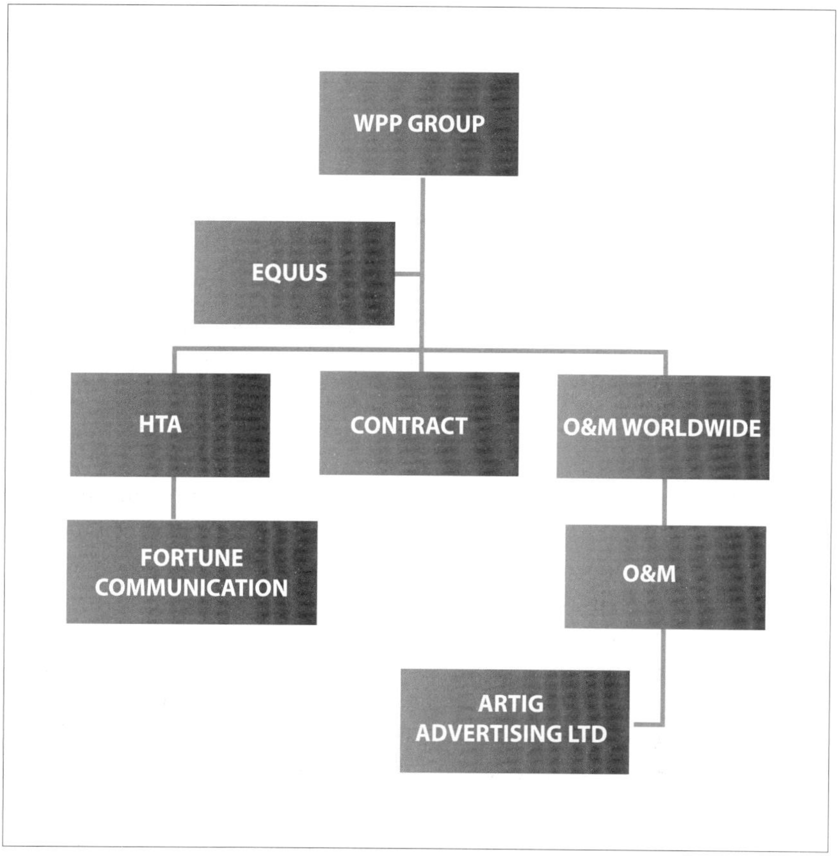

Among the agencies he bought, HTA had the strength of size and presence. HTA was India's biggest agency in billing terms. The company had fully-staffed offices in all the five metro cities. Subhas Ghosal was a respected leader in the profession in India. But, paradoxically, HTA did not produce too many eye-catching campaigns. That was not its style. It produced steady and effective ad campaigns; not dull but not brilliant. For a company operating in India for around 80 years there had to be some good work; here's a quick re-cap of the more memorable campaigns.

[6] I picked up this line from an article in *A&M* magazine dated 31 December 1999.
[7] *A&M*, 31 December 1999 issue, p. 68.

From the 1950s till the late 1990s, Air India ads were perhaps the most remarkable in the agency's account roster. The Tata Steel corporate campaign with the celebrated line 'We also make steel' was another memorable effort. So also was the job the agency did in establishing Wills Filter as the most sold cigarette in its category with the catch-line 'Made for each other'. For smaller regional brands such as Kwality Ice Cream, HTA came out with not-to-be-forgotten outdoor advertising that used double-decker buses in Calcutta. Buses were fully painted, for the first time in Calcutta, with cartoon illustrations of children carrying the line 'Health that melth in your mouth'—just as a child might say it. That turned a summer brand into an all-seasons brand. It brought Kwality Ice Cream into focus, which later resulted in a hostile takeover by HLL. Good advertising for Kwality helped to establish the brand, which in turn led to a more powerful company effect a hostile takeover. Who says advertising does not work?

But for an agency that retained its position as the number one agency for close to 80 years, the few campaigns that we mentioned, and even if we include another three or four more that we did not, the volume of work that may be classified as brilliant is rather small. Clients and agency heads should really think whether steady work produces better results in establishing and maintaining brands rather than brilliant advertising.

In terms of presence in India through ownership of Indian agencies, the Interpublic Group ranks second after Sorrell's WPP Group. The former also enjoyed a long association with Indian advertising, when it was not fashionable for large ad conglomerates in the USA to establish connection with Indian ad agencies. McCann Erickson had a tie-up with Clarion in the 1970s.[8] It broke up with Clarion and transferred loyalty to Tara Sinha Associates in which it took a minority stake in the 1990s.[9]

The agencies that the Interpublic Group bought in India were among the strongest. Enterprise-Nexus with Muhammed Khan was reputed for its bold creative work. Lintas, which had Alyque Padamsee as CEO in the early 1990s, had become very aggressive in its work as well as in market presence. Padamsee entered into a no-holds barred feud with HTA to prove Lintas was the bigger agency. Mike Khanna proved no match for Padamsee's verbal assault, which livened up the pages of *The Economic Times* and other business dailies.

The Interpublic Group also bought out the house agency of Kirloskar, which was first known as Pratibha and then re-named Quadrant. It was

[8]I joined Clarion in 1974. The appointment letter had the McCann name besides Clarion.

[9]After her first tenure in Clarion, Tara Sinha joined Coca Cola, where she proved her mettle. It is not unlikely that McCann shifted loyalty because of Sinha's connections in Coca Cola company and McCann.

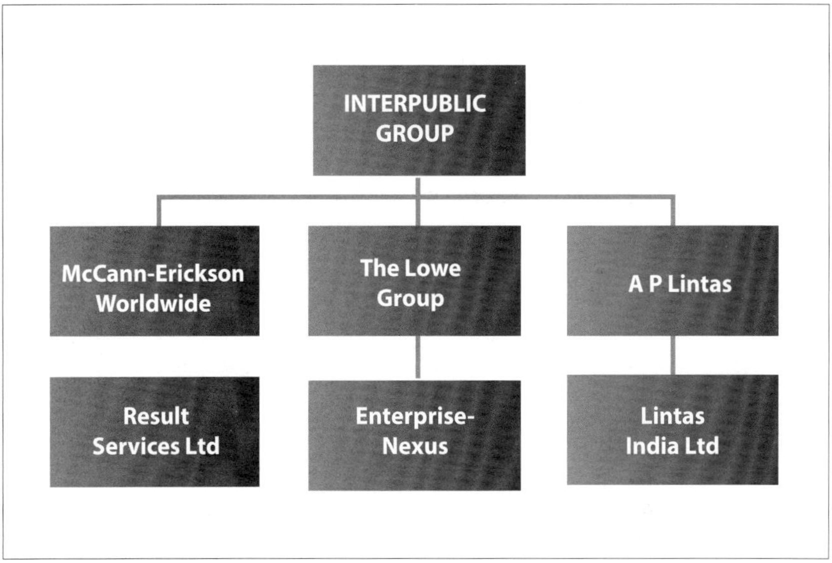

not a remarkable company. Kirloskar was going through a bad financial crisis and Pratibha was naturally facing bad times because much of what it handled pertained to Kirloskar brands.

Strangely, the world's largest ad agency conglomerate, the Omnicom Group, with reported billing of around $4 billion in 1998, did not have a strong India presence. BBDO, belonging to the Omnicom Group, was a big agency in the USA. It initially bought 20 per cent of R.K. Swamy in 1990, which it subsequently raised to 50.1 per cent by the end of the decade.[10] R.K. Swamy was then the seventh largest agency in India in terms of billing. The Omnicom Group also bought a majority stake in TBWA Anthem, a lightweight agency ranked 21st in the country. The sad part of the Omnicom story in India is that DDB Needham, which had an ongoing relationship with Mudra (the number four agency in India in terms of size), did not take off as Mudra insisted that 'globally aligned' accounts did not interest the agency much. Of course Mudra, unlike any other agency in India, with its Reliance background, could always count on financial support from the Reliance Group, which had by then grown into one of India's biggest industrial groups. In 2012, DDB Needham finally netted Mudra when Anil Ambani, the owner, decided to move out of advertising.

[10]Having interacted with Swamy during my four-year stint in his agency, I feel it must have taken a lot of persuasion from his family, especially his two sons, to get him to agree to the tie-up with BBDO.

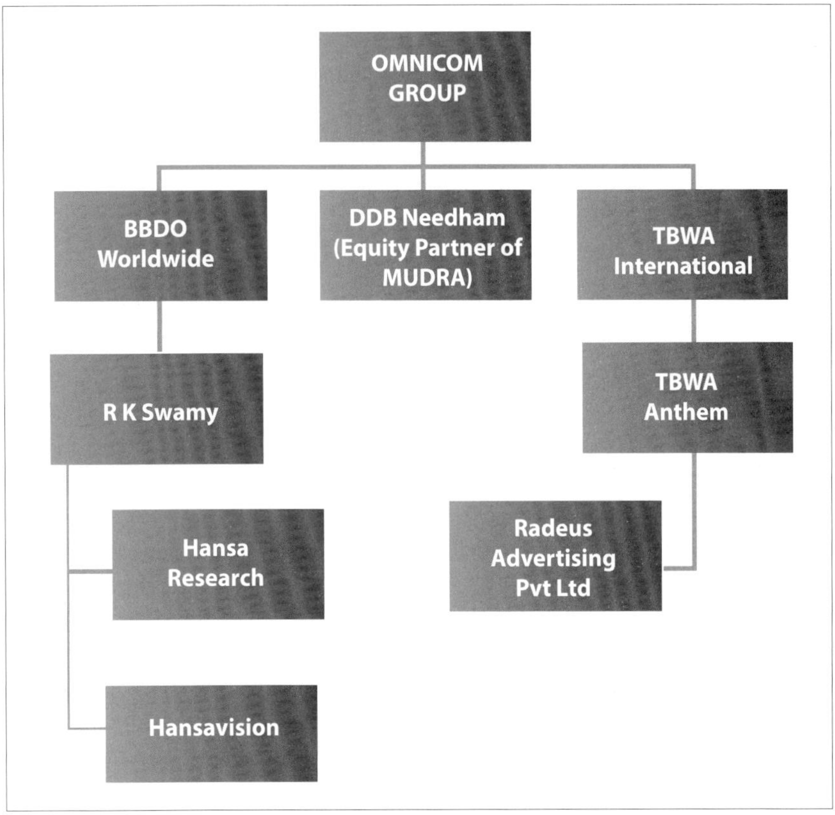

There were three other international ad agency conglomerates with tie-ups with the larger agencies in the country. Of these conglomerates two were fairly major in their India association.

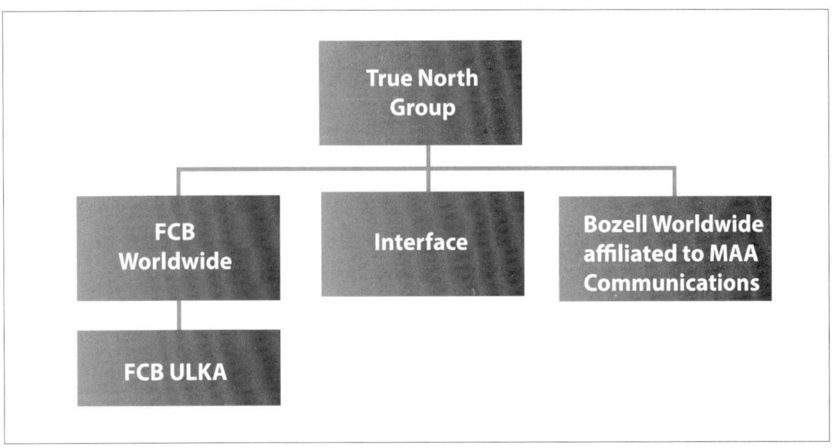

FCB Ulka was the new name for Ulka Advertising, which had rendered great service to clients ever since it commenced operations under the stewardship of Bal and Anne Mundkur in the mid-1960s. Interface and MAA were smaller agencies; Ulka alone figured among the leading agencies in the country and opened the doors of some of the biggest companies such as ITC and the True North Group. What was Ulka's gain from the tie-up?[11]

Dentsu, the biggest among the Japanese agencies, had a cross-holding with Young & Rubicam of Rediffusion. Rediffusion has been a leading agency in the country and has always been known for high creative standards. The profile of the agency has been far above Chaitra, which took on the Leo Burnett tag and later merged with Leo Burnett. Chaitra in the late 1980s and early 1990s was strong in the financial advertising sector. Financial advertising was generally associated with companies that actually indulged in ripping off unwary investors. Agencies such as Chaitra and Pressman excelled in advertising of this nature. They followed a three-stage process:

1. The first stage centred on a corporate image exercise. Initially the size of each corporate ad was large and both agency and national dailies made good money. Besides, a corporate campaign was not restricted to a single advertisement. They normally went to town talking about all the

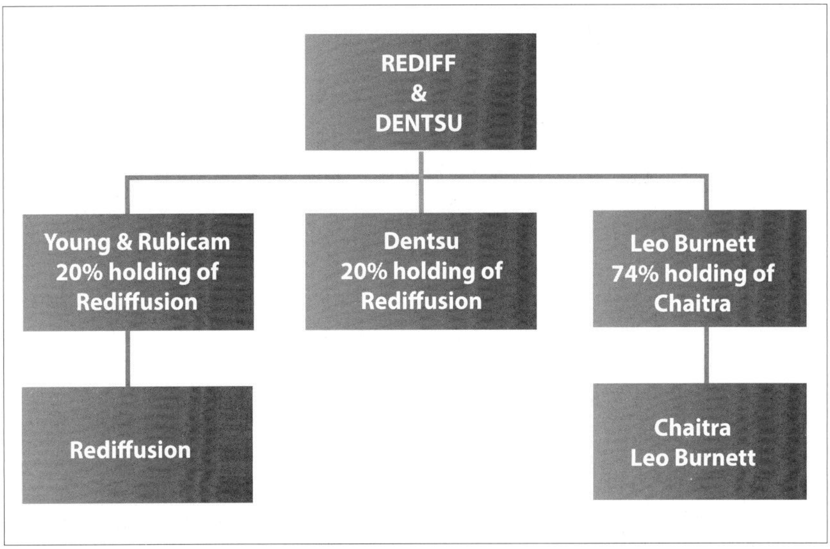

[11]I asked this question in 2000 when I interviewed Bal and Anne in New Delhi. They confessed that Ulka had gained nothing from this association with FCB. Only the management had changed. A foreign company was raking in the profits. I believe this is true of all other ad agency tie-ups as well. There is no rocket science involved in advertising, and there is nothing that foreign agencies can lay upon the tables of Indian agencies that is unknown to them.

wonderful things—mostly imaginary—that the company achieved and the profitability of the business it was into, along with its near invincible status in its chosen business line. So there was a series of ads built on a theme. Later the general hue and cry raised by millions of credible people who lost their life savings believing ads compelled the government and stock exchanges to lay down guidelines. The campaign amount was restricted to a fraction of the amount being raised from the market. The government also stipulated that the risks had to be clearly mentioned. These were mentioned in almost illegibly small type and written in legal jargon that hid the risks more than making the investor weigh the risks before showing his money.

2. This corporate campaign was followed by a detailed investor presentation at the bourses. These agencies concentrated on financial advertising. As a result they learnt the intricacies connected with the investor community. They had contacts with big-league investors who could make or mar a share issue. If the initial investment was good, the share issue was bound to be oversubscribed.
3. A strong financial advertiser could persuade the lead banks to insist that only this company be chosen to undertake the share issue campaign. Gradually other ad agencies that did not specialise in financial advertising were left out of a potentially rich business.

That was an unsavoury part of Indian advertising history. It proved advertising works; advertising can become a powerful tool to influence gullible investors. In India the propensity to get rich quickly through the magic of high yield investments that defy logic is higher than in any other country in the world.

The infamous Harshad Mehta was the most visible face among villains who built fortunes on the backs of non-existent companies that existed only in the corporate campaigns released in newspapers. Ad agencies which concentrated on financial advertising presented dream companies; investors were only too ready to believe what the ads said and put in their savings into worthless scrips. Apart from the ad conglomerates mentioned here, there was the Havas Group, which had a majority stake in Euro RSCG, a single-client agency. It was not a major ad agency in India.

Is there a real need for foreign associates?

The advertising profession in India is often featured along with society coverage on the third page of national and business dailies. Predictably, the same faces from the same leading agencies in the same postures—holding a half-empty glass of whisky—and interacting with the same crowd of business leaders and politicians is presented.

Over the years the ad agency has been loosely linked with the glamour world. Between the 1970s and 1990s, the presence of a number of ad personalities such as Alyque Padamsee, Shyam Benegal, Govind Nihalani and a few others who converged to film direction or directing and acting in plays has only reinforced the image of advertising as glamorous. The dynamic growth of MCM as an agency was the result of positioning the company on the fast track party circuit that gave an impression that advertising was almost as glamorous as Bollywood.

Leaders in the agency business are gradually taking their rightful position in the international arena through the conglomerates they serve. Many of the conglomerates now have Indians on their main boards with designations that are high sounding. Is all this the result of great advertising in recent times? Or is this phenomenon a reflection of the increase in value and volume of the Indian market? With an average year-on-year growth of around 7.5 to 9 per cent, are global brands forced to pay heed to this growth? But when the growth comes down to 4 per cent, does the Indian market attract overseas investors anymore? In 2014, we are witnessing a steady decline of foreign investment.

There is a change in the basic structure of advertising. Once dependent on words to convey a brand promise, it has evolved into expressing transient emotions and fads that capture the imagination of the youth for a moment, only to disappear the very next moment. The ad agency rarely scripts films. These are now scripted and directed by ad film-makers, who have been elevated to the position of 'famous ad men'. Prahlad Kakkar, for example, is quoted by society papers as a famous ad personality.

Do they service accounts such as ad men do? Every day? Month in and month out? Do these ad men have a stake in the brand's performance in the marketplace? Does the client deduct his fees if the film does not generate sufficient interest? Or does he find an easy excuse by pleading that the media plan did not give the film sufficient exposure?

These are issues that big spending advertisers need to confront. Since the expense incurred on TV is many times more than other media (for most FMCG brands), the TV producer-director-organiser is perhaps more central to the client than is the ad agency for so many FMCG accounts. Is he providing the service back-up that an agency provides such as brand positioning; developing a holistic view of the brand's market presence; studying consumer preferences; advising the client on evolving a brand portfolio when the brand reaches a stage of maturity; looking at every experiential point where and when a brand touches the consumer?

In a broad sense, as the Indian economy reaches a stage of maturity, consumers move up from physical needs to psychological needs, according to

Maslow's theory. This theory applies equally to mental satisfaction criteria. For example, consumer satisfaction derived from seeing a film in an old style cinema hall is not the same as seeing it in a multiplex. This is why a ticket for a film seen in a multiplex is no longer 10 or 15 or 20 rupees but is closer to 80 or 100 rupees or more. This is just an example. As consumer satisfaction parameters become more 'self-image'-driven and influenced by peer group usage, people no longer buy shirts or trousers, wrist watches and handbags, furniture and home exercise equipment, cars and motorbikes, they buy brands. But the Indian market is not a homogeneous market where societal divisions are uniform across the subcontinent. The Indian subcontinent is a politically unified geographical entity (at least we hope that is so) where there are umpteen demographic divisions that are often mutually disruptive and cause social tensions. At the same time, there are many points of social unification; for instance, the general love of cricket and the iconic status given to cricket players across the nation. So also the general preferences for peace that the political class do not allow the common citizens to enjoy as they wilfully sow seeds of discord, pitting one demographic group against another.

Given the prevailing state of society, TV has come to enjoy a central position in our lives. The importance of advertising cannot be over-emphasised. The most-seen faces on TV are faces in commercials. Whether it is the superstar in Bollywood or the superstar in the Indian cricket 11, they appear more often in commercials than they do as actors and players. How many times is the superstar in Bollywood seen in films in which he plays the lead role compared to the number of times he is seen every day endorsing multiple brands? Hair oil in one commercial, followed by a particular brand of fabrics in the next, a balm in a third, or endorsing enamel paint for your home in another? There is never an end to what he endorses.

With advertising taking the centre stage, the profession is no longer faced with the challenge to prove that advertising is socially relevant. While advertising, media and public relations are now looked upon as different professions, entailing different skills of specialisation, the three are interconnected in building and maintaining the brand image.

Summing up, what does the foreign ad or media company buying a big Indian agency or media company lay on the table? Capital. Those who have built the agency and cared for the business over the years of forced controls get enough to retire with and live life happily ever after. Advertising is not rocket science. A foreign tie-up can only add so much to an Indian company that operates within an Indian social structure, the nuances of which are best understood by Indians rather than foreign nationals.

Media agencies get enriched through foreign associations; they get the capital with which they buy media in bulk and sell media bought at a profit. Here the game is not so simple. As events such as the Cricket World Cup, Football World Cup, the Olympic Games, the Asian Games and the Commonwealth Games grow in importance for brand presence it is the TV channels that enter into negotiations with the organising committees and buy exclusive time—in a bidding process—to ensure that the channel that is the highest bidder bags the sole rights to all the commercial time. Media agencies next enter into contracts with the TV channel and buy time in bulk against their media plans for specific brands.

Why clients agree to pay huge amounts through event-related ad presence is not always clear. The new millennium has witnessed a drastic fall in viewers even for cricket matches. Advertisers have asked TV channels to pay back their initial investment since the number of viewers fell short of their projection. Media agencies carried on a thankless battle to help their clients. Viewers who have not heard of advertising clichés such as '360 degree connect', weary of seeing the same cricket matches replayed in different places by the same teams, look elsewhere for entertainment.

New age media

However, there has been a tremendous growth in interactive and more intrusive media. The internet and the cell phone are the most used among new media. They are intrusive because these media are targeted at individuals. Both have no fixed hours of reach. The youth do not sleep at night any longer. The office does not close for the day at 6 pm in the evening. The boss sends sms messages or e-mails long after he has returned home. He has no problem doing that as the spouse does the same—sending sms messages to the underlings who report to her. They are a working couple and together make a happy home communicating with all and sundry. In fact, the concept of home is undergoing a change.

Interactive websites such as Facebook invite individuals to post their own picture albums, leaving no part of themselves in the private domain. Companies revel in participating through these websites, hoping to make a profit from the consumer's personal interactions.

From the mid-1980s, Indian companies have increasingly posted their corporate profiles on the internet. Unfortunately, the look and feel of these corporate websites is too close to the print medium for comfort. Companies and ad agencies are aware that an interactive medium such as a website should be regularly updated and people who log in and ask questions must be replied to promptly. Rarely is a company website regularly updated or managed well.

Most large ad conglomerates such as the WPP Group have started companies to address the advertiser's need for digital advertising. Forced messages annoy people and they are not the most effective way of drawing the consumer's attention. The fact that even the finance minister of India lodged a protest stating that he was receiving unsolicited sms messages indicates that the dictates of business in this country respect no man.

Indian advertising, unlike advertising in the USA or Europe or other parts of Asia, continues to be brash but colourful. The ads that are remembered are not necessarily the most artistic. They are ads that tend to be the loudest in announcing the supremacy of a brand over all others. They are ads that connect with a large segment of the population rather than a small select group of moneyed people. Global ad conglomerates that rule the roost today are leaders because they have an easy way in acquiring global accounts, which are won not in India but elsewhere in the world. But as Indian companies begin to take their first steps in international business they too will, sooner than later, empower Indian ad agencies to turn global and evolve into global conglomerates.

6

2001–The Present Time *Ahead*

Every preceding decade shapes the decade following in many ways. For some decades the changes are not so obvious; while for others the changes are far-reaching. The decade of the '90s of the last century was truly momentous. The economic churn led to India becoming a country that the major economic powers of the world were keen to enter.

By the end of the '90s advertising in India had largely passed into the hands of multinational agencies. With the new millennium all the large Indian agencies passed through takeovers by foreign companies. Most takeovers were smooth; a few were troublesome.

The most dramatic change that happened in the nineties, however, was the break between the media and creative services that were offered by full service agencies to advertisers. In the '90s it was P&G that first brought about this change internationally. Whether there was any merit in the change and re-structuring is still a matter of debate.

Media outfits started as poor cousins of ad agencies in India. The initial phase lasted well past the middle of the first decade of the new millennium. But capable media experts gradually asserted their independence. Clients relied upon them more as the focus shifted from media planning to bulk media purchase. Advertisers started consulting media companies on a day-to-day basis as their operation led to quantifiable savings in media spend for advertisers. As for creative agencies, they lost the entire chunk of work on television that passed into the hands of professional TV producers, under companies that were floated by Bombay film stars.

Digital media began to draw the attention of advertisers; specialised agencies emerged. These were small outfits to start with, but the multinational groups started buying up these companies so that thcy were not found wanting in the new arc of advertising.

Public relations was no longer considered part of ad agency operations. PR companies had been doing business independently since the eighties. However, after the economic liberalisation of the nineties, these companies had come under the lens of multinational PR firms. There were tie-ups; takeovers; adjustments in dealing with multinational clients.

Markets expanded exponentially. The economy registered around 6.5 per cent growth per annum. The unpretentious Hindu rate of growth at below 4 per cent was a thing of the past. India was beginning to be seen as the emerging economic powerhouse along with China. However, the euphoria of an economic resurgence faded. During the last Lok Sabha election, voters rejected the BJP national campaign crafted by Grey Advertising that was built on the platform, 'India shining'.

The government of India in New Delhi had by then become a coalition of political parties led by the Congress Party. The Opposition, too, was a coalition of political parties led by the BJP. There was increasing importance of regional political parties across the subcontinent. Congress and BJP, undoubtedly the two major political parties in India, ran state governments in only a few states.

The highs of the economic resurgence saw airfares tumbling as many companies entered aviation. Price wars between airlines brought airfares within the reach of the middle-class Indian. Indians began travelling abroad on holidays with the Reserve Bank of India (RBI) removing stringent restrictions on the issue of foreign exchange. Young Indians born in the early or mid-1980s enjoyed a lifestyle that their parents had never had. Chaebols from Korea asserted dominance in consumer durables. Samsung and LG became household brands. Older companies, including Indian consumer durable companies such as Onida, Videocon, Sonodyne, Televista and others, gave up their marketing space.

We will cover the story of the new Indian consumer in this chapter and try and uncover what these new consumers regarded as meaningful. We will talk about persons who created and crafted advertisements for them. We will also cover in greater detail the new companies that now only concentrated on media for clients.

Indian advertising went through a period of complete change, which started in the early 1990s and continued at a fast pace till the end of 2010. Indeed, this phase of change has not stopped; nor is the rate of change expected to abate in its intensity so long as advertising in the country keeps pace with the growing needs of advertisers. While we have briefly mentioned the changes that shaped Indian advertising post the economic liberalisation initiated by Prime Minister Narasimha Rao, in this chapter we will dwell upon these changes at length.

1. Indian language advertising began to shape advertising impact. This was a major development. Economic liberalisation opened up the market, bringing within the fold of the consuming class people who lived in large non-metro towns as well as men and women residing in villages. These newer classes of consumers thought and spoke in the vernacular. Hindi, which men and women had begun to use as a link language across the country, benefitted most from this fundamental change. In the corridors of power in New Delhi where it mattered most, the lingua franca was now Hindi. In Bombay, which remained the economic capital of India, Hindi was widely used.
2. Among FMCG brands there were many new entrants that broke the monopoly of niche ownership of markets enjoyed by HLL and P&G. This had started with Nirma in the 1980s. A small Indian company designed the sachet pack in which it began selling small quantities of shampoo for Re 1 a pack. The company made a windfall, bringing in consumers who wanted something just like this.
3. Among large organisations, ITC entered a wide array of markets, successfully competing with old entrenched FMCG brands from HLL and P&G. Ready-to-eat snacks; branded rice, wheat and edible oils, in bulk and in smaller packs; various packaged pre-cooked food preparations; garments under the Wills brand name sold from exclusive retail outlets; and hotels catering to the needs of the super rich were some of the businesses that ITC went into so that its dependence on cigarettes came down considerably.
4. FMCG markets remained buoyant, encouraging the entry of smaller brands. Traditional brands such as Dabur modernised. There was a large untapped market for traditional herbal and ayurvedic/unani products, which was upgraded with smarter packaging, modernised manufacturing processes and eye-catching advertising that ensured that the earlier impression of cheap products was gone forever.
5. On consumer durables, the older companies, including Philips, lost ground steadily as they were unable to cope with the aggressive marketing of Korean and Japanese companies. Established brands such as Videocon, Onida, Sonodyne and Televista lost sheen. These brands were repositioned to serve the lower end of the market spectrum, but even here they steadily lost ground as new multinational Asian giants built up their respective brand franchises with aggressive marketing supported by heavy advertising.
6. In advertising, the separation of creative and media became permanent. Large agencies restructured; medium to small agencics continued to offer full service to clients but among major clients there were no takers for full service agencies. This total bifurcation has to be covered in a way that gives us the scope to discuss the important developments in creative and media separately.

7. Advertisers began observing the growth of social media, which gave them an opportunity to engage with current and prospective users in a manner that was totally new to advertising. Advertising historically meant a path of communication that flows in a single direction—from the advertiser to the consumer. Social media opened up a two-way path of communication, giving the consumer or the prospective buyer an opportunity to respond either affirmatively or otherwise.
8. There were major developments that are interconnected with social media but are bunched together under the acronym of digital media. Within the digital media space there are multiple options; every option entails specialist understanding of the technology that drives each option. The difference between conventional and digital media may be likened to the difference between the bullock cart and the motor car with regard to the speed with which a message is conveyed. That apart, unlike conventional media, digital media is totally measurable in the response generated. Neither creative agencies nor media agencies are equipped to tackle these new media yet. Therefore, in this period we also see multinational ad agencies buying up small shops where a few specialists with entrepreneurial flair combine to make profits from digital media.

The agency business, whether in India or anywhere else in the world, is dominated by personalities. That is how it has been and is likely to continue in the foreseeable future. The characters who seem to influence advertising most in the new millennium are Piyush Pandey and Prasoon Joshi. Both these men feature regularly on page three of major English dailies, including financial dailies, which seem to savour their presence. They have merely stepped into the shoes of their predecessors who were page three favourites prior to the nineties—Alyque Padamsee and Ranjan Kapur. So from what do the new incumbents derive their fame?

When these men entered advertising they brought some special talent as they were small-town residents. Initially, Joshi worked under Pandey in O&M, moving out to a new agency when he realised he had enough talent to compete with his peer on his own terms. Pandey in an interview, published in the *Brand Equity* section of *The Times of India*, once observed that he had developed his skill and confidence having assisted Suresh Mullick, who was creative director in O&M until his retirement from the organisation in the early '90s. Having worked in OBM Calcutta when Mullick was the creative director, I can assert that he was a disorganised person. In Calcutta we got to see little of the creativity he had, though everyone agreed that was remarkable. When Mullick was transferred to Bombay, he must have got exciting frontiers to conquer as the city had the best accounts. In Calcutta he had little sympathy for account executives who were held responsible by clients for not delivering jobs as promised.

While I have no direct knowledge of Pandey's famed leadership in O&M, I am aware that for servicing executives in the Bombay head office of the agency today, not much has changed from the conditions prevailing some 40 years ago. Every agency operates in a *gharana*-like environment. Servicing executives in O&M continue to be treated like slaves, putting in long, unpaid and thankless hours. Fortunately, 40 years ago there were no mobile phones or computers. Nowadays youngsters in advertising are on duty 24 x 7, like TV stations. God help them since our laws won't!

But while the grind is supposed to be part of agency life, which ad people believe makes them stand apart from all other professionals, though for the life of me I do not see why that should be so, men and women who make big names are seen to be very sociable in nature—unfailingly, team leaders. In an interview Joshi admitted that his ex-boss Pandey revels within a social setting. He likes people around him; he inspires art directors and copywriters to produce stimulating advertising.

The funny thing about the ad business is every campaign is the culmination of team effort. It is difficult to single out individual contributions in a campaign. You cannot say, 'Ah! This is Piyush's headline' or 'This other campaign is certainly Prasoon Joshi's'. But having such men surely motivates other team members to excel. Advertising celebrities such as Pandey and Joshi act as touchstones professionally, just like celebrities of the past did in their heydays.

The difference between the modern greats and those who belonged to the earlier periods of advertising is that post-1990s the new writers brought in a freshness of ideas in the vernacular. As the environment had changed and media in vernacular outstripped media in English in terms of viewer/reader preference, new ads, whether for TV or for print, were more appreciated if they were conceived in the vernacular as opposed to being translated into the vernacular from English. Pandey came from Jaipur; Joshi from a small town in Uttarakhand, which at the time was part of Uttar Pradesh. They were at ease in using the vernacular, which helped them create advertising that had an immediacy of appeal for the new generation of Indians who had become consumers.

However, the points noted above do not make the generations that entered advertising in the '80s and '90s very different from the preceding generations. Subhas Ghosal and copywriters in JWT in the '50s and '60s, men such as Shiben Dutta, were equally adept at writing Bengali as they were in English.

Of course, there were men and women such as Alyque Padamsee who have never been linked to advertising in the vernacular although that by itself does not take away anything from their greatness.

Art directors as a breed, whether in Bombay or Madras or Calcutta, had to be briefed very patiently in the vernacular; few were proficient in English. One of the reasons obviously was that they generally came from lower middle-class backgrounds; few went to public schools; in school those who excelled in art were not always good in other subjects. Admissions to an art college could be got even without obtaining a first division pass in the school-leaving exams. Those who cleared the entrance tests were accepted.

Therefore, advertising, when it made an impact with the target audience, was a cumulative effort of the copywriter and the account manager successfully explaining the basic positioning/promise to the art director in the vernacular even when the campaign was conceived in English. Only when the art director was taken into the cognitive loop he felt inspired and produced campaigns such as 'Utterly butterly delicious Amul', 'Made for each other', Wills Filter, the memorable Air India ads and 'Hamara Bajaj'.

Post the 1990s, Indian advertising saw the Fevicol campaigns breaking into TV unforgettably. Some of the cola ads from Thums Up, Coke and Pepsi were, likewise, eye-catching. These campaigns were short-lived, lasting through one or two seasons, not because the target audience was bored with the ads, but because most of these campaigns were event-specific. For example, 'Nothing official about it', the guerrilla attack by Pepsi on Coke, the official sponsors of the World Cup in cricket, was an event-specific campaign. Film production had already moved out of the ambit of the ad agency and films were being made by companies that focussed on commercials, which helped to Indianise both the content and language of the films/TV commercials they made with the advertiser's consent.

One TV commercial that deserves special mention was a Coca Cola ad featuring Aamir Khan that took the locale to an Indian village, depicted village situations, while introducing a smaller pack, therefore a pack that was priced lower than the normal one, with the aim of increasing the distribution spread of the brand. What was equally significant was the introduction of low-cost refrigerating/cooling units that enabled distributors to serve the cola cold to the consumer. Otherwise there would be no enjoyment in drinking Coke on a summer day. I recall the way this was shown in the commercial. Aamir Khan drew up a bucket from a deep well with Coke bottles, opened one, and quenched his thirst before passing on other bottles to a bevy of attractive girls waiting there. The setting of a village well with a typical filmy village backdrop established the claim that the brand was now available everywhere.

By then Coke had bought over Thums Up, which continued to be the preferred cola drink in India despite the presence of both Coke and Pepsi in the country. Coke came up with the humdinger ads for Thums Up with an action star as hero. He exhibited the agility of a monkey, more strength than King Kong and less sense than the latter as he jumped from a building to the lorry carrying bottles of Thums Up and gulped down the contents of a bottle, looking at a nubile actor chasing him. I am not sure who was chasing whom and why ... most action-packed advertising these days are not to be judged anyway.

The impress of great sociological changes in India influenced the behavioural patterns of different socio-economic groups profoundly. The decay of the so-called Gandhian way of living life unostentatiously culminated in a vulgar display of ill-gotten wealth. Advertising reflected these changes not only in developing brand messages that appealed to the new consumers, but also in producing ads that saw expenditures in making TV commercials reach astronomical heights. Of course, under the new dispensation, the evolution of media changes began on the premise that that would lead to large savings for the advertiser.

In reality, what the advertiser saved in terms of media bargains was a trifle compared to what he spent in creating ever-new campaigns with a promotional slant. The intent was that through keeping up a barrage of promotions the consumer would not only stay with the brand but would inspire other consumers—like-minded people, friends, colleagues, his larger social circle—to gather around his brand, because the new consumers, so sociologists believe, exhibit herd instincts rather than individuality in making a purchase decision.

The modern sociologist would also take an interest in observing consumers who do not belong to social groups. These consumers buy from the immense virtual market where almost anything a person can imagine is readily available. Through the internet every product can be seen in all its dimensions, in all the colours in which it is available, with a pre-fixed price that is agreeably lower than the price at which the same products are sold from shops. For such a consumer the occasion of purchase is in the house, very likely in his bedroom at wee hours in the night when he is undisturbed while searching the virtual market for a suitable brand. Is his decision to purchase always rational? Or does he look at advertisements, reading the small print, scanning the visuals to see whether the brand fits in with his lifestyle? Where does he come across ads?

These questions are being mulled over by experts in sociology, psychology and after a manner by marketing professionals who have the most to gain or the most to lose, depending on their reading of market developments.

Under the new dispensation, media planning accounts for 'smart buy' of media, while the creative labour of advertising is more intensely involved with getting the consumer emotionally engaged with the brand wherever he stumbles upon its ad.

So we come to a stage in the lifecycle of advertising that may be described as trying to do the best in an environment of irreconcilables. All because P&G and HLL together started a movement that took sense out of the way the advertising business was run. All because the two FMCG behemoths spanning continents wanted a share of the commission that was earned from the media by agencies.

Advertisers should ask whether this new system where the media pays the advertisers cut money is beneficial to them or to the system. This system in which the media pays the advertisers discounts/commissions on the basis of bulk purchase is rather similar to the distasteful system that prevails in the medical profession in India. Every doctor earns money from every medical service that a patient has to buy in the course of his treatment. Diagnostic clinics keep a close tab on prescriptions; they ensure a certain percentage of the amount charged goes back to the prescribing doctor. Every medical shop sends cut money on prescriptions received. Nursing homes/private hospitals are not exempt from the system if they care about the business. In the same way, I would say the advertisers entering upon an agreement with a TV channel/a daily/O-O-H media for their ads receive cut money that is negotiated by their media agencies that are retained on *their* willingness to negotiate the meanest media rates. These agencies operate on a commission that may be as low as 0.25 per cent or as high as 2.5 per cent. I have no idea how they manage on thin margins and manage well enough to pay professionals a good salary.

When P&G and subsequently HLL questioned the age-old practice of the agency earning a commission of 15 per cent from the media, it was said that 15 per cent was too large a sum. These companies felt that the agency gained a tidy sum without taking any risk in the business. Whether the advertisement succeeded or failed in the market, it was the advertiser who stood exposed to risk; the commission, therefore, rightfully belonged to the advertiser. Ad agencies, true to their form, fell in line without a murmur, accepting broadly the charge that 15 per cent was sinfully high; that the poor advertisers had been given the short shrift all along; it was time that they considered their services in the light of the risks they shared in their client's business.

Agency heads did not ask why they should share the risks of the advertiser's business. Agencies provided services that the advertisers needed; if advertisers felt they had greater competence in meeting these needs then they would not hire agencies. Besides, if none of their other vendors, such as auditors, lawyers, import-export companies or advisors in various streams, could be engaged in a business relationship without them, sharing the risks of the business, then why should ad agencies alone be singled out?

I had hoped in the 1990s that since India had a number of eminent ad personalities who were known to speak their mind in defence of the profession, they would resist this change. Unfortunately, agencies accepted the change too meekly; probably most of them shared the view of Sir Martin Sorrell who observed in an interview that since the advertiser wanted change, it was inevitable. However, in a business-to-business relationship there is always scope to debate, to mull over the pros and the cons with an open mind and to persuade the advertiser to change his mindset if the case could be presented convincingly. That never happened because P&G and HLL held a gun to the temple of the agency, 'Either you agree; or you are dead!'

Indian advertising had a number of eminent people in the early years of the 1990s who were active though old; who were combative; who had a large number of professionals swearing by them; and who had some clout with the media. Subhas Ghosal had argued on behalf of Indian advertising in forums at home and abroad numerous times. R.K. Swamy was never a person who could be slighted or who would willingly yield to an unfair proposition. Subrata Sengupta, with his cool rationale, could out-argue the glibbest among clients. But the opening up of the economy and the consolidation of the advertising business with multinational agencies taking over India's premier agencies probably created a situation in which protest was futile. Indian agencies had to accept what had already been adopted in the USA and in Europe.

Media costs spiralled upwards from the late '90s. This was in keeping with the sudden economic boom in the country following the opening up of the economy from official interference to a degree that seemed safe for the Congress Party. Production costs also rose; in fact, the rise was astronomical for the production of TV spots. TV had become the primary medium for most campaigns. One of the characteristics of media planners is that they seem to tread a common well-worn path that most media planners prefer in choice of media either because by doing so they face the least resistance from clients or because they think that following a prevalent trend is the safest thing to do for themselves within their companies.

In any case, why TV production cost rose phenomenally may be understood if the reader looks at a recent article that appeared in *The Economic Times*, on the occasion of Sachin Tendulkar's retirement from cricket. I reproduce the article (on the next page) prior to discussing the subject in detail.

WWW.ECONOMICTIMES.COM

Scoring it Right in Ad World, Too

PRITHA MITRA DASGUPTA
MUMBAI

Sachin Tendulkar made a fairly innocuous debut into the world of brand endorsements with a television commercial for adhesive bandage Band-Aid in 1989.

24 years later, he leaves the crease as the blue eyed boy of Indian marketers; the one Indian sporting star whose clout is likely to survive retirement. While more than enough has been written and said about his performance on the field, these are stories from an entirely different location: the ad film sets where Tendulkar would go on to become the spokesperson for everything from cars to credit cards to insurance and colas.

ADIDAS; Director: Ram Madhvani, director, Equinox Films

We carried out trials for two months while making the Adidas film. The shoot involved 50 cameras and it took us 10 hours to install them. Sachin's shot required him to step out of the crease and lift his feet above the ground to take a winning stroke. After we finished, the client told me that it will be good if Sachin could raise his feet higher in the air. After two months of trial and 10 hours of camera installation, we had just one day to reshoot. I went back to ask Sachin and he said.

"Yes, I can make the stroke better." I was really surprised by his honesty. Just as we started installing the cameras the next day, it began to rain. And the next date we got was after two months. But when we finally shot the film, the sun was brighter, the lights were better, and Sachin made it so much more dramatic. I honestly felt that he was protecting the film.

MUSAFIR.COM; Director: Shirsha Guha Thakurta, Native Films

We prepared three sets of costumes. We were apprehensive if he would do all the trials or if he would even put on a fake moustache. But he was a pleasure to work with. One look definitely suited him and throughout the shoot he was fooling around and twirling about in the costume. In the commercial, he portrayed a character and had to act a bit. But it was good fun and he made it really easy for us. He didn't mind giving us as many takes and was continuously checking, giving his inputs or telling us to retake a shot.

AVIVA; Director: Anupam Mishra, Crazyfew Films

I shot two films with Sachin for Aviva Life Insurance for IBIS Productions. I was relatively a newcomer. I had heard how difficult it is to shoot celebrities and was extremely apprehensive. But Sachin proved me wrong. He made me feel extremely comfortable. And after that it was a smooth ride. There is one memorable incident when we were shooting the second film. We shot it in an old age home in Australia and no one knew Sachin was coming. They are also a cricket crazy nation and when one lady standing in the corridor saw Sachin walk in, her expression changed to admiration, adoration.

PEPSI; Director: Prahlad Kakkar

In the old film with Sharukh Khan opting for the Pepsi can instead of the cricket bat with the 'I'll take it from here' was Sachin's idea. He also suggests alternatives to scripts he isn't comfortable with. The original iteration of Sachin Aala Re actually had him dancing with the fishermen and dhobhis but he changed it to what he does best: playing cricket.

Director Ram Madhvani recounts, for one Adidas film they needed a particular shot to be played by Sachin. In this he would step out of his crease and hit the ball. For one shot the producer set up 50 cameras. And, unbelievably, the world's greatest batsman and India's famous film producer could not get the shot right on the first take. So they arranged a re-take. I guess with the same 50 cameras set up at different angles. If the client who passed the bill was not an idiot, I have never seen an idiot in my life!

This is not the only eye-opener. Read on and you will see one of the other famous producers telling you how Sachin altered the storyline to improve the film. If a film producer allows a cricket player to alter a film script, the less said about the film producer's professionalism the better. But clients want this arrangement; they would rather trust a producer who does not understand the value of money to produce a film than trust the agency where the training of personnel from the beginning focuses on stretching the advertising rupee and thus doing the creative in a manner that avoids wastage.

Celebrities charge a large sum. In an environment in which a few celebrities endorse many different brands, each celebrity charges a fee commensurate with his market demand. Actors and celebrity batters have crossed the lakh threshold years ago; they now charge in crores. Where the film producer gets an opportunity to work with a celebrity, his fees are pegged at a level that makes him a top-of-the-line producer. If the advertiser derives far less value in terms of impact on the target audience does he then ask the producer or the celebrity to justify their cost? The way he asks his agency to justify which half of the advertisement campaign they really produced; the half that worked or the half that did not create an impact.

If we were to tabulate a list of dos and don'ts for the advertisers and their ad agencies, we will see why the situation today is such as it is:

- If you keep your storyboard simple, you will spend far less in production.
- If your film includes a lot of graphics, production cost will be high.

- If you shoot in or around Bombay, you are going to get the most professional support staff in India. They will ensure far less expenditure on overtime.
- If you shoot abroad, as seems to be the trend these days, cost will be high. Your budget will include additional expense if the client travels with spouse and children, which happens rather frequently. Most times, accompanying baggage with the production teams comprise CEOs of organisations. No one questions bills, but such bills get added on to the film budget. Therefore, to advertising.
- If your film includes music especially composed by A.R. Rahman your film will not be a budget film.
- If your film includes Amitabh Bachchan or any of the other illustrious members of his family, Sachin Tendulkar, any batter who is the current heart throb of a million cricket fans, you will not make a budget film.
- If your film is produced by production companies that were set up by successful Bollywood stars, your film will not come cheap.
- If you are focussed on big names in TV film production, men such as Prahlad Kakkar, you will have to accept that they will charge a substantial fee for their professional input. That might make you happy, but the price goes up!
- More time spent on post-production work increases cost.
- If you centralise your script around action shots, such as the Thums Up TV shows, the end cost will be high.

This evening as you watch a television show, if you remember these points observe how many of the ad films telecast fall into one of the categories described above. And how few TV commercials you see do not fall into any one of the categories.

The buying age of media has heralded the end of fair market competition in the country. The market is today governed by an oligopoly of companies who totally dominate an entire industry span with their no-holds barred spend on brand management. Advertising has moved from purely brand advertising that was common 20 or 30 years ago to brand promotion advertising with the stress on promotion. A recent example would help to illustrate this point better. Tata Motors did a wonderful job in making the least expensive automobile in the world. It was named Nano. But the brand did not do well in the market. The company tried to move a dormant brand with a promotional campaign in which it stated that a buyer may go to the Tata showroom and drive out with a Nano without paying anything; the buyer will start paying six months later. The company will, in addition, pay for fuel for many years (I forget how many), bear the road tax and additionally extend warranty and free service.

Tata Motors is not alone in trying to pump adrenaline into a stagnant market. Tata Motors has slipped and is among the also-ran companies in India although market reviews indicate that its brands in Europe—thanks to its acquisition of Jaguar—are doing better. In the home market, the Korean and Japanese companies are cornering a major share despite the slowdown. For all the companies that are doing better not only are they introducing new brands, positioning them as aspiration brands that people strive to own, but are spending adequately across the media spectrum, maintaining a share of voice. It is important for any brand to be seen across all media including TV channels.

When you talk about FMCG brands, there is no place for small companies any more. ITC succeeds because it has deep pockets to match HLL. ITC or HLL are not presenting stunning creative in their campaigns. Compare the Vivel TV ads of 2013 with the Lux TV spots of the 1990s; you will notice no difference in treatment, in the storyline, in the way the brands are presented. You could replace one brand with the other and it would not make a difference! That in a way sums up the presentation of brands in an oligopolistic situation. So, you might ask, is there no competition? Yes, there is competition because the consumer's fickle-mindedness keeps the same brands alive. Boredom moves the consumer from one brand to the other, not the heavy advertising. Are there no small brands then?

With the start of globalisation in the 1990s the trend was for multinational giants to enter or consolidate their market status in India. Between 2000 and 2010, these companies managed to expand the market by bringing in new consumers, upgrading consumers from products to brands, by realising that there was a lot of hot air being blown about a bottomless Indian middle class with a huge unfulfilled desire to consume since it had so long been starved of market choice. They learnt fast that the Indian consumer is rather difficult to define. The so-called middle class itself is divided into multiple demographic segments. Even the rich class is not homogeneous in terms of preferences, aspirations and lifestyles. Within the middle class there are women and men who are extremely conscious of value for money in their purchase decision. There are, similarly, a growing number of youngsters for whom the real value of a purchase is in owning brands that their peer groups are proud to flaunt.

The new millennium and beyond pose a number of big questions with regard to the evolution of consumer psyche in the current Indian market. Lack of research hamstrings the understanding of professionals in media or creative. Fortunately, the new crop of advertising professionals, whether in creative or media, are more educated, more vocal and more aware of international developments, as they are free to travel abroad, than advertising professionals 20 years ago.

Social advertising is the flavour of the moment. Through the social media the consumer is sought to be persuaded in a manner that makes him believe that he has decided to engage with a brand rather than being nudged to own or use the brand. Advertisers perhaps even now look at consumers as rather pitifully inept to guard against their guile. Some advertisers are shaken awake rudely when they realise it is dangerous to misjudge the consumer or to take the consumer for granted. However, a lot of water has flowed underneath the bridge, removing some of the flotsam that was considered important in advertising in the last century. Let us consider what has happened to Indian advertising in the past 63 years:

- Corporate campaigns are now restricted to a few businesses only. These businesses that rely on corporate advertisements for marketing their services include the most highly advertised businesses in the print media. Such businesses are: (1) Educational institutes offering professional courses (2) Financial companies offering mutual funds (3) Private hospitals (4) Real estate developers (5) *Babas*/*mataji*s heading religious groups that use TV heavily, some also run their own TV channels.
- Newspapers once again carry full-page advertisements on the first page, like they used to in the early years of the twentieth century. *The Hindu* had advertisements on the first page till about 1950. Now leading dailies carry front page ads almost every day. Few newspaper readers expect to catch the headlines on the front page.
- Media is separated from creative. Further, in a few leading media companies, planning has been separated from the buying function. How all this helps the advertiser to derive an integrated perspective on brand advertising is more than I can tell.
- Creative is no longer confined to first ideating in English and then translating into the vernacular. This is a wonderful development. Language copywriters are quite proficient in English. Some regional languages suffer in translation but if most big brands happen to be located in Bombay then this is bound to occur as those working in regional languages are cut off from the place where a particular regional language is supreme. I can say a TV script dubbed in Bengali in Bombay, not infrequently, sounds peculiar. May be Tamilians in Chennai feel the same way about Tamil dubbing!
- Printing has improved immensely. Brochures and folders look so beautiful these days. Unfortunately, copywriters have lost the art of writing long copy. Corporate brochures are a thing of the past.
- Radio has become a vibrant medium with so many FM channels competing in every major metro. Radio has also captured the ears of the younger population as they drive to work.

- Media is emerging as an exact/predictable science, given the predictability of the kind of products or services that are seen in the major mediums.
- Print: The following products are most seen—mobile phones, mutual funds, motor vehicles (both cars and scooters), admission to MBA courses, jewellery brands or shops, hospital services, consumer durables (particularly during festival seasons), computers, fashion wear, car loans or home loans from banks.
- TV: FMCG brands predominate. Consumer durables buy slots during festival times. Cars and scooters buy heavy presence across channels during their launch. Thums Up, Coke, Pepsi and Sprite/Limca take many spots during the summer months and festival times. Suiting brands also buy TV spots.
- Out-Of-Home: Hoardings/outdoor have evolved into O-O-H media. The activation of brands now requires effective back-up from O-O-H media. Ad agencies have opened their own ancillary companies to sell hoardings/O-O-H to the advertisers directly. Agencies normally buy space from recognised outdoor companies that have invested in infrastructure. Outdoor media services require a combination of infrastructure with engineering support to ensure visibility and efficient servicing.
- The social media is fast emerging as the future destination of both advertisers and agencies. How to use the social media is a subject of acute interest; it is not fully understood. Advertisers are beginning to invest around five to seven per cent of their budgetary allocation in social media. This is likely to go up significantly in the next five years.

Advertising has moved from product to brand building to positioning. The trend seems to be moving towards connecting the brand with the consumer emotionally. Indian advertising is loud, in-the-face advertising that repeats, 'This brand is the greatest ever' without regard to the finer sensitivity of the consumer. A consumer may not like vociferous claims nor may he think that a claim adds to the credibility of what the brand distils in a campaign.

Someday, not too far away, many more people will enter the net of the consuming class. Urbanisation is already driving more people from villages to cities. Tier 2 and Tier 3 towns are improving and there seems to be a preference among people of settling down and building careers in these towns instead of heading towards the bigger metropolitan centres. Marketers are veering to exploit the opportunities that are coming in the wake of modern retailing. Consumers as a class, if they are more educated, will certainly be more discerning. The advertisers and the ad agencies will need to contend with these challenges. They will have to initiate research into consumer habits, spend patterns, usage behaviour, beliefs and lifestyle changes as they create new campaigns to support their brands.

Index

Q

R

S